UNIVERSITY PRESS OF FLORIDA

Gainesville · Tallahassee · Tampa · Boca Raton

Pensacola · Orlando · Miami · Jacksonville · Ft. Myers · Sarasota

Onramps and Overpasses

Florida A&M University, Tallahassee
Florida Atlantic University, Boca Raton
Florida Gulf Coast University, Ft. Myers
Florida International University, Miami
Florida State University, Tallahassee
New College of Florida, Sarasota
University of Central Florida, Orlando
University of Florida, Gainesville
University of North Florida, Jacksonville
University of South Florida, Tampa
University of West Florida, Pensacola

UNIVERSITY
PRESS
OF
FLORIDA

ONRAMPS
AND
OVERPASSES

A Cultural History of
Interstate Travel

Dianne Perrier

Copyright 2009 by Dianne Perrier
Printed in the United States of America. This book is printed on Glatfelter
Natures Book, a paper certified under the standards of the Forestry Stewardship Council (FSC). It is a recycled stock that contains 30 percent post-
consumer waste and is acid-free.

14 13 12 11 10 09   6 5 4 3 2 1

LIBRARY OF CONGRESS CATALOGING-IN-PUBLICATION DATA
Perrier, Dianne.
Onramps and overpasses : a cultural history of interstate travel /
Dianne Perrier.
p. cm.
Includes bibliographical references and index.
ISBN 978-0-8130-3398-3 (acid-free paper)
1. United States—Description and travel—Anecdotes. 2. Interstate High-
way System—History—Anecdotes. 3. Express highways—United States—
History—Anecdotes. 4. United States—History, Local—Anecdotes.
5. United States—Biography—Anecdotes. I. Title.
E161.5.P47   2009
917.3—dc22
2009017145

The University Press of Florida is the scholarly publishing agency for the
State University System of Florida, comprising Florida A&M Univer-
sity, Florida Atlantic University, Florida Gulf Coast University, Florida
International University, Florida State University, New College of Florida,
University of Central Florida, University of Florida, University of North
Florida, University of South Florida, and University of West Florida.

University Press of Florida
15 Northwest 15th Street
Gainesville, FL 32611-2079
http://www.upf.com

Contents

1. Early Road Travel: Pluck, Patience,
   and Profanity 1

2. Interstate Commerce Develops:
   This Little Piggy Went to Market 61

3. Roads Cross the Continent:
   Root Hog, or Die 155

4. Coast to Coast Automobile Traffic Begins:
   Get Out and Get Under 239

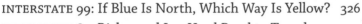

5. The Interstate Highway Era:
   Motorvatin' Over the Hill 313

6. The Red Trace of Taillights 377

Interstate Highways

"[We ate] ham and hard boiled eggs while our spiritual natures revelled alternatively in rainbows, thunderstorms, and peerless sunsets. Nothing helps scenery like ham and eggs . . . and after these a pipe— an old rank, delicious pipe . . . they make happiness. It is what all the ages have struggled for" (Mark Twain as quoted in Ward et al., 2001: 34). The illustration is from Mark Twain's 1871 version of *Roughing It*.

OUR MORNING RIDE.

While traveling west in 1861, Samuel Clemens and his brother found that the passing landscape could best be appreciated by sitting in their underwear on top of the stagecoach, smoking a pipe and eating ham and hard boiled eggs. After sweltering inside the coach through the desert heat over a route similar to today's Interstates 70 and 80, the brothers shed as much clothing as modesty permitted and climbed on top of the coach in their long underwear to contemplate the scenery. With their physical discomfort eased, the brothers could appreciate what passed before them as the coach continued its westward progression.

For novelist Pat Conroy, enlightenment about the passing landscape came in 1972. Having taught on an isolated island off the South Carolina coast for a year, Pat decided to reward his class with a field trip to Washington, D.C. They crossed by boat to Beaufort, South Carolina and piled into a station wagon for the trip up I-95. It didn't take long for one young boy to ask what the lines were on the road. "I sat there trying to comprehend what had just happened. I had seen the lines so often that they had disappeared from sight and were no longer part of my consciousness." Conroy explained the lines, but realized the interstate landscape had ceased to exist for him. "I regretted that I could not be making this trip with the freshness of insight and beautiful innocence of . . . the others. I regretted that I was old, that I could no longer appreciate the education afforded by an American highway, and that I could not grasp the mystery of a single line painted down a road going north."[1]

Robert Louis Stevenson, author of such classics as *Treasure Island* and *A Child's Garden of Verses*, also felt strongly about road travel. While Pat Conroy believed age had diminished his awareness and appreciation of the open road, Stevenson thought quite the opposite: before reaching middle age the traveler does not have the accumulated life experiences and wisdom to appreciate the passing landscape. Stevenson firmly believed in a magic time around middle age when the hair starts to thin and the waistline thickens, but the eyesight is still good. Those sharp eyes combine with a lifetime of experiences to put individuals in top form when it comes to observing, appreciating, and understanding a passing landscape. Pat Conroy, at the time a young man, had not yet reached that magic age. With his focus on getting his young charges to their destination, the interstate landscape before him had paled.

Conroy's experience is all too common, especially today. In the rush to get to the office, the beach, to visit family, are motorists—including those in their middle years—really able to see anything besides the taillight boogie happening on the road ahead? Can they truly appreciate what was hailed in 1956 as "the greatest public works program in the history of the world"[2] and the foresight of two middle-aged presidents with a well-defined sense of the past and the vision to push, prod, and cajole a nation into remaking the very fabric of its landscape? For modern-day travelers, the sense of anticipation that once marked travel in America has dimmed. The interstate highways are a means to an end: fast, efficient, concrete and asphalt ribbons and, in the seeming isolation of today's vehicles, motorists sit alone. Yet as Stevenson liked to point out, someone traveling by road is never alone: the road itself is always with the traveler, frequently the only companion.

Stevenson was well aware that in traveling by road he followed in the footsteps of all those who had passed that way before him. The road and its landscape displayed to him the signatures of those previous travelers, whether in a place-name along the way, a rest stop overlooking a valley, or the physical placement of the road itself. The earliest occupants of this land admired the same green mountains, crossed the same blue rivers—and they all had their own story to tell. While only a handful of those tales are retold here, these snapshots over time and distance highlight the various elements of the road landscape, interstate by interstate. They have been grouped into five eras of road travel in America.

Chapter 1 looks at the earliest days of road travel, from the trails created by Native Americans to the first European arrivals in North America to capture that sense of precarious adventure inherent in any trip on the earliest interstates. Here are the ladies in hoop skirts and Mark Twain on the perils of nineteenth-century fast food. But, whether it was Cochise acting as a tour guide along the I-25 corridor, Davy Crockett ambling toward the Alamo on what is now Interstate 30, or landscape architect Frederick Law Olmsted getting excited about stopping for fuel along a route similar to today's Interstate 24, it was very much a case of pluck, patience, and profanity.

Chapter 2 introduces Charles Dickens stuck in pig traffic, interstate travel by mule, and the best way to travel with Texas longhorns, as interstate commerce began to develop. Here was Yankee ingenuity in inventing products and methods of producing them and in creating a fledgling tourism industry. Here also the reader can find a town that decided to move down what is now Interstate 82 to be closer to the promised commercial glory of a railroad line. The stores stayed open for business while they rolled collectively, on logs, down the interstate of that era.

Hezekiah, Ezra, Gary, Horace, and Frances take over chapter 3 as hundreds of thousands of settlers clogged the roads beginning to cross the continent. Hezekiah and Gary survived thanks to the kindness of strangers along what is now Interstate 40. Horace and Frances recorded the disappearance of creature comforts along the future Interstate 70 corridor with more good humor than travelers could probably muster today, and Ezra lived to be the only man to cross the continent on the

Oregon Trail so many times by so many means of transportation. Interstate 84 West traces part of his journey. The chapter ends in Chicago with the introduction of motorized transportation at the Columbian Exposition.

In chapter 4, Jules Verne writes of a cross-continental race against time along a trace similar to today's Interstate 80, and George Carlin helps introduce an interstate with a stoplight on it: Interstate 78. Depression-era families take to what is now Interstate 20 and a young woman by the name of Mattie makes an ocean voyage to Arizona before the creation of the Interstate 8 corridor across Southern California. The chapter ends with the construction of the first superhighway of the modern era: the Pennsylvania Turnpike, its sleek engineering reflecting a road designed to best serve high-speed automobile and truck traffic, rather than the traditional approach of making the road fit the existing landscape.

By 1956, Chuck Berry's Maybellene was "motorvatin' over the hill" and the nation needed a fast, efficient network of interstate highways; the Eisenhower System of Interstate and Defense Highways was about to become a reality. Bureaucrats scrambled to invent a signage and numbering system, engineers worked to develop durable asphalts and concrete—and the equipment to undertake massive public works—and planners worked to learn from mistakes and get it right. Roads built originally for national defense became evacuation channels for those fleeing coastal storms and freeways to wonderlands built amid orange groves in Florida.

The book ends with a look back and a sense of anticipation for what lies beyond the next bend in the road.

While the travelers' tales are not always in strict chronological order, one story frequently leads into another, waiting for the curious to rediscover that sense of adventure that once marked travel along these traces in the American landscape. Together, these travelers and their stories form a more complete picture of interstate road travel in America: they give back a sense of prospect, of grand adventure and discovery. They provide color to the red trace of taillights.

Early Road Travel

Pluck, Patience, and Profanity

Pluck, patience, and profanity in New York, 1909.
(Courtesy of the Library of Congress.)

In 1899, John and Louise Davis decided to see America from their brand-new horseless carriage. They set off from New York, bound for Syracuse and then Chicago. Near Syracuse, a one-armed bicyclist, who had left New York ten days after the Davises, passed them on the roadway. Shortly thereafter, the Davises abandoned their trip, plagued by too many breakdowns and the poor condition of the roads. At the time, John Davis probably echoed the sentiments of every road warrior who had passed before him—and many of those yet to come—when he commented that a road trip requires "plenty of pluck, patience and profanity, and I think I am becoming proficient."[1]

On leaving New York, John and Louise Davis headed up the Hudson River valley, on a road built along one of the great natural conduits of the eastern United States. Sculpted by ice sheets of past millennia, the valley provided a natural trace for the migratory wanderings of animals and early North Americans seeking the path of least resistance. Here also was a natural opening for the first Europeans. In 1609, Henry Hudson sailed up the river that would eventually bear his name looking for the elusive passage to the Orient and all its riches. Instead, he found a valley that so captivated him that he kept going, even when the river narrowed and it became apparent he would not reach the Orient. Here was a lushly forested landscape and fertile meadows, riverside cliffs and the nearby mountains of the soon-to-be-named Catskills. For the beau monde of the 1800s, Henry's river, and the roads that eventually flanked it, led to the Springs—as in Saratoga Springs—where mothers scanned the field for eligible sons-in-law over high tea, dandies pranced to catch the eye of an heiress, and race horse fanciers bet on the track. Today, I-87 traces the Hudson River to Saratoga Springs and beyond.

The pattern repeated itself all over North America. Natural channels in the landscape became trails for wandering animals—buffalo and deer looking for grazing lands and naturally occurring salt licks—usually along the lines of least resistance. The first peoples followed the trace of game and seasonal vegetation. Centuries later, in the Southeast, the wild progeny of pigs introduced to North America by the early Spanish explorers added to the network of deer trails winding through the landscape. Many of these trails through the swamps and hammocks became early colonial roads. Southern tobacco farmers later etched some of these pig trails deeper into the landscape when they started rolling tobacco barrels down them to navigable streams for shipment to markets.

Further west, America was a pathless desert, with the rivers serving as the great interstates of the time. On land, the heights provided the best path: fewer fallen timbers and less erosion on windswept trails. Here, signal fires could be seen from a greater distance and lookouts kept to guard against intrusion. While the first villages sheltered in protective valleys or on the sides of cliffs, early thoroughfares for hunting, commerce, plunder and warfare, and sometimes religious celebration, sought the high ground—when not using the rivers and lakes. Some of these trails led to sacred sites and sources of water. Other roadways evolved as seasonal traces in the landscape for harvesting plants, nuts, and fruits, or following the migrations of game animals. Still others were simply a means of "passing through" an area on the way to someplace else. The Lenape of the New Jersey area, for instance, created a web of trails crisscrossing their territory that supplemented travel on the rivers and lakes. In Michigan, the Native American trail across the lower peninsula from Lake Michigan to Lake Erie eventually morphed into I-96. Along the Gulf Coast, trails ran inland for trade and warfare. It was here that the Spanish first made contact with Native Americans. Today, I-10, the most southerly of the transcontinental highways, crosses the traditional lands of many of the tribes the Spanish first encountered. Parts of I-91 through Connecticut and Vermont follow a trail carved out by the Iroquois and Mohawk for trade and mayhem between the St. Lawrence and Connecticut River valleys.

The first European settlers—Spanish, Dutch, English, French—followed these rudimentary trails. The path the Spanish took north from their Mexican colony in the late 1500s into what is now Arizona to set up missions and look for precious metals gradually widened and improved with increased traffic. As the man on foot or horseback evolved into a man sitting in a wheeled vehicle, this trace in the landscape became known as the Nogales Highway connecting Tucson with Nogales on the border with Mexico. Eventually, even the Nogales Highway became a numbered highway—I-19.

Interpretations of what constituted a road varied for colonial governments, as did the definition of a road in good condition. In some places, a blazed trail with any fallen timbers hauled out of the way was deemed acceptable. In the Massachusetts of 1639, a road had to be wide enough for two lanes of traffic. Pennsylvania and New York insisted on wide trails with stumps and shrubs in the pathway cut close to the ground and rudimentary bridges over waterways. Virginia decreed that roads leading to churches and county courthouses had to be forty feet wide. Spillways and dams also had to be fitted with a passageway on top, and every iron furnace had to have a good road leading to it. In the Virginia hill country, settlers frequently found themselves unloading and dismantling their supply wagons, carrying everything over the worst hills and then reassembling and repacking the wagon on the other side. In Tennessee, the main road between Nashville and Knoxville had to be fifteen feet wide; bridges could be twelve feet wide. (Twelve feet is the width of one lane on an interstate highway.) The year was 1802. Frequently, a road was in better condition if used as a post road. In 1806, the United States Postal Department cleared a horse path from Athens, Georgia, through to the army post north of Mobile, Alabama, and then on to New Orleans, following a trace similar to an old Lower Creek trading path. The army subsequently widened this path in 1811. In Tennessee, the government used parts of the famous Natchez Trace to deliver mail, but by about 1828, it had become more expedient to send mail by steamboat; the Trace's general condition declined.

In the South, sand made it difficult for both man and beast to walk. However, it did drain quickly after a heavy rainfall, even on hard-packed roadways. The Southern swamps, though, were an entirely different story. In 1711, John Lawson, Surveyor-General of Carolina, reported back to the English proprietors regarding his travels on their behalf. John attested to "good and pleasant" roads in and around the thriving settlements, but once he left these little islands of "richness and grandeur," conditions changed dramatically. In his travels around the colony, John usually walked, sometimes navigating a stream with a raft or dugout. Near the Santee River, much to his disgust, he reported "a prodigious wide and deep Swamp, being forc'd to strip stark-naked, and much a-do to save our selves from drowning in this Fatigue. We, with much a-do, got thro'."[2] Today's I-95 crosses the flooded version of the Santee River in South Carolina. The stumps sticking out of the artificially created Lake Marion and the low-lying shoreline hint at what Lawson's "prodigious wide and deep Swamp" might have been like three hundred years ago.

In 1743, John Bartram of Philadelphia headed northward to a spot near present-day Syracuse to attend a meeting of the chiefs of the Iroquois Six Nations on behalf of the British Crown. Together with a handful of other men anxious to meet with the chiefs, and guided by the famed Lenape chief, Shickcalamy, the small party made its way through Pennsylvania and New York over the trail of the time. On July 6, 1743, John described his travels through Pennsylvania on roads that were "[f]ull of scrubby bushes, and still poor and stoney to the last great ridge, which is composed of large gravel . . . the descent of the north side is very steep and rocky, large craggy rocks are disposed on all sides, most part of the way down, which brought us to a fine vale, where we lodged by a creek . . . and were grievously stung all night with small gnats."[3] Today, John could admire the craggy rock cuts on I-81 and presumably spend a bug-free night in a motel at some anonymous interchange.

Other roads were forced through the forests for military purposes. General Braddock cut into the Appalachians of Pennsylvania with a small army in 1755 to reach the French fort near present-day Pittsburgh. Because the existing trail was too narrow and rough for the army wagons and artillery, the roadway had to be widened and cleaned up. Braddock also brought with him a corps of seamen to raise and lower his supply wagons over steep inclines with a block and tackle. The French and their Indian allies ambushed the advancing troops in a bloody rout that left the British forces decimated and Braddock fatally wounded. A young George Washington accompanied Braddock on that ill-fated mission, and he saw to Braddock's burial in the middle of the road his army had helped create. After the interment, Washington had the soldiers march over the grave site in formation to hide any evidence of its location.

The same conflict that sent Braddock and Washington west along a course similar to today's I-76 sent Benjamin Franklin northward in December 1755. Always appreciative of a fine meal, Ben asked his wife

Braddock's Road as it appeared around 1908. While the road is not completely erased from the landscape, the photo hints at the magnitude of the task Braddock and his men faced in cutting a road through the wilds of Pennsylvania. (Courtesy of the Library of Congress.)

to cook and bake some meals to go, bought a cask of wine for the trip, paid six months of rent on his house in Philadelphia, and set off with 150 cavalry to survey the safety of the frontier and see what he could do to protect settlers from Native American raids. It was the wettest time of year to be traveling. An ensign accompanying the wagon train wrote of "the worst country I ever saw. Hills, like Alps, on each side, and a long narrow defile, where the road scarcely admitted a single wagon. At the bottom of it a rapid creek with steep banks, and a bridge made of a single log."[4] It took the convoy two days to get from Philadelphia to Easton, Pennsylvania, a distance of about sixty miles.

In the 1790s and early 1800s, more stone roads were built outward from New York, Philadelphia, and Baltimore, usually by corporations set up to make money off the road by charging for the privilege of using it. These high-speed interstate highways, known even in the early 1800s as turnpikes, replaced thoroughfares described just a decade earlier as heavily rutted, clay tracks with fallen trees frequently blocking the path. Turnpikes of that era typically had a crushed stone roadbed about twenty-four feet wide and cost between eight thousand and ten thousand dollars per mile to build. Tollbooths every few miles turned tidy profits of over fifteen percent for the primary shareholders. The stone roads made safe, rapid, all-weather travel a reality. They also raised the bar for road expectations.

In the South, heavy rains frequently made building, maintaining, and using roads a monumental challenge. New Orleans, for instance, did not have a storm sewer system to handle waste and runoff from the fifty-seven inches of rain the city receives each year. In 1805, a young lady visiting New Orleans stood at her host's front door wondering how they would cross the city to reach that evening's ball, given that there were no carriages for hire. To her horror, her hostess asked her to remove her shoes and stockings, which she then carefully tied up in a silk handkerchief. With ball gowns tucked up under their cloaks, the partygoers set out through the muddy streets barefoot, their way lit by slaves carrying lanterns. At their destination, the ladies dipped their feet in a nearby pool of water to remove the accumulated mud. Slaves then toweled their feet dry, and helped their mistresses put their silk stockings and satin slippers back on before entering the ballroom.

Elsewhere in Louisiana, travelers along the major thoroughfares now replaced by I-10 sometimes found themselves chest deep in water, but still on the marked roadbed, keeping an eye out for water snakes and alligators. About 350 miles to the west, in Galveston, Texas, the problem wasn't so much the rain and mud, but the sand. Those charged with looking after the thoroughfares within the town's limits tried crushed oyster shells and wooden blocks covered with tar. The blocks were easy

Some Native Americans collected tolls from settlers crossing their lands. The Cherokees of what is now Tennessee routinely charged tolls, and it was a case of pay up or die. Understandably, potential settlers tended to detour around the area, finding other routes west. The Cherokee continued to collect tolls and harass travelers until 1799 when George Washington intervened.

on horses' hooves and quiet, but tended to float away when it rained. Sometimes, heavier plank roads floated away as well. Dry sand roads could be just as onerous. Regular stagecoach service came to parts of Arizona in 1857, but passengers frequently found themselves doing more walking beside the coaches than riding in them thanks to the fine, loose sand covering the road that often bogged down both coach and horses. Frances Trollope, chronicler of social mannerisms and mother of novelist Anthony Trollope, advised anyone with an aversion to dirt to remain home. Some stagecoach companies even recommended passengers dress in clothing of brown or gray so the dirt would not show.

Frances described a trip to Niagara Falls as becoming "wilder every step, the unbroken forest often skirted the road for miles, and the sight of a log-hut was an event. . . . We were most painfully jumbled and jolted over logs and through bogs, till every joint was nearly dislocated. Yet the road was, for the greater part of the day, good, running along a natural ridge, just wide enough for it."[5] She was even more disparaging of New Jersey. "At Trenton . . . we left our smoothly-gliding comfortable boat for the most detestable stage-coach that ever a Christian built to dislocate the joints of his fellow men."[6] She was kinder near Memphis.

> We soon lost all trace of a road, at least so it appeared to us, for the stumps of the trees, which had been cut away to open a passage, were left standing three feet high. Over these, the high-hung Deerborn, as our carriage was called, passed safely; but it required some miles of experience to convince us that every stump would not be our last; it was amusing to watch the cool and easy skill with which the driver wound his horses and wheels among these stumps.[7]

Around 1840, the federal government turned responsibility for highways over to the states. Federal funding dried up until the invention of the bicycle and the automobile created a public outcry for better roads

AMERICAN STAGECOACH.

(From "Forty Etchings, from Sketches Made with the Camera Lucida in North America in 1827 and 1828," by Captain Basil Hall, R. N.)

Rebecca Latimer Felton had already written her memoirs when she briefly served as America's first female senator in 1922. A Georgia native, she described the stage from Nashville, Tennessee, to Augusta, Georgia, as it would have been around 1845. "These coaches were ponderous affairs with a big leather boot on behind and a little banister around to hold baggage. There were regular stage stands ten miles apart, where a relay of four horses were constantly stabled . . . the stage driver's horn would be sounded so that the hostler would be ready with fresh horses on his arrival. . . . It cost ten cents a mile to travel on the stage coach and it required ten cents to send a letter" (Felton, 1919: 57). Today, Interstates 75 and 20 serve part of the route Rebecca described. (Courtesy of Documenting the American South, University of North Carolina at Chapel Hill.)

some fifty years later. States and counties already had responsibility for most roads, but maintenance and construction was usually undertaken very haphazardly by private citizens with very little road know-how. In North Carolina, all white males eighteen to forty-five years of age and free African American males and male slaves sixteen to fifty years of age had to work on the state's roads under a court-appointed overseer. Those who could afford to sent a slave in their stead or paid the one dollar a day fine for not working. As a result, roads usually needed repair and bridges were built slowly, if at all. Towns had the authority to keep streets and sidewalks cleared for traffic and in good repair. Residents could not place wood piles on the sidewalks or in the streets, or "dump clay or pour washings from their kitchens or shops in the streets."[8] They also had to drain any stagnant water off their land. With the introduction and growing popularity of rail travel, roads fell into further disrepair.

The colder states had one advantage when it came to road travel—winter. Snow filled in the ruts and frozen streams formed a hard surface, making the transportation of heavy freight safer and easier. In other instances, the roadway simply shut down for the winter, with no attempt to keep it open. Settlers drove their carioles over the frozen rivers and lakes. These sleighs were the eighteenth-century version of a sports coupe on today's interstate: light, streamlined, speedy vehicles usually powered by two sturdy horses. In Grand Rapids, Michigan, the ferry service across the Grand River—a flatboat poled across the channel—gave way to an ice road in the winter months. Accounts exist of heavily loaded wagons using the ice above and below the rapids to cross the river as

"Nothing, certainly, can be more agreeable than the gliding smoothly and rapidly along, deep sunk in soft furs, the moon shining with almost midday splendour, the air of crystal brightness, and the snow sparkling on every side, as if it were sprinkled with diamonds": Frances Trollope (1832: 130 of 186) discussing the joys of a sleigh ride in America. Print by Joseph Hoover, circa 1867. (Courtesy of the Library of Congress.)

Interstates of
chapter 1

late as the end of March in the 1830s. Today, travelers on I-96 cross the Grand River in Grand Rapids at Mile Marker 31.

Of course, the snow and ice also precipitated more mud with the coming of the spring thaw. In Grand Rapids, a clerk named Frank Little described the river of mud in front of the store where he worked. "This mud was frequently from six to eight inches deep and the whole width of the street, and thick like hasty pudding. . . . in the early morning could

be seen unmistakable evidence that, during the night, the whole viscous mass of mud to the depth indicated had, like an immense Swiss glacier, moved bodily down the hill ten, fifteen or twenty feet."[9]

Goods were now coming thousands of miles into the frontier area to stores like the one where Frank Little clerked. And, as the people living all along the American frontier shifted from subsistence existence to having excess produce to sell, they needed avenues to the outside world. They also needed a means of building a solid manufacturing base of their own rather than constantly importing even the basics. But that was beginning. By 1805, for instance, on the Monongahela River in Western Pennsylvania, boats loaded with flour, iron, pottery, cabinetry, and whiskey made their way south through the various waterways to markets in places like Kentucky and Louisiana. Still, if people living in Western Pennsylvania or Michigan were to enjoy the benefits of a prosperous society, better and more numerous avenues of commerce were required. Ironically, the network of Native American trails throughout the country was about to become the greatest legacy the native peoples bequeathed, however unwillingly, to the young nation.

Interstate 10: Melodious and Mellifluous

"There is no part of the world where nomenclature is so rich, poetical and picturesque as in the United States of America."[10] Or so Robert Louis Stevenson believed. He loved the place names he found in America. They flowed, they presented images in the mind, and enriched the landscape. It almost didn't happen. In *The American Language*, H. L. Mencken, well-known editor and critic of the 1920s, bemoaned the lack of imagination of the very first settlers in New England, calling it their "poverty of fancy." If they didn't name something after a place back home, as in Cambridge or New London, they named it for what it was, as in Plymouth Rock. Or, they named it after a person. First name, last name; it didn't matter. Attach a suffix, as in borough or ville or town, and a community was born. Then, as settlement moved inland, the early colonists

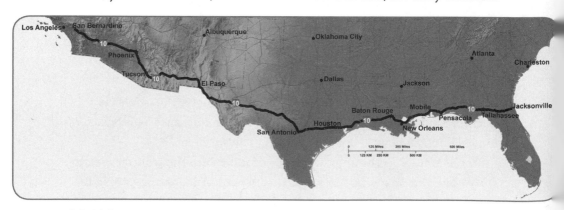

Interstate 10

First Man and First Woman created the mountains from the underworld. In the East, they held them down with a sheet of dawn. Then came a ray of sunlight from the south to pin down the southern heights and cover them with a blue sky. To the west, a sunbeam held down the mountains, a yellow cloud draped over the snowy mountaintops. To the north, a beautiful rainbow arched downward, pegging the mountains into the earth. Photograph by William J. Carpenter, circa 1915. (Courtesy of the Library of Congress.)

began to pay more attention to the more melodious, descriptive names Native Americans gave their landscape features and settlements: Mississippi, Potomac, Susquehanna, Chicago. The names flowed from the tongue and gave the place or geographical feature a special meaning. They gave color to the landscape.

Native Americans venerated their environment, entwining their lives and beliefs with the natural elements of their surroundings. All things lived in harmony and to upset this balance was to disrespect nature. Whether it was a sacred mountain, a spider responsible for teaching the art of weaving, or a cactus that gave nourishment and fibers, the landscape provided the essentials of everyday existence: physically, socially, and spiritually. Everywhere on the continent, native peoples responded to the challenges of their environment and carved out a space for themselves, making the most of the resources nature proffered. Along the

Southern coast, for instance, tribes depended on the waters of the Gulf of Mexico and on the rivers and streams flowing into it for their sustenance. These first fluvial highways connected tribes all along the coast to the interior.

For the first Europeans, the landscape along America's Gulf Coast was more about personal gain and finding the route to the Orient. For some, it was rumors of gold and how fast you could get across the terrain to find it. For others, tales of silver caches or that elusive fountain of youth drove them onward. Soon, Spanish slave ships began raiding along the coast. Contact with Native Americans had been made. The Spanish set up missions in what is now Northern Florida. Priests walking from mission to mission through the forests and swamps created a well-established trail extending into the Panhandle. In doing so, these priests were the first to travel along a trace now served by Interstate 10. The Deep South Freeway was about to become a reality. Today, you can drive from coast to coast—Saint Augustine, Florida, to Santa Monica, California—along a route partially created by Spanish priests.

As the Spanish moved farther afield, their missions and presidios along the Gulf Coast unfolded into the territories of various Native peoples. Towns along I-10 reflect this heritage: Pensacola (Exits 17–10) combines the Choctaw words for "hair" and "people"; Tallahassee (Exits 209–196) is Muskogee for "old town"; and Alabama is Choctaw for "vegetation gatherers" or "thicket clearers." Pasadena (Exit 26) is Ojibwa for "key to valley" or "valley town." Here also were the Mobile (Exits 15–26) Indians, the Biloxi (Exits 44–46), and Pascagoula (Exit 69) in what is now Mississippi, the Houma (Exit 220) in Louisiana, and the Yuma (Exit 19) in Arizona. Priests tried to gather the various tribal peoples up into missions to convert them to Christianity, but also to get them to do all the manual labor, including crop production. This proved unsuccessful, however, and the good fathers at the mission in Saint Augustine, for instance, ended up sending to Cuba for their foodstuffs.

Then the French became interested in the Gulf Coast. In 1682, Robert de La Salle claimed the lower Mississippi River valley for France; settlements followed at the mouth of the Mississippi and at Biloxi. The I-10 corridor continued to unfurl westward. Soon, Spain, France, and England were all active in the area—all with a political desire for land, but not necessarily for the elements of the landscape so intrinsic to the Native Americans.

Small-time traders discovered the priests' trail between Saint Augustine and New Orleans; traffic increased. Those with larger volumes of trade goods or more money who wanted to go all the way to Pensacola or on to New Orleans usually opted to sail around the Florida peninsula, but traffic still continued to increase along the overland route once taken by the priests. The swamps and forests gave way to an established interstate of its time.

At first, Spain generally ignored the region between the Mississippi River and the Rio Grande. Their first contact with this area seems to have been when four Spaniards, sole survivors of a gold-hunting expedition that left Sarasota Bay in 1528 and ended up shipwrecked on the Texas coast. The four men stumbled into the Avavares Indians, who took them in as healers. The men stayed with the tribe for several months before making their way south into Mexico.

The I-10 corridor was about to expand into what would later become Texas. In 1685, France established a fort along the Texas coast, reasoning that it would be a good place from which to invade New Spain. The Spanish learned of the fort and started paying closer attention to Texas. But as soon as they started opening up Texas, traders of other nationalities worked their way into the area, many by water along the coast and along the coastal trail unwinding westward through what is now Mississippi and Louisiana. Spain tried to keep them out of Texas, but couldn't and eventually gave up trying. Further west along the future I-10 corridor, the Tonkawa tribe ranged across South-Central Texas. Similar to Plains Indians in that they wore buckskin and lived in brush tipis, they did not practice agriculture but harvested a great deal from the wild.

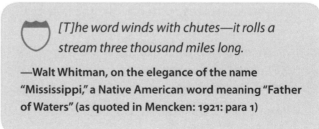

[T]he word winds with chutes—it rolls a stream three thousand miles long.

—Walt Whitman, on the elegance of the name "Mississippi," a Native American word meaning "Father of Waters" (as quoted in Mencken: 1921: para 1)

In September, with its cooler nights and the rains that revive the grasses for horses to graze on, Comanches used the bright light of the full moon to raid settlements for slaves, horses, and revenge. The full harvest moon became known as a Comanche Moon.

Several Native American tribes of the parts of Western Texas, New Mexico, and Arizona that include today's I-10 corridor were named by Spaniards trying to distinguish between the tribes. The Navajo may derive their name from the Spanish word for "knife" or the word *navaju*, which means cultivated land in a canyon. Both the Navajos and their neighbors, the Apaches, had arrived in what is now West Texas and Arizona shortly before the first Europeans did. The more aggressive Apaches fought in small parties, usually striking at night or just before dawn. The Apaches' neighbors, the Comanches, were so skilled at stealing horses that they could sever the rope tied to a sleeping man's wrist and make off with the horse without waking anyone in camp. For the Comanches, the Southwest was all about another element of the desert environment: dust. The Great Spirit had gathered swirls of dust from the east, south, west, and north to create the Commanche people. Because they were formed from earth, Commanches had the strength and ferocity of mighty storms.

In 1749, the Spanish formed an alliance with the Apaches to protect early settlers along the future I-10 corridor in Texas, but the Comanches, traditional enemies of the Apaches, disliked the agreement and continued to raid Spanish settlements until they reached their own accord with the Spanish in 1785. After Mexico gained independence from Spain, Americans poured across the Sabine River into Texas. (Interstate 10 crosses the Sabine at the Louisiana–Texas border.) Between 1821 and 1830, more people settled in Texas than in the previous three centuries of Spanish control.

The canyons of Eastern Arizona made it very easy for Native Americans to raid and then disappear; warfare continued at a violent pace until the late 1800s. To the east of Tucson (Exits 268–248), I-10 finds itself squeezed between the Little Dragoon Mountains to the northwest and the Dragoon Mountains to the southeast as it passes Dragoon (Exit 318). Here, Cochise, the legendary Apache leader, found refuge and a stronghold that could not be penetrated by the regiments out looking for him. Cochise had not been at war with the settlers until he was accused of leading a raiding party, a charge he denied. Seeking revenge, he spent the next eleven years waging war on settlers, attacking stage-coaches and wagon trains passing through his territory. Peace came at last through a negotiated settlement with Cochise, who eventually died undefeated in his mountain stronghold. Supposedly, his tribe buried him in Stronghold Canyon (now in Coronado National Forest, Exit 331) and then raced their horses up and down the canyon all night to erase any trace of his grave. Stronghold Canyon is considered hallowed ground for Apaches, who respect Cochise's memory and consider the place imbued with his spirit.

Another legendary Apache fighter, Geronimo, became infuriated after Mexicans killed his wife and children. His retaliatory raids, some taking place along the present-day I-10 trace in Arizona and West Texas, became so successful that the Apaches made him a war chief. In 1876, the U.S. government tried to force all Apaches onto a desert reservation east of Phoenix. It was an arid wasteland, lacking any kind of game, pasture, or food. The only thing on it was cacti. Rather than go to the reservation, many Apaches, including Geronimo, fled to Mexico. From time to time, Geronimo made peace with settlers, but he was eventually captured and jailed. He died at Fort Sill in Oklahoma in 1909.

In what is now Arizona and California, Native Americans first came in contact with Spanish adventurers and military commanders coming overland from Mexico in the mid-1600s. Here, in the drier landscape of the Southwest, native peoples made use of what was around them, now also along the I-10 corridor. Saguaro cactus fruit was eaten raw or dried, used as a sweetener, or as a base for wine. Saguaro fibers could be used for construction, and when a woodpecker drilled a hole in the cactus, the plant filled the opening of the hole with a harder fiber. Native Americans then carefully carved out this fiber for a drinking cup.

Piñon trees provided nuts; prickly pear cactus, like the saguaro, bore fruit, and the yucca root could be worked into a lather—symbolizing the clouds—for use as a mild soap. Its leaves provided the fibers for rope and also had curative properties. Pima and Papago Indians used the yucca to make baskets, nets, thread, and shoes. Its leaves thatched their cone-shaped homes. Mescal cactus crowns could be roasted and pounded into cake slabs, which were rolled up for easier transportation back to the permanent settlement. But if anyone dared to have sex while the crowns baked, the mescal would become inedible!

As at the Florida end of today's I-10 corridor, Spanish priests in California gathered Native Americans into missions where they were expected to work hard, study Spanish and European customs, and become good Christians—all on a strict schedule. Disease routinely decimated their ranks. As in Florida, the system did not work, but the heritage of California's missions remains in many place names as it does all across the Southwest: Amarillo, Texas (named for its yellow soil), Alhambra, California (from the Arabic word for "red" and the name of a city in Granada, Spain), and Los Angeles, "the city of angels." Mencken called these Spanish names some "of the most mellifluous"[11] of all American place names; the Native American names he found as melodious and charming as running water.

Sometimes names combined European and Native American words. Arizona, for instance, could come from the Mohave word *ari*, meaning "beautiful," and the Spanish word *zona*, meaning "area," to form an overall meaning of "beautiful land." Or, the name could be the stuff of legends. Arizumma, the beautiful daughter of one of the thirteen deities who ruled in the sky, descended to Earth. Pleased by the world, she stayed as its lone inhabitant. One night, while she slept, a drop of dew fell on her from the heavens, and she gave birth to a son and a daughter from whom have sprung all mankind.

Whatever their origins, the Native American and Spanish place names along today's I-10 corridor and throughout the nation transformed the American landscape, giving it color and charm. In the politically incorrect language of his time, Mencken called it a "barbaric brilliancy."[12]

Interstate 19: Perseverance and Patience

Soldiers in fine red uniforms sit atop prancing horses waiting to step into formation. The sun glistens on the lances, decorated for the occasion with rich banners. Blue-frocked priests gather for a final mass. Women weep, some children run around; others refuse to leave their

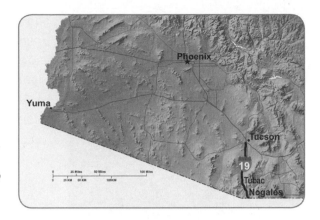

Interstate 19

mother's side. Men check the packs holding their family's possessions, cinched tightly to a mule. The nervous excitement in the air can barely be contained. King Carlos III of Spain has asked the twenty-nine families gathered by the mission to move to a place called California. Lieutenant Colonel de Anza takes his place at the front of the caravan and gives the command. It is time to depart.

In October 1775, Lieutenant Colonel Juan Bautista de Anza, his soldiers, servants, priests, and twenty-nine families, together with hun-

"I exhorted everybody to show perseverance and patience in the trials of so long a journey . . . they ought to consider themselves happy and fortunate that God had chosen them for such an enterprise" (as quoted in Sharp, no date). Friar Pedro Font, a priest with the de Anza caravan, which is shown here in a painting by Cal Peters. (Courtesy of the National Park Service.)

A portrait of Juan Bautista de Anza, commander of the Presidio of San Ignacio de Tubac.

dreds of cattle, and supplies began the long trek to California on orders from the King. California was to be colonized and Lieutenant Colonel de Anza, commander of the Presidio of San Ignacio de Tubac, was a loyal officer. He had dutifully scouted the route the year before, gathered up impoverished Mexican families with childbearing potential and nothing to lose, and acquired the supplies he thought they would need for the next few years in California, including six tons of food. He had even brought a supply of chocolate! Priests, including Friar Font, accompanied the caravan to oversee the spiritual needs of the new settlers. De Anza considered a march cross-country from Arizona easier than attempting to sail up the Pacific Coast from Mexico. Now, on this October morning, he was about to put his careful planning to the test. Soldiers, priests, families on foot, and pack animals fell into line behind him— along a trace that today includes Interstate 19.

Only sixty-three miles long, I-19 connects the Mexican border town of Nogales with Tucson, along a trail that is quite literally centuries old. Native peoples used that trail for hunting; so did Apache war parties. Spanish priests walked northward along this trail; Juan Bautista de Anza rode north to Tubac along this trail. Young children and their families walked out of Tubac that October day in 1775 along this trail, bound for California, where they were about to found San Francisco.

By the time Juan Bautista de Anza first arrived in Tubac in 1760, the trail along the Santa Cruz River was well established. An ancient people known as the Elephant Hunters inhabited this area over eleven thousand years ago, the dense forests and many streams that once blanketed Southern Arizona providing lush feeding grounds for wandering herds of mammoths. Even as the landscape continued to evolve, sculpted by the elements and climate change, the Santa Cruz River valley remained a fertile oasis amid the sand and rock. Native peoples migrated in and out of the valley. Some farmed, camping in small settlements along the river; others simply followed game. Inter-tribal warfare frequently sent them fleeing. A trail evolved along the bank of the Santa Cruz River, which flows north—when it flows; the riverbed is frequently dry. Between the Mexican border and Tucson, the Tumacacori and Sierra Mountains flank the river and present-day I-19 to the west, with the Patagonia and Santa Rita Mountains to the east.

While the Spanish are thought to have visited the Santa Cruz valley as early as the 1500s, the Jesuits were the first Europeans to put

Many people consider the White Dove of the Desert the most beautiful Spanish mission church in the Southwest. The interior is Mexican folk-baroque, displaying one of the nation's finest examples of folk art. Painted mud simulates everything from marble tiles to crystal chandeliers. Samuel Cozzens described it as "the most beautiful, as well as remarkable, specimen . . . nor have I ever seen a building in such perfect harmony with its proportions as this" (Cozzens, 1876: 155). (Courtesy of the National Park Service.)

down roots. They trekked northward from Mexico along the river in 1691. Once within this new territory, they built missions, farms, and ranches. Northeast of present-day Nogales they planted vineyards to provide wine for church sacraments. Arizona's wine industry continues to flourish in this area thanks to these early vines. At what is now Tubac (Exit 34), the Jesuits founded Mission Guevavi in 1732, creating what is now the oldest European settlement in Arizona.

Native Americans rarely greeted Europeans arriving in their midst with any kind of enthusiasm. After the Pima Indians revolted in 1751 against the Spanish interlopers, the Spanish military built a fort to guard against future insurrections—the Presidio of San Ignacio de Tubac. By the time the Presidio was complete, Apaches had taken over the area, terrorizing both the Spanish and the Pima, the latter of whom were moved to what is now nearby Tumacacori National Historical Park (Exit 29) for protection. The Spanish eventually abandoned the Presidio in Tubac, redeploying its garrison to Tucson. Ironically, after continued attacks from Apaches, Pima Indians moved in to staff the Presidio beginning in 1787, something they apparently did with distinction.

On that October morning in 1775, the de Anza caravan headed north along the trail at a pace of about two and a half miles an hour. Some children rode on the horses with soldiers, while others walked. The first night, a pregnant woman in the caravan gave birth, and though the child survived, the mother did not. A priest accompanied her body to San Xavier del Bac for burial; her family stayed with the caravan.

Construction had not yet begun on the church that would become the centerpiece of San Xavier del Bac (Exit 92). The mission had been founded by Jesuit Father Kino in 1692 to bring Christianity to the Pima Indians. Designed and built by Franciscan missionaries, the famous church was begun in 1778, and would soon be known as the White Dove of the Desert for its brilliant white adobe walls. To build the dome, laborers filled the entire church with sand, which they then molded into the shape of a dome. Masons built the dome on top of the sand. One legend claims that the priests salted the sand with gold coins to encourage the laborers to dig the sand out faster once the new masonry dome had dried. Adobe statues of a cat and a mouse adorn the top of the church; legend has it that if the cat ever catches the mouse, the world will come to an end.

The town of Tubac in 1864, as illustrated in *Adventures in the Apache Country: A Tour Through Arizona*, by John Ross Browne.

After arranging for the burial of the dead woman, the de Anza caravan continued its journey. Just south of what is now Tucson, Friar Font commented that Apaches had not yet attacked them. Given the great number of pack animals loaded with everything a colony would need for a few years, this surprised him. Many of de Anza's soldiers had two or three children riding along with them, and were obviously not in a position to fend off a sudden attack. The priest attributed their good fortune to the Holy Virgin of Guadalupe. One hundred years later, tourist Samuel Cozzens reported boards with the inscription "killed by Apaches" everywhere along the roadside de Anza's caravan had taken from Tubac. "Ruined ranches, deserted haciendas, and untilled fields stare you in the face whichever way you turn, and tell a story that cannot fail to awaken in the mind of the beholder the most melancholy reflections."[13]

North of Tucson, the caravan turned west for California. They eventually reached their destination on March 28, 1776. Only one person perished along the way—the woman who died in childbirth the first night. Several more women gave birth on the trail, so more settlers arrived in the new colony than left Tubac. After helping his charges settle in, Juan Bautista de Anza returned to Tubac with only enough soldiers and servants to ensure his safety and comfort. Friar Font settled into an Arizona mission to write his memoirs about a road trip of perseverance and patience. Many of the settlers, particularly their children, became leading citizens and major landowners in San Francisco. The trail they followed to California became known as the Anza Trail and continued in use for five more years until hostile Yuma Indians shut it down. Still, that was long enough to establish more colonies throughout Southern California.

Tubac eventually became a ghost town as more and more people fled Native American attacks or headed to the gold rush in California. A mining boom in the 1860s proved short-lived, and the town again reverted to the ghosts.

Even as Tubac was quite literally falling apart, the road south to Mexico continued to improve. By 1877, a weekly stage ran from Tucson through Nogales at the border and on into the Mexican state of Sonora. To its credit, despite various dangers, the stagecoach company managed to keep the stages in service for some time, along a road that now had a name: the Nogales Highway. Tucson of 1877 did extensive business with Mexico, much of it moving along what is now I-19 south through the Santa Cruz valley to the border. Many wealthy and successful businessmen resided in Tucson, and were identified as having made "handsome fortunes, in trade, government contracts, and general business enterprises."[14] Travelers stopping in Tucson could choose between two hotels. Two breweries kept the town's ten saloons amply supplied.

Today, the interstate version of the trail de Anza's settlers walked from Tubac to Tucson is traveled by over sixty-two thousand vehicles every day. South of Tubac, near the border, traffic is much lighter at about six thousand vehicles per day. The National Park Service works with all levels of government and private property owners to preserve de Anza's trail, now a national historic trail. A 4.5-mile portion of the original path in Tumacacori National Historical Park (Exit 29) near Tubac gives history buffs a chance to experience what it was like to walk across Arizona to California. The 4.5 miles represents about a third of the distance the 1775 caravan covered every day, regardless of weather, blistered feet, or whether they even felt like walking that day. Perseverance and patience. The distance to California was about twelve hundred miles. Could you have done it?

Interstate 30: The Road to Political Glory

"Raised in the woods so he knew ev'ry tree, Kilt him a b'ar when he was only three."[15] Davy Crockett, 1786–1836: frontiersman, congressman, legend. Crockett referred to himself in a more humorous fashion as "half-horse, half-alligator, a little touched with the snapping turtle; can wade the Mississippi, leap the Ohio, ride a streak of lightning."[16] He was also blessed with the ability to string words together that had people flocking to hear him whenever he spoke in public. So many people in his home district of Tennessee took notice that Crockett served two terms in the Tennessee Legislature (1821–1822 and 1823–1824), and was elected to Congress three times (1827–1831 and 1833–1835). Congress-

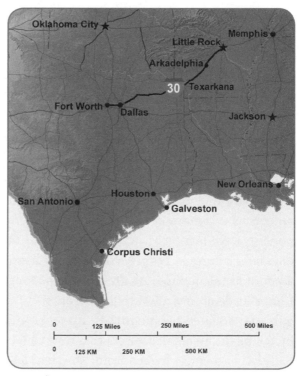

Interstate 30

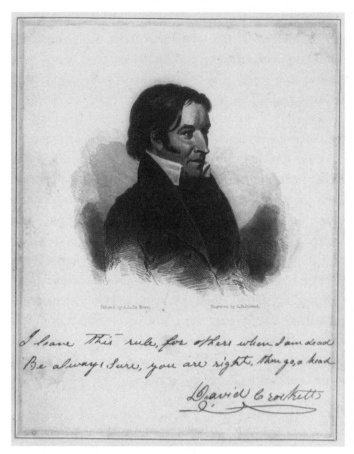

The caption, in Davy Crockett's handwriting, reads: "I leave this rule for others when I am dead. Be always sure you are right, then go ahead. David Crockett." (Courtesy of the Library of Congress.)

man Crockett was so successful that he felt others seeking public office could benefit from his experience on the hustings.

In the election of 1834, Davy Crockett opposed the policies of presidential candidate Andrew Jackson, who also had Tennessee roots. It was a hard-fought election. Davy liberally flattered, bribed, imbibed, and promised whatever it took to win a vote. Apparently, so did his opponent. Davy lost by 230 votes and did not take defeat lightly. A few days later he wrote: "I confess the thorn still rankles, not so much on my account as the nation's. As my country no longer requires my services, I have made up my mind to go to Texas."[17] Davy visited his constituents and declared his intentions in a final address, ending his speech by telling the assembled voters that they could go to hell while he went to Texas to free its citizens from "the shackles of the Mexican government."[18] Political glory would be his once again.

In this day and age, Davy would probably hop in his pickup truck and head west out of Tennessee to Little Rock, Arkansas. From there he would take Interstate 30 through to Dallas, Texas, then head south on another interstate to his eventual date with destiny at the Alamo in San Antonio. Such a trip would take eight hours at the most. In the 1830s, the journey was a bit more circuitous. After saying goodbye to his wife and children, Davy walked west to the Mississippi River, where he boarded a steamer that took him to the mouth of the Arkansas River. Here, he switched to another steamer headed for Little Rock. Once word spread that Davy Crockett was in town, the delighted citizens of Little Rock invited the legendary hero to a shooting match, which he naturally won. An "uproarious" good time was subsequently had by all, thanks to plentiful whiskey and wild game. Despite pleas to stay, Davy was determined to liberate Texas and off he went the next day, this time on a fine horse presented to him by Little Rock's residents. The road Davy took tracked southwest through Benton (Exit 114), Rockport (Exit 98), Arkadelphia (Exit 73), Washington (Exit 30), and Fulton (Exit 18), much as I-30 does today. As one biographer described the journey, Davy met up with an itinerant preacher who spoke of the many blessings bestowed upon them. "We were alone in the wilderness, but as he proceeded, it seemed to me as if the tall trees bent their tops to listen . . . and the

Get up on all occasions, and sometimes on no occasion at all, and make long-winded speeches, though composed of nothing else than wind.

Promise all that is asked . . . and more if you can think [of it]. . . . Promises cost nothing, therefore deny nobody who has a vote or sufficient influence to obtain one.

When the day of election approaches, visit your constituents far and wide. Treat liberally, and drink freely.

—**Congressman Davy Crockett (as quoted in Abbott, 1874: chapter 11)**

fading flowers of autumn smiled, and sent forth fresher fragrance, as if conscious that they would revive in spring; and even the sterile rocks seemed to be endued with some mysterious influence."[19] Davy was so moved, he hauled out the whiskey jug and offered it to the preacher. "[I]f he had ever belonged to the temperance society, he had either renounced membership, or obtained a dispensation. Having liquored, we proceeded on our journey."[20] The two men later parted company near Gurdon (Exits 63 and 54).

When Davy passed through Arkansas, about twenty-one thousand people called the territory home. (Arkansas was admitted into the Union in 1836.) His travels toward Texas took Davy through countryside that varied between hilly and flat, forested and treeless prairies. At the town of Fulton, he again received a warm reception from the local citizens. After visiting for a few days, he continued on to Texas. This is where his travel plans deviated from what he'd probably do today. In 1835, things were a little different. Texarkana (Exits 2–1) did not exist and the road from Fulton jigged southward before eventually jogging westward across the Red River into Texas. Once in Texas, the road forked, with the northern branch tracing through Mount Pleasant (Exit 160) before reaching Dallas (Exits 56–38). The southern branch crossed the state in a southwesterly direction.

Instead of more road travel, Davy disposed of his horse and boarded a steamer that took him down the Red River to Natchitoches, at that time a small village in Louisiana of about eight hundred people. From there his route took him overland along an old Spanish trail to Nacogdoches, Texas, bringing him ever closer to San Antonio and the Alamo. Would the Davy Crockett of today get distracted by Texas politics, setting his sights on Austin instead? Perhaps he would have become a motivational speaker after his election defeat. Television cameras and the Internet would have loved him. In 1835, however, the forks in his life course and in the I-30 corridor of that time became very much a case of the road not taken.

Interstate 81: Peas Porridge Hot

Interstate 81 travels eight hundred and fifty miles through six states, stretching from New York to Tennessee. Most interchanges along the

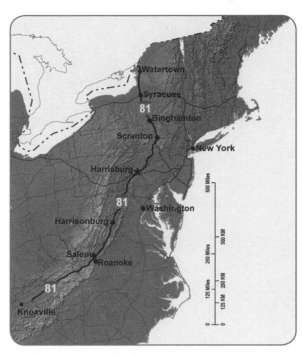

Interstate 81

way offer up at least one option for a snack or meal. Some restaurant chains even do a fairly good job of serving regional specialties. But, in the very earliest days of travel in America, most wayfarers were not as well provisioned as the caravan of settlers that trekked from Tubac, Arizona, to San Francisco. Instead, travelers often had to settle for eighteenth century versions of the old nursery rhyme:

> Peas porridge hot,
> Peas porridge cold,
> Peas porridge in the pot
> Nine days old.

In early colonial days, if you were well-to-do, you typically rode on a horse or in some sort of conveyance pulled by a draft animal. However, the vast majority walked everywhere they had to go, carrying their own food with them. Not only could they not afford a horse, the roads of the time were little more than rough trails through the bush. It was tough slogging. Taverns became important way stations for all classes of travelers. Generally spaced every two to three miles along popular thoroughfares, much like today's I-81 interchanges, taverns offered a meal and a bed to the traveler who could afford it, as well as a place for

OYSTER SOUP

An illustrator for *Harper's Weekly* took a few moments to sketch three men at this 1887 version of a roadside fast-food outlet. Two customers enjoy some oyster soup while the proprietor looks on from behind his makeshift counter. (Courtesy of the Library of Congress.)

draft animals to be fed and watered, or exchanged for fresh horses. The wayfarer on foot stopped in for a tankard of cheap whiskey or rum, or carried it with him, as Davy Crockett had done on his trip to Texas.

Enter the old nursery rhyme. Peas porridge hot, peas porridge cold was an early version of road food for the masses. Without rice cakes or granola bars to stash in their knapsacks, early travelers sometimes boiled a pot of dried peas until they thickened to the consistency of stick to the roof of the mouth, too thick oatmeal porridge. If it was cold weather, all the better. The congealed porridge could be kept cold, even frozen, then thawed and eaten cold or reheated in its pot, presumably for at least nine days.

Peas porridge hot took on a different meaning in a tavern. Usually little more than a log shanty, possibly with a table, sometimes even a bench to sit on, many taverns were identified "by an earthen jug suspended by the handle from a pole; the pip of the chimney never rising above the roof; or a score of black hogs luxuriating in the sunshine and mud before the door."[21] Guests usually ate whatever the owner ate. One big pot hung over or sat in the flames of the fireplace in the main room. The pot contained a stock enriched with dried peas, beans, and whatever other vegetables the cook had on hand. Meat was tossed in as it became available. From meal to meal, the cook threw whatever into the pot. The resulting stew or "porridge" had to be thick, because most people still ate with their fingers or a knife. In the days before paper-wrapped hamburgers and disposable cutlery—and government food inspection—people ate off of wooden trenchers that were not washed between diners. Those eating could only hope that whatever came out of the pot was no more than nine days old and that the trencher had been washed at some point in the last week or so.

In 1743, when John Bartram, noted botanist and resident of Philadelphia, traveled north along a route traced, in part, by today's I-81, eating at and lodging in taverns was not an option. For the most part, there weren't any. Instead, he camped out and occasionally stayed with a friendly trapper or Native American family. John's destination was a council of Iroquois chiefs near present-day Syracuse, New York (Exits 29–16). At one point, he was invited to a feast served to the attending chiefs.

> [T]his repast consisted of 3 great kettles of *Indian* corn soup, or thin homony, with dry'd eels and other fish boiled in it, and one kettle full of young squashes and their flowers boiled in water, and a little meal mixed . . . last of all was served a great bowl, full of Indian dumplings, made of new soft corn, cut or scraped off the ear, then with the addition of some boiled beans, lapped well up in *Indian* corn leaves. . . . near sun set . . . we regaled on a bowl of boiled cakes 6 or 7 inches diameter, and about 2 thick, with another of boiled squash.[22]

Today, after saying his farewells, John would probably grab some bottled water and head back to Philadelphia, down I-81 to the Pennsylvania Turnpike into Phillie, stopping at family restaurants at interchanges for his meals. In 1743, John had to replenish his food supplies before

At Cornell University, just to the west of I-81 at Binghamton, researchers have long been interested in the apple. In 1915, they introduced the Cortland apple, a cross between a Ben Davis and a McIntosh. An all-purpose apple, the Cortland is known for its crisp white flesh and is named after the town of Cortland, New York (Exits 10–11).

he could start the return trip home. For two days, he slogged through heavy bush, making portages around rapids and experiencing generally unpleasant conditions, to get to the trading post at nearby Oswego, New York (Exit 34). There, he purchased dried beef, a gallon of rum, and some biscuit for his trip back to Philadelphia.

In New York State, much of the area I-81 crosses today was settled in the 1700s and early 1800s by disaffected New Englanders looking for land of their own when their home states started to get crowded. The apple had always been an important staple in New England households and it too migrated into the I-81 area. The earliest settlers used apples to make cider and vinegar. They also dried apples for winter use. This time-consuming activity often provided an excuse for a community party with an apple-drying bee. Hard cider was even used as a form of money. In some instances, a settler had to plant an orchard to satisfy the conditions of his land claim. George Washington imposed these conditions on settlers occupying lands he owned near Winchester, Virginia (Exits 315–313). In the Virginias, apples were also turned into apple butter, which was spread on everything from biscuits to sausage.

In Northern Pennsylvania, I-81 winds through the Endless Mountains toward Scranton and Wilkes-Barre. This was once coal country, where eastern European immigrants flocked to work in the mines. They settled into the towns like Avoca (Exit 178) that had been settled by the Irish before them, but added their own culinary heritage to the mix. The flour pancakes of Russia called blini, served with caviar, became potato pancakes in Pennsylvania, served with strawberry jelly called bleenies. This deep-fried mixture of grated potato, onion, egg, and flour was popular at community events throughout the area; people lined up around the block for a good plate of bleenies.

South of Harrisburg, I-81 skirts the edge of Pennsylvania-Dutch country, where regional diners still serve shoofly pie. Frances Trollope deemed American eating habits "abundant, but not delicate." On her travels across Pennsylvania, the menu of an 1830s version of a family restaurant met her needs, if not her sensibilities.

> They consume an extraordinary quantity of bacon. . . . Ham and beef-steaks appear morning, noon, and night. In eating, they mix things together with the strangest incongruity imaginable. I have seen eggs and oysters eaten together . . . ham with apple-sauce; beef-steak with stewed peaches; and salt fish with onions. . . . They are "extravagantly fond" to use their own phrase, of puddings, pies, and all kinds of "sweets," particularly the ladies.[23]

Twenty-five years later, her son Anthony encountered the high-volume equivalent of a modern interstate diner at the breakfast hour. "They fill your cup the instant it is empty. They tender you fresh food before that which has disappeared from your plate has been swallowed. They begrudge you no amount that you can eat or drink; but they begrudge you a single moment that you sit there neither eating nor drinking."[24] You can almost hear his every synapse begging for peace and quiet while he nurses that morning cup of coffee, cradled in his hands.

On and on I-81 goes through endless acres of corn fields in Southern Pennsylvania. Whether it's the stubble of winter fields or the summer stalks stretching skyward, the evidence is everywhere. Corn was a staple of the Native American diet, and European settlers quickly adopted it in all its varied possibilities. They also adopted the names of the various corn dishes. Some words that we use today to describe edible corn are the words used by the Algonquians. Cornpone, for example, originates from *poan*, Algonquian for a cornbread baked on a griddle or in hot ashes. Hominy is a variation on *uskatahomen*, also an Algonquian word. Many early travelers like John Bartram carried ground corn with them for a fast meal over a campfire.

South of the Mason-Dixon Line at the Pennsylvania–Maryland border, food takes on a decidedly regional flavor and, as the Department of Tourism for Virginia likes to point out, it is about more than just peanuts. Interstate 81 travels down the middle of the Shenandoah Valley, past towns like Strasburg (Exits 298–296), Lexington (Exit 188), and

Roanoke-Salem (Exits 143–137). By the Civil War, the Shenandoah had become well known as the garden of Virginia. As such, it became a major target of Union forces. Here, much of the early cooking was done in the Native American style, corn being the primary staple year-round—corn meal, dried corn, corn flour, corn grits, popped corn—along with meat from hunting. In summer, additional vegetables—turnips, pumpkins, potatoes—enhanced the diet, as well as fresh fruits. The forest also provided wild leeks, berries, honey, maple syrup, sassafras, ginseng, and other herbs. Travelers described typical rural fare as something not soon forgotten: "buckwheat cakes with . . . butter, mountain honey or maple syrup . . . savoury venison or the luscious trout, all of which are commonly found."[25]

In the fall, travelers stopping at a tavern in the Shenandoah feasted on fresh pork. This meant ham, roasts, sausage, spare ribs, pigs feet, and head cheese. Meat was stored in smokehouses for the winter; bins in the cellar stored root vegetables, cabbages, and apples. There were also barrels of sauerkraut and salted fish. In the spring and summer, veal, chicken, and lamb appeared on the table. Produce could be swapped for groceries at the local general store including cane sugar and molasses.

While this kind of bounty was certainly available, it was not always served to strangers or presented in an appetizing fashion. On his way south in the 1850s, landscape architect Frederick Law Olmsted discovered what was to become the bane of his existence.

> At this dinner I made the first practical acquaintance with what shortly was to be the bane of my life, viz., corn-bread and bacon. I partook innocent and unsuspicious of these dishes, as they seemed to be the staple of the meal, without a thought that for the next six months I should actually see nothing else. . . . Taken alone, with vile coffee, I may ask, with deep feeling, who is sufficient for these things?[26]

Charles Dudley Warner, friend and co-author of Mark Twain, traveled through Southern Virginia and Eastern Tennessee in the 1880s. In the absence of conveniently spaced motels at exits along the Shenandoah interstate of his time, he took what he could get at an inn or from homeowners who provided a bed and an evening meal. The quality varied dramatically, and he found out where to stay by word of mouth or by stopping at the farm gate and asking. One meal in particular proved memorable.

Alas! The supper served in a room dimly lighted with a smoky lamp, on a long table covered with oilcloth, was not the sort to arouse the delayed and now gone appetite . . . and yet it did not lack variety: cornpone (Indian meal stirred up with water and heated through) hot biscuit, slack-baked and livid, fried salt-pork swimming in grease, apple-butter, pickled beets, onions, and cucumbers raw, coffee (so-called), buttermilk, and sweet milk when specially asked for (the correct taste, however, is for buttermilk), and pie. This was not the pie of commerce, but the pie of the country,—two thick slabs of dough, with a squeezing of apple between.[27]

As I-81 heads southward, it slips deeper and deeper into the land of biscuits and gravy, collards and turnip greens, grits, country ham, and redeye gravy. Here the country fare of settlers blended with that of African Americans with foods such as okra appearing in rich country stews. Black-eyed peas and chitterlings entered the American vernacular. In Eastern Tennessee, near the end of I-81, the interstate passes by Jonesborough (Exit 50). This was once the home of Andrew Jackson, hero of the Battle of New Orleans and future president. As the story goes, Jackson asked his military cook to prepare a meal for him. He wanted a slice of country ham with gravy as red as the cook's eyes. The cook, it seems, had had a rough night with the moonshine and had very hungover eyes. Nearby officers heard Jackson make his request and redeye gravy was born. To make redeye gravy, thicken the grease from a slab of fried country ham with a bit of flour and use day-old coffee in place of water. Serve on biscuits with the fried ham. It is guaranteed to get rid of red eyes.

Some like it hot,
Some like it cold,
Some like it in the pot
Nine days old.

Interstate 83: Rocking Chairs, Dining Tables, and Small Boys on Top, Please

In 1842, Charles Dickens set out from Baltimore, Maryland, bound for Harrisburg, Pennsylvania, via York, along a route traced very closely by today's Interstate 83. He rode the train sixty miles to York, leaving Baltimore in the morning and arriving at York in time for the evening meal. From there, he was to proceed via stagecoach to Harrisburg. Dickens had already seen his share of American roads, and was hardly averse to naming a pothole for what it was, but this time he focused his pen and wit on the conveyance itself, something he likened to a barge on wheels. At York, this corpulent giant rumbled to a stop in front of the hotel. Twelve passengers packed themselves inside and all luggage—including a rocking chair and a good-sized dining table—was strapped to the top. Dickens chose to sit on top with the driver and rocking chair rather than try to squeeze inside. At one point, an intoxicated gentleman climbed on top amid the luggage, but apparently fell off as he "was seen in the distant perspective reeling back to the grog-shop where we had found him."[28]

His routing that fall of 1842 was probably the most expedient at the time between Baltimore and Harrisburg. The road Dickens did not comment on wove its way north from the coastal plain to the gently rolling hills of the piedmont, across countless small runs (creeks) and rivers. Gunpowder (Falls) River in Maryland did not actually have a waterfall on it, but was so named because the river crossed from the rocky piedmont onto the coastal plain. All along the Gunpowder Valley, early settlements sprang up around mill sites. At the Jerusalem Mill on the Little Gunpowder Falls River, a firearms factory helped supply soldiers with weaponry during the American Revolution. In other places, ironworks and a copper factory harnessed the river's power. Roads soon connected

Interstate 83

the small settlements in the valley. Today, I-83 crosses through Gunpowder Falls State Park at Exit 27 in Maryland. The sixteen thousand acre park protects the Big and Little Gunpowder Falls Rivers, the Gunpowder River, and their valleys. Some of the park's trails follow the corridor carved out by the railroad Charles Dickens took.

On Charles Dickens' way to Harrisburg from York that fall day in 1842, it rained. Dickens got very wet and cold, exposed as he was to the elements from his seat on top of the coach. The frequent stops at wayside taverns allowed him to "swallow the usual anti-temperance recipe for keeping out the cold."[29] The coach followed the Susquehanna River as it wound its way northwestward to Harrisburg. (Today's I-83 travels in a more direct line toward Harrisburg.) At one point, Dickens climbed back on top of the coach to find what looked like "a large fiddle in a brown bag." But the fiddle appeared to be wearing muddy boots and a cap. Suddenly, the fiddle "upreared itself the height of three feet six, and fixing its eyes on me, observed in piping accents, with a complaisant

The countryside and the Baltimore to York road, as viewed from the Bushongo Tavern in July 1799. The tavern was located about five miles from York. The artist is Philip Vickers Fithian. (Courtesy of the Library of Congress.)

yawn, half quenched in an obliging air of friendly patronage, 'Well now, stranger, I guess you find this a'most like an English afternoon, hey?'"[30] At Harrisburg, Dickens found a comfortable hotel in which to rest and dry out from his English afternoon with a fiddle before proceeding westward on the Susquehanna River by canal boat.

Interstate 87: Fops and Flirts

The trouble with most of us Southerners, is that we either don't travel enough or we don't profit enough by our travels. Now of course all you gentlemen are well traveled, but what have you seen? Europe and New York and Philadelphia and, of course, the ladies have been to Saratoga.
—Rhett Butler in Margaret Mitchell's *Gone with the Wind*

Rhett Butler was referring to Saratoga Springs, New York, a combination mineral waters spa, glittering resort, and gambling center of 150 years ago. Many Southern ladies, even before Rhett's time, used ill health or the fear of malaria as an excuse to escape the antebellum mansion they called home and head north to a health spa like Saratoga during the summer months. To get there, Southern belles packed their Saratoga trunks—a domed trunk designed to accommodate hoop-skirted ball gowns—and, together with their maids and family members, took the train or coastal steamer to New York. From New York, the second leg of

Saratoga Springs on July 4, 1865, *Harper's Weekly*. (Courtesy of the Library of Congress.)

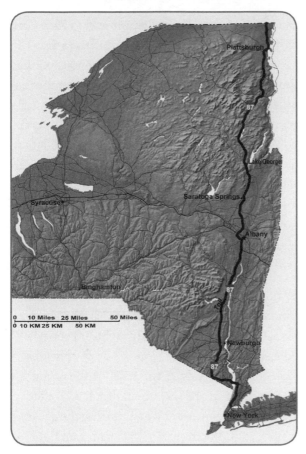

Interstate 87

the journey involved either a trip by boat up the Hudson River or by rail along the banks of the river.

Once at Saratoga Springs, the ladies enjoyed the beau monde: literary salons, art lessons and rounds of music recitals, croquet on the lawns, theater, grand balls, and afternoon tea. Gambling reached new heights with cards, boxing, and horse racing. It was also a good place to find a husband!

> To girls who go there with trunks full of muslin and crinoline, for whom a carriage and pair of horses is always waiting immediately after dinner, whose fathers' pockets are bursting with dollars, it is a very gay place. Dancing and flirtations come as a matter of course, and matrimony follows after with only too great rapidity.[31]

In the spring of 1835, one Southern belle, Caroline Howard Gilman, made the trip to Saratoga at a time when the resort was becoming popular. Caroline and her entourage had already made their way to New York and faced two options for the balance of the journey. A road ran up the Hudson River valley, on the opposite bank to today's Interstate 87, but travel by boat was the preferred option, as it was considered more secure and leisurely. From the river, the big estates springing up along the Hudson could be admired, as could the rock formations, West Point, the Catskills, and the villages lining the shore. This area was also the home of Washington Irving's "Rip Van Winkle" and of James Fennimore Cooper's *The Spy*, two bestsellers of their time with which Caroline would have no doubt been familiar. To the Native Americans of this area, the Catskills were the home of spirits. Washington Irving described their ability to influence the weather.

> [A]n old squaw spirit . . . dwelt on the highest peak of the Catskills, and had charge of the doors of day and night to open and shut them at the proper hour. She hung up the new moons in the skies, and cut up the old ones into stars. In times of drought, if properly propitiated, she would spin light summer clouds out of cobwebs and morning dew, and send them off from the crest of the mountain, flake after flake . . . to float in the air; until dissolved by the heat of the sun, they would fall in gentle showers, causing the grass to spring, the fruits to ripen, and the corn to grow an inch an hour. If displeased, however, she would brew up clouds black as ink, sit-

The Mohawk and Hudson Railroad's cars and engine as they appeared at the time of Caroline Gilman's visit to Saratoga Springs. Illustration from *Scribner's Monthly*.

ting in the midst of them like a bottle-bellied spider in the midst of its web; and when the clouds broke, woe betide the valleys![32]

At Troy (Exit 7), the Gilman party switched to rail for the final sprint to Saratoga. Caroline described the railcars as whirling by "mocking the slow canal boats, that peep up from the banks like tortoises."[33]

Once at Saratoga Springs, Caroline was exceedingly amused by those "whose heads appeared to turn on pivots in their zeal to recognize and be recognized."[34] While the ladies thoroughly enjoyed Saratoga, this genteel atmosphere was not everyone's idea of grand adventure. "There are more forlorn looking people than I have ever met with, if you watch faces; and there is nothing in the whole compass of yawns like a Saratoga yawn, if you hear one when a gaper is off his guard. The whole man is stretched, inwardly and outwardly. Let no one who values a small mouth risk a gape at the Springs."[35]

Caroline Gilman and her party enjoyed their stay. "[I]t is a glorious place, and in fifty years, palaces, and fountains, and gardens will burst forth on its now rude location, and rival in beauty the healing power with which God has blessed it so richly."[36] Saratoga would also become famous as the place where the potato chip was invented, a snack Caroline would probably have enjoyed.

By 1870, when Mrs. Samuel Colt visited Saratoga, things were much livelier. Caroline Gilman's imagined palaces had indeed been built—to

house the throngs now streaming into Saratoga every summer to gamble. Mrs. Colt, who was busy writing a tourist guide to the Empire State, took it all in.

> There are really a half dozen different Saratogas, and each one attracts its own "set." Here, young men come with "fast" teams and a keen interest in pretty faces and the races. Hither wend the fop and the flirt, who's paradise is the ball-room; this realm is ruled by the millionaire and the managing mother. Then too, there is a Saratoga of the sportsman. Also a Saratoga of the invalid. Outside of all these Saratogas, there is still another, which attracts thousands of sensible, healthy, but busy and overworked people, who come here every year for genuine recreation.[37]

To reach Saratoga, a steamboat up the Hudson River continued to be the preferred mode of travel along what Mrs. Colt called the great thoroughfare of summer pleasure travel. Once in Saratoga, however, the horse-drawn carriage took over.

> The most fashionable drive is the new boulevard to the lake. This drive is four miles in length, with a row of trees on each side and one in the middle. Carriages pass down on one side and return on the other. . . . Until recently there have been few attractions besides the gay and brilliant stream of carriages with their fair occupants and superb horses. Since last season immense sums of money have been extended on the avenues and roads in the vicinity of Saratoga, and this new boulevard is a magnificent drive.[38]

By the 1930s, Saratoga had lost some of its luster. But at a time when every job was needed, the State of New York stepped in and spent six million dollars restoring and expanding facilities at the Springs; twenty-five thousand visitors were expected annually. Spas charged $1.25 to $1.75 for a bath; a colonic irrigation was $1.50 to $2.00. For a penny, visitors could purchase a glass of mineral water guaranteed to cure "heart diseases, constipation, gout, rheumatism, nervousness and a stack of diseases which have not yet been catalogued."[39]

While many travelers still enjoyed the boat ride up the Hudson River, the train took over in the latter years of the nineteenth century as the preferred mode of travel. The *Saratoga Special* left Grand Central Station in New York every afternoon, bringing its passengers to Saratoga in time for dinner. By 1910, the automobile ruled. Saratoga boasted that it was the "automobiling center of the East" and "the mecca of every automobile tourist."[40] Federal monies in the 1920s and '30s helped improve that old roadway up the Hudson River Valley, transforming it into U.S. Route 9.

In 1944, Governor Dewey of New York authorized construction of the New York Thruway, from New York to Buffalo—as funds permitted. The Thruway followed the western shore of the Hudson River to Albany, where it then broke away to Buffalo. The New York to Albany section opened to the public in stages between October 1954 and August 1956. With the advent of the interstate system, the New York Thruway was quickly split in two. In 1958, the section from New York to Albany became I-87, which then continued on from Albany, skirting Lake Champlain to march onward to the Canadian border.

Saratoga Springs came alive every August for the annual races. Built in 1864, the racetrack there is the oldest in the United States. It was at Saratoga in 1930 that Jim Dandy beat the Triple Crown winner at one hundred to one odds. The legendary Man o' War suffered his only defeat here in 1919. Clarke Gable (who had not yet immortalized Rhett Butler in the film version of *Gone with the Wind*) and Jean Harlowe even came to town in 1937 to make *Saratoga*, a comedy about the horse-racing season and the foibles of love when you least expect it. The illustration by Winslow Homer depicts a crowd at the Saratoga Track in August 1865 (*Harper's Weekly*).

Native Americans were the first to take advantage of the natural conduit created by Lake Champlain, Lake George, and the Hudson River. Early European explorers followed suit, and the route soon became an important link between the French settlements surrounding the St. Lawrence River and the Dutch communities in the Hudson River Valley. This natural route between countries frequently in opposition to each other led to the construction of forts along the route now occupied by I-87, and several pitched battles, notably at Ticonderoga (Exit 28), Lake George, and Saratoga during the French and Indian War, the American Revolution, and the War of 1812. Many Loyalists also fled along this route to Upper Canada (now Ontario) at the outset of the American Revolution.

During her stay in Saratoga in 1870, the intrepid Mrs. Colt took a trip northward to Lake George (Exit 22). She found it to be a "strange lull in excitement after Saratoga . . . its tranquility is something like the morning after a ball. There is nothing but to croquet or sit on the piazza, or go boating or fishing upon the lake. It is a good place to study fancy fishermen who have taken their degrees in Wall Street."[41] However, she did caution: "Lake George may be reached by more than one route, but there is an inevitable stage ride of nine miles to be encountered or enjoyed—according to the temperament of the traveler."[42]

In 1870 to get to Lake George, travelers first took the train from Saratoga north to Glens Falls (Exit 18).

> Three coaches await the arrival of the train, and give promise of ample accommodation. Alas, for our expectations! All the passengers bound to Lake George are packed into and upon a single coach, until there is not an inch of room to spare, and trunks upon trunks are fastened behind. The drive . . . is said to be charming—in scenery—and so it is but if tourists are liable to be packed like sardines in a box, we recommend . . . taking a private carriage thence to the Lake.[43]

At Lake George, the gentility of the spa resorts gave way to the raw and rugged beauty of the Adirondacks. "It is our own opinion, dear reader, that if you have never been a 'Tom-Boy,' either male or female, at some period in your career that you will never be of those who find the

Adirondacks truly enjoyable."[44] Mrs. Colt must have had a little tomboy in her, for she tried her hand at poetry to describe how she felt.

Tumbling over ridges,
Driving under fir boughs,
Tilting on log bridges.
Wheezing up the hill-side,
Drinking at the fountain.
Bless me, this is pleasant,
Climbing up the Mountain![45]

To the north, I-87 skirts what has become Adirondack Park, a six-million-acre preserve between Lake Champlain and the St. Lawrence River. Lake Champlain, at the very northern end of I-87, is named after Samuel de Champlain, who explored the lake in 1609, ironically, within a few weeks of Henry Hudson sailing up the Hudson River as far as present-day Albany at the other end of today's I-87. One hundred and seven miles long, Lake Champlain provides an essential part of the link between the St. Lawrence and New York harbor for both commercial and pleasure boats. Many of the towns served by I-87 were once important industrial and shipping points along the lake. Plattsburgh and Rouses Point (Exits 39–36 and 42), for instance, took advantage of plentiful water power and lake travel to become industrial centers with iron ore production and lumberyards.

The journey today from New York to the Canadian border along I-87 can be accomplished in about five and a half hours. Caroline Gilman spent days just reaching Saratoga in 1835, but she had no complaints. "What can be said in a journal when one's carriages roll along over good roads, when boats are safe, and waters clear, and skies blue, and fish willing to come to the hook, and company good-humoured? Absolutely nothing. One can only fold arms quietly, be grateful, and fall asleep."[46]

Interstate 24: Water and Weather Permitting

What do you do when you want to go somewhere and the road doesn't exist? Today, we tend to take the availability of a nearby road, even an interstate, for granted, but in 1856, when landscape architect Freder-

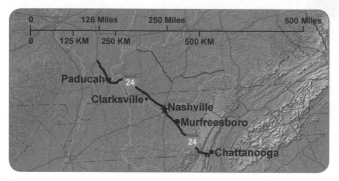

Interstate 24

ick Law Olmsted decided to see Nashville, Tennessee, a riverboat on the Cumberland River was the only viable option. While the fops and flirts heading to Saratoga Springs in New York had three choices—boat, rail, or stagecoach—in sparsely settled parts of the country, roads were impracticable. At a time when private citizens generally maintained roads near their property, it was a waste of time to look after roads hardly anyone used, especially when, as Frederick commented, "farmers not working themselves, are generally addicted to sporting, and to all easy views of life."[47] So, Frederick chose river travel to cross the then sparsely populated part of Kentucky and Tennessee now served by Interstate 24.

Today's I-24 begins just across the border in Georgia and then tracks in a northwesterly direction for downtown Nashville (Exits 54–44), where it follows along a route similar to that of the Cumberland River toward Paducah, Kentucky (Exits 16–3), on the Ohio River. In 1856, Frederick got on a riverboat at Smithland, Kentucky (Exit 4). The *D.A. Tomkins*, a flat-bottomed scow, drew about a foot of water. Freight, boilers, and wood for fuel occupied the first floor; a second floor provided a saloon and rooms for about twenty passengers. The captain told Frederick that they would be in Nashville the next day, "water and weather permitting."[48] Today's I-24 traveler can make the same trip in about ninety minutes, traffic and road construction permitting.

What today would be considered a road trip from hell was taken in stride in 1856. It wasn't so much road construction that held them up as it was boat re-construction. After pit stops to make repairs to the boat's wheel, damaged when it snagged a tree floating in the river, and getting stuck on the 1856 version of coming to an abrupt standstill on the interstate because of an accident—a river shoal—the *Tomkins* sounded its whistle four days later and with that shriek of excitement bumped against a levee in Nashville to unload its cargo and give passengers a chance to stretch. In an era without iPods or on-board DVDs, Frederick had whiled away the extra hours on board by studying a Spanish grammar book he had with him.

After taking four days to get there, Nashville turned out to be a disappointment, Frederick's anticipation fueled by a travel guide describing the city's "palatial magnitude and splendour."[49] Instead he found the place "quite uninviting," many of its homes neglected, and the town of eighteen thousand generally of a dull character. The architect in him was, however, thrilled to see what he called a "rare national ornament"— the capitol building. After a couple of days of sightseeing, Frederick returned to the docks, boarded another steamer, and headed back to the Ohio River. This time, his trip was uneventful, taking only a couple of days. In Paducah, he caught another riverboat and sailed down the Mississippi to New Orleans.

A steamboat similar to the type Frederick Law Olmsted took on the Cumberland River in 1856. (Courtesy of the Audio-Visual Archives, Special Collections and Digital Programs, University of Kentucky Libraries.)

If Frederick made the same trip today, would the couple of hours it takes to drive I-24 between Nashville and Paducah allow him to see the countryside as he did in 1856? Would he have time to admire the ancient trees overhanging the interstate right-of-way? Today's ribbon of concrete and asphalt certainly would not be the "placid surface" he found on the Cumberland in 1856. Still, after four days, even the scenery along the river grew tiresome. The creator of many of the late-nineteenth century's most beautiful cityscapes, including New York's Central Park, was unimpressed. Frederick began to sound like a modern-day car passenger after a long trip on an interstate. "You turn again and again from listlessly gazing at the perspective of bushes, to the listless conversation of the passengers, and turn back again."[50] With perhaps more excitement than someone pulling off an interstate into a gas station can muster today, Frederick also described a "wood-up." In the steamboat era, people living along navigable rivers, especially if their land was forested, made a decent living by providing fuel for passing boats. When supplies ran low, boats routinely nosed up to a stack of wood along the shore, and crew and able-bodied male passengers alike sprang over the side to load up. "Making a landing, or stopping to wood-up, become excitements that make you spring from your berth or your book."[51]

Frederick's lasting impression of his trip along part of the I-24 corridor evoked another sense: sound. "Two sounds remain still very vividly in my ears in thinking of this sail—the unceasing 'Choosh, choosh; choosh, choosh,' of the steam, driven out into the air, after doing its work; and the 'shove her up! shove her up!' of the officer on the deck, urging the firemen to their work."[52] Would the Frederick of today notice the steady thrum of the various engines on the interstates? Choosh, choosh has become the soft gentleness of a small car tiptoeing by in the passing lane, the deeper thrum of a transport diesel. It's pedal to the metal all the way—traffic and road construction permitting.

Interstate 43: 'Tarnal Bad Roads

Around 1840, a "merry Briton" using the pseudonym, Morleigh, decided to explore Wisconsin. To get there, Morleigh traveled over the worst road he could remember. "[T]he trees have been just cut down and pulled aside, and the stumps, rocks, and ruts, render it almost impossible for

Interstate 43

the horses to tug the wagon along."[53] He found Milwaukee (Exits 89–57) to be a cheerful place with neat homes and stores that had evolved to the point that they even had signs above their entrances. From the front stoop of his hotel, he could look toward Lake Michigan and see "a marsh, through which a road has been made and lots conveyed—and the main street. In another direction we see the light house, the Episcopal church . . . the sundry gay white cottages rising out of a scrubby sort of jungle which grows in the high bluff above the lake."[54] He was less

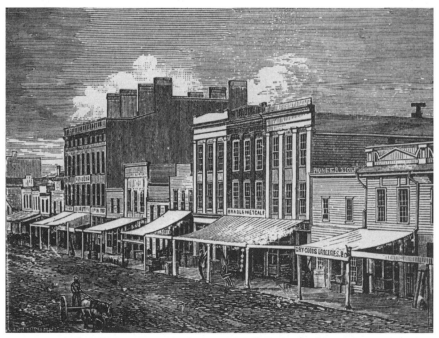

Downtown Milwaukee as it appeared in Morleigh's time, complete with signage above the stores. (Courtesy of the Wisconsin Historical Society, Image WHi-5226.)

kind about his fellow wayfarers at the hotel. After wolfing down their dinner, the men at the table typically started whittling toothpicks, spitting tobacco juice, and slugging back gin.

Morleigh explored Milwaukee for a few days, then resolved to head north into the Green Bay area (Exits 189–181), but he'd heard about the road. "Some wayworn and weather-beaten travelers have arrived from Green Bay; they declare the road to be in a dreadful state; between floods and sloughs, and fallen timber, they were obliged to fag along on foot, leading their horses, and occasionally camping out, when they found it impossible to kindle a fire, owing to the rain and damps."[55] Morleigh waited for the weather to change, enjoying some good conversations around the hotel fireplace and checking out boats at the town wharf. Here, he found the steamer *Columbus*, and decided to head for Green Bay by water instead, skirting around the Door Peninsula. The weather continued soggy and it took him several days to reach his destination. Today, Morleigh would probably think nothing of renting a car for the three-hour trip on Interstate 43.

From Green Bay, Morleigh decided on a hiking excursion, but the "road was full of mudholes and most execrable."[56] He soon secured a ride aboard a wagon driven by an old Frenchman.

> Jolting along the road, through rain and mud, and branches of trees, and fallen trees, and bottomless sloughs, I listened to the rambling conversation of my whip. He seemed delighted to have found a good listener. . . . In the midst of one of his rigamaroles, three deer . . . burst into the road before us. Thus at a moment when I never expected to see a deer, cramped in a wagon with a noisy old Frenchman, and totally unprepared, a splendid shot escaped me.[57]

After leaving his noisy old Frenchman, Morleigh continued on foot. At a tavern not far from Green Bay, he met up with an acquaintance he had encountered on the road, who, with his wife, was traveling west by horse and buggy. The couple had decided to rest for the night in the tavern to nurse their aches and pains. The husband declared the road the most "'tarnal bad road" he had ever encountered. Morleigh, hardly enamored with the couple, painstakingly pointed out that the road into Green Bay was a bowling green compared to what they would encounter a little further west. That, Morleigh declared, was "a regular wagon-splitting, racking road,"[58] and really, the best way to travel on the frontier was on foot. With this independence, a man "has no incumbrance—no lumbering wagon—no lame horse—no awful mud-holes, to retard his progress. He carries his blanket, his fire-box, his rifle, on his shoulder, jauntily; he crosses the deep rivers in a log canoe; he basks upon the sunny side of flowery banks, and snaps his fingers at the world."[59] Morleigh had learned to appreciate what was passing before him; he had discovered the freedom of the open road.

Interstate 96: Uncle Dan's Semi-Historic Side Lights

"My parents were endowed with a nomadic disposition." So begins *Pioneer Recollections* by Daniel Mevis, an early settler of Lansing, Michigan. Probably aware of his own ability to spin a fine yarn, Daniel subtitled his book, *Semi-Historic Side Lights on the Early Days of Lansing. A Tale of the Life in Lansing when Wolves Howled Near Doorsteps*. Published in 1911, the book gathered together columns published over the years, under the

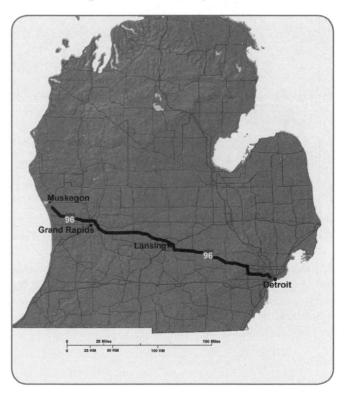

Interstate 96

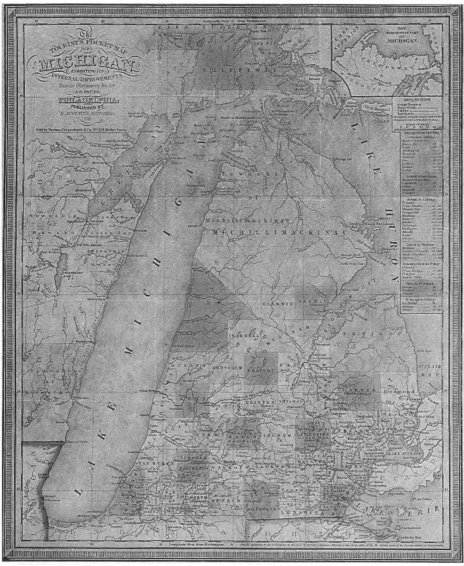

This pocket map for tourists was still in use when the Mevis family headed into the wilds of Michigan to homestead. From Detroit at the southern end of Lake St. Clair, Daniel's family headed cross-country in a northwesterly direction to the corner of Ingham, Eaton, and Clinton counties, the location of present-day Lansing. While rivers are clearly marked on the map, roads are less discernable, even in the more settled southern part of Michigan. (Courtesy of the Archives of Michigan.)

pseudonym of Uncle Dan, in *The State Journal*. Daniel recounted how in 1847, in Buffalo, New York, his family had boarded the first steamer they found headed up the Great Lakes.

> The captain asked father where we wanted to go.
> "Oh, almost anywhere" was the reply. "Where are you going?"
> "To Detroit and on up," the captain answered.
> "All right, we'll go too."[60]

The Mevis family disembarked in Detroit. "The household goods all being well packed and in movable condition, it was decided to go on as far as we could get public conveyance."[61] In 1847, this meant Pontiac, Michigan, about twenty miles beyond Detroit. But Daniel's father wasn't satisfied. A new state capital was to be built in the wilderness west of Pontiac. Father and the eldest son set out on foot, through the bush. After two days, they met a long-whiskered gentleman promising to sell them the best real estate in all of Michigan. Here was water, lumber, and the promise of factories, the man said. The father was excited; the son had obviously read "The Old Woman and the Three Bears" (Goldilocks did not become part of the story until around 1900) and persuaded his father that this location just wouldn't do. Father and son continued west. The next day, they were cordially welcomed by another gentleman telling them they would be fortunate indeed to buy a lot near his high and dry juncture of two rivers. The father was convinced, but his son again advised holding out for a better "bed." They walked further and came to the place where the new capital was being built. By now the pressure was on; Mother and the remaining children were set to arrive in two weeks with a couple of wagonloads of household furniture. She expected a place to put that furniture and a bed for her children at night. As Daniel commented in his reminiscences: "My mother was not a suffragette nor an Amazon, but she was the head of the family all right."[62] After a two-week struggle over nearly non-existent trails, no one wanted to see Mother disappointed. Father looked at the new town under construction, declared that this place was just right, and got to work. After purchasing a lot, father and son felled the trees to build a cabin. The extra sideboards on the wagons became the doors, and Mother brought the windows with her from Pontiac. Daniel declared his new home in the middle of the vast wilderness novel and romantic.

Serenaded every night in summer by the denizens of an immense frog pond near the cabin and with clouds of mosquitoes indoors and outdoors adding their plaintive thrills to the grand jubilee of welcome to the "early pioneer"—these and other romantic sights and sounds, such as the snarling of wolves, the distant cry of the panther—like a woman in distress—and watching the pretty deer as they fearlessly browsed among the newly made brush heaps, made for us a new and novel experience.[63]

Anyone passing through downtown Lansing today on the Interstate 96 Loop (Exit 104) passes within a couple blocks of the lot Mr. Mevis bought in 1847. Exiting the I-96 Loop west onto Saginaw Street takes you over the Grand River and past Durant Park. This is where Daniel Mevis lived in 1847.

The Mevis family appears to have thrived. So did Lansing. As the new state capital, the town grew quickly from a handful of individuals when Daniel and his family arrived in 1847 to three thousand residents by 1859. Meanwhile, Mr. Mevis opened a bakery, Mrs. Mevis bought some chickens and a pig to keep the family fed, and Daniel and his siblings started a Tom Sawyer kind of existence, albeit a few years ahead of Tom's debut. Daniel became friends with some local Native American boys who taught him the ways of the woods, had a one-seater walnut canoe built for him, and took him home to meet their folks. In this case, one of the folks was Chief John Okemos, an Ojibway of the Ottawa tribe. The nearby town of Okemos, Michigan, at Exit 110 on I-96, honors Chief Okemos.

One of Uncle Dan's side lights involved the story of his ride home from seeing the circus in nearby DeWitt. He had walked the distance between the two towns to go to the circus against his father's wishes and now wanted to get home before he was missed. An "eccentric" German gentleman called Old Sag offered Dan a ride with his family. They took off at a runaway gait over the rough road "passing everything in sight regardless of ruts, holes, logs and stumps."[64] A tavern owner, hearing the commotion, rushed out to stop the runaway team, but Old Sag just yelled at him to get out of the way. At one point, the wagon rolled over a log in the road. Down went everything in the wagon into a heap on the floor for the remainder of the trip. "[W]e pounded around, so mixed that it was hard to establish our own identity or to escape serious injury among broken glass, fans, parasols, lunch baskets, etc. and then the atmosphere, the aroma of high wines added to the sulphurous stream of profanity and our madman driver's yells."[65] Daniel got home safely, but did not say whether he had been caught by his father.

As the young town grew, things weren't always easy for the representatives gathered at the new Michigan State Legislature. Housing was so scarce in Lansing that it was not uncommon for representatives of different political persuasions to end up sharing a bed in a rooming house. At one point, the legislature ordered the construction of a sidewalk from the town's main hotel. The sidewalk consisted of two-inch thick white oak planks spiked down to sturdy oak logs underneath. Difficulties in getting to Lansing also prompted the legislature to authorize funds for road construction in 1848.

Surrounded as it is on three sides by water, travel in Michigan had always been concentrated along the shores of lakes Erie, Huron, and Michigan. Inland travel tended to follow the rivers and streams. Luckily, east-flowing streams frequently found their source not far from that of west-flowing streams in the center of the Michigan Peninsula so, with a short portage, Native Americans could cross the state easily by canoe. In other places, wide, well-maintained trails connected native communities. These traces on the landscape usually followed the path of least resistance with easy changes in elevation, crossing streams in the shallowest spots. Settlers soon adopted these native highways as their own. Daniel and his family used one of these trails in 1847 to reach Lansing. Known as the Grand River Road, it ran from Detroit through what is now North Lansing to Grand Rapids and finally the mouth of the Grand River. As a main thoroughfare, it was one of the roads earmarked by the state legislature in 1848 for upgrading. The section from Howell (Exit 137) to what is now Grand River Avenue (Exit 90) in Lansing opened in 1849.

A private corporation took over the Grand River Road in the 1850s and rebuilt it with two-inch oak planking. It soon became a toll road. The plank road gradually improved, acquired a better surface, and, in 1918, gained a number as part of Michigan Highway 16, which ran from Detroit through Lansing and Grand Rapids. In 1926, M-16 became U.S. Route 16, and acquired a freeway designation in 1957. Interstate 96 designations started appearing in 1961, with further upgrades to the free-way occurring over the next few years to complete all of what we now know as I-96. Today on I-96 in a rented truck, Mrs. Mevis could drive from Detroit to Lansing in just under two hours—if the traffic cooper-ated. Chances are, in 1847, she didn't get caught in too many wagon jams during her two weeks on the trail. Traveling with Daniel, however, must have been the equivalent of getting stuck in traffic with no way out and a bored ten-year old in the back seat.

In Daniel's time, the Grand River Road had already extended west-ward to Grand Rapids and beyond. Not only was Grand Rapids served well by water transportation, but the terms of an 1836 treaty with the Native Americans of Western Michigan made Grand Rapids an im-portant center for an annual gathering. The 1836 treaty agreed to pay a total of eighteen thousand dollars over twenty years to the Native Americans listed on the treaty. A few weeks before the day of the payout, agents started spreading the word to be in Grand Rapids at a certain date. But the signatories did not come alone—their wives and children also traveled to Grand Rapids, where they camped alongside the river. Traders joined in the cavalcade, wanting to buy furs and other goods and, of course, relieve the men receiving the annual stipend of their coins through consumer purchases. Those who could travel by water did so; families walking overland wanted trails suitable for the young and old alike; hence, the relatively good condition of the Grand River Road, I-96's precursor, during the initial years of settlement in mid-Michigan. Perhaps the Native American figuring in one of Uncle Dan's side lights was on his way to Grand Rapids for the annual gathering. As told by Daniel, the encounter involved a man by the name of Oliver Rice, who was grading down a sand hill with a rudimentary grader and a team of horses.

> He ran his scraper plump under the skeleton of an Indian that had been buried there, the skeleton heading straight for Oliver's face. Having the lines [from the team of horses] around his neck he could not extricate himself in time to avoid a collision with the ab-origine, and he fell face foremost on top of what there was of this noble redman. To say that there were no bones broken would be a mistake. There were, but the breakage was wholly sustained . . . [by

the skeleton] whose long black hair decorated Mr. Rice's face for about a minute.[66]

Mr. Rice recovered and the skeleton, complete with its turtle-shell adornments, was reburied safely out of the path of Mr. Rice's scraper. As for Daniel Mevis, he appears to have lived well into the twentieth century. His writing reflects a contented individual who probably enjoyed life to the fullest, if his own reminiscences are to be believed. He did state near the end of his book of side lights that everyone should say only what they know to be true. However, he added a codicil of sorts that if everyone did tell the truth all the time "[m]ountains would shrink again to molehills, and fish stories would cease to interest."[67] Presumably this also applied to his tales of adventure along the I-96 of one hundred and sixty years ago.

Interstate Commerce Develops

This Little Piggy Went to Market

THIS WAGON CARRIES
INTERSTATE COMMERCE
TRAFFIC ONLY

ADAMS
EXPRESS
COMPANY

ADAMS EXPRESS COMPANY.
SOUTHERN EXPRESS Co. 495

"INTERSTATE" SIGN ON EXPRESS WAGON

Interstate transport. George Grantham Bain Collection.
(Courtesy of the Library of Congress.)

IN 1784, George Washington, with the wisdom of middle age, retraced the route he had taken in 1755 with General Braddock through Pennsylvania. Instead of the memories of "singing bullets" and "the bright face of danger" a younger George Washington had written about, the middle-aged Washington now saw meadows that would be good for grain and navigable streams that connected to the Potomac River. Here was a future avenue for commerce, where the produce of the interior could be carried to Atlantic ports and manufactured goods could be sent inland. Here also was a way to unite a new nation, provided the vast distances could be overcome. He wrote to Henry Lee, former cavalry officer (also known as Light Horse Harry), fledgling politician, and future father of General Robert E. Lee. "Open ALL the communication which nature has afforded . . . between the Atlantic States and the western territory, and encourage the use of them to the utmost . . . and sure I am there is no other tie by which they will long form a link in the chain of Federal Union."[1] Washington's vision of a national road over the Appalachians, into the Ohio Valley and points further west was taken up by Thomas Jefferson, who appointed a commission to select the route. Construction began in 1811 to widen the road Braddock had cut through the wilderness and lay down a proper roadbed of rock, covered over with sand, gravel, or clay. By 1825, you could ride from Baltimore to the Ohio border on the National Road, as it came to be called. Eventually, this interstate highway of its time extended from coast to coast as U.S. Route 40.

But not everyone enjoyed such modern commercial thoroughfares. In Northern Louisiana, near today's Interstate 20, wagons taking cotton bales to market kept sinking into the muddy roadway up to their axles. Finally, someone had a eureka moment, and the farmers banded together to build a shed over nine miles of road creating the world's longest covered bridge. While the shed is long gone, the name stuck. Shed Road is accessible today from Exit 15 on Interstate 220. In North

Carolina, a wagon on its way to market with two hogsheads of tobacco fell into the river while crossing the bridge over the Neuse River. The driver and three horses drowned. The accident, wrote the *Raleigh Observer*, "was owing to the very shameful state of the bridges, the planks covering which, lying aslant and loose, gave way. How can those who have the charge of public bridges acquit themselves for suffering them to remain in such a state?"[2] The year was 1800.

Throughout the country, many early roads followed Native American trading paths and the traces cut through the landscape by wandering pigs, deer, and buffalo. Shells, pottery, copper, deerskins, and salt had been important trading commodities to the Native peoples willing to travel long distances between the seacoasts and the interior to acquire these commodities. Europeans added dyes, firearms, and gunpowder, beads, and liquor to the trade over these rudimentary traces in the landscape. Charlotte, North Carolina, for instance, sits at the confluence of older trails for commerce between Catawba villages. Gradually, new trails began to radiate out from this crossroads of commerce. Now, Interstates 77 and 85 serve the Charlotte area, facilitating trade with the coast and the Great Lakes region, as happened hundreds of years ago.

In the West, one early trail for interstate commerce ran from Southern Mexico, through what is now known as the Chihuahuan Desert of Mexico, northward through the lands of the various Native Americans then inhabiting the Rio Grande Basin and the Rocky Mountain area. From here, other trails continued northward and onto the Great Plains. All kinds of goods made their way up and down this interstate route: turquoise, shells, copper, macaws, salt, hides, bone fishhooks, pottery, and slaves. Goods traveled these early Southwestern trails, usually in great baskets on the backs of traders capable of carrying an extremely heavy pack up to thirty or forty miles a day. These traders sometimes traveled in groups or with family. Native American communities welcomed them, but still took the precaution of holding a purification ceremony to ward off any evil spirits that might accompany the traders. The introduction of the horse and mule by the Spanish made commerce more efficient and added another commodity to early intertribal trade. At first, Native Americans ate the horses and mules, but then they discovered how much bigger their world could be if they used them for travel and to transport goods.

Trails carved into the landscape for commercial purposes included the Chisholm Trail for cattle and the Santa Fe Trail for trade goods, both now partially served by Interstates 35 and 25 respectively. In and around Cincinnati, the desire to bring large droves of hogs to market and hams to customers created a hub-and-spoke with slaughterhouses taking advantage of river, road, and rail to get bacon into the frying pans of a nation. Many early thoroughfares around Cincinnati were toll roads, built by private companies, since state and local governments did not yet see the point in investing public funds in roads. But by 1851, county officials had come to see the importance of roads for something other than hog thoroughfares and macadamized all roads of "any importance" leading out of Cincinnati. In the city, the main streets were paved with bricks.

In the case of the Santa Fe Trail and its shorter Cimarron Cutoff, a small group of men itching to turn a tidy profit, but with more bravado than good sense, decided, in 1821, to attempt an overland crossing of the Kansas Territory with pack animals loaded with trade goods. Their destination was Santa Fe, a mission town served by annual caravans of traders from Mexico. The men faced hostile Native Americans and an uncertain route that included desert lands with limited access to water. For the residents of Santa Fe, who only saw trade goods about once a year, it must have felt like the 1821 equivalent of waking up one morning and finding a Wal-Mart had opened overnight on their deserted island, when the little convoy showed up unannounced with the likes of dress fabric, kitchen goods, and foodstuffs. By 1830, about a hundred men a year crossed over what had become known as the Santa Fe Trail. With the introduction of the wheel to the trail, the route suddenly became an important interstate for commerce.

The Mexican government reacted much the same as local stores do today when a Wal-Mart appears in their midst: it got mad. Mexico imposed tariffs on goods arriving in Santa Fe from the United States: the equivalent of $500 per wagon. It didn't matter what was loaded on the wagon or its value, the tariff was still $500. The wagon master also had to pay a duty on any gold or silver he took out of Santa Fe. Inbound wagon masters minimized the impact of the tariff by stopping just outside Santa Fe and loading as much as they could into one wagon. Someone stayed behind with the empty wagons while the caravan made its

> *The occupants of the rude shanty . . . freely offered us a pot of pumpkin they were stewing. . . . We looked more like skeletons than living beings. . . . We had to refuse some salt meat which they had also proffered, as our teeth were too sore to eat it. . . . We had subsisted for eleven days on one turkey, a coon, a crow, and some elm bark, with an occasional bunch of wild grapes.*
>
> **—Traders returning to civilization after traveling the Cimarron Cutoff in August 1828 (as quoted in Inman on the Legends of America Web site)**

way into the city with the overloaded wagon. Outbound wagons usually had a false bottom for concealing most of the gold and silver received in payment for the goods traded while in Santa Fe.

Imagine for a moment what life would have been like as an 1840s "trucker" on this particular interstate: the constant threats of attack, dehydration, snakes, and other wildlife, and a diet of strong coffee, dried corn, peas and beans, and any "meat" they killed on the trail.

Add to this, ornery mules, a baking sun, and a few hours' sleep each night rolled in a blanket under a wagon, as opposed to today's comfortable bunk in an air-conditioned cab of a tractor trailer. Before getting underway each day, the mechanical check of equipment and starting the engine involved a bit more than inspecting tires and cables, and then turning the key in an ignition. Mule power had its own routine.

> [T]he hallooing of those in pursuit of animals, the exclamations which the unruly brutes call forth from their wrathful drivers, together with the clatter of bells, the rattle of yokes and harness, the jingle of chains, all conspire to produce an uproarious confusion. . . . I have more than once seen a driver hitch a harnessed animal to the halter, and by that process haul his mulishness forward, while each of his four projected feet would leave a furrow behind.[3]

Wages averaged twenty-five to fifty dollars a month and it typically took about three months to bring a load of goods from Kansas or Missouri to Santa Fe. Monthly stagecoach service between Independence, Missouri, and Santa Fe, established in 1850, included mail delivery. Eight men guarded each coach. A contemporary account described each man as armed with a Colt revolving rifle, a Colt long revolver, and a small Colt revolver in addition to a hunting knife. This gave the guards the ability to fire 136 shots without reloading, a feature guaranteed to protect the mails from whatever befell them. A few passengers rode along on each trip. It took about two weeks to make the run and cost each passenger two hundred and fifty dollars, but this included food, such as it was at way stations. Today's I-25 traveler can experience part of this early stage route northeast of Santa Fe. To the south, I-25 traces part of the route the Spanish caravans followed as they made the annual journey to Santa Fe.

As settlers opened up an area, a second type of citizen followed very quickly—those folks wanting to provide a good or service to settlers. Blacksmiths were so essential to the local nineteenth century economy that they were frequently lured with offers of free land and other enticements. A storekeeper, saloon operator, and doctor also were important to the well-being of the residents. The general merchant supplied everything from medicines to bullets with some settlers paying for these goods through barter with eggs, firewood, butter, or moonshine. You could generally barter for just about everything—taxes excepted. As farms matured, people gradually began to grow and produce much more than they needed for a subsistence existence. More trade goods headed west to meet the demand, and the early interstates improved to get this excess produce to market.

In 1874, outside Austin, Texas, Edward King, a journalist writing for *Scribner's Monthly*, encountered "long wagon trains, drawn by oxen, and loaded with barrels and boxes, with lumber and iron, toiling at the rate of twenty miles a day towards the west." Behind each of these nineteenth century versions of a string of semis on an interstate marched "a tough little horse, saddled neatly; and a forlorn dog who has a general air of wolfishness about him, brings up the rear, showing his teeth as we dash past."[4] Mark Twain described the dust kicked up by the long processionals of loaded wagons making their way over the mountains from California into Nevada as a writhing serpent, visible from miles away.[5]

In New England, logging trails evolved into railroads or roadways for hauling timber to markets. Scenery along today's I-89 through New Hampshire and Vermont belies the fact that this area was once stripped to bare rock.

Roadways into and out of places like Baltimore, Philadelphia, New York, and Boston evolved as trucker thoroughfares with all kinds of goods from fresh strawberries to coal and firewood making their way into urban centers. Horse manure from the hundreds of thousands of horses working in the cities frequently made the return trip in the truckers' wagons to fertilize those same strawberry patches. As wagons and roads improved, the distance outward from the urban cores increased for carting fresh produce to market. Today, produce from Florida travels up I-95 to sit alongside potatoes from Maine, and vegetables from other continents in those same markets.

To the west, boosters of cities like Detroit, Chicago, and Minneapolis proclaimed their particular urban areas—where many boosters just happened to own land—the best place on the planet to build that new factory or make a living as a laborer. Bigger, better, grander; boosters shouted to one and all. The trouble was, sharp wits like Mark Twain were not averse to putting their thoughts into print: "When you feel like telling a feller to go to the devil—tell him to go to Chicago."[6] Today, I-94 connects Mark Twain's idea of hell with Minneapolis to the west and Detroit to the east.

In Georgia, the need to bring cotton and tobacco to port cities resulted in former pig trails through the bush and Native American trading trails becoming more identifiable in the landscape. Interstate 16 from Macon to Savannah, Georgia, evolved out of pieces of one of these trails. But while the roads frequently improved with increased commerce, the vehicles along those roads did not always keep pace. In Northeastern Georgia in 1867, noted naturalist and pioneer of the conservation movement, John Muir came across a ramshackle wagon whose three occupants—an old woman and a young couple—were possibly headed to the nearest market town. Two mules pulled the wagon.

> In going down hill the looseness of the harness and the joints of the wagon allowed the mules to back nearly out of sight beneath the box, and the three who occupied it were slid against the front boards in a heap over the mules' ears. Before they could unravel their limbs from this unmannerly and impolite disorder, a new

ridge in the road frequently tilted them with a swish and a bump against the back boards in a mixing that was still more grotesque. [As the occupants slid back and forth courting disaster with every change in elevation of the roadway], they engaged in conversation on love, marriage, and camp-meeting, according to the custom of the country. The old lady, through all the vicissitudes of the transportation, held a bouquet of French marigolds.[7]

In Kentucky's case, poor roads led to the creation of one hundred and twenty counties in a state only 40,411 square miles in size. (Only Texas and Georgia have more counties.) Early in Kentucky's development, legislators decided that every resident should be within an easy day's journey of their county seat, but the roads were either nonexistent or notoriously bad over very hilly terrain. The county seat was where you had to go to look after land titles and wills, or get a license. It was also the home of the county court and usually the nearest point to go to market or sell or barter farm produce. Every time a group of residents petitioned the government, saying it was too difficult to get to their appointed county seat, instead of improving the roads, the government subdivided the county, creating a new county and county seat that was presumably easier for these residents to access. When Kentucky entered the union in 1792 it had nine counties. By the beginning of the Civil War, there were 110 counties. But as roads improved, the expansion in the number of counties slowed to a crawl. Only 10 have been added in the last 140 years. Improved highways made it easier for those in rural Kentucky to acquire city-made products and for the rural residents to go to more urban centers. Today about 1,500 miles of interstates capitalize on Kentucky's position in the middle of the Eastern United States, making it a major transportation and distribution center.

Throughout the Appalachians, improved roads opened isolated areas up to the goods and services available in more accessible parts of the country, and created markets for the resources of states like Kentucky, Tennessee, and West Virginia. In West Virginia's case, county roads eight to twelve feet wide with an inclination of no more than ten degrees were built if one or more settlers petitioned for a road to get to the local mill or county seat. A guide, published in 1870 to attract immigrants to the Mountain State, boasted that one mile of road could be found for every square mile of land in the state, but felt it prudent to add that,

Interstates of
chapter 2

"the quality is not generally in proportion to the quantity."[8] But under no circumstances were these developing networks of roads to be considered backward. A connection to the world, whether by river, rail, or road, was essential for a community to thrive, and the more connections, the better. Transportation links also increased property values, a fact not lost on many early land developers. But the community also had to promote itself as a commercial center. Consequently, to attract desirable

commerce, a church, library, school, and opera house were frequently the first public buildings constructed in many fledgling frontier towns.

Often, the arrival of a good transportation connection spelled the end of the traditional barter system used in many rural areas. In Clarksburg, West Virginia (Exit 115 off I-79), for instance, stores had long accepted farm produce in exchange for market goods, but that ended in the 1860s when the B&O Railroad arrived in town. Commerce switched to a cash-only basis. The existence of a road or railroad usually meant more sophisticated commerce, but sometimes, the chief means of transportation in and out of an area bypassed an established settlement. In 1878, when the Denver and Rio Grande Railroad passed thirty miles to the west of one small, recently established town in Colorado, townsfolk simply dismantled the town and moved it—wooden sidewalks and all— to the railroad to found Alamosa (Exit 52 off I-25). In Washington State, Yakima residents pulled up stakes and moved everything to the town's present location (exits 33–34 on I-82).

Along some routes, the U.S. Army either established garrisons to protect commercial trade or the commercial trade came to an existing garrison with some enterprising businessman setting up a trading post near the fort. Sometimes, unscrupulous traders made the Army's job all that much harder. And, inevitably the garrison attracted other businesses: a saloon, a dance hall, perhaps a brothel. Kearney, Nebraska (Exit 272), and Fort Bridger, Wyoming (Exit 34), both off I-80 flourished as military outposts. Because garrisons were considered a fairly safe place, immigrant trains and traders frequently made them a stopping point. Again, the hub-and-spoke effect occurred, with trails fanning out from both centers. And, as more and more people traveled these rudimentary interstates, things like deadwood for campfires and grazing grass became scarce, creating another market for enterprising businessmen. Elsewhere on the Great Plains, the spacing of settlements generally depended on a farmer being able to get into the nearest town and back home again all in one day. This was particularly important if he had livestock to tend. As a result, small towns sprouted up about every ten miles along thoroughfares to provide basic services.

Back East, that same restlessness that infected the pioneers heading west sent city folk off to experience nature and see what the backcountry of New England had to offer. In 1861, Anthony Trollope, British author and son of Frances Trollope, made his way through New Hampshire.

> That there was a district in New England containing mountain scenery superior to much that is yearly crowded by tourists in Europe, that this is to be reached with ease by railways and stagecoaches, and that it is dotted with huge hotels almost as thickly as they lie in Switzerland I had no idea. Much of this scenery, I say, is

superior to the famed and classic lands of Europe. . . . October, no doubt, is the most beautiful month among these mountains."[9]

Today, leaf peepers, skiers, and hikers clog the likes of I-89 through New Hampshire and Vermont, taking over the bed and breakfasts, antique stores, craft shops, and factory-outlet malls on weekend jaunts to enjoy the landscape that so surprised Anthony Trollope.

In his ramble through the South in 1870, author E.A. Pollard could not understand why otherwise intelligent people had not made the link between good roads and prosperity. "It is said that our Virginia farmers spend about four times as much power to cart the same amount of produce as a New England or a Pennsylvania farmer does—all owing to bad roads; the stoutest vehicles are torn to pieces over the stumps and through the quagmires; neighborhoods are comparatively isolated from the want of roads, and all intercourse within spaces of a few miles is sometimes suspended for weeks from the effects of a freshet."[10] He did acknowledge, however, that the roads had improved since colonial times. These improvements, "as if by magic enchantment," had given many areas "a close and lucrative connection" with the large population centers along the Eastern seaboard. The "journey over the mountains, formerly considered so long, so expensive, and even perilous, is now made in a very few days."[11] The pig trails and horse paths of his father's generation, along which the first rudimentary interstate commerce developed had evolved into wagon roads, and then into the "substantial" macadam turnpikes of Pollard's own time. George Washington's future avenues of commerce were indeed unfolding as he had envisioned.

Interstate 25: Hokey Pokey Winky Wang

In the late 1870s, Ernest Ingersoll worked throughout the Rocky Mountains surveying roads. Since roads did not exist yet in many of the locations where he and his fellow surveyors worked, the work crew did all its travel by mule, mules being better suited for carrying loads on rough trails. Ernest soon discovered that the high price of a mule reflected its value: while a good pack pony cost $50, a good mule cost $150. During the two years he spent on this assignment, Ernest got to know his long-eared "de-e-vlishly sly" mule quite well.

The first day's ride through the miserable outskirts of civilization is likely to be tiresome and unsatisfactory. You have not become accustomed to your mule, nor he to you. You are sun-burned, and your eyes smart with the alkali dust. . . . Going through a town or past a ranch the mules have exerted themselves to enter every gate and door-way, to go anywhere and everywhere but where they ought; and the amount of caution, invective and hard-riding necessary to keep them together and under their respective packs has been vexatious and fatiguing, conducive neither to observation of scenery nor to the cultivation of Christian virtues.[12]

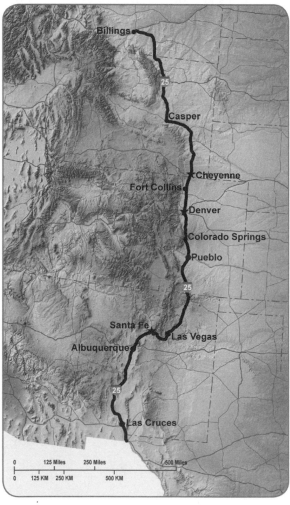

Interstate 25

PIKES PEAK EXPRESS.

A photo of the Pikes Peak Express taken circa 1890 by William H. Walker. Note the mule in the middle of the image carrying a wagon wheel. (Courtesy of the Denver Public Library, Western History Collection, X-21771.)

For Ernest, travel acquired sound—the bell on the lead animal. Over and over, day in and day out, "all life centers about that tireless hammering and . . . in unison with the ceaseless copper-clatter of that ding-dong bell, your mind loses itself in Hokey pokey winky wang."[13]

The survey crew worked in an area at the top of today's Interstate 25, fanning out from Denver (Exits 225–201) or Cheyenne (Exits 9–13) with their mules to survey possible transportation routes for the commercial traffic that would inevitably follow. All along the trace I-25 now cuts through Wyoming, Colorado, and New Mexico, that de-e-vlishly sly mode of transportation was the preferred way until supplanted in Ernest's time by rail, where possible, and later by the advent of the automobile after roads were cut through the landscape Ernest helped survey.

The story of mules along the I-25 trace starts with the Spanish. They were the first Europeans to make use of the trails northward from Mexico carved out of the landscape by Native Americans. The Spanish turned one such trail into a major thoroughfare in 1581 and called it what they called all their roads in North American: El Camino Real. Those using the road gave it another name: the Chihuahua Trail. Colonies sprang up along the trail as far north as the present-day Colorado–New Mexico boundary area as the Spanish hunted for that elusive pot of gold in the New World. Santa Fe was founded during this period when settlers congregated for safety from the Pueblo Indians who weren't too welcoming, probably because the Spanish had come in, settled on their land, and then demanded the Pueblo Indians provide food and labor for the Spanish. At Santa Fe, Spanish and Pueblos routinely massacred each other. When the Pueblo's anger against the Spanish incursion into their territory boiled over in the 1670s, Spanish settlers in Santa Fe and on ranches along the Rio Grande withdrew south on the Chihuahua Trail to El Paso, Texas.

The Chihuahua Trail became the first European road in what is now the United States. Caravans of wagons pulled by mules usually covered eight to twelve miles a day. From Chihuahua, Mexico, it took about forty days to reach Santa Fe along a trace winding through the Rio Grande Valley. Today, I-25 motorists zip along the same river valley at a significantly faster pace traveling from the Mexico border to Santa Fe in about five hours. In addition to spare mule teams, caravans also carried a supply of wagon parts and the implements to repair wagons. It was not uncommon to repair every part of a wagon at least once in a round-trip. Nearly every trade good brought into the area came up the Chihuahua Trail on the back of a mule or in a wagon pulled by a mule, whether it was a bolt of cloth, a window, pots for the hearth, or a harpsichord for the parlor. Chihuahua, Mexico, merchants had a monopoly on trade and they knew it, charging high prices for the goods shipped north to Santa Fe yet paying very low prices for the goods they took in return as trade. Produce making the return trip to Mexico included hides, candles, pine nuts, and salt gathered from dried up lakes. Spanish caravans traveling up the Chihuahua Trail arrived in Santa Fe every two to four years.

Today's I-25 heads northward from I-10 at Las Cruces, along the old Chihuahua Trail, following the Rio Grande. The Franklin and Organ Mountains dominate the view. Traveling through this area in the 1870s, Samuel Cozzens, a retired judge from Tucson, Arizona, described large irrigation ditches on each side of the river. Here, farmers grew corn, rye, barley, wheat, figs, pears, apricots, grapes, and peaches. While Jesuits

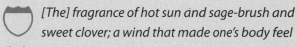
had planted the grapes in 1680 to provide wine for church sacraments, by the time Sam visited in the 1870s, the vines produced about one hundred thousand gallons of wine a year—quite a bit more than required by the church. Samuel reported that it tasted like a fine port or burgundy.

Apache Indians regularly terrorized the caravans on the Chihuahua Trail, especially in the Jornada del Muerto, literally translated as "Dead Man's March" or "Journey of the Dead." A trip across this desert was ninety miles shorter than going around it, but there was no water. Samuel Cozzens described the Jornada del Muerto as a valley or plain only because mountains surrounded it. Cochise, the legendary Apache leader, acted as Samuel's guide. "To your uneducated eye, it presents a smooth and unbroken surface, yet there is hardly a level spot upon its face. It is a mass of canions, ravines, ridges, gullies, chasms, and mountains, piled one above another in inextricable confusion, in all conceivable shapes, towering above and around you on all sides."[14] Samuel described the trail across the desert as constantly "impeded by huge boulders of granite, blocks of sandstone, fissures and chasms worn into the earth by floods ages ago."[15]

Trade along the Chihuahua Trail continued to increase, despite the hardships and continuous raids by the Apache and Navajos on anyone using the trail or living along it. From nearby peaks, Apaches could see for miles up and down the trail, as they watched for possible raiding targets and threats to their territory. A series of brilliant warrior strategists, including Cochise and Geronimo, continued this reign of terror for decades. Sometimes, the raiding parties toyed with travelers in a terrifying game of cat and mouse.

The next day we made but five miles; it was a continuous fight, and a very difficult matter to prevent their [Comanches] capturing us. This annoyance was kept up for four days; they would surround us, then let up as if taking time to renew their strength, to suddenly charge upon us again, and they continued thus to harass us until we were almost exhausted from loss of sleep.[16]

Forts sprang up along the way: Fort Thorn at the southern end of Jornada del Muerto (twelve miles north of Las Cruces) in 1853 and Fort Craig at its northern end in 1854. Fort Craig's ruins still exist on the west bank of the Rio Grande (near Exit 115). Fort McRae opened in 1863 in the Fra Cristobel Mountains. Its site now sits at the bottom of Elephant Butte Reservoir (Exit 83). Fort Selden replaced Fort Thorn and was garrisoned by the Buffalo Soldiers—the African American 125th Infantry.

Rather than crossing the Jornada del Muerto as the Chihuahua Trail did, I-25 curves west, around the Caballo and Fra Cristobel Mountains. It rejoins the old Chihuahua Trail north of the Jornada del Muerto. The interstate then heads up the Rio Grande Valley for Albuquerque. All along the highway, Pueblo Indians once farmed. Pueblo is the Spanish word for a village; the Pueblos were "people of the village." Albuquerque is named after the Duke of Alburquerque (minus the first r in his name).

North of Santa Fe, New Mexican traders started a trail of sorts as they traded with the Plains Indians, but it was not until 1821-22 that William Becknell pieced together the trails northward to the Missouri River that became known as the Santa Fe Trail and the Cimarron Cutoff. The Cimarron Cutoff more closely approximates today's I-25 as it climbs through Glorieta Pass northeast of Santa Fe, skirts the Sangre de Cristo Mountains, and then follows the Canadian and Cimarron River valleys before crossing a very dry stretch of desert that ended many dreams of fortune. American traders using the Cutoff typically packed everything on mules, which were later sold off once the destination was reached, the trader keeping only the animals he needed to get him and any trade goods he acquired back up the Cutoff again. As the trails improved, trad-

> The sun darts its perpendicular and scorching rays on the arid and barren rocks, which sparkle by day like gigantic diamonds.
>
> —Sam Cozzens, describing the road he took north along the Rio Grande (1877: 273)

A mule on the Santa Fe Trail typically carried about four hundred pounds. It would take about one hundred and forty-five mules to haul the load carried by one transport truck on today's I-25. Once traders switched to wagons, it only took about twenty-three wagons to equal one transport truck of today.

ers switched to wagons, pulled by mules. As with the mules, the trader usually sold off the wagons at the end of the journey.

In 1846, Susan Magoffin accompanied her husband, Sam, on a trip to Santa Fe. She found her first glimpse of the Sangre de Cristo Mountains to be in stark contrast to what she had become used to seeing. "We are surrounded, in the distance by picturesque mountains, a relief to the eye when one is accustomed to behold nothing save the wide

A photograph of Santa Fe's San Francisco Street, taken by William Henry Jackson circa 1895. "To dignify such a collection of mud hovels with the name of 'city' would be a keen irony; not greater, however, than is the name with which its Padres have baptized it" (as quoted in Inman, 1897: 58). When founded, Santa Fe's full name was La Villa Real de la Santa Fe de San Francisco de Asis. (Courtesy of the Denver Public Library, Western History Collection, Z-4106.)

plain stretched far on all sides meeting the edges of the bright blue sky and appearing more like water than land."[17] That same year, U.S. troops marched unopposed down the Santa Fe Trail and into Santa Fe during the war with Mexico. The trail was used again during the Civil War, with battles at Apache Canyon (Exit 294) and Glorieta Pass (Exits 307, 299) to stop a Confederate attempt to march north and capture the gold regions around Denver and Pikes Peak (Exit 122) in Colorado. Pecos National Historic Park protects the Glorieta battlefield as well as the ancient pueblo of Pecos and two Spanish colonial missions. A little further north, Fort Union National Monument (Exit 366) preserves the largest network of Santa Fe Trail ruts still visible. Built in 1851 to protect travelers from attacks by Jicarilla Apaches and Utes, Fort Union became the largest garrison in the Southwest. But, the advent of the railroad spelled the end for the fort in 1891. The railroads also spelled the end to overland freight caravans and to mules along the I-25 trace.

In 1846, twenty men from Bent's Fort, Colorado (near La Junta, Exit 15) were on their way on horseback to Taos, New Mexico, following a route that cut kitty-corner across today's I-25, probably somewhere near Trinidad, Colorado (Exits 13–14) from which they could go through Raton Pass, as I-25 does today. The men were not going to be gone all that long, by 1840s standards, so they did not take a change of clothing. But, they forgot one very important fact of interstate travel in 1846: mules don't always do what you want them to do. Three days into the journey, the mules carrying their food balked at going any further and refused to budge. In the absence of cell phones and fast-food restaurants conveniently spaced along the route, the men were in a bit of a quandary. Then, the commanding officer ordered all his men to take off their undershirts and drawers, in other words, their long underwear—their three days on a horse, sweaty, dusty, haven't had a bath in ages underwear. The men tied up the sleeves and legs of the underwear, poured their allotment of flour for the trip into the resulting bags, and tied the bags and their ration of bacon to their saddles and proceeded on the way, safe in the knowledge that they would be able to eat for the rest of the trip.

In her travels through the American West in 1873, Isabella Bird rode along part of what is now the I-25 corridor by rail, not a mode of travel she necessarily recommended. "An American railway car, hot, stuffy, and full of chewing, spitting Yankees, was not an ideal way of approaching

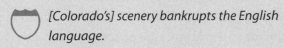
this range [the Rockies] which had early impressed itself on my imagination."[18] At another point, although she had paid full fare, she rode on the floor of a baggage car. Sitting by the open door, she could see the passing landscape of "primeval forests, with their peaks of rosy granite, and their stretches of granite blocks piled and poised by nature in some mood of fury."[19] At Denver, she could not bear to stay in town. "The sight of those glories so near and yet out of reach would make me nearly crazy."[20] Up close, "they looked not of this earth, but such as one sees in dreams alone."[21]

Katherine Lee Bates, a professor in literature at Wellesley College in Massachusetts, also appreciated the glorious Rockies. While working as a summer lecturer at Colorado College in Colorado Springs (Exits 140–150), she accompanied friends on an outing to the top of Pikes Peak (Exit 122). For her, the glories of the landscape Isabella Bird so eloquently described became:

> O beautiful, for spacious skies,
> For amber waves of grain,
> For purple mountains majesty
> Above the fruited plain.

Her poem, "America the Beautiful," was later famously set to music.

Isabella Bird also included what is now the northern end of I-25 on her travels in 1873. Isabella stopped over in Cheyenne, Wyoming. She described it as a "godforsaken, God-forgotten place,"[22] owing its existence to the railroad. From the station in Laramie, goods were loaded onto wagons, usually pulled by a team of mules, for the journey to the isolated communities scattered as far as three hundred miles away. Isabella described as many as one hundred wagons trying to load at the depot at one time, creating a state of lawless pandemonium. Ernest Ingersoll, who spent time in Cheyenne a few years after Isabella visited, declared that the mule packers and drivers were the "most desperately profane men I have ever met; they exhibit a real genius in 'good mouth-filling oaths.'" In Ernest's "honest and serious opinion, founded upon much observation, that so long as any considerable numbers of mules are employed there, it is utterly useless for missionaries to go to the Rocky Mountains."[23] Not much had changed since Isabella's visit when she commented that the "roads resound with atrocious profanity."[24] Created on July 4, 1867, as the first terminal on the Union Pacific Railway in Wyoming, Cheyenne's population grew by the thousands almost overnight. Isabella described six-year-old Cheyenne as an "ill-arranged set of frame houses and shanties, and rubbish heaps, and offal of deer and antelope, produce the foulest smells I have smelt for a long time. Some of the houses are painted a blinding white; others unpainted; there is not a bush, or garden, or green thing; it just straggles out promiscuously on the boundless brown plains, on the extreme verge of which three toothy peaks are seen."[25]

As for the plains outside of town: "Plains, plains everywhere, plains generally level, but elsewhere rolling in long undulations, like the waves of a sea which had fallen asleep. They are covered thinly with buff grass, the withered stalks of flowers, Spanish bayonet, and a small beehive-shaped cactus. One could gallop all over them."[26] Ernest Ingersoll could not quite contain his enthusiasm either. "Mile after mile . . . right-foot, left-foot, right-foot, left foot. . . . The sun beats down, the dust rises up and your only entertainment is the cowbell hung on the neck of the leader. . . .

Hokey pokey winky wang
Linum lankum muscodang.[27]

Interstate 37: Cart Wars

Spanish authorities didn't like poachers, as in non-Spanish citizens, in what is now Texas. This included non-Spanish traders. Authorities went to extremes to keep what they considered the best grasslands in the world and the people inhabiting the area between San Antonio and the coast dependent on Mexico and on the tortuous overland trade route to Mexico. While less than one hundred and fifty miles from the Gulf, all trade goods and supplies still went overland in convoys that frequently

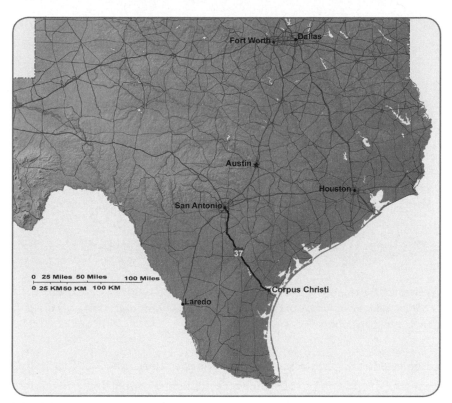

Interstate 37

took several months to make the trip. Not only could residents not get supplies on a regular basis, but they had limited means of shipping their excess produce to market. A port outlet on the Gulf made sense, but Spain refused to relent, fearing smugglers and inroads from the French and Americans on their border.

Today, a direct route exists between San Antonio and Corpus Christi, Texas: Interstate 37. While a seventeenth or eighteenth century equivalent of the interstate would have made sense from the point of view of San Antonians, it did not make sense to the Mexican merchants benefiting from their monopoly on trade with the growing colony. Overland caravans continued. Not until Texas gained independence from Mexico did north–south roads really open up, linking interior settlements with the Gulf to the south and the United States to the north. But even then, San Antonio's port city did not become Corpus Christi, the most direct link; a settlement had not formed there yet, due to the shallow harbor and lack of potable water. Instead, goods bound for San Antonio

A carter and his team, near San Antonio, as drawn for the January, 1874, edition of *Scribner's Monthly*. (Courtesy of Documenting the American South, University of North Carolina at Chapel Hill.)

came into Matagorda Bay, further to the east along the Gulf Coast. This beautiful deepwater port became an established supply depot in the late 1840s. It even had steamship service to New York. Cargo bound for San Antonio was carted over a road from Indianola on Matagorda Bay to Goliad on what is now Route 59 and then up to San Antonio. (This routing tracks to the east of today's I-37 corridor.) Mexican residents soon controlled the bulk of traffic over this 1850s highway using carts pulled by oxen to haul freight. Prices were high due to the distance and the condition of the roads, but the Mexican-Texan drivers did it cheaper than their Anglo-Texan counterparts. There was also tension over Mexican support for the abolition of slavery, something that did not sit well in the South of the 1850s. Harassment of Mexican drivers turned into cart burnings and reports of carters being killed. The Cart War of 1857 had started. Those who were against discrimination worried that other groups, such as the Germans living around San Antonio and Austin, could be the next targets. Consumers worried that the hostilities would result in increased prices. Finally, the Mexican envoy to Washington complained about the situation to the secretary of state who, in turn, complained to the Texas governor. Governor Pease wasted no time declaring: "It is now evident that there is no security for the lives of citizens of Mexican origin engaged in the business of transportation, along the road from San Antonio to the Gulf, unless they are escorted by a military force."[28] In the 1857 equivalent of calling up the National Guard to protect truck convoys on an interstate today, the Texas legislature approved the appropriation of $14,500 for "subsistence and forage" and ordered the militia to escort the carters over the road. Prices would not go up and supplies would continue to reach San Antonio. It took a month or so, but tempers cooled and the Cart War of 1857 came to an end.

Meanwhile, Corpus Christi, the logical coastal port for San Antonio, had acquired a reputation as a rough-and-tumble place. Drunkenness and lawlessness ruled in a settlement inhabited mostly by people passing through town, usually heading west. A yellow fever epidemic decimated the local populace in 1854, and bombardment and occupation during the Civil War hampered its economic development. But, gradually, more ships dropped anchor in the harbor, their goods and passengers tendered in to shore. In 1874, authorities had the harbor dredged to accommodate larger ships. Ranchers along what is now the I-37 corridor realized that Corpus Christi made sense as a shipment point for their wool and cattle. Stockyards, packing houses, and rendering plants soon appeared in Corpus Christi, but the roads there were still in deplorable condition. The rolling landscape of the coastal prairie also resulted in the cart pitching as if on a sea and the ox or horse struggling to control the constant rise and fall of the pitching cart.

In 1886, San Antonio businessmen built a railroad to Corpus Christi, providing a more direct link with a Gulf Coast port. The rail line generally followed what is today the I-37 corridor to connect the two cities. The San Antonio Lone Star Brewery (started by Adolphus Busch), flour mills, local foundries, brick and cement plants, and the flourishing mohair industry now had an export outlet for their product. Best of all, in building their own railroad, San Antonio businessmen could thumb their noses at those Matagorda Bay and Galveston companies that had monopolized the transportation industry in this part of Texas. Carts had lost the technology battle to the iron road, and caravans of carts along what would become the future I-37 corridor came to an end. Carts now only hauled goods to and from railroad stations. Railroad companies began aggressively promoting the Gulf Coast as an all-year resort and the rail line to Corpus Christi flourished. As for the once-prosperous Indianola on Matagorda Bay, hurricanes pretty much destroyed it—one in 1875 and another in 1886. And, perhaps justifying the decision of those San Antonio businessmen of the 1880s to create a direct link with Corpus Christi, the road the carts had traveled in the 1850s to Matagorda Bay evolved into state and U.S. highways, but the businessmen's rail link with Corpus Christi became an interstate highway with another important mission: the main evacuation route for the entire South Texas coastline.

San Antonians can now load up their modern-day equivalent of the cart and, in a couple of hours, drive down I-37 to the coast and its many recreational attractions. Their drive takes them through the sea of grasslands so prized by the early Spaniards. Oil rigs appear like ocean buoys amid the roiling waves of the endless landscape on both sides of the interstate. As vehicles rush past at speeds possibly dreamed of by those 1880s San Antonio businessmen, but certainly beyond the comprehension of those 1850s carters, the rigs bob a greeting—and nod farewell.

Interstate 35: Pardners of the Wind and Sun

Cowboys taking the time for a group photo near the Oklahoma–Texas border, circa 1904. (Courtesy of the Library of Congress.)

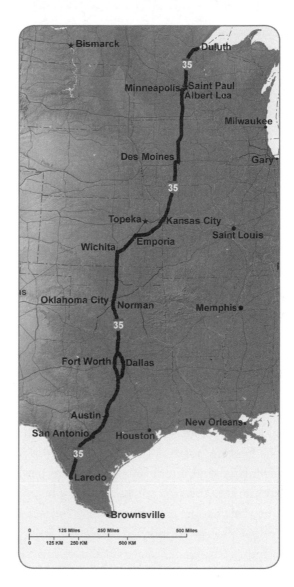

Interstate 35

By the end of the Civil War, the Texas economy was in a shambles. As in many other Southern states, its residents looked around at what they had to offer that would relieve the economic hardships of a long war and Reconstruction. Some states saw a future in cotton mills and furniture manufacturing. In Texas the answer was a good beef stew.

In South Texas alone, an estimated five million longhorn cattle roamed free. If you could catch them, they were yours. A little farther north, thousands of settlers were pouring into the grasslands of Kansas, Iowa, Nebraska, and points west. Cities all along the East Coast were expanding. Cattle herds in the other Confederate states had been decimated to feed starving troops and civilians, or slaughtered to prevent them from being used by the enemy. Cities along the East Coast needed beef, the South needed beef and the settlers of the Great Plains needed beef. Those same people also needed leather.

Today it would be called a no-brainer, and that is exactly how Texans saw it. Longhorn cattle had evolved in the wild from the domesticated cattle brought over by Spanish explorer Francisco Vásquez de Coronado in 1541. Over the centuries, they naturally adapted into the ideal open-range cow. Not only were they very hardy, but their long legs enabled them to walk great distances, they could live without water for long periods, eat cactus if they had to, and were generally very adaptable. They could also withstand both heat and cold. Their horns, extending as much as eight feet between points, were ideal for fending off predators. The Spanish missions in Texas had begun keeping herds of these cattle in the 1730s. (Priests at one mission had amassed forty thousand head of cattle by 1770.) The only drawback to the longhorn was their lack of beef; they were all bone. Still, there was some meat. All you had to do was round them up and get them to market. But market prices varied depending on the location. Slaughterhouses in Chicago paid about forty dollars a head for beef; in Texas, the price was about four dollars. If you could get the beef up north, a tidy profit could be made. Businessmen in Texas calculated that it took about one dollar per head to walk the cattle north to market. The concept had already been tested before the Civil War, but ended soon once hostilities erupted. The early cattle trails north followed trails established by Native Americans, buffalo, and traders in wagons. One trader, Jesse Chisholm, ran a wagon from Wichita, Kansas, to Washita River in what became Oklahoma. It was a general store on wheels and his route became known as the Chisholm Trail.

Interstate 35 traces Jesse's trail south from Kansas through Oklahoma and then south through Texas cattle country. From San Antonio to Fort Worth, I-35 follows the main part of the trail. South of San Antonio, the Chisholm Trail branched out into feeder trails serving the state as far south as Brownsville and Laredo. Here, in the sparse lands near the Mexican border, the Spanish *vaquero* morphed into the western buckaroo of song and movie fame.

If you expect to follow the trail, son, you must learn to do your sleeping in the winter.

—Advice to a young cowboy in *The Log of a Cowboy*
(Adams, 1903: 79 of 136)

Today's I-35 begins in Laredo, Texas, just north of the border with Mexico—and near one of the points of origin for longhorns in the 1860s, many of which were rounded up in Mexico and driven across the border. From Laredo, I-35 heads into the heart of Texas, cutting in a northeasterly direction toward San Antonio, Austin, and Dallas before heading to Oklahoma City and then into Kansas. At Wichita, Kansas, I-35 again turns to the northeast and makes a beeline for Kansas City (exits 235-220). For many of the millions of longhorns driven over this route in the 1860s and '70s, Kansas was generally the end of the line in massive slaughterhouses. Other herds were shipped north by rail to slaughterhouses in Chicago. In the late 1860s, it took about three months to drive a herd a thousand miles north to Kansas City. Today, the same drive north in a cattle truck on I-35 takes about fifteen hours— less time than the cowboys on the trail worked in a day.

Driving cattle on the Chisholm Trail was a hard way to earn a living, but it soon became a badge of honor among cowboys. The young men earned fifteen to twenty dollars a month, often working thirty-six-hour shifts, grabbing a few hours sleep when they could. Older, more experienced wranglers made as much as forty or fifty dollars a month. The heyday of the trail drives and the need for cowboys coincided with the end of the Civil War—a time when many disillusioned young men fled the Southern states for greener pastures in places like Texas. For these young "greenhorns," a day typically began about 3:30 in the morning when the cook roused them for breakfast. They would then drive the herd north until sunset when a grazing ground was found for the night. Cowboys, anxious to keep the massive herds of longhorns heading in the right direction, frequently sang to them, particularly the calves or dogies, as they were called. Those unable to carry a tune, talked to their cows, hoping their soothing voice would keep the animals content. The cowboy ballad and the singing cowboy became fixtures of the Chisholm Trail, spawning the likes of Roy Rogers and Gene Autry. (Exit 40 in Oklahoma leads into the town of Gene Autry. When Autry bought the nearby Flying "A" Ranch in 1939, townsfolk honored him by renaming their town.)

After stopping for the night, each cowboy rode guard duty for a couple of hours, which typically interrupted any sleep he managed to get. Even the horses got more of a break than the wranglers. Extra horses were driven north with the herd so the cowboys could change to fresh horses when needed. The diet was simple: lots of coffee to wash down beef, wild game, molasses, cornbread, and beans. Heavy dark-roasted, almost smoky coffee hid any unwanted "flavoring" in the water. It took about twelve men to wrangle three thousand head of cattle northward.

Despite the working conditions, somehow the underpaid, overworked, lonely cowboy on the trail became a romantic image of the excitement and adventure of the Wild West. Andy Adams, considered one of the best chroniclers of true Western culture and the trail days, described the mule and horse requirements for a cattle drive in his 1903 book, *The Log of a Cowboy*: four mules for the chuck wagon and ten horses per cowboy with two extra for the foreman. Fresh supplies were purchased when possible in towns through which the drive passed. This included everything from replacing worn out work clothes to purchasing fresh produce. And, it didn't take long for clothing and boots to wear out on the trail. A young man by the name of Herman Justin set up a boot-making business in his home in Spanish Fort, Texas (Exit 498), to capitalize on the potential business riding past his front door. Cowboys stopped to order custom boots on their way north and picked them up on their return a few months later. Herman made good boots. His home-based business evolved into the Justin Boot Company, still in operation in

Fort Worth and still considered one of the leading boot manufacturers in the country.

In 1866, cowboys rounded up two hundred and sixty thousand longhorns along what is today the I-35 corridor in Texas and drove them north. But there was a problem. In places like Kansas, the herd crossed settled farmland. The longhorns trampled the crops, and sometimes the cattle had ticks, which could be lethal if they spread to Kansas cattle. Kansans called it "Texas fever." Kansas farmers frequently objected—sometimes with violence—to Texas cattle infesting their land. Eventually, Kansas passed a law only allowing Texas cattle into Kansas in the coldest months after frost had killed off the ticks. More grazing lands and cattle yards sprang up just beyond the Kansas border—usually in the Indian Territory, now Oklahoma. These holding pens solved another problem plaguing Texas cattlemen: the reputation longhorns had as inedible. With a bit of rest and relaxation bovine style and a supply of grass, the longhorns forced to wait at the border until winter became fatter and thus more edible as far as the Eastern palate was concerned. The other problem involved how to deal with a large herd at the end of the trail. An Illinois cattle broker by the name of Joseph McCoy solved the problem by setting up a cattle market in Abilene, Kansas (Exit 275 off I-70). From here, McCoy could connect with stockyards further north, including Chicago slaughterhouses. McCoy bought land in Abilene in 1867 and started to advertise his new stockyard in Texas. In his brochure, he pointed out the advantages of the Chisholm Trail. As well as having streams that were smaller and easier to cross, "[i]t is more direct. It has more prairies, less timber, more small streams and fewer large ones, altogether better grass and fewer flies—no civilized Indian tax or wild Indian disturbances—than any other route yet drived over. It is also much shorter because [it is] more direct from the Red River to Kansas."[29] His promotion worked. Over the next twenty years, an estimated six million longhorn cattle passed through Kansas stockyards.

Geologically, I-35 divides East and West Texas. The springs and caves, and the change in topography along I-35 between San Antonio and Austin result from something called the Balcones Fault, which I-35 traces from Mexico to Oklahoma. From the Spanish word for balconies, the ground to the west rose up millions of years ago. The springs in this area gush out of fissures created by the fault. These springs make the

The town of West, Texas (Exit 353), between Hillsboro and Waco, has problems with its name. When residents declare they are from West, Texas, people think they mean the western part of Texas. The local solution: "I'm from West, comma, Texas."

fault area good for cattle and became a stopping point for the vast herds headed north. Nearby Temple (Exits 300–305) and Waco (Exits 334–345) developed around holding pens for the cattle on the trail and a few general stores that opened to meet the needs of the passing cowboy traffic. Waco had long been a cattle stop, because of its springs. The city takes its name from the original inhabitants, the Waco Indians, who lived here until forced out by Cherokees from further east, who had also been forced out of their homes.

Once across the Red River, the Chisholm Trail cut north through the Oklahoma Indian Territory, along a trace very similar to today's I-35. Forty years later, another breed of cowboy—the roughneck—came to these plains when the first commercial oil well, the "Nellie Johnstone," came in, in 1897. Today, oil refineries and wellheads dot the passing

While the U.S. Army had supposedly cleared everyone out of the Oklahoma Territory before the great land grab of April 1889 to give everyone a fair chance, some people snuck back into the area "sooner" than they should have to stake a claim. From that day onward, Oklahomans have been known as Sooners and Oklahoma as the Sooner State. Oklahoma is a combination of two Choctaw words: *okla* for "people" and *humma* for "red."

Taillight boogie, 1889 style. Boomers heading into the Oklahoma Territory from Arkansas City, by artist Albert Richter. (Courtesy of the Library of Congress.)

An 1889 version of an ATM along I-35 along what is now I-35 in Guthrie. The bank teller sits on the ground in the middle of the illustration, his customers lined up a few feet away. The image is a wood engraving published in the May 18, 1889, edition of *Harper's Weekly*. (Courtesy of the Library of Congress.)

landscape along I-35 where longhorns once trudged. At the border with Kansas, I-35 passes to the west of Arkansas City (Exit 4). In April 1889, a huge race started from this modest border town. The federal government had just opened up the Oklahoma Territory for settlement and thirty thousand people showed up in Arkansas City to register to claim land. Once the signal was given (a cavalry bugle) they were off, over the border, to claim what they could. In one day of pandemonium, the face of Oklahoma changed forever. Guthrie (Exits 153, 157) went from a population of zero in the morning to ten thousand by nightfall. One journalist wrote of the thousands of campfires "gleaming on the grassy slopes of the Cimarron Valley, where the night before, the coyote, the gray wolf, and the deer had roamed undisturbed."[30]

In 1920, Tom Henry of Arkansas City, Kansas, invented a candy bar he named the "Tom Henry"; the name later changed to "O Henry."

For some cattle, Wichita (Exits 42–57), or Abilene to the north, marked the end of the trail. Others continued on through this more settled part of the country to Kansas City. A contemporary description exists of the pandemonium a cattle drive could create when the longhorns reached an urban area. Picture busy city streets clogged with pedestrians, carriages, men on horseback, and wagons loaded with produce driven by teams of mules. The streets are dusty and narrow,

> the tatterdemalion drivers urging on the plunging and kicking mules with frantic shouts of "Look at ye! You dar!" These wagons, in busy days, were constantly surrounded by the in-coming droves of stock, wild Texas cattle, who with great leaps and flourish of horns objected to entering the gangways . . . and now and then tossed their tormentors high in the air; and troops of swine bespattered with blood drawn from them on the thrusts of the enraged horsemen pursuing them. Added to this indescribable tumult were the lumbering wagon trains . . . the loungers about the curbstones . . . the nameless ebb-tide of immigration scattered through a host of low and villainous bar-rooms and saloons, whose very entrances seemed suspicious; and the gangs of roustabouts rolling boxes, barrels, hogsheads and bales.[31]

For Kansas City, cattle were a big business. An 1874 account identified Kansas City, Missouri, as the leading packer of beef in the United States, with four packing houses that could handle two thousand cattle daily, their interiors so vast that they were "imposing as well as disagreeable."[32]

By 1872, railroads extended into Texas and cattle no longer had to walk to Kansas. At Fort Worth, Texas (Exit 465), stockyards allowed cattle to fatten up before being herded onto railcars. Fort Worth already had a reputation on the Chisholm Trail as a brawling, whoring, whiskey-drinking cow town where the wranglers could take a break from the hot, dusty trail. But about the same time as the railroads showed up, barbed wire was invented, and farmers now used it to stop herds from crossing their lands. Northern herds were becoming larger and Texas cattle no longer had a ready market. People living along the trail also became more resistant to large herds of cattle passing by their homes. By 1884, the Chisholm Trail had come to an end. The cattle drives almost spelled an end to the longhorn as well. By the late nineteenth century, only a few remained. The U.S. Forest Service preserved a small herd in Oklahoma in 1927, and in the 1940s, two Texans placed another herd in Fort Griffin State Park near Albany (Interstate 10). Today, the same characteristics that led to the longhorn's popularity on the Chisholm Trail have made the breed popular again; its hardiness and resistance to disease have attracted the attention of top breeders and scientists.

Many of the cowboys who had made their living on the Chisholm Trail headed north and west to frontiers opening up in such places as Minnesota and Montana. Zane Grey, the creator of the cowboy novel genre, described the Chisholm Trail as a hard place that frequently left its mark on those who traveled it. "To come from Texas was to come from fighting stock. And a cowboy's life was strenuous, wild, violent, and generally brief. The exceptions were the fortunate and the swiftest men with guns; and they drifted from south to north and west, taking with them the reckless, chivalrous, vitriolic spirit peculiar to their breed."[33]

The same pressures that pushed land-hungry settlers out of New England in the early 1800s pushed them out of Kansas and Illinois fifty years later. As settlers headed for Iowa and Minnesota, they brought the rough and rowdy spirit of the old cow towns and the cowboys of the Chisholm Trail. Years later, I-35 would again trace their path, this time northward from Kansas City through Iowa and Minnesota to the tip of Lake Superior at Duluth. That's how Badger Clark ended up in Iowa. His family left Missouri when being Abolitionists made leaving town expedient. They settled near Albia (Exit 33) where Badger was born in 1883. The name Badger Clark might not mean anything to most readers, but Badger grew up to be a cowboy with a secret vice—he loved to write poetry, and went on to publish several small volumes of poems. Many of his poems ended up as classics to be recited while sitting around a campfire and influenced the early country and western singing stars. Tex Ritter liked to recite "A Cowboy's Prayer" with music playing in the background.

I thank You, Lord, that I am placed so well,
That You have made my freedom so complete;
That I'm no slave of whistle, clock or bell,
Nor weak-eyed prisoner of wall and street.
Just let me live my life as I've begun
And give me work that's open to the sky;
Make me a pardner of the wind and sun,
And I won't ask a life that's soft or high.[34]

Another famous cowboy from the same era as Badger Clark swaggered into this world in nearby Winterset, Iowa (Exit 56), where a museum in the house where he was born honors the celluloid king of the cowboys, John Wayne.

Perhaps Zane Grey, creator of some of John Wayne's most memorable characters had it right. The Chisholm Trail and the wranglers who made a living riding its length had a huge impact on the West. "The pioneers and ranchers of the frontier would never have made the West habitable had it not been for these wild cowboys, these hard-drinking, hard-riding, hard-living rangers of the barrens, these easy, cool, laconic, simple young men whose blood was tinged with fire and who possessed a magnificent and terrible effrontery toward danger and death."[35]

Interstate 71: Bricks, Hurry, and a Muddy Roar

If you had been a hog living in Kentucky, Ohio, or Indiana in the nineteenth century, you stood a very good chance of visiting Cincinnati. Here, in the heart of what was quickly becoming the American Corn Belt, farmers had figured out the value-added element for farm produce. It was much easier and more profitable to let the corn they were growing walk to market in the form of a hog nicely fattened for slaughter or to distill that corn down into whiskey and other forms of alcohol for various medicinal and manufacturing purposes. To add to the profit margin, hogs ran free most of the year, eating acorns and beech nuts,

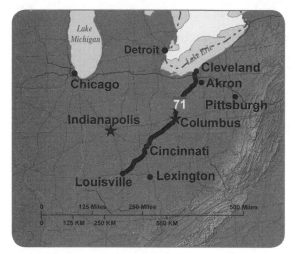

Interstate 71

A Cincinnati pork-processing operation circa 1873. From the top down, the illustrations show the killing on the upper floor, followed by cutting and fat rendering on a lower floor and, finally, salting the pork cuts in the cellar. (Courtesy of the Library of Congress.)

and anything else that caught their fancy, only receiving a feast of corn a few weeks before the trip to Cincinnati and that big smokehouse in the sky.

The city where all pig trails seemed to lead started life as a military fort in 1789 and became incorporated as a town in 1802. (Its name comes from a society of officers from the Revolutionary War, named after Cincinnatus, a Roman statesman.) Given its ideal location on a navigable river, in the heart of good farmland, and at the center of the settled area of the country at that time, Cincinnati thrived, particularly its slaughterhouses. Just as the farmer added value to his corn by feeding it to pigs, Cincinnati businessmen added value to those pigs by butchering, then curing, pickling, smoking, grinding into sausage—whatever it took to make a profitable finished product. They rendered the lard down for cooking and manufacturing purposes; the bones and other waste were turned into fertilizer—to grow more corn and start the cycle over again. Nothing went to waste. Processed Cincinnati hogs ended up as far away as Europe. By the 1840s, Cincinnati boasted that it was the largest pork market in the world.

In the early days, hogs walked to Cincinnati, sometimes with a short trip on a river barge thrown in to speed up the process. Droves of a thousand or more hogs, clogging roads into the city were fairly common. Anyone traveling in the Cincinnati area frequently found the way obstructed by pigs. Charles Dickens, rode along the 1840s version of what is today Interstate 71 and found pigs everywhere. "The road was perfectly alive with hogs of all ages, lying about in every direction fast asleep; or grunting along in quest of hidden dainties."[36] Frederick Law Olmsted passed through Cincinnati on his way to Louisville in 1856, also on a route similar to today's I-71. He soon found his stagecoach slowed by "droves of hogs grunting their obstinate way towards Cincinnati and a market. Many of the droves were very extensive, filling the road from side to side for a long distance. . . . I venture to say we met as many hogs as trees."[37]

While today's I-71 cuts a fairly direct line diagonally across Ohio from Cincinnati to Cleveland, hogs in 1851 rooted along many of the country roads that cross the interstate today. South of Cincinnati, the 1851 roads followed the river or radiated outward like spokes from places like Louisville. Finished goods generally left town via the river. Later on, seven railroad companies took Cincinnati hams to markets east and west, north and south. One line tracked northward toward Lake Erie along a trace similar to today's I-71.

Hogs generally made their way to Cincinnati in late October and early November. By the mid-1800s, five hundred thousand hogs a year trotted into the city. The 1851 Cincinnati directory described one typical "pork house" as being 360 feet long by 160 feet wide with two stories. Hogs were driven onto the roof by means of a ramp and held there until they could be taken to the second floor and slaughtered. The roof and slaughtering floor could accommodate four thousand hogs. Butchers on the first floor then cut the sides into pork and ham products. Packers filled wooden barrels with the pork cuts before sealing and lowering them into one of fifteen basement cisterns full of cool water for storage. The hams and bacon headed for the smokehouse and the fat into the rendering tanks. Some products left the city on barges a few months later, but the hams and bacon were held back for curing; corn figured in the process, with corncobs and hickory wood burned to smoke the meat. The smoked pork continued to cure until July, when flotillas of barges left the city loaded with ham and bacon for East Coast tables.

Those five hundred thousand hogs generally yielded about 180,000 barrels of pork, 25 million pounds of bacon and 16.5 million pounds of high-quality lard suitable for cooking, baking, and as a butter substitute. Lower grades of lard produced an additional 6.2 million bars of regular soap, 8.8 million bars of "fancy" soap, 2.5 million candles, and 1.2 million gallons of lard oil. In addition to the official figures from companies in the city, many Cincinnati residents had the space in the backyard and the wherewithal to slaughter a pig for home consumption. Thousands of hogs ended up curing in cellars and on back porches all over the city each winter.

To put these figures into perspective, the twenty-five million pounds of bacon would fill about 440 semitrailers on today's I-71. Enough high-quality lard was produced every year to pave I-71 northbound for fifty-four miles, shoulder to shoulder, with a half-inch thick layer of fat. That is more than half way to Columbus (Exits 101–119) from the Kentucky border.

But the value-added to those ears of corn grown by the farmers in Ohio and Kentucky did not stop with bacon and hams. Butchers and laborers were needed for slaughterhouses; other laborers rendered down the fat and turned the waste into fertilizer. Coopers built barrels; carpenters constructed the wooden boxes used to pack the bacon; still others dressed the bristles into consumer products. Factories turned out candles and soap. Transport companies shipped the finished products to markets. All those laborers needed housing, food, clothing, consumer goods, and public services. The city flourished and with it, the transportation networks needed to get pork products out of the city and consumer goods to the laboring public. Laborers looking for work flooded into the city along those same transportation networks.

Barges and boats filled the harbor; roads radiated out from the city proper. In 1828, Frances Trollope traveled between Louisville and Cincinnati, the road of that era hugging the Ohio River a little more closely than today's I-71 does. She was delighted with what she saw. "I have rarely seen richer pastures than those of Kentucky. The forest trees, where not too crowded, are of magnificent growth, and the crops are gloriously abundant where the thriftless husbandry has not worn out the soil by an unvarying succession of exhausting crops."[38] Frances was on her way to Cincinnati with her family where they planned an extended stay. She found a city "finely situated on the south side of a hill that rises gently from the water's edge; yet it is by no means a city of striking appearance; it wants domes, towers, and steeples; but its landing-place is noble, extending for more than a quarter of a mile; it is well paved, and surrounded by neat, though not handsome buildings."[39] The main street was the only one with pavement.

> The "trottoir" [of the main street] is of brick, tolerably well laid, but it is inundated by every shower, as Cincinnati has no drains whatever. What makes this omission the more remarkable is, that the situation of the place is calculated both to facilitate their construction and render them necessary. . . . [S]howers wash the higher streets, only to deposit their filth in the first level spot; and

this happens to be in the street . . . containing most of the large warehouses of the town. This deposit is a dreadful nuisance, and must be productive of miasma during the hot weather.[40]

Frances rented a house for her family. In asking about garbage disposal, she was advised by her landlord to put all the family's garbage in the middle of the street "but you must mind, old woman, that it is the middle. I expect you don't know as we have got a law what forbids throwing such things at the sides of the streets; they must just all be cast right into the middle, and the pigs soon take them off."[41] While she thoroughly disliked Cincinnati's pigs, complaining that it was impossible to keep her skirts and shoes clean when walking on the streets because of pigs brushing against her, she was well aware of the Herculean service the pigs performed in keeping the city clean—at least as far as garbage was concerned. "[T]hough it is not very agreeable to live surrounded by herds of those unsavoury animals, it is well they are so numerous, and so active in their capacity of scavengers, for without them the streets would soon be choked up with all sorts of substances in every stage of decomposition."[42]

By the time Charles Dickens passed through the city in 1842, Cincinnati had apparently transformed from a sow's ear into a silk purse. "Cincinnati is a beautiful city: cheerful, thriving, and animated. I have not often seen a place that commends itself so favourably and pleasantly to a stranger at the first glance as this does: with its clean houses of red and white, its well-paved roads, and footways' bright tile. . . . The streets are broad and airy, the shops extremely good, the private residences remarkable for their elegance and neatness."[43] Dickens found Cincinnati's residents to be quite proud of their city, which Frances Trollope also observed, if on a more limited basis.

On the 4th of July the hearts of the people seem to awaken from a three hundred and sixty-four days' sleep; they appear high-spirited, gay, animated, social, generous, or at least liberal in expense; and would they but refrain from spitting on that hallowed day, I should say, that on the 4th of July, at least, they appeared to be an amiable people.[44]

To the north, Frances found the city "bounded by a range of forest-

> *A ceaseless energy pervades . . . [Cincinnati] and gives its tone to everything. A profound hurry is the marked characteristic of the place. . . . Men smoke and drink like locomotives at a relay-house. They seem to sleep only like tops, with brains in steady whirl. . . . What more need be said of Cincinnati? Bricks, hurry, and a muddy roar make up the whole impression.*
>
> **—Frederick Law Olmsted (1857: 8)**

covered hills, sufficiently steep and rugged to prevent their being built upon, or easily cultivated, but not sufficiently high to command from their summits a view of any considerable extent. Deep and narrow watercourses, dry in summer, but bringing down heavy streams in winter, divide these hills into many separate heights, and this furnishes the only variety the landscape offers for many miles round the town."[45] Today, suburban sprawl has turned the forest-covered hills into a tangle of concrete and asphalt thoroughfares that ring the city and then radiate off, seemingly in all directions. Interstate 71 continues across the Little Miami River through miles and miles of farmland to Columbus, and onward across more farmland to Cleveland, where it marches north through the city to abut I-90 in coils of concrete and asphalt on the shore of Lake Erie. From start to finish, traveling the highway takes about six hours—a far cry from the 1800s when it took a week or so to drive hogs forty miles into the city that thrived on ham.

Interstate 49: Interstate Gridlock

It will eventually connect Kansas City with New Orleans, but for now, Interstate 49 contents itself with joining Lafayette and Shreveport, Louisiana, carrying "one pleasantly from swamp to scrub to suburb,"[46] as author Larry McMurtry put it in his book on America's great highways. A relatively new addition to the transportation network of Western Louisiana, for most of its length, I-49 traces the Red River—a waterway

Visualize four lanes of traffic at a standstill. Interstate gridlock on the Red River circa 1873. (Courtesy of the State Library of Louisiana.)

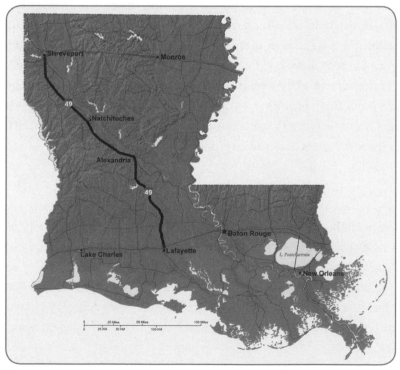

Interstate 49

> *The first hundred miles looks like a little deep and winding canal finding its way through a forest so thickly set, and of such heavy foliage, that the eye cannot penetrate.*
>
> **—Ulysses S. Grant describing travel on Louisiana's Red River in January 1846 (as quoted in McFeely, 1990: 26)**

that was the nineteenth century equivalent of a freeway. This interstate of its time was considered so essential to the welfare of anyone investing in the cotton exchange of New Orleans that when the river experienced the equivalent of transportation gridlock nineteenth century style, in the form of a massive logjam (timber was another source of wealth in Western Louisiana in the nineteenth century), officials ordered a crew of engineers to clear up the mess so cotton and grain could once more flow freely downriver to markets, and investors in the New Orleans cotton exchange could expand their business.

The first time a logjam happened in the 1830s, the U.S. Army Corps of Engineers arrived on the Red River to clean up a one hundred and eighty mile-long jam. Captain Henry Mille Shreve commanded the unit, and grateful shareholders of the newly incorporated company formed to build a town at the juncture of the Red River and the trail west to Texas named their new village Shreve Town in his honor. The name officially changed to Shreveport in 1839 in recognition of the increased importance of river travel to the area's well-being. In the 1800s, the swamp, to scrub, to suburb of the 1990s I-49 corridor, was prime agricultural land with sugar, cotton, grains, and corn production on the alluvial soils along the river. Grain crops in parts of Louisiana, including the Red River area, were a post-Civil War phenomenon. Places where cavalry horses had been fed during the war subsequently sprouted lush fields of wheat and rye. Not wanting to look a gift horse in the mouth, locals harvested the bonus crop and, what they did not consume, they shipped to markets along routes that included today's I-49 corridor.

All was well until the 1870s when logs once again clogged the Red River. As the river was now busier than ever, the logjam created transportation gridlock of massive proportions. Settlers now used the Shreveport area as a staging ground into Texas, and commerce along the river

Interstate repairs, 1870s style. Workers aboard a barge use a crane to clear logs from the Red River in 1873. (Courtesy of the State Library of Louisiana.)

had rebounded from the Civil War. The jam of walnut, oak, and ash logs was only thirty miles long this time, but it effectively stopped all traffic. Once again the U.S. Army Corps of Engineers came to the rescue. But once they broke up the logjam, it was not necessarily smooth sailing. Patience was the order of the day as it took six "toilsome" days to get from Shreveport to New Orleans, along a river that "only a flood renders worthy the name of a stream."[47] Indeed, it was almost easier to get a letter from New Orleans to Liverpool, England, than it was to get one to Shreveport. Today, the trip can be accomplished along I-10 to Lafayette and then up I-49 to Shreveport in less than six hours.

The Red River remained a major transportation route until the early part of the twentieth century when railroads took over much of the commercial business in and through this part of Louisiana; truck transport traffic on the interstates would do the same thing to the viability of the railroads. The Red River began to fill with silt. But everything that goes around comes around, and the Red River is once again being used as a transportation route with development in Shreveport to improve the facilities that put port in the town's name and made fortunes for those long ago cotton merchants in New Orleans.

Interstate 16: Five-Cent Cotton, Forty-Cent Meat

In the days when cotton was king, farmers in central Georgia brought their crops by wagon and mule, to shipping points, like Macon, Georgia, where they loaded the cotton bales onto flat barges that could navigate shallow rivers, such as the Altamaha, and floated them downstream to coastal ports, which expanded rapidly to handle all the cotton floating their way. By 1820, in Savannah, cotton represented eighty percent of all agricultural shipments. At that time, the Port of Savannah shipped about fourteen million dollars worth of goods every year. Cotton had become so important to Savannah and Savannah so important to cotton that traders frequently set global cotton prices at the Savannah Cotton Exchange.

By the 1840s, a railroad had been built to handle cotton freight. It

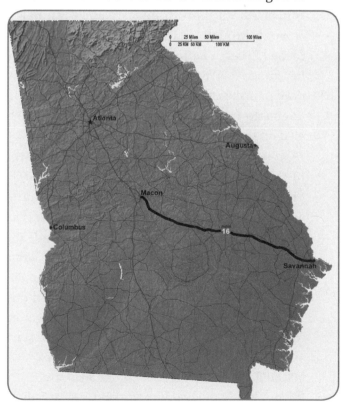

Interstate 16

Cotton bales being shipped from Savannah Harbor. Published in *Frank Leslie's Illustrated Newspaper*, 1865. The wood engraving was created by W. T. Crane. (Courtesy of the Library of Congress.)

connected Macon with Augusta and Savannah. More cotton could be shipped through Savannah. In the summer of 1846 or '47, a young girl named Rebecca Latimer took that train from Macon to Savannah with her father.[48] "We . . . left Macon Friday morning and traveled until after dark to make the trip to Savannah. A tremendous rain storm overtook us and the track was often under water. The train hands frequently shoveled off the wet sand from the rails."[49]

In its march to the sea in 1864, Sherman's army destroyed 110 miles of the rail line between Macon and Savannah. By 1866, the track had been reconstructed and once farms in the countryside recovered, cotton again flowed into Savannah by rail. "The [1874] journey from Savannah to Macon carries one well out of the lowlands into a high rolling country, admirably suited to cotton raising. . . . The smaller towns around about [Macon] . . . are not very promising in appearance." Macon, in that era, was described as "picturesquely perched on a hill around which a densely wooded country stretches away in all directions."[50] Macon's iron foundries and cotton mills gave the town of ten thousand a "sprightly appearance."[51] It had been founded fifty years earlier and named after Nathaniel Macon, a states' rights advocate and friend of Thomas Jefferson. Roads did connect Macon to Savannah, but it was much easier and more economical to ship cotton by rail. The road of 1870 almost duplicated present-day Interstate 16, running from Macon to Dublin and then straight into Savannah.

By the 1870s, the Port of Savannah had regained its status as a major port, primarily through the shipment of cotton and naval stores, such as turpentine and timber. A visitor to Savannah in 1874 reported: "As we walked, day by day, through the Savannah streets, late in autumn, we were amazed at the masses of cotton bales piled everywhere. They lined the commercial avenues . . . down by the water side they were heaped in mammoth piles, and the processions of drays seemed endless. The huge black ships swallowed bale after bale, gaping for more; the clank of the hoisting crane was heard from morning till night."[52]

By 1905, exports through the Port of Savannah were greater than for all other southern ports combined. But the Great Depression started in Georgia a full decade before the rest of the nation, largely due to the boll weevil, which destroyed much of the cotton crop. And what the boll weevil did not damage was reduced in value by the Depression to the point that a common refrain throughout the cotton belt became: "Five-cent cotton, forty-cent meat; how in the world can a poor man eat?"[53]

Farmers along what became I-16, turned to other crops and livelihoods. Just south of what is now Exit 84, a farmer near Vidalia, Georgia, on pulling his crop of onions, discovered they were not quite what he thought he had planted. They were very sweet and mild, thanks to the soil in which they were grown. At first he had trouble selling them, but was soon getting more than the normal price for onions, even in the depths of the Great Depression. Consumers soon clamored for those Vidalia onions and the name stuck. Today, only onions grown in

> *In dust, in rain, with might and main,*
> *He nursed his cotton, cursed his grain,*
> *Fretted for news that made him fret again,*
> *Snatched at each telegram of Future Sale,*
> *And thrilled with Bulls' or Bears' alternate wail—*
> *In hope or fear alike forever pale.*
>
> **—From "Corn," by Macon, Georgia, poet Sidney Lanier (1842–1881) (1885: 58)**

a twenty-county region of Georgia can legally be called Vidalia onions. Along I-16, this area stretches from near Exit 32 to just beyond Exit 137 where 225 farmers grow about seven hundred million Vidalia onions every year.

While some farmers managed to rebound from the devastation to the cotton crop, the Port of Savannah took the demise of cotton in stride and switched to goods from other industries, such as pulp and paper and sugar refining. World War II brought shipbuilding and further expansion of port facilities. But with the end of the war, much of this activity ceased. Then along came President Eisenhower's plans for a national interstate highway system. The interstates turned out to be essential in the revitalization of Georgia's postwar economy. In the case of the proposed I-16, it would provide a limited-access, direct link between the Port of Savannah and I-75, which led directly to Atlanta, a city quickly becoming the center of the Southern universe.

Interstate 16 replaced a portion of U.S. 80, formerly known as the Dixie Overland Highway. U.S. 80 had been a key transportation route for its time, but in the postwar years, as truck transportation increased and technological advances in trucks brought bigger and heavier vehicles to the nation's highways, the trace of U.S. 80 through the small Georgia towns along its path slowed down the forward march of interstate truck commerce. Main streets in places like Statesboro (Exit 116) and Swainsboro (Exit 90) were difficult to navigate in a larger truck, never mind the constant gear shifting required to accelerate and decelerate. The proposed I-16 was also much straighter; it was to be built in as direct a line as possible. Travel time from end to end of I-16 is now a little over two hours. Technological advances of the postwar era also put new pressures on the Port of Savannah. Larger ships, and more of them, docked in Savannah, and not just from Europe or other North American ports. Ships originating in Asia now unloaded cargo in Savannah. New facilities were built and the harbor dredged.

Construction of I-16 began near Dublin in March 1963, with the entire interstate open to traffic by 1978. Its impact on Georgia's economy cannot be underestimated. Savannah has been called the most logistics-friendly city in the nation, and I-16, with its quick access to Atlanta, plays a huge role in this accolade. Between 1980 and 2003, the amount of container traffic flowing through the Port of Savannah increased sevenfold while nationwide container traffic in the same period increased fourfold. Over fourteen million tons of freight passed through the port in 2004. In response, large retail distribution centers have come to the Savannah area as have heavy industries that depend on truck transportation, such as pulp and paper facilities. And those old cotton warehouses along the waterfront have evolved into trendy boutiques and bars.

As one of the top container-shipping ports in North America, the Port of Savannah continues to expand. Plans are afoot to dredge the harbor yet again to accommodate even larger vessels. When the first settlers landed in what is now Savannah, the harbor was about eighteen feet deep. It is now forty-two feet deep and some want to make it forty-eight feet deep although more shore erosion and the destruction of nearby freshwater marshes are a major concern if this happens. The debate continues.

Interstate 89: Leaf Peepers

In northern New England, Indian summer puts up a scarlet-tipped hand to hold winter back for a little while. She brings with her the time of the last warm spell, an unchartered season which lives until Winter moves in with its backbone of ice and accoutrements of leafless trees and hard frozen ground.[54]

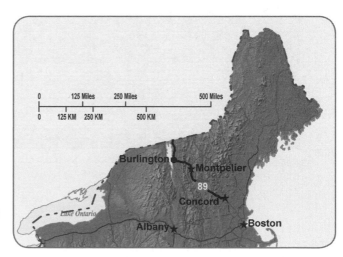

Interstate 89

Leaf peepers enjoying the autumn woods in their brand new Franklin automobile, 1909. This illustration appeared in an automobile advertisement. (Courtesy of the New York Public Library.)

In mid-September, the freshly painted, scarlet-tipped hands begin beckoning leaf peepers out of their natural habitat in places like New York, Boston, and Philadelphia. On fine fall weekends, they dig out their rural chic wardrobe, climb into vehicles and migrate north along Interstate 89 to see the scarlet lady, her finery draped over the plump New England mountains. During this migration, a few million leaf peepers clog I-89 through New Hampshire and Vermont to the Quebec border, as it winds for 191 miles through some of the prettiest hill country of New England, across the Connecticut River valley, past the Green Mountains, and along the eastern edge of Lake Champlain.

Early settlers looked at those same plump mountains and saw something else. It had not yet occurred to anyone that these forested hills were good for anything besides timber and firewood, and with typical New England determination, they sharpened their axes and went to work clearing land for farms. The income from forest products helped them through the early years. By the 1800s, Vermont and New Hampshire had lost great swaths of their scarlet-tipped landscape, the plump mountain slopes left bald. Timbers were either floated down the Connecticut River to paper and saw mills in the more settled areas or driven northward on Lake Champlain to the St. Lawrence River. In clearing their land, farmers also made potash. It took a ton of wood to make seven pounds of potash. In turn, a ton of potash was worth as much as three hundred dollars, a lot of money in the early 1800s. (Potash was used to make soap, and in the textile industry in processing yarns into fabrics. It was also used in dyes, glass making, and some drugs. These days, potash is used extensively as an ingredient in fertilizers.)

While New Englanders could clear the land of trees, the boulder-strewn fields represented their own challenges and by the mid-1800s, many settlers had given up attempts to farm in parts of Vermont and New Hampshire and headed further west, abandoning their land. Lumber companies simply went in on these abandoned farms and clear-cut the timber. And then there were people like lumber baron J. E. Henry who supposedly declared: "I never seen the tree yit that didn't mean a damned sight more to me goin' under the saw than it did standin' on a mountain."[55] Advances in technology further compounded the problem. Steam engines were brought into lumber camps to mill the timbers;

This load of timber, on its way to the mill, contains one thousand feet of spruce. Many of these logging roads subsequently became overgrown, while others became side roads now crossing I-89. (Courtesy of the U.S. Forest Service.)

railroads were built into forested areas that had been uneconomical to harvest.

If there was an up side, the money flowing into Vermont and New Hampshire from the sale of timber products built better homes and community facilities, such as schools and churches. It also bought more consumer products for households making money from lumber. Some logging trails evolved into roads that today cross I-89; others gradually reforested themselves once J.E. Henry's crews had moved on to other stands. Vermont even put its prisoners to work processing timber into wood products. Just south of White River Junction (Exit 1), state prisoners made handles for scythes in the 1860s. But as one writer mused: "Is not Vermont setting a bad example by teaching her 'crooked sticks,' who are sent to prison to be made straight, to make straight sticks crooked?"[56]

The lumbering continued to destroy old-growth forests as did massive forest fires. Governor Woodbury of Vermont started agitating for change. In an 1894 speech to the state legislature, he bemoaned the wanton destruction of the forests. "Every decade will see timber more valuable and it is of great importance to the state as a whole . . . that some measure should be adopted."[57] Others also recognized the consequences of deforestation. Societies sprang up to save the forests and in 1911, the federal government established a national forest on 722,000 acres in the White Mountains of New Hampshire. The Green Mountain National Forest in Vermont was established in 1932.

Today, leaf peepers heading north connect with I-89 at Concord, New Hampshire, an area first settled by Native Americans because of the fertile soil in the Merrimack River Valley, where they raised squash and corn. Settlers from Massachusetts formed a settlement here in 1725, and the New Hampshire legislature named Concord the state capital in 1808. From Concord, I-89 heads northwest across the middle of the state toward the Connecticut River Valley, crossing both the river and I-91 at White River Junction. In Vermont, I-89 tracks northeast past the Green Mountain National Forest toward Montpelier (Exit 8), the state capital. Like so many other mountain chains in Eastern North America, the Green Mountains were formed about four hundred and fifty million years ago, but the Ice Age and time wore them down to the boulder-strewn landscape you see today.

Montpelier does not look much like a capital city, with fewer than nine thousand residents. It is, in fact, the smallest state capital in the

The Reverend Samuel Peters stood on top of Killington Peak one day in 1763. As he admired the dark green mountains, he decided to christen the land *vert mont*, French for "green mountain." Rev. Peters later complained when the "t" was dropped from *vert*, because *ver* meant maggot, so Vermont really meant the "mountain of worms."

Vermont humor: A traveler comes to a fork in the road and asks a local resident: "I'm going to Montpelier; does it matter which road I take?" The Vermonter responds: "Not to me it don't."

nation. Founded in 1781, Montpelier seems to have been named after Montpelier, France, because the town's founder liked the sound of the name and all things French were in vogue, with France assisting the colonies during the Revolution.

After leaving Montpelier, I-89 heads northwest toward Lake Champlain and Burlington, Vermont. Here, the interstate crosses the Green Mountains. The huge stacks of firewood beside many of the rural homes along the highway attest to the ongoing importance of forest products in a corner of the country where they still joke that there are only three seasons: getting ready for winter, winter, and recovering from winter. Vermonters were always well aware of the natural attributes of their state, but they didn't always know how to exploit that bit of wisdom. Somewhere in the civil service, an idea clicked and Vermont became the first state to open a state tourist agency. In 1911, the Vermont Bureau of Publicity started telling people what a fine place Vermont was for a vacation, good for more than leaf peeping in the fall. Soon, residents of Vermont caught on, opening hotels and their homes to accommodate visitors. Ski resorts and summer camps began trumpeting the soft powder and pristine lakes of the state and its reforested slopes. The fledgling Green Mountain Club blazed a hiking trail through the Green Mountains. The 262-mile long trail opened in 1928.

New Hampshire and Vermont also work hard to attract another form of leaf peepers: those with a sweet tooth. Maple syrup is big business in both states, but in a state where sixty percent of the trees are maples, Vermont leads as the largest producer by far in the United States with

In 1934, a resident of Woodstock, Vermont (Exit 1), figured out how to hook a rope up to a Ford Model T's engine to pull skiers uphill.

about five hundred thousand gallons of syrup boiled down from about twenty million gallons of sap every year. It takes cold nights and days above freezing to make the sap run. The maple syrup season generally extends from early March to mid-April in both states. But before the sap can run, the maples need their winter sleep. The god of the north world sits in the golden warmth of an autumn day admiring the scarlet-tipped crown of autumn. He grows pleasantly drowsy watching people feasting after the harvest. Often, the first frost rouses him just enough to enjoy a leisurely smoke before his annual hibernation. When this happens, there is a spell of smoky, mellow weather until the god dozes off contentedly and winter begins.

Interstate 84 East: Yankee Doodle Ingenuity

During his visit to King Arthur's court, Mark Twain's Connecticut Yankee proudly spoke of his Hartford, Connecticut, roots. In telling his story, he recounted how he had gone to work in Hartford's great arms factory and "learned to make everything: guns, revolvers, cannon, boilers, engines, all sorts of labor-saving machinery. Why, I could make anything a body wanted—anything in the world, it didn't make any difference what; and if there wasn't any quick new-fangled way to make a thing, I could invent one."[58] It was no accident that Mark Twain chose a Hartford, Connecticut, resident as his hero to visit King Arthur. A long-time resident of the city, Twain developed a character who typified the stereotypical Yankee: industrious, inventive, honest, shrewd, and decidedly set in his ways. Frances Trollope, early travel writer and social commentator, met quite a few New Englanders in her North American travels from 1828 to 1830, but she typified a Yankee a bit differently. "I like them extremely

Interstate 84 East

Roads passing the Hotchkiss & Merriman Manufacturing Company of Waterbury, circa 1850. The company manufactured men's suspenders. (Courtesy of the Connecticut Historical Society.)

well, but I would not wish to have any business transactions with them, if I could avoid it, lest, to use their own phrase, 'they should be too smart for me.'"[59]

Today, Interstate 84 East serves this hotbed of Yankee shrewdness as it traces a path from Scranton, Pennsylvania, through the Poconos, across the Delaware and Hudson River valleys, and then into the gently rolling hills of the Connecticut countryside, through Hartford, and onward for a few miles in Massachusetts. The Hartford of Mark Twain's time was already the leading insurance center in the country. Businessmen played the odds that a house would not burn, a husband would not die before his time, a traveler would not have an accident on a railroad. Records for 1867 indicate eighteen insurance companies in operation: eleven providing fire insurance, six offering life insurance, and one selling accident insurance. The accident insurance company was the first of its kind in the United States. Manufacturing and commercial enterprises also attracted workers to the city.

"Yankee Doodle" became Connecticut's official state song in 1978. The term "Yankee" may have Dutch origins: when the first English settlers moved from Massachusetts to the Connecticut River valley circa 1635, their new Dutch neighbors referred to them rather sarcastically as John Cheese—"Jan Kees" in Dutch.

While Dutch settlers founded the town that later became Hartford in 1633, English settlers from Massachusetts discovered the waterpower potential of the Connecticut River and mills soon followed, among them various firearms manufacturers and textile mills. In 1867, Hartford had good streets, generally macadamized, and a population of about forty thousand. It was, per capita, the wealthiest city in the United States. Between the insurance industry and two arms manufacturers—Colt revolvers and Sharpe rifles—the city thrived during the Civil War. A subsequent Colt innovation—the six-shooter—became the firearm of choice in the West. At nearby Enfield, the Hazard Powder Company produced twelve tons of gunpowder a day during the Civil War. At Manchester, an employee in a silk factory invented the Spencer repeating rifle. Even a local harness maker landed some lucrative contracts to supply the Union Army.

Samuel Colt's firearms plant pioneered many of today's manufacturing methods. Among his modern innovations was the idea of interchangeable parts for various models, the assembly line, and more attention to employee welfare than was common at the time. The Colt plant soon became a training school for many of the next generation's industrial leaders, including the future founders of Pratt and Whitney Company. Many early factories foundered as the times changed; others learned new skills and took up the challenges of a new era. In Manchester (Exits

The first automobile insurance policy issued in the United States was written in Hartford in 1898.

Noah Webster, a Hartford native, published the first American dictionary of the English language in 1828. It was the first dictionary listing American usage and spelling, and included technical terms not found in other dictionaries of that time.

59–63), a company known for its innovations in the manufacturing of silk became a parachute factory during World War II. Pratt and Whitney made airplanes, and a propeller factory opened up to serve the war effort. The eventual demise of New England's textile industry led to depressed local economies, one being that of Manchester, but Yankee ingenuity soon attracted manufacturers and companies looking for skilled workers. Sturbridge (Exits 2–3), just across the border in Massachusetts, become known for optical instruments and cutlery.

Development in New England tended to begin at the coast and move inland along the rivers. By 1830, Hartford, on the Connecticut River, had been around for almost two hundred years. But to get from Hartford to Waterbury, the next major center to the southwest on today's I-84, was not a simple thirty-mile cross-country trip over the rolling hills. In 1830, there were a couple of choices: down the Connecticut River to the coast, along the coast to the Naugatuck River, and up the Naugatuck to Waterbury, or by road to New Haven on the coast and then by road inland to Waterbury, a distance of about eighty miles. The same Yankee ingenuity that overtook Hartford, also infected the Waterbury area. Here could be found factories mass producing everything from hooks and eyes to suspenders and clocks. Someone speeding along on I-84 today tends to take the digital clock on the dashboard for granted, but until the 1800s, unless you were fairly comfortable in life, you did not have a clock, because they were too expensive for the average household. Then, in the early 1800s, clockmakers from Connecticut developed the ability to mass produce clock parts and suddenly a clock for the mantle was within the reach of everyone. Clock prices plummeted from about twenty-five dollars to five dollars.

A little further southwest along I-84, Danbury, Connecticut, billed itself as the hatting capital of the world. In the Danbury of one hundred

> Other notable Connecticut firsts: American-made steel, axe factory, bicycle factory, carpet mill, cigars, commercial telephone exchange, condensed milk, copper coins, cotton thread, cylinder locks, football tackling dummy, friction clutch, gun silencer, knockdown furniture, lollipop-making device, machined bolts, machine to cut teeth in combs, mechanical player piano, nails, packaged garden seeds, plow, shaving soap, silver-plated spoon, spool-wound silk thread, accurate measuring machine, steam-powered manufacturing, tacks, tinware, trading stamps, vulcanized rubber (which made the automobile tire possible), and the whiffle ball. All of the above were either invented or first manufactured in Connecticut.

years ago, they made felt hats, fur hats, beaver hats, wool hats, derby hats, hats, hats, hats. As with a road trip from Hartford to Waterbury in 1830, a road trip from Waterbury to Danbury meant going down to New Haven on the coast and then taking another road from New Haven inland to Danbury. For I-84 motorists today, it is a distance of seventeen miles. From Danbury, I-84 crosses into New York through the cities of Newburgh (Exits 10–7) and Middletown (Exits 4–3). All thrived in the 1800s as manufacturing centers. Newburgh, from its position on the west bank of the Hudson River, was also home port to a whaling fleet. The town subsequently became the major market center for the surrounding area, capitalizing on its position on the Delaware and Hudson Canal and, subsequently, the Erie Canal. After crossing into Pennsylvania, I-84 heads west past Milford (Exit 46) across the ridge and valley topography of Northeast Pennsylvania for fifty-five miles. The route is sparsely settled and almost entirely forested, crossing through the Delaware State Forest, around the Bruce Lake Natural Area, and over the Moosic Mountains before abruptly meeting up with I-81 in a tangle of overpasses outside Scranton.

Mark Twain's Connecticut storyteller made no apologies for being a Yankee. "So I am a Yankee of the Yankees—and practical; yes, and nearly barren of sentiment, I suppose—or poetry, in other words."[60] But, if you needed a "new-fangled way" to do something, he was your man. Frances Trollope might have disagreed. "It is by no means easy to give a clear and just idea of a Yankee; if you hear his character from a Virginian, you will believe him a devil: if you listen to it from himself, you might fancy him a god—though a tricky one."[61]

Interstate 86 East: Chimerical, Impracticable, and Useless

Its own self-congratulatory guidebook called it "one of the grandest achievements of modern intellect,"[62] comparing it to the Egyptian pyramids and the Roman aqueducts. The book went on to note that in these modern times—the 1850s—patience and a lever would eventually move just about anything, but why bother? Just blast right through it! Time was of the essence and patience in short supply.

This miracle of modern technology, "this splendid homage to our memory,"[63] was a railroad connecting New York City with Erie, Pennsylvania. This paean to mankind, the New York and Erie Rail-Road, passed through country that "was thought insanity to talk of building a rail-road through."[64] Today, Interstate 86 East generally crosses the same terrain. With the exception of each end, where I-86E is a few miles away from the original roadbed of the New York and Erie, the two roadways share the same trace through Southern New York State between I-87 to the east and I-90 to the west. In the 1830s, it was thought to be an impossible trace. It crossed mountains deemed impassable and traversed valleys where "timid men said it would cost billions to fill in; it leaps ravines where bold engineers paused, shook their heads, and turned back."[65]

Interstate 86 East

Two men look out over a section of the New York and Erie Rail-Road from a spot east of Binghamton. (Courtesy of the Library of Congress.)

Indeed, it took a lot of convincing to get the railroad built in the first place. From a security standpoint, the importance of a road connecting New York with Lake Erie through the valleys of the Delaware, Susquehanna, and Allegheny Rivers had been proposed by two generals at the end of the Revolutionary War. No action was taken. Politicians and local community boosters proposed other routes but, in most instances, the costs of crossing the formidable terrain of swamps and mountains were untenable. New York's legislature advocated a route as early as 1832, but no one could see any reason why a thoroughfare through the southern counties connecting New York, specifically its harbor, with Erie, Pennsylvania, again specifically its harbor, was necessary. After all, the Erie Canal tracking through Albany and Syracuse was doing well. And there wasn't even anything in the southern counties of New York to justify the cost of a road. A consultant hired to study the matter concluded that the southern counties were "mountainous, sterile, and worthless, affording no products requiring a road to market."[66] All in all, the whole undertaking was "chimerical, impracticable, and useless."[67]

The railroad's backers persevered, but construction was not an easy task. Work crews encountered all kinds of hazards; one, of the bovine variety, made it into the 1854–1855 guidebook. It seems a bull objected to the workers being in his field and had to be led away by the farmer. But the bull did not forget the indignity. "[W]hen the first locomotive appeared on the scene of his defeat, he lay in ambuscade for the unconscious engine, and rushing toward it, they met in full career, and his bullship was converted into fresh beef on the spot!"[68] Every mile of the finished line attested to the physical challenge of laying the rail bed, with rocky rubbish and scattered and splintered trees lying along the margins of the right of way. Eventually, on a stormy night in late December 1848, the first train on the New York and Erie Rail-Road reached Binghamton (Exit 75). As the guidebook pointed out, the "conquerors of space" who had succeeded in building the road were now the welcome "harbingers of trade, intercourse, and civilization."[69]

> Old hunters . . . stood . . . in the snow-storm, lit up by the tar-barrels, leaning on their rifles, and watching with curious eyes the apparition of the iron steed and his splendid train. Troops of girls entered at one end, and walked through the whole row of cars, gazing with astonishment at the velvet seats and the cloaked citizens, who were no less astonished at the bright eyes and rosy cheeks that . . . could turn out in a winter storm to welcome strangers.[70]

The train engines of the New York and Erie Rail-Road apparently had a whistle that was quite different from the shrill pitch of early train engines. It was described at the time as an "unearthly hoarseness, as though it had a bad cold."[71] In rural New York, residents reported ungodly sounds emanating day and night from the surrounding forest. Stories of monsters and fierce wild animals soon spread. One town was convinced an ancient mastodon had somehow wandered into the area. One night, villagers gathered their "guns, axes and pitchforks in ambuscade at the hour he selected for his vocal exercises. At the usual hour the roar was heard, and so suddenly and so near that the party was about to hurry back to their anxious wives and mothers when, lo through the gloom of night issued the glaring Cyclops eye of the locomotive."[72]

Less than a decade later, the railroad's travel guide commented: "Since the introduction of roads . . . [the Binghamton region] has advanced in agricultural importance and in the richness and abundance of its product. . . . Though generally mountainous, there is hardly a hill not susceptible of cultivation to the very top."[73] The same guide quickly pointed out that the commercial traffic and hence the wealth that had formerly gone to other cities now poured into New York City, thanks in large part to the New York and Erie Rail-Road.

Towns all along the route thrived. Not only did they now have a means of getting goods to and from larger markets more economically, but the railroad encouraged passenger traffic. Middletown (Exits 121–118), for instance, got its start exactly as its name implies: it was half way between the Hudson and Delaware Rivers on a stagecoach route. Apparently a hotel, called the Half Way House served hungry travelers. The town thrived, especially when the New York and Erie Rail-Road arrived in 1843. Daniel Webster, the great American orator and politician, is said to have taken his first ride on the new railroad through Middletown seated in a rocking chair on a flatcar so he could enjoy the scenery without the walls of a coach in his sight lines. Today, Middletown continues its tradition of serving travelers with multiple exits on I-86E, all crowded with services for motorists.

In grandiose fashion, the 1855 guidebook credited the railroad with the flourishing trade across southern New York State. But it did not stop there. Places like Milwaukee and Chicago had been but tiny twinkles on the western landscape when the New York and Erie Rail-Road had been constructed. While the railroad could not take all the credit for their subsequent development, there was absolutely no doubt that this trace across Southern New York, now followed by I-86E, had "contributed more than any other single road or route of travel to these great results. . . . Future years will show great triumphs of art and perseverance of intellect, but no age will exhibit a greater contrast with that which preceded it than is presented by this . . . nor do we believe that the labor of man will ever produce a more magnificent result in filling valleys or hewing down mountains than is presented by the Erie Rail-Road."[74]

Interstate 88 East: Where Would Huck End Up?

If Huck Finn traded in his wooden raft for a neon-colored kayak and launched it into the Susquehanna River, where would he end up? Motorists on Interstate 88 East through central New York flirt with the Susquehanna and its tributary streams for the ninety or so minutes that it takes to make the journey from Binghamton to Schenectady. Some-

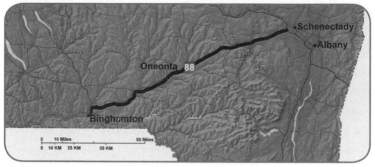

Interstate 88 East

times, it is only a glimpse of water. Then it becomes the panorama from a bridge (near Mile Marker 17) or the sinuous curves of the highway along the meandering stream, but the sense is there of an important element in the landscape. What would Huck think of the modern highway? Where would he end up if he decided to float downstream? Lake Erie sits to the north, the Mississippi River to the west; the Hudson River flows into New York to the east, and to the south, there's the Potomac River. A little further southeast lies Chesapeake Bay.

From the Algonquian words for "muddy river," the Susquehanna drains a prosperous agricultural area in central New York. Robert Louis Stevenson commented in 1879 that the "beauty of the name [Susquehanna] seemed to be part and parcel of the beauty of the land. . . . That was the name, as no other could be, for that shining river and desirable valley."[75] A few years later, writing about his canoe trip down the Susquehanna for a book called *Athletics and Manly Sport*, Irish poet, novelist, and editor John Boyle O'Reilly was shocked by the denuded hills along the river, referring to them as

> shorn like a stubble-field. The naked stumps are white and unsightly on the mountains, like the bones of an old battle-field. . . . A monster has crept into the valley. . . . The hills stand up in the sun, cropped and debased like convicts; their beauty and mystery and shadowed sacredness torn from them; their silence and loneliness replaced by the selfish chirp of the grasshopper among the dry weeds. Never did the hard utility of civilization appear less disguised and less lovely.[76]

The railroad monster cutting through central New York had destroyed large tracts of forest, for use in the construction of bridges and

Would Huckleberry Finn appreciate the idyllic scene portrayed in this 1887 print of the Susquehanna River? (Courtesy of the Library of Congress.)

as ties, but also in clearing the right of way. But, as in Vermont and New Hampshire, loggers had also been busy along the Susquehanna. In the subsistence economy of the early settlers, the extra money from timber and potash added greatly to a family's ability to survive with a few basic comforts. Settlers also had to clear the slopes before they could farm. The Susquehanna provided the means of getting to their lands and of floating timbers and rafts loaded with produce to market. But where would the produce—and Huck—end up if they floated down the Susquehanna? Huck would have had quite a ride! Waters of the Susquehanna River eventually flow into Chesapeake Bay near Havre de Grace, Maryland, about four hundred miles away. It was this link that led the first settlers into the Susquehanna Valley in 1791 as they followed the water trail northward. Timbers and farm produce could then float down river to markets and ship-building centers in New York, Philadelphia, and Baltimore. Produce included everything from salt pork to apples and whiskey, and the ever-popular potash.

While he was upset by the denuded appearance of the Susquehanna Valley, John Boyle O'Reilly was almost poetic and seemed to belie the "muddy" origins of the river's name. "The water was not three feet deep; clear as air—every pebble seen on the bottom, and none larger than your hand; and the whole wide river slipping and sliding like a great sheet of glass out of its frame! . . . Never have I seen river-water so clear and wholesome as the Susquehanna. One of our daily pleasures was to dip our bright tin cups into the river, drink a mouthful, and pour the rest into our mouths without swallowing."[77] Huck Finn would probably have enjoyed his ride.

Interstate 91: Manly Sport

In 1890, John Boyle O'Reilly, writer, editor, publisher, noted Fenian, escaped felon, and darling of the Irish literati of Boston, published *Athletics and Manly Sport*, a book in which he recounted his canoeing adventures on the Connecticut River. Canoeing had become quite popular and, in describing his trip along a river now traced by Interstate 91, O'Reilly portrayed the romanticized, idyllic view so prevalent in nature writing of that era—particularly male adventure in the great outdoors—whether fishing for salmon in California, hunting in Florida, or canoeing down the Connecticut River.

"Miles in a voyage are of no more account than years in a life: they may be filled with commonplace. Men live by events, and so they paddle" (O'Reilly, 1890). John Boyle O'Reilly, pictured above, on canoeing in *Athletics and Manly Sport*. (Courtesy of the Library of Congress.)

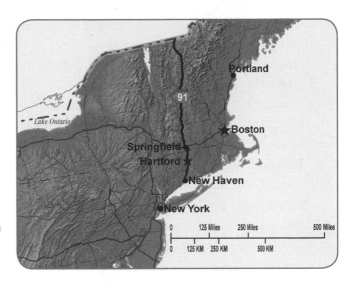

Interstate 91

At 407 miles long, the Connecticut is the longest river in New England and thus is aptly named: Connecticut is thought to be from the Mahican Indian word *quinnehtukqut* meaning "long river." The river forms the border between New Hampshire and Vermont before flowing through Massachusetts and Connecticut to the coast and Long Island Sound. It descends 1,618 feet and drains 11,000 square miles of countryside. As a result of this drop, it is one of the most heavily developed rivers in the country, its dams generating hydroelectricity and controlling the flooding that ravaged the area over the centuries. While other rivers, such as the Hudson, are deep enough to accommodate large vessels, along much of their length, a huge sandbar and salt marshes at the mouth of the Connecticut River prevented deep-draft vessels from navigating the river. This also meant the Connecticut did not become as important for the movement of people as the nearby Hudson. However, small ocean-going vessels can still navigate the river as far north as Hartford, a distance of about fifty miles.

An 1867 guidebook to the Connecticut River Valley characterized it as only recently becoming known thanks to improvements in transportation that "opened the doors to this elysian field, and thousands come with the recurring period of foliage and flowers, to worship at the shrine of beauty found in lofty mountains, broad meadows and a majestic river."[78] Here was a land meant for rest and inspiration. John Boyle O'Reilly and his canoeing companion found relaxation with a paddle in hand. They began their adventure in Boston at the train station, rail being the easiest way to ship their canoe to their starting point. The alternative was a wagon trip of an undetermined number of days along roads that wound along the riverbank. At that time, all roads in the Connecticut Valley were still a local responsibility and, generally, in poor condition. The roads that did exist generally traced ancient paths that connected Native American villages along the river. With the arrival of European settlement in the valley in the 1630s, these well-worn trails soon connected the fledgling commercial hubs forming along the riverbanks and provided trading routes away from the river. By O'Reilly's time, many of these towns had become vibrant commercial hubs.

A steamboat started operating on the Connecticut River in 1793, and the first canal in the United States was built on the river in 1802, around the Bellows Falls. By the time O'Reilly set out on his trip, the railroads in the Connecticut Valley had been in existence for about fifty years, but the same floods and heavy rains that sometimes wiped out the roads and left residents along the river stranded for extended periods also wiped out railroads. And, it was easier to patch a roadbed or create a detour than it was to get a rail line back in service. As the population centers along the river competed with each other for superiority, the road system improved, but standards varied. Road conditions and construction depended on the whims of locally elected officials. But the same restless need to experience nature and see what the backcountry had to offer that infected O'Reilly had caught up with many of his fellow urbanites. They came to fish, paddle, enjoy the scenery, get out of the cities along the coast, and spend money.

Today, the Connecticut River continues to be popular among canoeists and kayakers. If John Boyle O'Reilly was around today, he would probably strap his composite fiber canoe to the roof of a sport utility vehicle and head to Hartford and then I-91. From his loft apartment in Boston, the trip north up the Connecticut River Valley would probably take him about five or six hours depending on traffic and pit stops. In the late 1880s, O'Reilly and his friend told the train conductor where they wanted to disembark, and the train stopped. Their canoe was unloaded out of the baggage car for them and the train continued on its way. O'Reilly and his companion chose a white sandbank along the river north of White River Junction in Vermont (Exits 11–12) from which to launch their grand adventure. Here, they were upstream from a large log boom making its way down the river and could safely follow it. If he did the trip today, O'Reilly and his companion might go beyond White River Junction to Fairlee (Exit 15), where the palisades along the river are popular among rock climbers.

From White River Junction, I-91 stretches northward for another 107 miles parallel to the western bank of the Connecticut River until just south of Saint Johnsbury, Vermont (Exits 20–22) where the river bends to the east and the interstate continues to the north all the way to the Canadian border. Here, the landscape is a mixture of forests and meadows. Saint Johnsbury lies among the hills at the confluence of the Sleepers, Passumpsic, and Moose Rivers. Settled in 1786, the town is named after Ethan Allen's friend, Michel Guillame Jean de Crevecoeur. An iron foundry established here in 1823 helped turn the town into an industrial center. Vermont considers the Connecticut River its most important river but, technically, the river is not in Vermont at all. The U.S. Supreme Court ruled that the border between Vermont and New Hampshire is on the Vermont bank of the river. New Hampshire gets the revenue from the hydroelectric plants on the river but must pay for the upkeep of the three bridges across the river between New Hampshire and Vermont. Vermonters may not be able to claim the river as their own, but they still get to enjoy it.

That July afternoon, at White River Junction, O'Reilly and his companion headed downriver. "Hundreds of miles of beautiful water, splendid days, a new moon, a well-stored locker, and a boat that danced . . . like a duck"[79] lay ahead of them. At night, they slept on the bank of the river, without a tent.

> For an hour before rising, I had lain awake, looking out at the river, and listening to the strange country sounds around me. All over the grasses and low bushes, the spider's webs were stretched, glistening with dew. What a wonderful night industry! . . . The little night-toilers had woven them over our olive bottle, over the gun, over ourselves. The field above us was white as snow with this incomparable cloth-of-silver.[80]

Their daily routine consisted of alternating between two hours of easy paddling followed by two hours of strenuous paddling. They portaged where necessary to avoid waterfalls and rapids, and the occasional logjam. They stopped at farms along the way for fresh supplies and, occasionally, to see a town. O'Reilly and his companion paddled by Brattleboro (Exits 3–1), about to become home to the creator of *Jungle Book* and *Gunga Din;* Rudyard Kipling moved here with his American bride in 1892.

A few years before O'Reilly's canoe trip, a travel guide advised tourists to take in the view from Cemetery Hill in Brattleboro. Here was a panorama that included Wantastiquet Mountain to the east of the river, countless hilltops to the north and west and Brattleboro itself. "The drives in and around the village are remarkable, winding along the banks of impetuous little streamlets, through beautiful groves, and over high hills. A new drive can be taken every day for nearly a month, with out going outside of a radius of four miles, and all of them have peculiar features of interest."[81]

At Holyoke, Massachusetts (Exit 16), the Connecticut River falls sixty feet in one-and-a-half miles. A dam and three canals helped turn Holyoke, one of the first planned industrial cities in North America, into a thriving manufacturing center with dozens of textile mills and a handful of paper mills. At Springfield, Massachusetts (Exit 13), O'Reilly gave a previously arranged lecture. The Springfield of O'Reilly's day was perhaps best known as the home of Smith & Wesson revolvers. "We had been told that the beauty of the Connecticut ended at Springfield, but it is not so. Indeed, one of the loveliest stretches lies between Hartford and Middletown. . . . I never saw more delightful scenery than in the river valley just above and below Northampton."[82]

One for the bug, one for the crow, one to rot, and two to grow.

—Old saying about planting corn from the Connecticut River valley

After finding a campsite for the night in a pine grove or along a sandy bank, O'Reilly and his companion cooked dinner, enjoyed some claret, and ended the day with a cup of coffee and a good cigar. Ironically, they were paddling through what was to become prime tobacco country, famous for its shade tobacco leaves used to wrap cigars. In a small area of about sixty-one square miles in the Connecticut Valley, tobacco is grown under cotton blankets. In 1899, the U.S. Secretary of Agriculture imported some Sumatra tobacco, long considered the best leaf available for the outer wrapping on a cigar. Since Sumatra is overcast most of the time, planters in the Connecticut Valley shaded their plants with gauzy netting that filtered the sun in a manner similar to Sumatra's overcast skies. Those Connecticut farmers met with almost instant success. Native Americans knew how well the Connecticut Valley grew tobacco; they grew it along with squash, pumpkins, and corn. Onions also became a cash crop for the early settlers. These days, corn, Brussels sprouts, and potatoes are grown in the valley.

As for John Boyle O'Reilly, he continued to canoe and write. But he found himself missing the serenity of the Connecticut River, which he felt sure was guarded by water nymphs. "[W]e often missed the overhanging branches, the flash and twitter among the leaves, the shadows that made the river look deep as the sky, and the murmur of the little brown brooks that are lost in the great stream, leaving only their names, like Bromidon, clinging to the water like naiads."[83]

Interstate 95: Occupation: Trucker

An 1896 guide to North Carolina's resources admitted that at long last, residents of the state had turned their attention to good roads. "The question is of vital importance to the farmer and trucker, and indeed every industry."[84] But what did a trucker do for a living in the United States in the 1800s? Those fifty-three-foot behemoths clogging today's

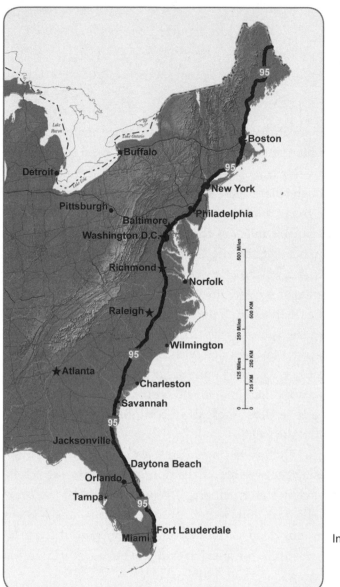

Interstate 95

interstates had not been invented yet. Henry Ford was still a few years away from the first Model T. How did a trucker make a living?

A "trucker" in the 1800s usually grew vegetables—so many vegetables that he had to find a market for them other than his neighbors or the local general store. As urban centers along the East Coast grew, city dwellers needed all sorts of country goods—vegetables, fruits, and feed for their horses, the cow in the stable behind the house, and pos-

This illustration of New York's Washington Market appeared in *Harper's Weekly* on September 14, 1878. A trucker leads his horse and cart loaded with produce into the market area. (Courtesy of the New York Public Library.)

sibly their chickens. They also needed firewood, and liked to splurge on freshly cut flowers. From the French word *troquer* meaning "to exchange or barter," the word developed into the anglicized spelling of today.

Interstate 95 connects those large urban centers along the Atlantic coast—Boston, New York, Washington, and Baltimore—with the tips of Maine and Florida, its northbound lanes clogged, depending on the season, with open trucks of watermelons, tankers full of orange concentrate, refrigerated loads of strawberries from Georgia, citrus fruit from Florida, peaches from the Carolinas, and other fruits and vegetables from all over the South. Potatoes, corn, strawberries, and other seasonal crops from New England also end up on New York or Boston tables. While truckers make up only eight to ten percent of the volume along the length of I-95, this still adds up to 2.5 million trucks a year along this most easterly of interstates.

> If you lined those 2.5 million plus trucks on the I-95 each year up end to end along the 1,920 miles of the interstate, they would completely fill a lane of traffic stretching from Maine to Florida twenty-four times over.

In the early 1800s, truckers lived and grew their produce within a day's journey of an urban center. Manure from city livestock kept the fields fertile, and an overnight journey by cart got the goods to urban markets when they opened in the early morning. Even with the introduction of commercial fertilizers, truckers around New York and Boston still insisted on good stable manure, and the distance Southern crops needed to travel to reach Northern markets meant Northern truckers still had the market pretty much to themselves. Many urbanites were also making a better life for themselves and now had the money to demand more fresh veggies. During her travels in North America, Frances Trollope visited the market in Baltimore. In her opinion, it constituted the "beau ideal" of what an urban market should be.

> [I]t is, indeed, the very perfection of a market. . . . The neatness, freshness, and entire absence of every thing disagreeable to sight or smell, must be witnessed to be believed. The stalls were spread with snow-white napkins; flowers and fruit . . . bright, fresh, and fragrant; with excellent vegetables in the greatest variety and abundance, were all so delightfully exhibited, that objects less pleasing were overlooked or forgotten. The dairy, the poultry-yard, the forest, the river, and the ocean, all contributed their spoil; in short, for the first time in my life, I thought a market a beautiful object.[85]

Truckers all along what would become the I-95 corridor began to experiment. In New Jersey, they added commercial fertilizers to the warm sandy soil and discovered that they could bring peas and potatoes to market a few weeks earlier than their northern counterparts. Northern truckers, however, stuck to manure, and while they lost the market for some crops, they still had protection with bulky crops: it was simply too expensive to cart a watermelon or a cabbage long distances, given the

A photograph of the Boston Market taken by Lewis Wickes Hines in October 1909. (Courtesy of the Library of Congress.)

state of transportation at the time. But as the urban population grew, so did the demand for fresh produce. At the same time, urban sprawl ate up more and more of New York's vegetable gardens. In turn, truckers moved farther out along the I-95 corridor.

And then there was the manure issue. While each of the one hundred thousand plus horses in New York produced about forty-three pounds of manure a day, that still wasn't enough to keep Northern market gardens fertilized. All of a sudden, horse manure became a hot commodity. Enterprising truckers set up market gardens around Norfolk, Virginia, where the growing season was longer and shipped horse manure from New York down the coast by barge at ten cents a bushel. But as transportation facilities improved, all of a sudden, it was not so far-fetched to sell produce grown in the Carolinas in New York. And Carolina truckers had the advantage of climate: they could provide New Yorkers with fresh strawberries long before they even blossomed in the North. Because they were ahead of season, fresh fruits and vegetables from the South commanded premium prices. More truckers started using commercial fertilizers. But because that same patch of land could now produce more crops, those Carolina truckers needed to find more markets. They also needed to be able to get the commercial fertilizers to their farms; that meant better transportation facilities. Trucking quickly became one of the most important industries. The fast age was on the doorstep of the Carolinas.

In 1856, tourist Charles Lanman headed south along a route similar to today's I-95. Once he crossed the Mason-Dixon Line, "[c]otton and corn fields came into view only at distant intervals; but then the cart-loads of sweet potatoes and ground or pea-nuts which were offered for sale at the crossroads, proved conclusively that there was no scarcity of the good things of life on the neighboring plantations."[86]

Further south he found evidence that foodstuffs were also making their way down the coast from Northern farms. One morning he took a stroll through a marketplace in Savannah, Georgia. "I found it abundantly supplied with vegetables, game and fish—sea-trout, whiting; and black sea-bass—and also with an occasional round of beef, all the way from New York."[87] But farther away from a population center, the more primitive transportation became, and the less available fresh produce became. Tourist Charles Clinton spent the winter of 1851–1852 in Northern Florida. He found very poor roads, and somewhat surprisingly, given the mild climate, a total lack of market gardens.

> There is no back country; few or no farms or plantations; no mills, turnpikes, plank roads, or canals. The country does not even produce sufficient for home consumption. There are no grasses for hay, no corn, none of the cereal grains; and the whole product may be summed up in fish and oysters from the bays and oceans, wild fowl from the swamps, venison and turkeys from the woods; dwarf cabbage, potatoes, cassava, arrow-root, and other esculents from the gardens; sugar-cane and syrup from two or three small plantations, and sour oranges. . . . Their groceries, furniture, store goods, preserved meats, luxuries, hay, clothing, salt, corn, flour, and butter, are all imported.[88]

It was Clinton's opinion that, given the beautiful locations and warmer winter temperatures, coastal Florida locations could become crowded in the winter months if markets in the area could solve the problem of obtaining fresh produce and ice, rather than importing them from Savannah.

Then the Civil War broke out. Northern urbanites used to receiving fruits and vegetables ahead of season had to do without. Southern truckers used to the lucrative Northern market were all of a sudden stuck with a crop that was not worth as much as it had been. Many abandoned the vegetable patch and marched off to war. Those left behind suffered through near starvation conditions with the destruction of crops and farmlands, and the lack of manpower to keep truck farms afloat. By the end of the war, Southern rail and road networks were also in ruins, but truckers in Northern Virginia did not let that deter them. They went back to gardening in a big way, their proximity to markets giving them an initial advantage with early vegetables and small fruits. But as the Southern transportation infrastructure was repaired, improved, and expanded, truckers all through the Carolinas, Georgia, and Florida could once again get their produce to port cities along the coast or towns with a rail link. First, watermelons were the lone fruit to break through the juggernaut Northern Virginia truckers had on the Northern market, but, bit by bit, growing other fruits and vegetables paid off. Northern urbanites began to expect a continuous supply. While Northern truckers could no longer expect to get the high prices they had once received for the first crops of the season, they soon found that people would pay for freshness.

Truckers also started experimenting with forcing vegetables and fruits under glass in winter, using hot water or steam pipes. Business was good and truckers in places like Rhode Island and Maine made a good living. "Cucumbers from hothouses in Vermont are now sold every winter in New York at fancy prices. In these northern sections the winters are characterized by long spells of dark and sunless weather, the intense cold demands double glazed houses, and a very complete and expensive heating apparatus, with an enormous consumption of coal."[89] Southern truckers refused to be outdone and began experimenting with forcing fruits and vegetables in the winter months. Floridians even grew pineapples under glass, selling them wholesale for $1.50 apiece.

North Carolina published an agricultural guide in 1869 in an attempt to attract people and capital to the state. The guide touted the advantages of the region through which I-95 now runs. "This whole eastern section, is flat and damp . . . finely adapted to truck farming. . . . It is perhaps superior to any section of the United States in affording a good living for the smallest amount of labor."[90] While some would call the millions of acres of flat, moist land a swamp, there were benefits: it was in its natural state and, therefore, very fertile. As the pamphlet claimed, most "of these lands can be bought from their present proprietors at nominal prices, not one-third their real value."[91] The North Carolina Land Company talked about how the entire coastal region was well suited for growing fruits including apples, pears, cranberries, and strawberries.

> The raising of vegetables to ship through Norfolk, to New York, is an established and profitable business. The seasons, it is computed, are about one week earlier for every half degree of latitude one goes South, but proximity to the sea, or a location on the south side of a wide water course, has much influence in this respect. The climate is favorable to the raising of all domesticated animals. Horses and mules thrive. Cattle keep fat on the native wild grasses for nine months in the year, and many never receive grain or hay or shelter, during the whole year. Hogs could keep fat all the year in the swamps on acorns and reed roots.[92]

Tourist Francis Moore visited Savannah, Georgia, in 1736. On viewing some local gardens he commented that the early settlers who had cleared their five acre lots had made a substantial profit out of greens, roots, and corn. In 1875, poet Sidney Lanier followed up by saying that it "would appear that the charming market-gardens of Savannah, whose products have such a reputation in New York, may claim an antique origin."[93] Antique origins aside, the trucking heritage of the I-95 corridor continues. Greens from Savannah can now be in New York the same day they are picked via the most-used of the north–south interstates as far as trucking is concerned. In 1875, truckers produced the goods and carted them to local markets. Those greens from Savannah headed from the garden plot to the Savannah market via a truck cart and then to New York via rail. While bits and pieces of road existed, they tended to track inland from the coast in a haphazard fashion. Even rail involved a bit of juggling from track to track, company to company, and frequently involved loading and unloading the freight into a wagon for a journey of a few miles from one company's tracks to another. Produce did not always arrive in the best condition. Not so today. With one direct route, Georgia greens can be in Northern markets at peak quality. The two-wheeled carts truckers once used to haul vegetables to market have given way to 18-wheelers on today's I-95.

Interstate 86 West: One Potato, Two Potato

Three potato, four. With fifteen percent of all income coming from spuds, Idahoans are happy to count potatoes. With average annual potato production of about 1.37 billion ten-pound bags in the grocery store, who can blame them. Idahoans like to bake, boil, scallop, fry, freeze, hash, flake, and dry spuds, and sock them away for seed for the next year's crop. They keep a nation in love with French fries and potato chips chugging along toward couch potato heaven.

From its intersection with I-15 at Pocatello, Idaho to its juncture with I-84 almost sixty-three miles later, Interstate 86 West passes through potato country. Here, in irrigated fields along the highway, potatoes find everything they could possibly need: rich volcanic soils, warm, sunny days and cool nights, and plenty of clean, clear water from local watersheds. Scientists at the University of Idaho supply farmers with the know how and companies, such as McDonald's, provide the incentive.

The first settlers in this corner of Idaho came up from Utah about 1860, bringing seed potatoes with them. They planted enough for their

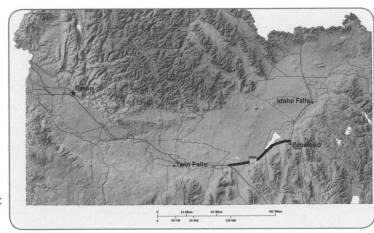

Interstate 86 West

Freight drivers relaxing at a truck stop in 1873. Today's long-haul trucker would have been known as a "freighter," as these men were, when this illustration was produced for *Scribner's Monthly*.

own use. Then a freighter—a truck driver in today's parlance—hauling foodstuffs from Utah northward, along what is now the I-15 corridor, convinced an Idaho settler that he should plant more than he needed and sell the extra crop. Soon, commercial potato production spread throughout Southeast Idaho, then to the rest of the state. By 1882, farmers had two thousand acres in the territory in potato production; by 1904 production was up to seventeen thousand acres. The value-added processing element of potato production developed with the two world wars and the need to feed a far-flung military. Dried potatoes and instant mashed potatoes entered the vernacular. Then along came the interstates and fast food. Idaho was ready. The average American consumes fifty-nine pounds of French fries and hash browns a year, plus seventeen pounds of potato chips. So, if ten thousand vehicles pass over I-86W every day, and each vehicle contains an average of two persons, how many pounds of Idaho French fries and potato chips do motorists on I-86W potentially consume every year? Five potato, six potato, seven potato more.

Interstate 82: The Town That Played Turtle

As the West opened up to settlement, people looking at newspapers and broadsides in the Eastern United States and Europe could read about faraway places called California, Kansas, and Oregon. Occasionally, a story like that of the doomed Donner party in the Sierra Nevadas fired up journalistic passions for several months. While sensationalism sold newspapers, these stories left average readers knowing just about as much about California or Oregon as they did about the moon. At least the moon could be seen in the night sky, but these places in the newspapers took months to reach. Yet, with the trails west gradually evolving into roads, and the advent of railroads, all of a sudden people had the means to head to the moon.

Unfortunately, this also meant some individuals wanted to sell you a piece of the moon. Speculation ran rampant. All it took was an official-looking notice in the paper, some rave reviews about the location, a map of the new "town," perhaps a drawing or two of its main street, and an address to which prospective buyers sent their money. In return, buyers were supposed to get a deed to so many acres or a town lot in this new Eden where all their dreams would come true and they would live happily ever after. Dream towns popped up all over the place, some in impossible locations deep in a swamp or other building-challenged terrain. Families sold everything they owned and headed west only to find that their particular piece of the moon did not exist. Some stayed and made

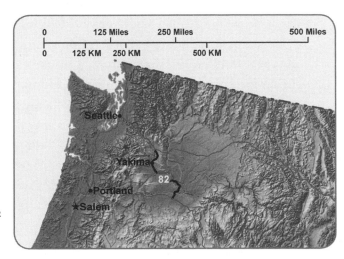

Interstate 82

Downtown Yakima, Washington, in 1883. (Courtesy of the Yakima Valley Museum.)

the best of their new swamp lands or desert acreage; others moved on to the next town that really existed—usually about as far as their available money would take them. Here, they could perhaps provide a service missing among that town's businesses or find work as a laborer.

Few Western towns in the early stages of development actually met the ideal wish list of any settler. Even so, there were a few essentials: a general store, a blacksmith, maybe a doctor, and definitely a cemetery. A local burying ground was considered just about as essential as a school or a church. There was something permanent about a cemetery—a sign that maybe this town was here to stay. The other essential for any town was a means of getting to and from it. Road, rail, or water transport provided the options. More transportation routes increased the odds that the town would thrive. Sometimes, a resource at a town site prompted the development of transportation to it, but more often, the transportation route prompted the development of a town.

But what happened to a town built on speculation that the transportation route would arrive—and it did not—or the town suddenly found itself bypassed by the chief means of transportation in that area? Ghost towns resulted. But sometimes, a town's residents did not give up so easily. Such was the case with Yakima, Washington (Exits 36–33). Today it is a thriving city in the heart of apple country. Interstate 82 provides the link to other interstates to get the produce from the very fertile and productive Yakima Valley to market in places like Seattle. In 1883, Yakima was a young town with stagecoach service to nearby communities via what had originally been a military wagon road. The town had a vibrant retail sector, hotels, and a growing population. Irrigation canals had turned the sagebrush and scrub of the Yakima Valley into a promising agricultural region. Yakima seemingly had everything going for it and was expected to get a big boost when the new railroad line being built through Washington State arrived in town. Then the unthinkable happened: the Northern Pacific Railroad picked a route four miles away, apparently because of better water and power supplies. The company also objected to the somewhat haphazard layout of the existing town, preferring a well-planned community with uniform streets and a proper municipal infrastructure.

After their initial anger, town residents held a meeting. Four miles represented half a day's journey away by road! People were not going to get off the train and come to eat in their hotels or shop in their stores when there was a four-mile drive in between. They might just as well have been in business on the moon! Residents talked and blustered. What could be done? The first train passed over the new track in December 1884. The rail company had laid out a town along the track. A livery, two eateries, and two saloons were already open for business; a boardinghouse tent had sixteen guests. To sweeten the pot, Northern Pacific offered free lots to anyone who moved to the new town site. Townsfolk talked and blustered some more. The railroad then agreed to pick up the cost of the move as well. Residents made a decision. Those who wanted to move jacked up their houses and stores. All through the summer and fall of 1885, fifty to sixty houses and stores rolled down the four miles of road to the new town site. It took about two weeks for a building to make the journey, and the main street of Yakima became a rolling retail district on logs. While the hotel was being moved, it stayed open. Its guests never missed a meal or a good night's sleep. Wherever the hotel happened to be, guests climbed in and ate or went to their room. Stories abound of farmers hitching their horse and wagon to the general store as it rolled along, making their purchases and, after loading the wagon and untying the horse, riding off home. It was the same story for the bank and courthouse.

Everyone and his buildings arrived safely. The new town was incor-

A photograph of Yakima's Adams Hotel, circa 1884. (Courtesy of the Yakima Valley Museum.)

porated in January 1886 as North Yakima. In 1918, North was dropped from the name and it became Yakima. What had been Yakima, now the old town, was officially called Union Gap.

Imagine for a moment having almost an entire town roll down I-82 between Exit 38 (present-day Union Gap) and Exit 34 (to Yakima's business district). Visualize having the ability to somehow attach your vehicle to a rolling fast-food outlet and stop in for a hamburger. (That brings new meaning to a drive through.) How about getting a good night's sleep in a motel rolling down the interstate in the same direction you are traveling? All over America throughout the 1960s and '70s, the new interstate highways bypassed towns. Some communities faded away, others decided to shoot for the moon. While they did not exactly play turtle as Yakima had done, physically moving homes and companies to locations along exit ramps, business districts frequently migrated into new buildings along thoroughfares connected to an interstate. It continues today with more and more commercial enterprises clustering along roads served by an interchange. Like the Yakima of 1884, it boils down to economics and survival. At a time when many people rarely traveled more than a few miles away from home, it must have been a huge decision to move a town. People needed to work to support themselves and the businesses employing those people needed customers to survive. Yakima shot for the moon and won.

Interstate 94: Rounding Into Form

In the nineteenth century, as Americans continued their restless search for the best that life could offer, cities and their boosters vied for attention on the public stage. They wanted their share of Americans on the move and the immigrants pouring into the country. It was generally believed that some things were just naturally preordained. If God had seen fit to create an area with really good natural transportation routes and with weather and soils conducive to human habitation, then obviously a city at that location was destined for greatness.

Interstate 94 across the top of the country connects several cities that were very much works in progress in the nineteenth century, each vying to be the biggest, the most successful, and the best place to live and work on the planet. Detroit, Chicago, Milwaukee, and Minneapolis all enjoyed excellent transportation facilities via water, and if you overlooked swampy conditions in places like Chicago, and did not question the weather factor too closely, they had everything going for them. Unfortunately for the cities and their boosters, some of the sharpest and most popular literary minds of the nineteenth century took it upon

Interstate 94

themselves to visit these growing metropolises and skewer them in print. Anthony Trollope, Mark Twain, Robert Louis Stevenson, and Rudyard Kipling among others took aim with zingers, particularly aimed at Chicago, guaranteed to make prospective visitors, residents, or investors take notice. Comparisons of the cities inevitably made their way into print. Others like John Greenleaf Whittier, one of the most popular American poets of this era gave voice to the thoughts of everyday folks struggling with this new wave of urban industrialism. In Whittier's world, he could hear the tread of pioneers, the

> far-off voyager's horn;
> I see the Yankee's trail,—
> His foot on every mountain-pass,
> On every stream his sail.

Here was a world where

> The steamer smokes and raves;
> And city lots are staked for sale
> Above old Indian graves.

The urban empires being constructed in Whittier's West were "plastic yet and warm," but progress was inevitable amid the chaos. Things were

> rounding into form!
> Each rude and jostling fragment soon
> Its fitting place shall find,—
> The raw material of a State,
> Its muscle and its mind![94]

Interstate 94 begins its cross-country trek through these jostling urban empires in Port Huron, Michigan (Exits 275–271), where it serves the petrochemical industry in that area and connects with a bridge into Canada that is heavily used by truckers going both directions, fulfilling one of the tenets of the interstate system—road connections to both Canada and Mexico. In the nineteenth century, anyone visiting Port Huron with the wherewithal to write about it was probably about to embark on a summertime cruise. Such was the case for Johanna Wisthaler, who in July and August 1893 sailed on a private yacht from Schenectady,

The Chicago River became the "big stink" for real as a growing city dumped raw sewage and industrial waste into it. Environmental awareness in the 1950s and '60s led to antipollution laws and the river was cleaned up. This photo, circa 1900, shows conditions near 12th Street. Interstate 94 today crosses over 12th Street near Exit 52. (Courtesy of the Library of Congress.)

New York, to Chicago to visit the Columbian Exposition. At Port Huron, Johanna and her party found a prosperous city, advantageously situated to capitalize on the busy traffic on Lake Huron, with sawmills, lumberyards, dry docks, flour mills, beautiful broad streets, and elegant residences. Today's I-94 cuts in a fairly straight line from Port Huron to Detroit (Exits 236–198), where it skirts the western edge of Lake St. Clair for about half of the fifty-six miles between the two urban centers.

Johanna sailed across Lake St. Clair, and, looking west where I-94 is today, she remarked that "the uplands wore a tinge of tenderest blue . . . [the shore ringed by] superb summer residences, tasty villas, and elegant hotels . . . interspersed between romantic hills and tufted groves. The horizon was of a fine, golden tint, changing gradually into the deep blue of the mid-heaven."[95]

Johanna found Detroit to be a thriving city with extensive commercial facilities and an "attractive appearance," with wide, tree-lined boulevards and beautiful buildings. Anthony Trollope, visited Detroit in his explorations of North America for a two-volume series he was writing. He found the Detroit of 1861 to be "a large, well-built, half-finished city lying on a convenient waterway, and spreading itself out with promises of a wide and still wider prosperity." While he saw the promise, he wasn't all that favorable about its appearance. "It is not so pleasant as Milwaukee, nor so picturesque as St. Paul, nor so grand as Chicago, nor so civilized as Cleveland, nor so busy as Buffalo. I will not say that it is uncivilized; but it has a harsh, crude, unprepossessing appearance."[96]

From Detroit, Anthony Trollope continued westward across Michigan. He described the route as "a country that was absolutely wild till the railway pierced it. Very much of it is still absolutely wild. For miles upon miles the road passes the untouched forest showing that even in Michigan the great work of civilization has hardly more than commenced."[97] Today's I-94, passes through Anthony's wild country, the untouched forest having given way to miles and miles of beef and dairy production, and corn and grains to keep the cereal capital of the world—Battle Creek, Michigan (Exit 92)—in business. Settlers heading west largely ignored Michigan, tucked as it was between the lakes, preferring instead to try their luck in Indiana and Illinois.

Once it reaches Lake Michigan, and a rich fruit-producing belt, I-94 hugs the lakeshore for its trip around the bottom of the lake, past what is today the Indiana Dunes National Lakeshore (Exit 26) and into Chicago (Exits 74–53). Here, in Anthony's time, railways from Wisconsin, Iowa, Illinois, and Indiana converged, bringing produce into Chicago harbor for shipment east. Unlike his confrères to come, Anthony was surprised by what he saw.

Chicago is in many respects the most remarkable city among all the remarkable cities of the Union. . . . Chicago may be called the metropolis of American corn. . . . In Chicago there are great streets, and rows of houses fit to be residences of a new Corn-Exchange nobility. They look out on the wide lake which is now the highway for breadstuffs, and the merchant as he shaves at his window, sees his rapid ventures as they pass away, one after the other, toward the East.[98]

The Chicago Anthony Trollope was so impressed with got its start in 1779 when a French-speaking Haitian built a trading post near the mouth of the Chicago River. Jean Baptiste Pointe du Sable moved on to Missouri in 1800, but by that time a permanent settlement had sprung up around his cabin. Jean Baptiste had selected a fairly low, swampy place to build a cabin. While it is generally agreed that the word "Chicago" sprang from the Potawatomi Indian word *checagou*, scholars disagree on its meaning. "Great, wild onion place" and "big stink" are all possibilities, big stink coming from rotting wild onions that like damp conditions. But it was a matter of location, location, location. Situated as it was on Lake Michigan, at the mouth of the Chicago River and in the heart of the Midwest, Chicago's destiny was assured. It quickly became a major shipping point for goods heading in just about every direction.

By 1837, Chicago had four thousand residents and was incorporated as a city. Ten years later, the city could boast that it had about seventeen thousand people and over four hundred and fifty stores. By 1860, one hundred thousand people lived in Chicago and by 1871, three hundred and thirty-four thousand. More vessels docked in Chicago than in New York, Baltimore, Philadelphia, Charleston, Mobile, and San Francisco combined. The Illinois and Michigan Canal, opened in 1848, connected the Illinois River to Lake Michigan adding to the boat traffic. But because of the city's fast expansion, buildings and the infrastructure were constructed hastily and cheaply. Sidewalks were wooden planks and some streets were paved with blocks of wood. Granted, there were factories, grain elevators, grand residential districts, and fine commercial streets, but there were also crowded working class neighborhoods, and a notorious red-light district. One tenement district was described as having the "dirtiest, vilest, most rickety, one-sided, leaning forward, propped up, tumbled-down, sinking fast, low-roofed and most miserable shanties."[99] Conditions were ripe when a fire started in Patrick O'Leary's barn in the fall of 1871 killing three hundred and making one hundred thousand people homeless. Newspaper editor Horace White described what he saw: "The dogs of hell were upon the housetops. . . . A column of flame would shoot up from a burning building, catch the force of the wind, and strike the next [building]. It was simply indescribable in its terrible grandeur."[100] Interstate 94 passes through the part of the city obliterated by the fire. As for Patrick O'Leary's barn, it sat closer to present-day Exit 52, just off Taylor Street, between I-94 and Lake Michigan.

The businessmen boosting Chicago quickly headed off to visit prospective investors trumpeting the opportunity for a bigger, better, grander Chicago and the potential for business as the city rebuilt. One businessman promoted a city that was not burnt up "only well blistered."[101] It did not take long. Much of the rubble was pushed into Lake Michigan, creating more lakefront real estate and more business opportunities; laborers and investors set to work.

Mark Twain, who periodically wrote columns for the *Chicago Republican*, had been adding lines about Chicago into his books for years. Pudd'nhead Wilson's new calendar, at one point featured Satan: "The trouble with you Chicago people is, that you think you are the best people down here; whereas you are merely the most numerous."[102] Robert Louis Stevenson entered Chicago dog-tired. When he finally found a place to sit, he "sank into it like a bundle of rags, the world seemed to swim away into the distance, and my consciousness dwindled within me to a mere pin's head, like a taper on a foggy night."[103] From her well-chaperoned, well-to-do vantage point, Johanna Wisthaler found Chicago of 1893 to be an astonishing city, clearly living up to its reputation as the second city of commercial importance as well as population in the United States.

Rudyard Kipling saw a different Chicago. He wrote of his visits to the windy city in his 1899 *American Notes*. "I have struck a city—a real city—and they call it Chicago. . . . This place is the first American city I have

Chicago as the second city comes from A. J. Liebling in *The New Yorker*. For many years, Chicago was the nation's second-largest city before being surpassed by Los Angeles in the 1980s.

encountered. . . . Having seen it, I urgently desire never to see it again. It is inhabited by savages."[104] After checking into a hotel, Kipling went outside to explore. He found a city of long, flat, endless streets. "Except for London . . . I had never seen so many white people together, and never such a collection of miserables. There was no color in the street and no beauty—only a maze of wire ropes overhead and dirty stone flagging under foot."[105]

Twentieth-century authors treated Chicago with more respect. While the city certainly had its highs and lows, it fared better in print. Norman Mailer called it "the last of the great American cities."[106] Wallace Stegner wrote the city into his 1973 best seller, *Big Rock Candy Mountain*.

> He visited Chicago, and the sight of that city roaring into incredible size and impressiveness on the shore of Lake Michigan left his mind dazed with grandiose visions. Here was really the big town, here were the gangs of men creating a city out of a windswept slough, here were freight engines, passenger engines, lake boats, nosing in smoking and triumphant from every direction, here was money by the millions, a future as big as the sky.[107]

Carl Sandburg called it the City of Big Shoulders.

> Hog Butcher to the World,
> Tool Maker, Stacker of Wheat,
> Player with the Railroads and the Nation's Freight Handler,
> Stormy, husky, brawling,
> City of Big Shoulders.[108]

From Chicago, I-94 continues up the western side of Lake Michigan toward Milwaukee, Wisconsin (Exits 314–305). When he visited Milwaukee in 1861, Anthony Trollope seemed a bit puzzled. "It stands immediately on the western shore of Lake Michigan, and is very pleasant. Why it should be so, and why Detroit should be the contrary, I can hardly tell."[109]

> The view from Milwaukee over Lake Michigan is very pleasing. One looks upon a vast expanse of water to which the eye finds no bounds, and therefore there are none of the common attributes of lake beauty; but the color of the lake is bright, and within a walk of the city the traveller comes to the bluffs or low round-topped hills,

from which we can look down upon the shores. These bluffs form the beauty of Wisconsin and Minnesota, and relieve the eye after the flat level of Michigan. Round Detroit there is no rising ground, and therefore, perhaps, it is that Detroit is uninteresting.[110]

Interstate 94 marches westward from Milwaukee to near Madison (Exit 240) and then onward to the Twin Cities. Anthony Trollope could not believe the good farmland west of Chicago. Of Minneapolis (Exit 225), he commented: "Till I got there I could hardly believe that in these days there should be a living village called Minneapolis by living men."[111] Nearby Saint Paul (Exits 249–226) was, at the time of Anthony's visit, a city of about fourteen thousand along the Mississippi. With the bluffs along the river, he found the setting "pretty, and almost romantic."[112] From Minneapolis, I-94 marches across North Dakota and Montana to Billings, Montana, where it meets up with I-90. Here, motorists can continue on to the coast or connect up with I-25 and head southward. In the nineteenth century, the trace I-94 now follows echoed with the footsteps of pioneers making their way to the cities along its length or to the countryside around these cities. Frequently, with an eye to the financial success of their own commercial or industrial endeavors, boosters promoting these cities worked long and hard to attract manufacturing, residents, railroads, canals, roads, opera houses, a world's fair—whatever it took to guarantee success, and their own financial well-being. In Whittier's words, they did what it took to mold these young urban empires into form.

I hear the tread of pioneers
Of nations yet to be;
The first low wash of waves, where soon
Shall roll a human sea.[113]

Roads Cross the Continent

Root Hog, or Die

"So we traveled across the country, and we got upon the ground, / But cold weather was ahead, the first thing we found. / We built our shanties on the ground, resolved in spring to try, / To gather up the dust and slugs, root hog, or die." The painting is by Frances F. Palmer, circa 1867. (Courtesy of the Library of Congress.)

To see a man squatted on a quarter-section in a cabin which would make a fair hog-pen . . . living from hand to mouth by a little of this and a little of that, with hardly an acre of prairie broken . . . with no garden, no fruit trees, "no nothing"—waiting for some one to come along and buy out his "claim" and let him move on to repeat the operation somewhere else—this is enough to give a cheerful man the horrors.[1]

The year was 1859. Horace Greeley, noted publisher of the *New York Tribune* and politician had decided to check out the American territories of Missouri, Kansas, and Utah for himself. This was the frontier, the land of dreams and legends, of Manifest Destiny and "Go West, young man"—of root hog, or die—fend for yourself or die.

By the late 1700s, the East Coast states had run out of available, potentially arable land. The lure of the trails unrolling westward—the interstates of their time—became an almost irresistible impulse for those driven by the constant need to be on the move and the quest for cheap or free lands to call one's own. All along the East Coast, restless settlers breeched barrier after barrier in the quest for space: the Appalachians, the Mississippi, the Great Plains, deserts, and Western mountain ranges. It started with New Englanders moving into the wilds of New York, and Pennsylvanians flooding into the Shenandoah Valley of Virginia and into Kentucky behind Daniel Boone. Trains of Conestoga wagons and livestock headed west. An account of a night spent on Negro Mountain in Southwest Pennsylvania, along the National Road, spoke of "thirty-six horse teams in the wagon yard, a hundred Kentucky mules in an adjoining lot, a thousand hogs in their enclosures, and as many fat cattle in adjoining fields. The music made by this large number of hogs eating corn on a frosty night I shall never forget."[2] After seeing to their teams, wagoners had supper and gathered in the bar for fiddle music, storytelling, and a place in front of the fire. Negro Mountain is visible to present-day motorists looking southwest as they approach Somerset, Pennsylvania (Exits 112 and 110 off I-76).

People looking for land of their own started drifting down the Ohio River on rafts to claim farmland in what is now Ohio and Kentucky. In Ohio, eighty acres sold for one hundred dollars. Many could not afford such a price, so they found land they liked and squatted. Usually, they could then buy the land once it was put up for sale. This process of squatting and then getting the first right to buy was called preemption and happened all over the west. By 1850, Ohio had a population of almost two million; in 1803, it had been seventy thousand. In the early 1800s, it usually took six weeks to get from New England to Ohio. This was the outskirts of civilization. The War of 1812 further fueled the processional west as the Eastern states suffered through a recession. With the arrival of railroads, goods could flow in and out of the Eastern states, but so could residents.

Politicians worried about their disappearing constituents. As early as 1818, Governor Branch of North Carolina urged his state's legislature to adopt measures at once to stop the flow of emigrants and entice North Carolinians to remain home. By 1834, the *Raleigh Register* was urging the state to do something immediately. "Our wealth is decreasing daily—our commercial towns present decayed wharves, dilapidated warehouses and untenanted dwellings; while in the country, may everywhere be found deserted plantations and abandoned settlements. Our roads are thronged with emigrants to a more favored Country."[3] Meanwhile, a correspondent to the *Western Carolinian* wrote that, "during the last four months the flow of emigration through Asheville has surpassed any thing of the kind the writer has ever witnessed. It was not uncommon to see eight, ten, or fifteen wagons, and carts passing in a single day. . . . The great body of the emigrants were from the middle or eastern part of the State, wending their way to the more highly favored climes of the West."[4] In Arkansas, people who could not afford land in the more developed area east of the Mississippi River, squatted on government land.

In the Southwest, the Mexican government tried to keep drunkards, gamblers, profane swearers, and idlers out of Texas.[5] But empty cabins kept appearing all over the Southern states with the letters "GTT" on a wall or door: Gone to Texas. By 1830, Anglo-Americans outnumbered Spanish-speaking Tejanos by about three to one; four years later the ratio had become five to one. Land in Texas cost 12.5 cents an acre and if you were going to ranch, you could buy as much as 4,428 acres. If you were going to farm, you got 177 acres. All a settler had to do was agree to become a Mexican citizen. With good land in Eastern Texas suitable for cotton production, the decision to emigrate became much easier.

It had taken about two hundred and fifty years to push this far west, but that was the limit of the technology of transportation at the time and of the roads to get to the frontier. Even New Orleans was considered a remote outpost of little consequence with no direct road link between it and East-Coast cities; steamer service between New York and New Orleans was finally established in 1848. Many settlers, especially from Georgia, Alabama, and South Carolina, arrived in Texas via steamer at Galveston, road travel still not being a viable option. Whether it was the development of the Conestoga wagon or improvements in road surfacing, the means of getting somewhere determined just how far westward settlers pushed. By the 1850s, well-worn trails crossed the Great Plains. Many former soldiers from both the Mexican and Civil Wars headed west for a new beginning. These veterans, particularly the Confederate soldiers, found they had very little to return to; freed slaves and equally disillusioned Yankees joined the exodus. Many former slaves also headed north to factory jobs in places like Chicago. Today's I-65 from Mobile, Alabama, to Chicago, Illinois, traces the route that many took with expectations and hope.

New immigrants pouring into East-Coast ports added to the rush for lands along the frontier. Social and political pressures in their home countries, aided and abetted by fired-up stories of the wonders of America pushed many desperate families onto ships bound for America. Like Horace Greeley, Robert Louis Stevenson, decided to see what the life of these potential settlers was like. Stevenson had few illusions about the picture of America these settlers held of "vast cities that grow up as by enchantment . . . forests that disappear like snow; countries larger than Britain that are cleared and settled . . . oil that gushes from the earth; gold that is washed or quarried in the brooks or glens of the Sierras." There was no mention of the travel conditions or the almost certain

Speculation is the fashion even at this early stage,
And corner lots and big hotels appear to be the rage.
The emigration's bound to come, and to greet them we will try,
Big pig, little pig, root hog, or die.

hardships. Stevenson's fellow passengers knew "nothing of the Maine Laws, the Puritan sourness, the fierce, sordid appetite for dollars, or the dreary existence of country towns,"[6] of root hog, or die.

Once in America, many immigrants chose to travel as far west as they could by train before buying their homesteading supplies. Others opted for stagecoach travel, but this could be expensive. For instance, the one-way fare from Iowa City to Des Moines in the 1850s cost ten dollars, a sizeable outlay, even if it was a twenty-hour trip. (Today's I-80 motorist would pay a similar amount for the gas to make the same two-hour trip of about 110 miles.) While stagecoach fares were high, meals and accommodations were more reasonably priced. Meals were served at predetermined station stops. If passengers were lucky, the cook served a choice meat with seasonal vegetables and a nice dessert, accompanied by wine or other spirits. More frequently, passengers got the 1850s equivalent of today's fast-food outlet: mutton or greasy pork with beans, and bread or biscuits, perhaps some soup. Dessert frequently consisted of two layers of pie crust with a thin layer of dried apples or peaches—all to be washed down with the latest distilled efforts from the local tavern. All this could be yours for twenty-five cents. Overnight accommodations, which included supper and breakfast, cost about fifty cents, but this was not the bargain it seemed; guests frequently shared rooms, sometimes beds—and more. Thirty to fifty men sharing a room also shared that

 One rain washes the just and the unjust, why not one wash-bowl?

—Frederick Law Olmsted (1857: 26)

room's one washstand, towel, and toothbrush. If the inn possessed a bathtub, the first person in the bathwater paid maybe a dollar for the privilege. The next person in the same bathwater paid a little less, and so on until everyone had a chance to soak in the tub.

One of the first inns west of the Rocky Mountains opened in Oregon City in 1842 (off I-84 and I-5). Guests paid five dollars a week, for which they received a blanket and were told to find a patch of floor no one else had claimed. The inn had no furniture. In furnished inns, many chose to sleep on the floor in their clothes anyway to escape the vermin already inhabiting the bed. Often, settlers camped outside, sleeping under the wagon at night and eating when they could. In September 1857, Joseph Trego of Rock Island, Illinois, headed into the Kansas Territory to homestead. He and his companion expected to eat and sleep at public houses along the way. Instead they found themselves sleeping on the ground, usually without any supper. The wagon driver served coffee and crackers for breakfast and then found a cabin willing to serve them a noonday meal: always fat pork, cornbread with fried butter, and lots of coffee.

Nebraska and Kansas opened up to settlers; the nineteenth-century interstates unrolled further west. Trails across the continent had to have three elements: wood, water, and grass. Today, we consider the three essentials restaurants, rest stops, and gas stations. As opposed to trails started strictly for commerce as were the Chisholm Trail and the Santa Fe Trail, other trails were carved into the landscape strictly for migration. The Oregon Trail and Mormon Trail were two such traces westward. The nineteen-hundred miles of the Oregon Trail, opened in 1841, stretched from Independence, Missouri, to Oregon, and was considered one of the best and safest. (The Santa Fe Trail also started in Independence.) Not only was the Oregon Trail the shortest, most direct road to the Pacific, but it was also one of the best-known. Animal forage was available from early May to mid-winter and water was readily found. While stories persisted of pioneers on other trails further south having to unload, take the wheels off the wagon, and dismantle the wooden frame, and then carry everything over the next incline piece by piece, a wagon on the Oregon Trail could negotiate the entire roadway intact, albeit with occasional help from a winch or a second team of oxen or mules. All able-bodied family members walked to relieve the burden on

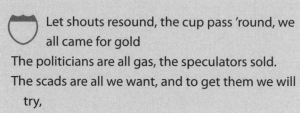
the draft animals and to escape the bone-rattling ride in the wagon. Today, I-84W traces the western end of the Oregon Trail.

Those who did not want to live on the Great Plains either pushed onward or returned home. Sometimes, as in the Dakotas or New Mexico, Native American uprisings forced settlers to flee. Droughts or other forms of severe weather were also a factor as were crop prices. Dakota-bound settlers frequently came from places like Iowa and Wisconsin, having originally come to Iowa or Wisconsin from Pennsylvania, New York, or New England. Still others flooded in directly from Northern Europe. Manifest Destiny became the unwritten creed that Americans were meant to inhabit this vast territory.

Everywhere, squatters ruled. Many, like the man squatting in the hog-pen, repeated the process over and over. To establish a claim, the squatter had to swear that he resided on the land, had built a habitation, and had made improvements. He also had to confirm that he intended to use the land and establish his family there. Horace Greeley was told of one squatter who carried a birdhouse from claim to claim. The man would swear before an officer that he had a house eighteen by twenty on the land and let the officer presume he meant eighteen feet by twenty feet. Once the claim was established the birdhouse owner then found

I tell you how it is when you first get on the road,
You have an awkward team and a very heavy load
You cut and you slash, if you swear it's on the sly
Punch along your team, boys, root hog, or die.

a speculator willing to pay him fifty to three-hundred dollars for the land. The squatter packed up his birdhouse and moved on to the next potential claim. Meanwhile, the speculator advertised and got two hundred and fifty to fifteen hundred dollars for the claimed land, usually a quarter-section.

One caravan reminded Horace Greeley of the days of Abraham and Lot. "It comprised six or seven heavy wagons, mainly drawn by oxen, with a light traveling carriage and pair of horses conveying the patriarch's family, some two or three hundred head of cows, steers and young cattle, with three or four young men on horseback driving and keeping the herd. Girls were milking, women were washing, children were playing—in short here was the material for a fair settlement, or quite an imposing Kansas City."[7] Horace found it hard to juxtapose this caravan with the wilderness of Western Kansas, in an area untouched by civilization, as he knew it. "But the utter absence of houses or buildings of any kind, and our unbridged, unworked road, winding on its way for hundreds of miles without a track other than of buffalo intersecting or leading away from it on either hand, bring us back to reality."[8]

As he traveled through Kansas, Horace carefully noted road conditions. He considered the roads primitive and kept to the highest "prairie swells," avoiding the lowlands along streams. In dry weather, the roads were "excellent, and in wet as good as possible."[9] But, in the absence of a legally established roadbed, anyone claiming land along the road was at liberty to run a fence across it if his land happened to cross the road. Many did just that, forcing trails to zig and zag through the countryside. On his visit to Kansas, in January 1859, lobbyist John Ingalls found himself on a road near Leavenworth that ran through a squatter's claim. The squatter had fenced across the road and threatened to shoot trespassers. Nevertheless, Ingalls' driver opened the gate and proceeded under the cover of darkness only to discover the next gate off the property had

On mountainsides, where trails wound precipitously close to steep ravines, Mormon travelers developed a novel way of compensating for the absence of guardrails—"dug-ways"—two deep ruts dug in the road that the wagon wheels sank into up to their hubs. This helped keep the wagon on the road. Crossing near Lake Tahoe, Nevada, in 1866. (Courtesy of the Library of Congress.)

been chained and locked. Since this gate was near the squatter's house, the men opted to remove the hinges on the gate and swing the gate open as quietly as they could. They were not quiet enough. The squatter soon showed up with "big dogs and big oaths" and a pistol. John and his companions managed to escape after "the matter was arranged."[10]

And then there was the problem of fording streams, bridges and ferries being singularly absent from these nineteenth century interstates. Stream banks were almost perpendicular, the bottoms of the streams muddy, and the streams themselves deep from bank to bank, making a crossing treacherous at the best of times. "A stream which a three-year-old child might ford at night will be running water enough to float a steamboat before morning."[11] It was not unheard of for stagecoach passengers to be forced to camp out by a rain-engorged stream waiting for the stagecoach to show up from the opposite direction. A passenger exchange took place between the two coaches, across the river in a small boat and then the coaches on each bank turned around and headed back to their point of origin. The mud posed another problem—extricating yourself and your team and wagon when a river crossing went wrong. In June 1859, James Griffing wrote home to Oswego, New York, describing the "nastiest, slimiest, greasiest mud . . . that sticketh closer than a brother."[12] It had taken the better part of a day for about two dozen men to rescue a team of horses and a wagon from the "bottomless sediment" of a stream near Topeka, Kansas. On bright dry days, the muddy roads baked into "a sort of adobe . . . though enough [mud] still remained in sunken holes and brook-crossings to remind us of what had been."[13]

Imagine, for a moment, walking across Kansas, Colorado, and Utah, alongside I-70 pushing a shopping cart holding all your belongings; you are homeless. The terrain beside the roadway is fairly flat, but still uneven with clumps of vegetation, rocks, and small inclines and declines. Among the thousands of people leaving Europe to settle in America were groups of Mormons, including many Scandinavians who had converted to Mormonism. Many of them reached the end of the lines in Missouri and their money ran out. The Governor of the Utah Territory and Mormons all over the territory came to the rescue, providing handcarts in which to place a few belongings, but winter set in before they reached Utah and hundreds died. Between 1856 and 1860, about four thousand people walked across the Great Plains pushing or pulling handcarts. Other settlers were fortunate enough to be able to afford a wagon and draft animals. In 1875, Isabella Bird traveled to Utah by train. The trail the Mormons had followed could be seen beside the railroad. "The wheel marks of the trail to Utah often ran parallel with the [train] track, and bones of oxen were bleaching in the sun, the remains of those whose carcasses fell in the wilderness on the long and drouthy journey."[14]

Crossing the deserts of Utah and Nevada posed the next challenge for California-bound travelers. On his trip to California along a route similar to that of today's I-80, Robert Louis Stevenson remembered the miles and miles of "desolate and desert scenes, fiery hot and deadly weary." He also remembered that his first glimpse of a pine-forested ravine and a foaming river made him feel more alive than he had felt in days. "Every spire of pine along the hill-top, every trout pool along the mountain river, was more dear to me than a blood relation."[15] Stevenson and his fellow passengers "threw off their sense of dirt and heat and weariness. . . . The sun no longer oppressed us with heat, it only shone laughingly along the mountain-side. . . . At every turn we could see farther into the land and our own happy futures."[16]

Horace Greeley commented on the diversity of those he met on his trip through the territories, which he attributed to the vagrant tendencies of Americans. At one point, Horace and his party spent the night at a way station—a tent pitched in the middle of nowhere—kept by an ex-lawyer from Cincinnati; his wife, an actress from New York, did the cooking.

Not everyone went West from the Eastern United States. These families settled in Wyoming after trekking overland from California in the nineteenth-century version of an RV. Today, they would probably follow I-80 into Rawlins, Wyoming (Exits 215–211). (Courtesy of the Denver Public Library, Western History Collection, Z-8843.)

Everywhere he turned, Horace found people from somewhere else, some other occupation. "Omnibus-drivers from Broadway repeatedly handled the ribbons [reins]; ex-border ruffians from civilized Kansas—some of them of unblessed memory—were encountered. . . . All these, blended with veteran Mountainmen, Indians of all grades . . . half-breeds, French trappers and voyageurs . . . and an occasional negro, compose a medley such as hardly another region can parallel."[17]

While today's interstate travelers frequently see roadside memorials of accident victims, many of those heading west in the early wagon trains remarked about the simple wooden crosses or piles of stone marking grave sites. Not all were the victims of hostile Native Americans; many died at the hands of robbers; even more succumbed to disease. Virtually no one had a proper diet, which compromised their immune system. Scurvy and malaria decimated the caravans, and a simple cut finger could lead to a serious infection, amputation, or death. Sanitation was another matter. It just was not a big factor on a road trip of that era. Mom would gather up the buffalo chips for a fire and then, unwashed, mix the ingredients for the evening meal with her hands before scooping it into the frying pan, again with her unwashed hands. Travelers shared plates and cups, if they existed. Knives and spoons were a luxury; most ate with their fingers at a time when the evening meal did not come wrapped in foil or paper as it might along today's interstates.

While Horace Greeley exhorted young men to "Go West," other American frontiers were also opening up. On his travels in 1852, tourist Charles Clinton noted that the "press to Illinois and Iowa still continues; the boats on the Mississippi and Red Rivers are filled with emigrants to Texas and Minnesota and the encampment fires of new comers nightly light up the woods of Florida."[18] About the same time as Horace Greeley and Charles Clinton explored the West, a landscape artist from Michigan, by the name of Charles Lanman decided to head off to the wilds of Florida for inspiration and possibly some rest and relaxation. At that time, the future land of Disney, Daytona, and space travel was a relatively new U.S. possession, having been acquired from Spain in 1821 and admitted as a state in 1845. Its long coastline served most travel needs quickly and efficiently. The sandy soils easily absorbed moisture when it rained, so while walking in sand was not always easy for man or beast, at least the trails and rudimentary roads were relatively dry. Florida's

Interstates of
chapter 3

interior was left to the alligators and the Seminole Indians, with only
a few rudimentary trails leading inland. Nevertheless, Lanman decided
to head into the panhandle from Saint Augustine. "I was compelled to
travel by private conveyance, and I managed to reach here in safety [near
present-day Gainesville]. The same feat, or something like it, has undoubtedly been performed by the officers of our army in former times,

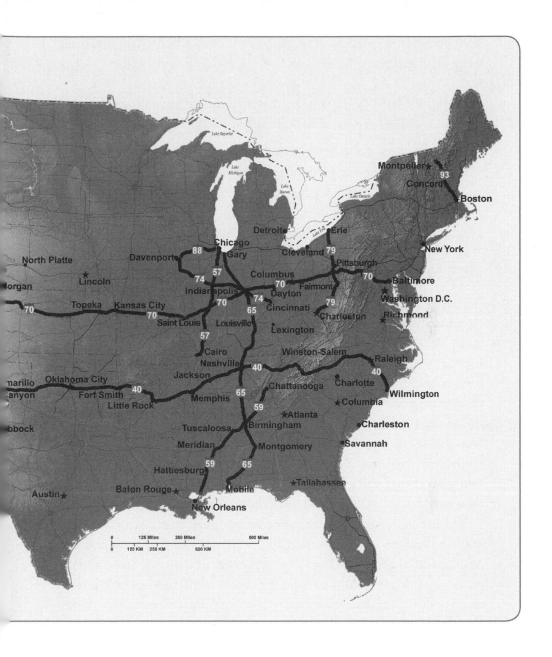

but their only enemies were the revengeful Seminoles; the dangers from which I have escaped were those of starvation and a rickety vehicle."[19] Further on, he hired another private buggy, whose driver anticipated twenty-first century gas prices. "[W]e drove . . . a distance of forty-eight miles, the cost of which journey was twenty-four dollars, or just about half the value of the horse and buggy. We only experienced one breakdown, but then the road was very good."[20] Today, Charles Lanman could leave his beachfront hotel near Saint Augustine and head up I-95 to I-10.

As Horace Greeley had done, Charles Lanman got to know the immigrant families he visited. In one encampment, he found a

> man and woman and fifteen children. They had built their watch-fire directly upon the bank of the stream, and as the woman was cooking their humble meal, children were playing with the dogs, the father cleaning his rifle, and the blue smoke ascended in the quiet air, to be lost among the neighboring cypress trees, the effect of the scene was picturesque in the extreme. The man informed me that he was a carpenter by trade, was born on the Atlantic coast, in one of the Carolinas.

Meanwhile, the states losing residents to the new frontiers fought back. North Carolina published statistics for potential farmers, noting the two-way traffic on those interstates unfurling westward; many former North Carolinians were returning to their home state. North Carolina promoted its swampy soil as more productive than the soils of Illinois, and claimed that people could live and work in a swamp without fear of disease. And besides, as North Carolina boosters slyly offered, the swamps were actually beneficial to farmers. The reeds in the swamps grew year-round and made excellent feed for cattle. Hogs could even be fattened "almost without feeding."[21] Root hog, or die.

Because of Horace Greeley's interest in these migratory Americans and the Western territories, his paper, the *New York Tribune*, published more material about the West than any other newspaper. These articles encouraged many young men to try their luck. (Horace's well-known catch phrase, "Go West young man, go West," also helped.) Because the *New York Tribune* was national in scope, it was popular in the territories where settlers could read about events back home. And, since you never threw anything out, once the papers were read, they frequently ended up being used as wallpaper to help insulate and decorate cabins. Many of those moving on to America's frontiers left fairly comfortable homes and good farms for parlors papered with newspaper and a sod hut. It was a time of expectation and hope. Charles Clinton attributed the traffic to the "enterprising character of our people; their natural restless-

I have finished now my song, or if you please, my ditty
And that it was not shorter is about the only pity.
And now that I have had my say, don't say I've told a lie
For the subject I have touched is root hog, or die.

ness, sanguine temperament, and migratory habits."[22] Horace Greeley added: "Was there ever another such vagrant, restless, discontented people, pretending to be civilized, as ours!"[23]

Interstate 79: A Sea of Billowy Hills

An 1870 guide designed to lure immigrants to West Virginia boasted that the hills of the Mountain State were much healthier than the coastal plain of Virginia. West Virginia's hill country was so beneficial that "gastric and pulmonary patients" from other states flocked there in large numbers "to renovate the juices of life, and nurse their returning strength" in the highland air.[24] Moreover, the entire state was so high up that that scourge of the lowlands—malaria—was unknown. But, with an eye to attracting potential farmers, the guide's author qualified his statement by pointing out that while the entire state was high enough to ward off the evils of malaria, no corner of the state was so high that you could not grow corn and sorghum. (Technically, this was correct, but

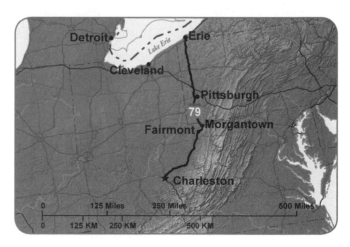

Interstate 79

Artist James Champney's tongue-in-cheek depiction of his and author Edward King's travails during their "road" trip to West Virginia. (Courtesy of Documenting the American South, University of North Carolina at Chapel Hill.)

the very hilly nature of the state meant cultivation was not always practical.) But the guide's author was adamant: West Virginia was "a land peculiar for its green pastures flowing with milk, for its bright flowers laden with honey, and its river slopes that promise to run with wine."[25]

This mountainous terrain kept most of what is now the Interstate 79 area isolated. There were not even many permanent Native American settlements. Tribes (Shawnee, Mingo, Tuscarora, and Lenape) treated the area as a vast game and salt preserve and lived elsewhere. Consequently, few trails crossed the region. This isolation kept the westward march of European civilization at bay; and when settlers finally did arrive, they followed the handful of Native American trails. Resulting conflicts with the Native peoples led to a series of forts, including Pricketts Fort (Exit 139) built in 1774 at a fur-trading post operated by Jacob Prickett. Nearby Fort Morgan (built 1772) evolved into Morgantown (Exit 152). A little further north, a young George Washington recommended a fort be built at the confluence of the Allegheny and Monongahela Rivers. The French thought so too, forced the British out, and built Fort Duquesne, soon to be reclaimed by the British and renamed for William Pitt. All

> West Virginia is so hilly and its valleys are so narrow that dogs wag their tails up and down rather than sideways.

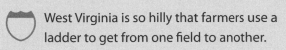
West Virginia is so hilly that farmers use a ladder to get from one field to another.

three forts were along the frontier of the 1770s—the land I-79 crosses today.

West Virginia is the only state lying entirely within the Appalachian Mountains. As a result, its average height is fifteen hundred feet above sea level. But, West Virginia and the western part of Pennsylvania were not always mountainous; prehistoric seas once covered this area. Gradually, sediment in these seas built up to depths of thirty-thousand feet and turned to rock. The Appalachians, once taller than the Swiss Alps, formed out of this rock during a period of geologic upheaval, and erosion gradually wore them down to what you see today. In Pennsylvania, I-79 hugs the border with Ohio, as it travels through the ridges and valleys of the Laurel Highlands, the forested slopes fed by the many creeks and streams that rush out of the mountains. Researchers, with far too much time on their hands, calculated that if someone took an iron to West Virginia and ironed the whole state out flat, its 24,232 square miles would be smoothed out to an area larger than the United States (that is, more than three and a half million square miles).

With few roads, the timbered wilderness remained sparsely settled, but those billowy hills yielded everything a settler needed. The 1870 immigrants' guide to West Virginia boasted: "Game and fish and even wild fruit and honey were everywhere abundant, and the slovenly cultivation of a few half cleared acres in this genial climate, furnished in abundance the bread and other necessities of the settler's frugal fare."[26] To reach this Eden, potential immigrants were advised to take the Baltimore and Ohio Railroad west across Maryland into West Virginia. The B & O stopped in Clarksburg, West Virginia (Exit 119) and from there immigrants could head northward either by road or on the Monongahela River into Western Pennsylvania and up to Lake Erie. A connection to Lake Erie had always been important, as a major military and economic thoroughfare to and from the port at Erie, Pennsylvania. Commodore Perry certainly thought so, when he marched a crew of shipbuilders and sailors north to Erie, to build the fleet used in the Battle of Lake Erie against the British in the War of 1812. To signal his victory, Commodore

Perry sent the now famous message: "We have met the enemy, and they are ours."[27]

Southward from Clarksburg railway station, potential settlers could claim land along the way or keep going to Charleston (Mile 0) and possible homesteading sites along the Kanawha River. Over the next one hundred years, the trails these immigrants followed north and south from Clarksburg gradually evolved. In Pennsylvania, state officials widened and improved Commodore Perry's route into a two-lane road, known as the Perry Highway. With a few alterations, it evolved into U.S. Route 19. By the 1950s, U.S. Route 19 was again rebuilt—this time as a four-lane highway. With the passage of the legislation for the interstate system, Pennsylvania proposed a parallel interstate to U.S. Route 19 to deal with increasing traffic loads, and construction on I-79 began in 1961. It now extends for 343 miles southward from Erie, Pennsylvania, crossing I-90 before intersecting with I-64 and I-77 in that sea of billowy hills in West Virginia.

Settlers opting to head south from Clarksburg followed a road that paralleled today's I-79 as far as Weston (Exit 99). From there the road looped in a more westerly direction before curving back to Charleston. If they chose to stay in Clarksburg, those 1870 immigrants could expect to pay ten to fifty dollars an acre for improved land and five to fifteen dollars an acre for unimproved land. Or, they could go to work in the glass-making industry.

For 1870s immigrants heading north from Clarksburg, their first overnight stop was usually Fairmont (Exits 133–139), the 1800s version of today's I-79 interchange with its cluster of places to stay, eat, and buy fuel. Settled in the 1790s, Fairmont flourished as a way station on the road to Morgantown and as a major coal-mining town. With the discovery of coal in Fairmont in 1850, miners and their families flooded in through Clarksburg and Pennsylvania. The deadliest mining disaster in U.S. history occurred in 1907 at Fairmont's Monongah Mine; 361 miners lost their lives.

West Virginia quickly became a leading producer of coal, attracting even more coal miners and their families to the state. By 1923, more than nine thousand coal mines operated in West Virginia, with Pennsylvania and West Virginia vying to see which state could produce the most coal in the United States. Much of that coal fueled the steel in-

> West Virginia is so hilly that cattle's legs are shorter on one side so that they can comfortably graze (Leach: 163).

dustry in Pittsburgh, which soon gained a reputation as a blackened industrial wasteland. Coal mining continued to drive the economies of the I-79 area through World War I, but virtually ground to a halt with the onset of the Great Depression. Many mines closed and thousands lost their jobs. World War II renewed the demand for coal, and workers again found jobs in coal mines, in the steel mills of Pittsburgh, and further north in manufacturing plants at Erie. Coal production tapered off with the increased use of oil, only to rise again in the 1990s with increased energy demands. By this time, technology had caught up with a centuries-old industry and fewer miners were needed.

The 1870 immigrants' guide asked potential settlers to visualize their trek out from the railway station in Clarksburg. "As you descend the mountain path . . . and breathe the pure fresh air of the hills, cast your eyes upon the most impressive scenes, for Nature is there in all her glory."[28] For today's I-79 traveler, little has changed. "The sturdiness of the forests, the hardy vigor of all vegetable life, the munificence of all visible nature, impress the traveler accustomed to see[ing] bare rock and stinted vegetation amid mountain scenery. . . . few jutting crags are seen, unless hewn out of the mountain side in cutting the wild pathway of the railroad; and no rough rocks, piled heap upon heap, offend the eye as it sweeps the gracefully rounded knobs."[29]

Interstate 74: Knock, Knock

There are varying theories on how Indiana became known as the Hoosier state. Some say the word "hoosier" could be a derivative of "hoozer," an Old English word for "hill" in the dialect of many of the very earliest settlers in Indiana. Others refer to an Indiana resident by the name of Sam Hoosier who, in 1825, supposedly took a work crew out of the state to build a canal on the Ohio River. Other workers on the project referred to the crew members as "Hoosier's men" and the name came to mean Indianans in general. But the most colorful explanation comes from a

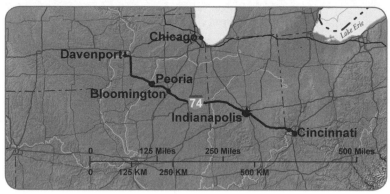

Interstate 74

A Hoosier as portrayed in *The Hoosier Schoolmaster*, by Edward Eggleston. Originally published as a magazine serial, the story proved so popular that its serial chapters were released in book form in 1871. Translated into several languages and made into a movie in 1935, *The Hoosier Schoolmaster* is generally credited with popularizing the term "Hoosier."

habit that apparently drifted into common usage by the very earliest settlers in what became Indiana. When a visitor knocked on the front of a cabin or on the door—if one existed—the occupant of the cabin frequently responded with "Who's here?" But the local vernacular had them saying the words so fast that the greeting sounded like "Hoosier."

The word "Indiana" itself means "land of the Indians," but that did not last long once transportation networks unrolled this far west. By 1816, there were sixty-four thousand people in the territory, enough to grant statehood. Indianapolis became the capital in 1825. By 1860, Indiana was home to more than a million people, mostly thanks to the state's transportation network; two major roadways (the National Road running east–west and the Michigan Road running north–south) and a network of wagon trails. Twelve different stagecoach lines ran through the state on the National Road. A canal, later made obsolete by railroads passing through Indianapolis, completed the transportation network. This convergence of transportation links meant Hoosiers were soon treated to the sight of wagon trains heading west across their state. A gentleman by the name of Maurice Thompson writing in *Scribner's Monthly* in 1878 had a more colorful description of Indiana's importance as a transportation hub. He explained that if Boston and New York were the two lobes of the national brain then Indianapolis was certainly a vertebra "through which passes the spinal marrow of the republic, the very life of which is that of a thrifty, ever progressive, honest, honourable rural population."[30]

Indianapolis continues as a "vertebra" in the nation's transportation system with multiple interstates diverging on the city. Interstate 74, one of the interstates passing through or around Indianapolis, cuts its own trace through the surrounding landscape approximating the general routing of the old Indianapolis and Cincinnati Railroad between those two cities. Elsewhere, I-74 cuts to the chase, heading westward to Illinois and Iowa in a more direct line than was the case in 1878. A tiny fringe of I-74 also exists in North Carolina, and plans are in the works to "connect the dots" in the coming decades.

In describing his visit to the state, Maurice Thompson seemed surprised by the sophistication of the rural people he met. He simply could not explain why Hoosier "tillers of the soil are to-day far ahead of the same class in Eastern states, as regards a broad, liberal knowledge of men and things, and a thorough-going, virile way of thinking and acting for themselves."[31] Maurice's attitude reflected the general opinion many people had of Hoosiers as uncouth, crude, somewhat ignorant rural rustics. His bias added weight to the argument for the Old English dialect explanation for the origin of the word Hoosier. Many of the earliest settlers did indeed come to Indiana from the part of England where the dialect was still spoken, and their speech pattern certainly set them apart as "different." Whatever the origins, Maurice went on to comment, somewhat self-importantly that a "competent observer . . . cannot fail to note the rapid growth of eloquence, art-culture, philosophical inquiry, and all else tending to a lifting of the masses to a high intellectual plane."[32]

And then there's the guy who walked into a tavern in early-days Indiana after a fist fight in which noses had been bitten off and eyes gouged out. While nursing his whiskey, the new arrival toed a piece of flesh on the dirt floor with his boot and called out: "Hey, who's ear?"

Interstate 88 West: Grass and Sky and Sweet-Breathed Giants

Few early visitors forgot their first glimpse of prairie. For some it was not as expected. Robert Louis Stevenson called it a "flat paradise."[33] Tourist Charles Clinton could not forget the endless horizon. "As far as the eye can reach, is one continued field of grass and flowers, waving in the passing breeze, and exhibiting the appearance of a country which has been cultivated for centuries, but now deserted by its inhabitants."[34] Captain Basil Hall of the British Navy remembered the flowers hidden in the grasslands. Few also forgot the smell of freshly tilled prairie soil—and the back-jarring, tedious work of prairie breaking. Grasses of the natural prairie can survive in very low rainfall areas, because of deep roots, but those same deep roots made it very difficult to turn natural grasslands

Interstate 88 West

into tilled field. Early settlers resorted to a big iron plow and a team of at least six with twenty oxen considered an even better option.

Today, Interstate 88 West from I-294 in Chicago to I-80, a few miles short of the Iowa border, passes through what was once tall grass prairie country. Now, that endless field of grass and flowers has given way to toll booths, concrete, and subdivisions—and miles and miles of corn-fields, waving motorists onward toward the distant horizon.

"The long line of oxen, each one leaning heavily away from his fellow as he slowly surges on, the ponderous plows steadily proceeding, with the strong masses of prairie grass roots snapping, and the black loam boiling beside the share, the sun-burnt man plodding behind, and the assistant or driver with his big whip—all these are in the foreground, while away to the horizon the green or brown billows of the prairie roll like those of the ocean . . . the plain homes of the farmers, like small arks adrift on the waves" (Thompson, 1878: 679). Illustration is from the September, 1878, edition of *Scribner's Monthly*.

"[D]ropping corn in the West is . . . what hay-making is in the East, a rare chance for lovers and love-making" (Thompson, 1878: 679). Illustration was published in the September 1878 edition of *Scribner's Monthly*.

To get from the prairie-breaker stage to the cornfields of today involved a certain amount of courtship. After plowing a field in one direction, the farmer then plowed it at right angles. This was an exact science with the best teams and their handlers able to plow a precise grid of furrows. Young men and women then walked side by side down the furrows putting four grains of corn at each juncture of the furrows. Since Illinois settlers planted corn in May and May was a month for romance, who knew how many "tender words and glances they exchange . . . only the breezes may know."[35]

Old-timers bemoaned the passing of this custom; they also missed the teams of oxen that had helped turn the I-88 corridor into the miles and miles of cornfields of today. "The great ox-wains will soon be no more forever. Beautiful high-bred horses and Studebaker wagons have crowded them to the wall,—those slow-going, lumbering vehicles drawn by those sweet-breathed giants of old."[36]

Interstate 84 West: Ezra and the Boys

Ezra Meeker firmly believed that to attempt the Oregon Trail with anything other than a good team of oxen was just plain stupid. Oxen were better at foraging on prairie, could ford rivers easier than horses and were a little more difficult for horse thieves to sneak off with in the night. Once settlers reached their new land, oxen also did a better job of plowing. Ezra also believed that all of those who had crossed on the Oregon Trail, and in many instances been buried beside it, and the trail itself, deserved to be remembered and not lost to history. Too many people had forgotten the role the trail played in opening up the American West. As Ezra explained, the "difference between a civilized and an untutored people lies in the application of experiences. The civilized man builds upon the foundations of the past, with hope and ambition for the future."[37] So, in January 1906, at the age of seventy-six, Ezra set out from his front lawn in Puyallup, Washington (a town he had founded), to retrace and mark the trail he originally crossed in 1852 with his young wife, Eliza Jane, and infant son. He built a replica of his 1852

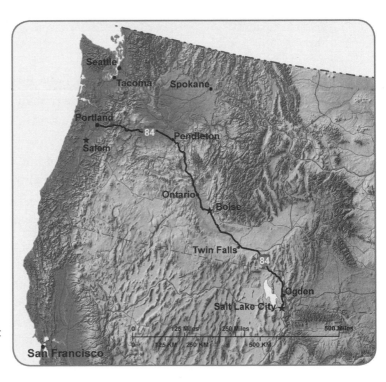

Interstate 84 West

The 1850s version of what happens to a road surface when there is too much interstate traffic: these ruts were carved in solid rock. "The tramp of thousands upon thousands of men and women, the hoofs of millions of animals, and the wheels of untold numbers of vehicles had loosened the soil, and the fierce winds had carried it away. In one place we found ruts worn a foot deep into the solid rock" (Meeker, 1922: 188). Ezra Meeker sits in one of these wheel ruts. (Courtesy of the Denver Public Library, Western History Collection, X-21915.)

wagon and, with his oxen "boys" Dave and Twist hitched up to it and his collie dog Jim for company, set out. He was a man on a mission. His friends and family thought he was certainly suicidal. It was too hard a trip for a man his age.

But, not only did Ezra survive, he managed to find and mark the entire length of the Oregon Trail, raising awareness all along its length by talking to schoolchildren and giving speeches in local community halls. By the time he made it to the East Coast even President Teddy Roosevelt wanted to meet the man single-handedly putting the Oregon Trail back on the map. Roosevelt also wanted to meet Ezra's boys and in an impromptu moment, grabbed his hat and hurried off to the stable where they were staying leaving assistants scrambling to keep up.

Today, Interstate 84 West, from Exit 222 in Idaho to Portland, Oregon (Exits 16–1), follows the western part of the trail Ezra so carefully marked in 1906. On his first crossing of the trail with his family in 1852,

Ezra reached the I-84W part of the Oregon Trail after traveling a northern branch of the trail through Wyoming. (Interstate 84 West also extends southeast from Exit 222 in Idaho to just beyond Ogden, Utah, where it meets up with I-80.)

Ezra and his wife, Eliza Jane, first went west in 1851 to Iowa from Ohio, but found the Iowa winter too cold for their liking. The next spring, with a one-month-old son, the couple again packed up and headed further west. In Oregon, the government was giving away 320 acres of land to each settler, but if they stayed in Iowa, they would have to pay for a farm. Given their opinion of Iowa weather, the decision was relatively easy. With no service centers or fast-food outlets to pull into for meals, Eliza Jane did the 1850s equivalent of packing the van for a road trip. She put butter in the center of sacks of flour, put eggs in cornmeal or flour, and loaded up enough dried fruit, pumpkin, and beef jerky to last five hundred miles. She knew how to make dried yeast cakes, and with a tin reflector for baking, they had fresh white bread to eat all the way to Oregon. The only non-essential was a bottle of brandy "for medicinal purposes." The Meekers joined other families heading west and as a group, traveled about fifteen to twenty miles a day. "Yet although we kept apart as a separate unit, we were all the while in one great train, never out of sight and hearing of others. In fact, at times the road would be so full of wagons that all could not travel in one track, and this fact accounts for the double roadbeds seen in so many places on the trail."[38]

At one point the Meekers' wagon had to stop, because Ezra's brother Oliver, who had joined them along the way, had become ill. While they nursed Oliver back to health, Ezra counted sixteen hundred passing wagons.

The pioneer army was a moving mass of human beings and dumb brutes at times mixed in inextricable confusion, a hundred feet wide or more. Sometimes two columns of wagons, traveling on parallel lines and near each other, would serve as a barrier to prevent loose stock from crossing; but usually there would be a confused mass of cows, young cattle, horses, and men afoot moving along the outskirts . . . a young girl, maybe, riding astride and with a younger child behind her, going here and there after an intractable cow, while the mother could be seen in the confusion lending a helping hand. As in a thronged street, no one seemed to look to the right or to the left, or to pay much attention, if any, to others, all being bent only on accomplishing the task at hand.[39]

Ezra found the dust of the trail intolerable. "In calm weather it would rise so thick at times that the lead team of oxen could not be seen from the wagon. Like a London fog, it seemed thick enough to cut."[40] They crossed the Snake River (I-84W crosses it at Mile Markers 215, 128, 122, and 0) and continued past the fort at Boise (Exits 54–52), over the Blue Mountains (summit at Mile Marker 241), past Pendleton (Exits 210–297) and onto The Dalles (Exits 88–83), a rock formation on the Columbia River where a town soon formed to serve settlers passing through the area. Here Ezra and his travel companions found a crowd of "travel-worn people."

> The appearance of this crowd of emigrants beggars description. Their dress was as varied as pieces in a crazy quilt. Here was a matronly dame in clean apparel, but without shoes; her husband perhaps lacked both shoes and hat. Youngsters of all sizes were running about with scarcely enough clothing to cover their nakedness. Some suits and dresses were so patched that it was impossible to tell what was the original cloth. The color of practically everybody's clothing was that of desert dust.[41]

From this point, travelers on the Oregon Trail could float down the Columbia on a raft or continue along the bank of the river to Portland. Ezra, Eliza Jane, and their son opted for the raft while the brother, Oliver, continued on by land with the wagon and livestock. The relief on boarding the raft and that knowledge that their journey was nearing an

Interstate 40

end washed over everyone in the group. "We were like an army that had burned the bridges behind it."[42]

As for Ezra, he seems to have thrived on the Oregon Trail. Not only did he complete the journey for a second time in 1906 to raise awareness about the importance of the trace it had left on the landscape, but he did it again several years later. He also did it by train, in an automobile and, just before he died, in an airplane. He is the only individual, walking the Oregon Trail in the 1850s, known to have traveled along it so many more times by so many different modes of transportation. As for the various incarnations of Dave and Twist that traveled the trail with Ezra, they also got to experience the route by train, enjoying their favorite hay and rolled barley from the baggage car on one of Ezra's many crossings. In looking out the train window, Ezra saw the landscape from a different perspective and began to realize the expansiveness of country the trail crossed. He wondered if he would have ever attempted the Oregon Trail if he had realized just how long it was going to be; it stretched endlessly before him like a panorama. "But where were the camp fires? Where was the herd of gaunt cattle? Where the sound of the din of bells? The hallooing for lost children? Or the little groups off on the hillside to bury the dead? All were gone."[43]

Interstate 40: How I Learned to Love America

It started with eBay. Gary explains: "I've been traveling around the U.S. on one highway or another for the better part of thirty-five years—up and down both coasts and across the top through some of the most beautiful country, meeting genuinely friendly people at every turn. My

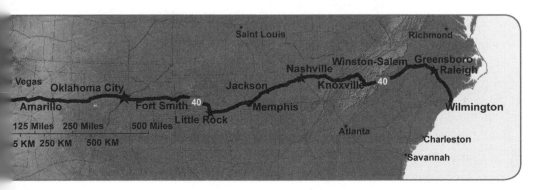

Gary posing at home with his motorcycles. The black bike prompted him to embark on his adventures on I-40.

last journey was one of those mid-life adventures that requires a bit of trust, well actually a lot of trust, and a small gamble." In April 2004, Gary bought a BMW motorcycle on eBay from a fellow bike enthusiast living in Louisiana. Having the bike shipped to his home in Canada would have deprived Gary of a road trip with his new wheels, so instead, Gary flew into New Orleans where the owner of the bike met him at the airport. "Over the next twenty-four hours we drank beer, ate crawdads, and generally swapped stories. I drove away on my new bike the next morning headed for a friend's home in Oklahoma, grateful for the meeting, sorry for the leaving." In Oklahoma, on Interstate 40, Gary found himself in trouble.

> I had been making time in a convoy of trucks when the heavens opened; rain coming at me from all directions and eighteen wheelers all around. I was just west of Fort Smith, Arkansas [Exit 1]. My bike died on the edge of I-40 right where they were making road repairs. I had a steep embankment on one side and semis going by at seventy miles per hour only feet away. Down the embankment and up a slight grade put me onto a new unopened highway. I got about six feet from that black tarmac before the red mud sucked my wheels under. I stopped dead in that thick goo and no way on this Earth was I going to be moving.

Construction trucks plied up and down the unopened highway too busy with their tasks to pay me much mind. I managed to get a rock under my side stand and went hiking through tall grass toward a chain-link fence and what looked like a small engine-repair place. Two elderly Southern belles greeted me with a sunny hello despite my soaked attire and several days of facial growth. They offered up that a BMW dealer just opened in Little Rock [Exits 159–153] and they'd be happy to get me the number. Shortly thereafter I was speaking to a friendly fellow who said he'd be out with his pickup shortly and to stand by. I headed back to my mired bike to wait.

About twenty minutes went by when I noticed a red Jeep turn off the main highway and head up the unopened highway toward me. It pulled up a few feet away, the driver and female passenger eyeing me as I eyed them. The driver, with a long moustache and too many tattoos to count, ambled over and opened the conversation with, "How y'all doing?" He was a member of a Christian biking group and he and his wife would be only too happy to help me out of my fix. I explained the imminent arrival of the pickup, but they wouldn't hear of me waiting in the muck, so, with me on the bike, he and his good wife pushed me up onto the new roadway and I coasted down to where they had entered the new road from the old road.

With a shake of hands and a wave of thanks they motored off, reaffirming my belief in decent folk. Right about then my other white knight showed up. He hitched my bike onto his trailer and headed back to Little Rock. After we'd pulled into the mechanic side of his business and unloaded my broken beast, the head mechanic came over and admired the bike, but not the muddy mess in his shop. He began pulling things off the bike, stripping everything down to the frame and motor. Twenty minutes into a diagnostic I was told the good news: "We found the problem." Seconds later they told me the bad news: "We just sold the last one of the parts needed to fix your bike." Did I mention that this was Saturday at about one o'clock in the afternoon? Now at most bike shops they'd tell you to come back in a few days when the part comes in and the bike is ready. I patiently and as cheerfully as I could explained that

I needed to be back in Canada by Tuesday night, and as much as I would like to wait, I had to be on the road. The whole business went into action. The sales manager and sales team started making telephone calls in search of a part. Hours slipped by and, as we approached five o'clock, with closing time looming and no part in sight, a slim ray of hope opened up. They could get a part shipped, but not today. It would be first thing Monday morning. I went outside and sat on a bench under the lone tree on the property and listened to the whine of the interstate cutting across Little Rock, wishing I were on it. It was crunch time. Decisions had to be made.

About one hundred miles west of where Gary broke down on I-40, Hezekiah Crumpton faced a similar dilemma. It was April 1849 and it was raining. Hezekiah had joined a wagon train in Fort Smith bound for California and the gold rush. At that time, Fort Smith was the main supply depot and departure point for travelers taking the southern route across the Great Plains to the fortunes awaiting them in California. All the dreams of a twenty-one year old rested on that trip, but, in the rain, that April day, in the low valleys of Oklahoma, a horse floundered in the mud. In trying to help the horse, Hezekiah seriously injured a leg. "Two reputable medical men in the train gave me kind treatment and

A photo of Hezekiah Crumpton (*right*) and his brother, taken circa 1849 and published in a book that they coauthored. (Courtesy of Documenting the American South, University of North Carolina at Chapel Hill.)

rather gloomy prognostications, hinting at the possibilities of amputation . . . everything tended to make me despondent."[44]

As with Gary, strangers stepped forward to help. Hezekiah's white knight was another young man traveling with the same wagon train. "Young fellow, you are in a bad fix. You had better return and let those Wheeler girls and their mother take care of you and you'll soon be as good as new—don't say you can't stand the trip—you can ride horseback. There is one of my best horses, saddle, bridle and lariat; take them and deliver them to my father at Ft. Smith."[45] Hezekiah had boarded with the Wheeler family in Fort Smith while waiting for a wagon train. John Wheeler had married a Cherokee woman and had a slew of pretty daughters, something Hezekiah appears to have appreciated.

On his way back to Fort Smith, a Choctaw family took Hezekiah into their home. They made him feel welcome, especially when they found out about his friendship with the Wheeler family. Under the family's care, Hezekiah mended to the point that when another wagon train passed by, he joined it. Unbelievably, in an era without cell phones and e-mail, and in a region without identified roads, Hezekiah found his benefactor still on the trail and returned the borrowed horse and gear. "I became a general chore boy, looking up camping sites, starting fires, procuring wood and water, driving team, or looking out for stock; most of the time traveled on foot. . . . I had learned to ride and stay on most any kind of a 'critter.' So while en route, I rode everything placed in my charge, steer, cow, mule or bronco, thus I had many a lift when tired of tramping."[46]

Wagon trains heading west generally followed the rutted trace of other wagon convoys across the territories of Oklahoma, Texas, New Mexico, Arizona, and California. Without the benefit of road signs and the limited-access ribbon of concrete and asphalt today's I-40 travelers take for granted, it was very easy to get lost, especially if the ruts you followed were of wagons that had also gotten lost. At one point, in following the trace previous wagons had made, Hezekiah discovered he was actually heading eastward back to Fort Smith. Beyond Fort Smith, the next large town was Albuquerque (Exits 167–155) in the New Mexico Territory. Today, Fort Smith to Albuquerque is a little over nine hours of driving on I-40; it took Hezekiah several days. Interstate 40 travelers crossing the Texas Panhandle can stop in Amarillo (Exits 73–71), but that was not an option for Hezekiah: Amarillo did not exist in 1849. In

Friendships often formed while on the road and around the campfire. This wood engraving by Albert Bobbett depicts a wagon train camped on the Great Plains; it was published on December 23, 1871, in *Harper's Weekly*. (Courtesy of the Library of Congress.)

Hezekiah's time, the panhandle was a gently undulating ocean of grass peopled by potentially hostile Native Americans. It was a case of proceed cautiously and as quickly as possible. Further down the road, Albuquerque, New Mexico today is a service center of almost half a million people for the nearby mining, timber, and ranching operations. Its dry, warm climate also makes it popular with tourists and snowbirds. In Hezekiah's time, it served as an important trading center on the trail south into Mexico and for those coming through the pass in the Sandia and Manzano Mountains. Interstate 40 motorists see practically the same landscape Hezekiah saw in 1849. Near Exit 175 to Tiheras, the Sandia Crest rises to 10,678 feet to the north of the highway; Manzano Peak sits to the south, off in the distance at 10,098 feet high. West of Albuquerque, I-40 crosses the Continental Divide then on to Arizona, passing through

Petrified Forest National Park and the spectacular Painted Desert (Exit 311) before reaching Flagstaff (Exits 201–191). In Arizona, much of I-40 sits on or beside the old roadbed of U.S. Route 66, a highway Hezekiah probably would have enjoyed, possibly on Gary's motorcycle, given his ability to ride whatever conveyance came his way. But in Hezekiah's time, road planners did not see much need for a proper road through Northern Arizona; after all, no one really lived there and those who did found it easier to get around on foot or horse, particularly with the sand, canyons, and dramatic changes in elevation. Railroads eventually crossed the area, providing links with the outside world, but it was not until the invention of the automobile that thoughts turned to building a roadway.

From Arizona, I-40 crosses into California and heads west to Barstow (Mile 0) in the Mojave Desert. In 1849, Hezekiah's wagon train left what would become I-40 and turned southward along a route traced by today's I-25 along the Rio Grande Valley to a spot just north of El Paso where they then turned westward through Tucson and Yuma and across the desert. Today, he would take I-10 and I-8. From there, Hezekiah traveled north to Los Angeles and employment not far from the end of today's I-40. Again, Hezekiah appreciated the kindness of strangers. Another white knight ignored Hezekiah's unkempt appearance and put him to work for a day at manual labor and then fed him. But, Hezekiah was determined to push on to San Francisco and the goldfields. His generous host paid him for his services and gave him a fine pair of Mexican blankets and provisions for the trip. Hezekiah had rough times and some luck in the goldfields before returning to Alabama and family in 1853, this time by steamer to New Orleans.

Back on I-40, in Little Rock, Gary also wanted to return to family.

I was afraid I'd have to pack the disassembled bike into a rental van and leave. I explained my situation to the owner of the company. Ten minutes later he came down the stairs and asked if I could delay leaving until noon the next day, Sunday. "But aren't you closed on Sunday?" I asked. "Yes," he said, "but we'd like to help you out, and I just got off the phone with a guy in Missouri who has two of the parts you need. He's coming down tomorrow to pick up a bike but said he'd leave early to make sure he got here by nine o'clock."

The next morning, Gary walked into the repair shop to find his bike ready to go.

> The mechanic had come in on his day off to repair and put the bike back together. The service manager had come from his sick bed to make sure the bike was to my satisfaction and prepare my bill. Their credit card reader was on the blink, so the owner said, "Don't worry about it, send me a check when you get home." I started up, shook hands all around, expressed my deep gratitude to one and all, and waved goodbye. Crosstown traffic, wheels whining over hot pavement, and I was back on the interstate homeward bound.

Gary's eastbound trek took him across the Mississippi River into Tennessee at West Memphis (Exit 1), then on to Nashville (Exits 221–199), before connecting with I-81. If Gary had continued on I-40, he would have crossed the Great Smoky Mountains into North Carolina, through Asheville (Exits 44–55) and the piedmont towns of Winston-Salem (Exits 188–192), Greensboro (Exits 216–217), Durham (Exits 259–279), Raleigh (Exits 285–299), and finally to the coast at Wilmington (Exit 420). Hezekiah wandered around a bit more before eventually becoming a medical doctor and returning to California to live. Gary reached home as originally planned. For both men, the interstate landscape of their time included strangers who offered a helping hand and quickly became friends. Gary continues to drive the interstates "not because big highways make better places to drive or make the driving more enjoyable, but because it links us as people in a common goal at times. Sharing and looking out for one another when lady luck turns her back. So thanks Jim, Mike, Julius Caesar, and the unknown Christian biker and his wife who took the time and made the effort to reach out to a neighbor."

Interstate 70

Interstate 70: Primitive Simplicity

Horace Greeley probably would have appreciated traveling along Interstate 70 in a recreational vehicle. The well-known publisher of the *New York Tribune* and politician could have stayed in touch with his office via the Internet and cell phone, filing his stories from the road à la Charles Kuralt, enjoying the same comfortable, bug-free bed at night in air-conditioned or heated comfort, an espresso with his morning paper, variety in his meals, and a nice glass of California merlot with his evening beef tenderloin and fresh salad. Instead, with perhaps more good humor than his picture belies, Horace found himself sleeping under a wagon, riding a mule, going for days without a bath, and eating endless rounds of dried biscuit and pork washed down with strong coffee. In doing so, he kept a journal of his descent toward "primitive simplicity"—his catch phrase for living the simple life without the social amenities he took for granted. Horace was forty-eight, his hair line receding—the perfect age to appreciate fully the passing landscape, at least according to his contemporary, Robert Louis Stevenson. The year was 1859, and Horace had decided to check out the American West for himself. He had written enough about it, exhorting young men to "Go West"; now it was time to experience the trip firsthand. So, Horace hopped on a train to Chicago, then down to Kansas City where he caught up with one of the popular routes west, traced today by the western half of Interstate 70.

Thirty years earlier, Frances Trollope, social commentator, well-known author, and mother of novelist Anthony Trollope, traveled extensively in the Eastern United States, including over a route traced by the eastern half of today's I-70. She also kept a journal of her spiral into primitive simplicity. Like Horace, Frances enjoyed a middle-age sensi-

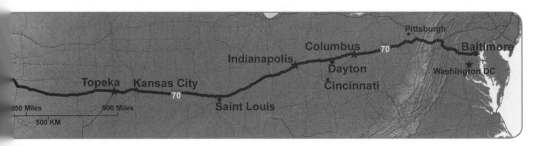

HON. HORACE GREELEY,
Our Next President.

"Go west, young man, and grow up with the country" (Horace Greeley). The above image is a Currier & Ives lithograph of Greeley circa 1872. (Courtesy of the Library of Congress.)

bility of the passing landscape; she also began her travels in America at the age of 48. This somewhat unlikely pair kept journals that cover most of today's I-70. While Frances complained about the lack of clean bed linens in the Alleghenies, Horace noted that chocolate and a morning paper last appeared at the breakfast table in Chicago. In Indiana, he last saw room bells and baths.

If Horace would have enjoyed an RV, the Frances of today, with her liberated sense of adventure, would have probably rented a comfortable minivan. Her family could watch movies in the back seat or play video games, leaving Frances in the driver's seat, possibly dressed in comfortable jeans and a shirt, to enjoy the drive and the passing scenery along I-70. The 1830 Frances traveled in less comfort, constricted by the gown, gloves, petticoats, and bonnet of her day. She found the road west of Baltimore in good shape, one of the best in the country. Despite the relatively smooth road surface, her carriage broke a wheel in the early hours of a March morning. There was no cell phone call to the American Automobile Association to come to her rescue. Instead,

> we decided upon walking to the next village, a distance, fortunately of only two miles, and awaiting there the repair of the wheel. We immediately set off, at the brisk pace that six o'clock and a frosty morning in March were likely to inspire. . . . When we had again started upon our new wheel, the driver, to recover the time he had lost, drove rapidly over a very rough road. . . . [An old lady traveling in the coach] fell into a perfect agony of terror, and her cries of "We shall be over! Oh, Lord! We shall be over! We must over! We shall be over!" lasted to the end of the stage.[47]

The first large town west of Baltimore on today's I-70 is Frederick (Exit 53), followed by nearby Boonsboro and Hagerstown (Exits 35 and 32). Here, in the Great Valley of the Appalachians, travelers had little idea of the conditions ahead. The first chore was to cross the Alleghenies. Today's I-70 smoothes out the landscape, reducing gradients, eliminating bad curves, and adding an element of safety in the form of guard-

A portrait of Frances Trollope. (Courtesy of the New York Public Library.)

rails; that was not the case in Frances' time. Despite her concerns about the road sometimes passing too close to the edge of a steep mountain-side, Frances still found time to enjoy the passing landscape outside her coach window. "As our noble terrace-road . . . rose higher and higher, all that is noblest in nature was joined to all that is sweetest. The blue tops of the higher ridges formed the outline; huge masses of rock rose above us on the left, half hid at intervals by the bright green shrubs, while to the right we looked down upon the tops of the pines and cedars which clothed the bottom."[48] A sunrise also caught her attention. "The vapours caught the morning ray, as it first darted over the mountain top, and passing it to the scene below, we seemed enveloped in a rainbow."[49]

Once across the Alleghenies of Pennsylvania, the road, like today's I-70, passed through Washington, Pennsylvania (Exits 17–15), on its way to Wheeling, West Virginia (Exits 2–1), the next major population center. The number of bridges along this stretch of the road impressed Frances. "I regretted not having counted the number of bridges between Wheeling and Little Washington, a distance of thirty-four miles; over one stream only there are twenty-five, all passed by the road. They frequently occurred within a hundred yards of each other, so serpentine is its course; they are built of stone, and sometimes very neatly finished."[50]

Today's, Frances could pull off the interstate when she wanted to, for a rest stop and meal; not so in her own time.

The stages do not appear to have any regular stations at which to stop for breakfast, dinner, and supper. These necessary interludes, therefore, being generally "impromptu," were abominably bad. We were amused by the patient manner in which our American fellow-travellers ate whatever was set before them, without uttering a word of complaint, or making any effort to improve it, but no sooner reseated in the stage, than they began their complaints— "twas a shame"—"twas a robbery"—"twas poisoning folks"—and the like. I, at last, asked the reason of this, and why they did not remonstrate? "Because, madam, no American gentleman or lady that keeps an inn won't bear to be found fault with."[51]

Near Wheeling, Frances Trollope found a beautiful countryside, but despite her appreciation of the landscape through which she was passing, Frances was not totally immune to the living conditions of the people she met. "[E]very trace of the art of man appeared to be confined to the individual effort of 'getting along,' which, in western phrase, means contriving to live with as small a portion of the incumbrances of civilized society as possible."[52] Here was primitive simplicity.

Wheeling's name conjures up images of a wheel, perhaps wheeling through town, or someone's last name. Not so. The name comes from a Native American word, *weeling*, meaning the "place of skulls." The very first Europeans to visit the area donated the skulls—much against their will. Skulls on poles warned other white settlers to stay away from Native American lands. It did not work. Enter the three legendary Zane brothers—Ebenezer, Silas, and Jonathan—who settled here in 1769. The town of Wheeling was subsequently laid out in 1793 and became a major trading center on the Ohio River, its commercial importance far outweighing that of nearby Pittsburgh for many years. A descendant of the Zane brothers, Grey Zane, reversed his name, and set about to become the father of the Western novel and cowboy movie. The Zane Grey Museum can be found at Exit 164 and Zanesville, Ohio at Exits 157–155.

Frances Trollope explored a bit of Ohio, but did not go much beyond Cincinnati where she rented a house. Interstate 70 continues on through Ohio, Indiana, and Illinois. In 1854, Charles Boynton accepted a commission from The American Reform Tract and Book Society and the Kansas League of Cincinnati, Ohio, to prepare a report on the prairie lands to the west, specifically those in Kansas. To this end, Charles described the Great Plains. "Everywhere the undulating outline of the plain touches the 'horizon's rim.' Over the vast plateau the heavens seem spread out on purpose to curtain it in."[53] The undulation that Charles noticed resulted from advancing and retreating glaciers during the Ice Age that left rows of glacial debris called till. Today's I-70 travelers can still see expanses of flatland interspersed with hills that look a bit like waves on the landscape.

On the road west, primitive simplicity really took hold for Horace Greeley. In Topeka, Kansas (Exits 365–355), horror of horrors, beefsteak disappeared from his menu possibilities. It was also the last time he saw anything other than a tin basin for washing. In other words, the china washbasins of his world were no longer available. It was also the last place he could find a barber. The disappearance of beefsteak in Kansas had to be one of the ironies of travel in 1859. Nearby Kansas City was about to become a major stockyard for the beef industry. Ironically, Horace was apparently still able to get his shoes polished.

Horace described pulling into a roadside tavern that already had five or six wagons in the "parking lot." Fifteen or twenty other wagons drove up after them. Not being one to miss an opportunity, after supper, Horace gathered everyone together at the schoolhouse for a "Republican talk." Horace continued to note disappearing amenities. At Manhattan, (Exits 313–303), "potatoes and eggs last recognized among the bless-

Although taken for granted today, potatoes and eggs were luxuries in the West of 1859. One egg commanded about a dollar; a bag of potatoes was worth about fifteen dollars. Gold miners in Colorado typically paid for their eggs and potatoes with gold dust. The amount of gold dust a man could pinch between his thumb and index finger was pegged at about twenty-five cents, so to buy an egg, a miner would have to relinquish four pinches of gold dust.

ings . . . chairs ditto."[54] By Junction City (Exits 299–296), even the opportunity to have his shoes polished had disappeared, and as he put it in his journal: "Beds bid us good-by."[55] He made another notation further down the road when benches for seats at meals disappeared; he now sat on a bag or box when he ate. Horace slept in the wagon, the prairie wind sometimes shaking it so violently that he made his nightly journal entries with difficulty. Sometimes, it was necessary to stake down the wagon at night.

West of Junction City, Horace and his party halted for an hour at an 1859 version of an interstate highway exit to change mules and dine. It was called Station 8. Here he found a meal of bacon and greens served with bread and applesauce with pie for dessert. The landlady apologized for not having butter as her cow had only just arrived and needed a few days of rest from the cross-country ordeal. This fast-food diner was located in a tent.

Kansas is a relatively flat plain that gets higher as you move from east to west. In Horace's time, this was known as the Great American Desert. It is now called the Great Plains. An early American explorer, Major Stephen Long, visited in the summer of 1820. He described it as uninhabitable and unfit for cultivation of any kind, and for the next few decades, the Kansas area was regarded as a wasteland. Near the Kansas–Colorado border, Horace and his party took a more northerly route to Denver (Exits 285–261) through a very desolate part of the country. "[T]he winds which sweep the high prairies . . . are terrible; and the few trees that grow thinly along the creek-bottoms rarely venture to raise

GREELEY'S RIDE.

Horace Greeley's ride across the Great Plains, as illustrated in Mark Twain's *Roughing It.*

their heads above the adjacent bluffs, to which they owe their doubtful hold on existence. . . . we seem to have reached the acme of barrenness and desolation."[56] As he approached Denver and the mountains, Horace took time to observe and appreciate the changing view before him. "[T]heir majesty was a bleak and rugged one; while the pines . . . lent a grace and hospitality to the landscape which only the weary and wayworn, who have long traversed parched and shadeless deserts can appreciate."[57]

As he approached Denver, Horace's wagon experienced the 1859 version of a vehicle in the outside lane on today's I-70 being passed unsafely, ending up on the shoulder, and rolling over into the ditch. Three friendly Cheyenne on horseback suddenly appeared beside his wagon, startling the driver and the mules pulling the wagon. The whole rig rolled down a steep embankment. Everyone escaped unscathed except Horace who was trapped inside. A nearby stationmaster's wife patched him up, treating his cut face and sprained leg. The wagon was righted and they carried on, but as Horace recorded on entering the Denver House Hotel: "I have in my mind's eye an individual who rolled out of . . . [Kansas] barely thirteen days ago in a satisfactory rig, and a spirit of adequate self-complacency, but who . . . dropped into Denver this morning in a sobered and thoughtful frame of mind, in dust-begrimed and tattered habiliments, with a patch on his cheek, a bandage on his leg, and a limp in his gait, altogether constituting a spectacle most rueful to behold."[58]

Despite the grandeur implied by its name, the Denver House Hotel of 1859 turned out to be a log cabin, its roof and windows covered by canvas. It did have six bedrooms, but they were partitioned off with cotton sheathing. As for food, things were looking up. Milk was now on the table and he had heard a rumor that eggs were about to be available at fifty cents a dozen. "On every side, I note signs of progress . . . there was a man about the city yesterday with lettuce to sell—and I am credibly assured that there will be green peas next month—actually peas!"[59]

Horace left Denver the next day riding on a mule to continue west through the Rockies. The first hill was steep, the ascent being "more than one foot in three. I never before saw teams forced up such a precipice; yet there were wagons with ten or twelve hundred weight . . . being dragged by four to eight yoke of oxen up that giddy precipice, with four or five men lifting at the wheels of each. The average time consumed in the ascent is some two hours."[60] Horace probably would have appreciated a lane for slower traffic so he could pass the larger rigs.

Despite his own difficult and uncomfortable ascent, Horace took time to admire the landscape. "A wilderness of mountains rose all around us."[61] He also visited the camps of men panning for gold in the Colorado gold rush of 1859. By the end of the day, Horace had to be lifted off his mule and wrapped in a blanket near the fire. His companions predicted he would be too stiff and sore to move the next day, but Horace surprised them and got back on his mule the next morning.

It was here that Horace really learned about primitive simplicity. Everyone lived in tents or in the open. There was not a table or chair to be seen anywhere and the diet consisted of salt pork, bread, beans, and coffee. Things did not improve with time. Another traveler a few years later and a few miles north of Denver found the diet nauseating. "It would

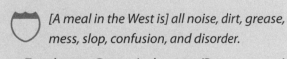

[A meal in the West is] all noise, dirt, grease, mess, slop, confusion, and disorder.

—Traveler near Denver in the 1860s (Brown, 1991: 34)

The gold diggers' camp Horace Greeley visited, as it appeared at the time of his visit in 1859. (Courtesy of the Denver Public Library, Western History Collection, X-11631.)

The highest point on the entire interstate system sits between Mile Markers 213 and 215 on I-70. Here, near the west portals of the Eisenhower Memorial Tunnel, the roadbed is 11,192 feet above sea level. This is the famous Continental Divide: everything west of this point flows west and everything east of this point flows east. The Eisenhower Tunnel itself is, at 1.7 miles, the longest tunnel in the interstate system.

have required a first-class quartz-mill to masticate the bread . . . and nothing more dainty than a buzzard could have eaten the other articles. The cook was an Irishman who was filthy enough himself to sell as real estate."[62]

A couple of weeks later, however, Horace found a very satisfactory supper. "Table, of course, there was none, and we had unluckily lost our fork; but we had still two knives, a sufficiency of tin cups and plates, with an abundance of pork and pilot bread, and an old bag for a table-cloth which had evidently seen hard service, and had gathered more dirt and blood in the course of it than a table-cloth actually needs."[63] Rather than continue along what would today be I-70, Horace returned to Denver to rest before heading north to Laramie, Wyoming. If Horace traveled I-70 today, his next stop west of Denver would most likely be Glenwood Springs (Exits 116–114) for some serious soaking in the mineral spas to ease his aches and overtaxed muscles. This section of highway challenged the talents of the engineers who laid out I-70 with every effort made to preserve the natural beauty of the valleys and canyons and the environmentally sensitive landscape. Interstate construction through Vail Pass and Glenwood Canyon resulted in more than forty bridges and viaducts, and a tunnel, to minimize the impact on the landscape. A section of I-70 just west of Denver called the Hogback, cuts away a section of the mountain to show the layers set down fifty million to eighty million years ago. From here, I-70 carries on into Utah where it connects with I-15.

Would Horace Greeley be astounded by traffic volumes today on I-70? Traffic along the route was heavy even in his time; Horace wrote repeatedly of overtaking large caravans of wagons or doing the 1859 version of pulling into a truck stop and discovering four hundred or five hundred mules already tethered there for a few hours of rest. Today, daily traffic ranges from about forty-five hundred vehicles a day in parts of Utah to about one hundred and fifty thousand vehicles a day through Indianapolis, Indiana (Exits 90–73). Horace would probably take it in stride, pulling into a truck stop in his RV and kicking back in a recliner to watch some TV, maybe enjoy a nightcap before wandering back to his well-appointed bedroom and a sleep in air-conditioned comfort. His situation in 1859 was somewhat different. "Thunder and lightning from both south and west give strong promise of a shower before morning. Dubious looks at several holes in the canvas covering of the wagon. Our trust, under Providence, is in buoyant hearts and an India-rubber blanket. Good-night."[64]

Interstate 76 West: Galvanized Yankees

Not everyone heading west necessarily wanted to go there. In 1863, thousands of men found themselves in a life and death situation: stay where they were and face serious deprivation, disease, malnutrition, and probably death, or head west to defend the frontier. For many, it was a very tough decision, because it called their own moral convictions into question and severed relations with family and friends, often forever. But it beat the status quo—starving to death in very dirty and primitive conditions.

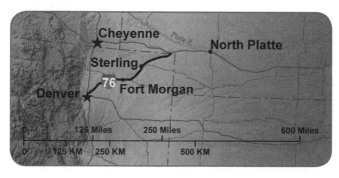

Interstate 76 West

GENERAL CROOK'S HEAD-QUARTERS, FORT FETTERMAN.

Marching in formation during a prairie snowstorm. The sketch appeared in *Harper's Weekly*. (Courtesy of the Denver Public Library, Western History Collection, Z-4026.)

In December 1863, President Lincoln made a tough decision with regards to manpower. Union lines needed more men yet soldiers were needed all through the West to deal with hostile Native Americans, and protect the territories and the settlers trekking overland to new beginnings. In the East, prisoner of war camps were dangerously over-crowded. After much deliberation, Lincoln authorized discussions with the Confederate prisoners being held in Union camps: take the oath of allegiance and enlist in the Union Army, take the oath of allegiance and go to work on public work projects in the North, or take the oath of allegiance and go home—if that home was now within Union lines. Facing certain condemnation if they returned home and not wanting to labor at public works in the North, thousands chose to enlist and, because they were essentially putting on a coat of a different color, covering or "coating" Confederate grey with Union blue, they became known as gal-vanized Yankees, a term meant as an insult by fellow Confederates.

Many of these newly minted Yankees recognized the opportunity be-ing offered to them and deserted as soon as they could, but thousands more stuck it out in a blue uniform and headed west. One unit ended up at a spot on the south side of the South Platte River that now sits about midway between Denver, Colorado, and the Nebraska border on Interstate 76 West. The location, on a plateau afforded a slightly elevated view of the north shore of the river and up and down the river valley. This was also the point where settlers using the South Platte River switched to the Overland Trail for a more direct route to Denver. The galvanized Yankees arrived here in 1864 to build a fort to house troops, who would then protect settlers and the mail service. The completed garrison was called Fort Morgan.

Today, the fort no longer exists, but the community that sprang up in its place is now also known as Fort Morgan. Interstate 76 West and the town obscure the view up and down the river from the old fort's site along what is now Railroad Avenue. Turning southbound on Colorado Highway 52 at Exit 80 or turning east on U.S. Route 34 from Exit 75 takes you past the fort's site near the municipal tennis courts. The fort itself was substantial—about one square city block in size with a parade ground surrounded by about twenty buildings. Settlers heading west were forced to wait at the fort until at least thirty men were available to act as an armed escort for the next leg of their journey.

By the mid-1870s, the area along the South Platte River had become relatively safe and the fort was no longer needed. The U.S. Army moved what it wanted to other forts in the system, sold off what it could at auction, and abandoned the rest to scavengers. A few years later, in 1883, a businessman laid out the town of Fort Morgan, gave the two railroads passing through his property land in return for a station, and set about attracting residents. As for the galvanized Yankees who built the fort, the biggest threat came from the elements, not Native Americans. They skirmished regularly with small bands, but had a tougher time dealing with the cold, especially with less than perfect accommodations the first winter and a diet that was greatly improved over their fare in prison, but salt pork, coffee, and hard tack still did not give them the sustenance they needed on a cold winter day. The fact that most of them were experiencing a bitterly cold winter for the first time did not help either. Scurvy and the cold took their toll.

The units of galvanized Yankees were mustered out of service in November 1866. Those who could, returned home, but many had nothing to return to; their homes had possibly been destroyed, their land confiscated, and they were unwilling to face the condemnation of family and friends, for having been "galvanized." Instead, they joined the throngs moving into the Western territories, sometimes even changing their names to erase former identities. Here, they shared in the hopes of so many others, settling down with a new identity and a fresh start.

Interstate 65: Riddle Me Free

In 1857, the Reverend Horace Atwater of Rhode Island toured the South where he came face to face with the realities of slavery. All that winter, Horace wandered through the Southern states, sometimes preaching, other times soaking up the Southern experience. He attended slave auctions and burials, but the most lasting impression seems to have been of the cavalcades on the roads, of young slaves tied or chained together, forced to walk hundreds of miles to their new masters on plantations in places like Alabama and Georgia.

Interstate 65

One of the sad sights which often meet the eye reminding the stranger that he is in a foreign land, is the slave coffles, on their sad march from the blue hills and sunlit valleys of Virginia, Kentucky, and Tennessee, where they have spent their childhood, and leave parents and friends, for the dreaded plantations of those States, bordering on the Mexican Gulf. The practice of collecting droves of cattle, horses, and hogs, in the free States, for the great markets of Philadelphia, New York, and Boston, is just the counterpart of the collecting of these droves, of human cattle, for the great markets, in the South and South West.[65]

While much of the corridor Interstate 65 occupies today from Gary, Indiana (Exits 262–253), to Mobile, Alabama (Exits 9–1), is a later trace on the landscape, sections, such as the Louisville to Nashville Turnpike, were well developed at the peak of the slave era and undoubtedly witnessed these tragic processions. In the 1800s, the I-65 corridor from Mobile, north through Montgomery (Exits 172–168) and Birmingham (Exits 264–252) to Tennessee, Kentucky, and Indiana did not exist as

A somewhat idyllic portrayal of runaway slaves crossing the Union lines, created by artist Edwin Forbes. (Courtesy of the Library of Congress.)

we know it today. Instead, spider webs of roads radiated outward from places like Montgomery, Alabama, and Louisville, Kentucky (Exits 136–125). In Kentucky's case, roads, such as the Cumberland Road and the Wilderness Road, tended to track east–west along the traces of the earliest pioneers. All along the I-65 corridor, water travel dominated in the early part of the nineteenth century, albeit in a somewhat disjointed fashion as travelers floated along interconnecting streams flowing in the direction they were headed. Interstate 65 crosses one of these streams— the Alabama River—at Mile Marker 173 and the Tensaw, Middle, and Mobile Rivers at Mile Markers 29, 28, and 25 respectively in Alabama. Further north, some roads, such as the Louisville to Nashville Turnpike, were privately developed for toll roads, which made road travel expensive. Built in 1833, the turnpike had toll booths every fifth of a mile. Stagecoach service ran three times a week with the three-day trip from Louisville to Nashville, Tennessee (Exits 88–82) costing twelve dollars. Then the railroads came along, supplanting river and road travel. From Northern Alabama onward, the I-65 corridor retraces these nineteenth century rail lines through Nashville, Louisville, Indianapolis (Exits 124–106), and onward toward Gary and Chicago.

By 1860, four million slaves kept the economies of fourteen states humming along, more precisely the livelihood of the hundreds of thousands of families who owned slaves. And then there were the thousands of small businesses that supplied goods and services to those slave-holding families. Throughout the South, slaves grew almost all the cotton, tobacco, hemp, rice, and sugar cane crops. Not all slaves worked in rural settings. Many found themselves rented out to factory owners to do the hard, often dangerous work in places like iron foundries. Riddles became a favorite of many slaves while they worked, the riddle itself being a wish for freedom. The person solving the riddle would be free.

Was 12 pear hanging high
And 12 pear hanging low.
Twelve kings came riding by.
Each, he took a pear.
How many pears were left hanging there?

Even before the Civil War broke out, many African Americans took the Underground Railroad northward to freedom, frequently traveling the interconnected waterways along the I-65 trace so they would not be detected by bloodhounds. One famous stop on the Underground Railroad sits about sixty-five miles east of I-65 in Indiana off Exit 112. Levi and Katie Coffin, of Fountain City, helped more than two thousand slaves escape between 1826 and 1847. Their activities were controversial at a time when Indiana, as a border state between the polarized free and slave states, was split in its support of slavery. Pro-slavery advocates even managed to make it illegal in Indiana to aid an escaped slave. Many Southern planters tried to relocate their slaves to "safety" as the war approached. (Texas was a popular choice.) But, if the slaves got wind of a relocation, they frequently ran away, rather than risk even worse conditions.

The trickle of slaves escaping northward became a deluge with the outbreak of the Civil War. While many accompanied their masters when they marched off to war, continuing in their role as a servant, others labored in the fields and factories to keep the Confederate Army provisioned. In some places, authorities put slaves to work building defenses. In the eyes of the North, this made them war booty when captured and therefore not something that needed to be returned. The Confiscation Act of 1861 made it official and those slaves and their families who did escape beyond Union lines were declared free. Many served Union forces as servants. African Americans were finally allowed to enlist in late 1862, but, if captured, Confederate soldiers refused to treat them as prisoners of war, frequently killing them or trying them as runaway slaves.

As the war drew to a close, many freed slaves found themselves working on confiscated plantations in much the same manner as they had before, only this time they were called sharecroppers. Others looked northward for a better life, aided by Emancipation in 1863. After the war, economic opportunities were few, least of all for African Americans— menial jobs, laborers, domestics, sharecropping—the bondage continued. Changes in agricultural practices also contributed to the migration to urban centers in the North. As horse and mule power gave way to gas or steam-powered tractors, fewer workers were needed. In the South, African Americans increasingly left rural areas and headed for the cities and industrial or service jobs. In Birmingham, Alabama, the African American population more than doubled from fifty-two thousand in 1910 to one hundred and nine thousand in 1940.

While the lynch mentality and worsening economic conditions, has-tened by the boll weevil, pushed, the lure of better homes and wages pulled thousands of African American families northward to the prom-ised land. This exodus between the end of the Civil War and the onset of the Great Depression became known as the Great Migration. Rail-roads tracing what is now I-65 became a major corridor in this migra-tion northward. Many African Americans hopped on board freight cars or rode in segregated train coaches. The railroads along the I-65 trace also proved to be a major conduit for word-of-mouth dissemination of information about the North from African American porters and train attendants. Not only were these employees important role models for those wanting to leave the South, they also spread the word all along the rail lines about opportunities in the North. Some distributed African American newspapers, such as the *Chicago Defender*, to passengers on their trains. The *Defender* urged African Americans to vote with their feet and head north. To help the process along, the newspaper routinely published thousands of job ads for all kinds of positions. Improved bus service and more affordable automobiles hastened the exodus. Near the northern end of I-65, Chicago's African American population grew from just over forty-four thousand in 1910 to over two hundred and seventy-seven thousand in 1940. Many others did not make it all the way to Chicago, preferring to try their luck in places like Indianapolis and Gary, Indiana. One African American by the name of O'Dell Willis remembered his trip north by bus. The driver turned to him and said, "You don't have to sit in the back anymore. We've crossed the Mason-Dixon line. You're free to sit where you want." O'Dell thought about it for a minute and then as he later recounted, he "sat in the front seat for the first time."[66] O'Dell had solved the riddle.*

Interstate 59: Pine Tonic

In 1827, Frances Trollope spent Christmas in New Orleans. While she enjoyed the novelty of fresh fruit and vegetables in December, and the pleasant temperatures, she found the incessant mosquitoes unbearable.

---

* There were twenty-four pears to start. A man named Each took a pear, which left twenty-three. As described in Hamilton, *The People Could Fly: American Black Folk-tales*, chapter 1.

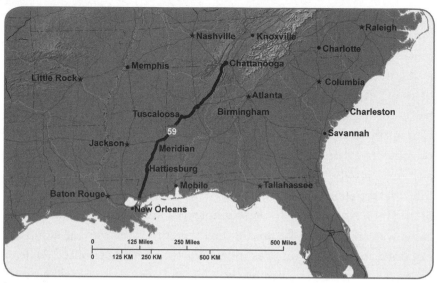

Interstate 59

In the summer, it was even worse. People also believed that the "prolific and exuberant" vegetation of the warmer months was naturally "counterbalanced by chills and fevers."[67] Anyone with the means escaped in summer for the cooler, presumably mosquito-free, and healthier pine-covered mountains of Georgia, the Carolinas, Tennessee, and Virginia. All over the South, well-to-do households packed up and headed inland in an annual summer migration to mountain aeries. "Here came in the summer-time the Southern planters in coach and four, with a great retinue of household servants, and kept up for months that unique social life, a mixture of courtly ceremony and entire freedom, the civilization which had the drawing-room at one end and the negro-quarters at the other."[68] Those making this great summer migration could take the waters of mountain springs, luxuriate in health spas of their day, and entertain themselves at well-appointed hotels. A mountain resort and spring could heal just about anything. They were

> cathartic, diuretic and tonic. Their main efficacy appears to depend on their laxative and purgative operations by which the alimentary canal is excited to copious secretions, and the secretory functions of the liver and pancreas are stimulated to pour out appropriate fluids. . . . This effect is the happiest sort. It may be said, in popular language, that the system is cleaned out and built up at the same

time and thus renewed by a process which is all the time exhilarating and agreeable.[69]

For those heading to the spa from New Orleans, the direct line northeast to these mountain retreats afforded by today's Interstate 59 did not exist. Instead, the journey involved coastal passage to Mobile and then up through Alabama on the Mobile River, or a steamboat trip up the Mississippi River to a place like Memphis and overland into the mountains. In later years, a railroad link from New Orleans, through Jackson, Mississippi, connected in Atlanta with stagecoach routes and other rail lines into the mountains. In January 1828, it took Frances Trollope about nine days to get from New Orleans to Memphis by riverboat. Here, she lost both her shoes and gloves to the mud in scrambling up the riverbank into town. Frances continued up the Mississippi, but most ladies

A packed coach heading into the mountains for some pine tonic.

*Here are belles from the city, with beaux in
their train,
Here are dowager dames, here are pretty and plain,
Health, pleasure, or fortune, each one tries to gain,
So they come to the Springs*

—**Gilman (1838: 348)**

of her era heading to the mountains climbed into a carriage in Memphis
for the cross-country trip. In her memoirs, New Orleans native Eliza
Ripley recounted her summers in the 1840s spent in hill country. Every
year, her family traveled up the Mississippi River, disembarked in Kentucky, and then headed cross-country by coach. "When I was a little girl
. . . mother made me, for the summer romps in the country, gloves that
well covered the wrist, had a hole for the thumb and a deep flap to fall
over the hand . . . I hated them and had a way of losing them in the currant bushes. . . . If I lost my scoop sunbonnet one day—and how easily
I lost it!—it was sewed on the next."[70]

By the time summer pilgrims like Eliza and her family arrived at their
mountain destination, they had skirted malaria-infested lowlands, been
scared to death by the narrow winding mountain roads, coped with broken wagon wheels and skittish horses, were frequently coated in dust or
mud, had dealt with motion sickness, spent about a week on a steamboat or train, another week being jostled about in a carriage, and had
slept in private homes along the way or in their carriage. They came in
droves.

It is a different story today. From just outside New Orleans, I-59 cuts
kitty-corner through the forested heart of Mississippi past Hattiesburg
(Exits 60–67), Meridian (Exits 150–154 on the combined I-59/I-20), and
Birmingham (Exits 132–124 on the combined I-59/I-20) and on into
the Appalachians in a fairly direct line, ending in the hills near Chattanooga, Tennessee. The journey that would have taken Frances Trollope two weeks can now be accomplished in less than a day. As for Eliza
Ripley, she continued to visit the mountain resorts well into her senior
years. But a lot had changed. Eliza was appalled at the freedoms her
granddaughters expected. While her mother protected Eliza's skin and

complexion from the sun, the Eliza of 1912 was shocked at the cavalier attitude of young girls vacationing in the mountains.

> I see young society girls, educated girls who ought to have known better, with bare head and arms playing tennis in the hot sun; and worse still, racing over the golf links. . . . I tell my grandchildren who want to "do like other girls" that is not the way "other girls" did in my day. Grandma may be so old that she forgets, but she moralizes all the same. These girls come back to city homes so sunburnt and with such coarse skin they have to repair to a skin specialist . . . and be polished up before the society season opens.[71]

Of the hundreds of mountain resorts and health spas that once nourished the souls of Southern planters and the local economies, only a few remain. The rest have disappeared; memories of some live on in the name of a country road or small hamlet. The Civil War and subsequent recession ended the viability of many of these resorts; others burned to the ground and were never rebuilt. For some, being bypassed by a railroad or upgraded road spelled the end, just as interstate routings one hundred years later ended the viability of many of the next generation of hotels in the towns and cities no longer on a main thoroughfare. The grounds many of these long-ago resorts occupied are now part of protected forests and state and national parks, attracting yet another generation of summer migrants, this time with camping gear or luxury RV, but still seeking the tonic of the mountains. "'Rest,' the pines say . . . 'the noises and the cares that have infested the life elsewhere come not here. Rest. And be healed by day. Sleep, and be healed by night.'"[72]

Interstate 27: The Sweep of a Hand

On the plains of West Texas they like to tell the story of the creation of their unique landscape. It seems God was nearing the end of a full workday. As dusk approached, he gave the earth one final creative sweep with his hand and, yawning, decided to finish the job the next morning. But come sunrise the landscape he had been working on the day before had hardened into a dry plateau. How was he going to add in lush forests and beautiful, blue lakes? After some thought, God decided the only solution was to create some people who would fall in love with this

Interstate 27

arid plateau. And that is how cowboys and oil workers came to populate West Texas.

That dry plateau, populated with just enough special people to make it work, is called the Llano Estacado. Interstate 27 from Lubbock (Exits 1–10) to Amarillo (Exits 116–123) skirts its eastern edge for one hundred and twenty-four miles. Also called the Staked Plains, this level, semi-arid plateau averages about 3,450 feet above sea level along I-27, increasing slightly in elevation from the southern to the northern end of the interstate. Here and there, small draws or creeks cross under the interstate, notably Palo Duro Creek just north of Exit 106 and Running Water Draw at Exit 49. While the soils are potentially fertile, there is so little rainfall—about nineteen inches a year along the I-27 corridor—and so much evaporation that much of the area is used for grazing, with some dry-land farming, sorghum production, and irrigated cotton, and of course the petroleum and natural gas industry.

In his travels through the South in 1873 with author Edward King, artist James Wells Champney interpreted his surroundings in finely detailed drawings for *Scribner's Monthly*, a news and literary magazine of its time. In their own ways with pen and ink, Edward and James recorded their impressions of everything they saw: landscapes, buildings, various means of transportation, and street scenes. But for both men, travel in America held a human element—the people they met along the way, whether it was sharing a meal with them, observations made at a distance, or individuals they stopped to interview. While Horace Greeley commented sometimes superficially on many of the people he encountered, James and Edward preferred to sketch more complete portraits of those they met at work and in various everyday activities. Some they skewered into caricatures or injected with the stereotypes of their day; others they portrayed with a great deal of empathy and sensitivity.

On a train ride through Texas, the two men observed one of those special people from West Texas—a drover. This was an opportunity not to be passed up since as Edward put it, West Texas seemed to produce a "more highly-colored, vivid, and dramatic manner of talk"[73] than anywhere else, probably, he assumed because of the Spanish and Mexican influence in that area. Edward described the subject of their interest as "robust and perfectly formed," with a "certain chivalrous grace and freedom" in his movements. "His cleancut face was framed in a dark, shapely beard and moustache, which seemed as if blown backward by the wind. He wore a broad hat with a silver cord around it, and I felt impelled to look for his sword, his doublet, and his spurs, and to fancy that he had just stepped out of some Mexican romance."[74]

A Texan Cattle-Drover.

James Champney's illustration of one of God's special people. (Courtesy of Documenting the American South, University of North Carolina at Chapel Hill.)

Edward and James continued to observe the drover's conversation with an acquaintance, making it part of an article they were preparing for *Scribner's Monthly*. "His conversation was upon horses, his clear voice ringing high above the noise of the car-wheels, as he laughingly recounted anecdotes of adventures on ranches in the west, nearly every third word being an oath. He caressingly cursed; he playfully damned; he cheerfully invoked all the evil spirits that be; he profaned the sacred name, dwelling on the syllables."[75] The conversation finally came to an end and the subject of their interest walked off cursing "as heartily as an English boatswain in a storm."[76] Edward and James continued westward seeing enough of Texas to make for entertaining reading for *Scribner's Monthly* subscribers. Their portrait of the West Texas cattle drover appeared in the February 1874 issue.

Interstate 17: The Veil of Mystery

Local residents boast that they can swim in an outdoor pool in Phoenix (Exits 195–215) in the morning in the hot dry desert environment and ski in Flagstaff (Exits 339–341) in the afternoon, switching seasons—

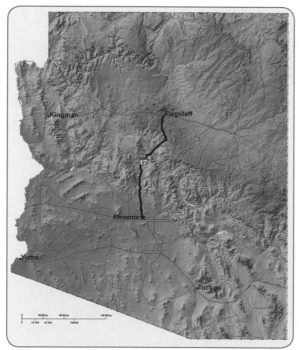

Interstate 17

The fictional Hettie and Ina Ide headed to Arizona in a rig similar to the one pictured here, perched at the edge of the change in elevation along the future I-17 corridor circa 1903. (Courtesy of the Library of Congress.)

and topography—in a couple of hours. Interstate 17 provides the seasonal progression between the two cities—and between the east–west I-10 at Phoenix and I-40 at Flagstaff. Along its 145-mile length, I-17 climbs over a mile in altitude, from 1,117 feet above sea level in Phoenix to over 7,000 feet in Flagstaff. The interstate travels through Black Canyon, wedged between the Bradshaw Mountains to the west and the New River Mountains to the east. Near the exit to Prescott (Exit 278), I-17 ascends the Mogollon Plateau or Mogollon Rim. Here, travelers leave the desert topography and continue the ascent into the forested landscape of the Coconino National Forest for the balance of the trip to Flagstaff. In a departure from usual interstate practices, scenic overlooks allow I-17 motorists to stop and take in the changing landscape.

But consider two descriptions from another era of the desert as it appeared south of Phoenix and as viewed from the Mogollon Rim. In the 1870s, Samuel Cozzens, a retired judge, decided to spend three years traveling through New Mexico and Arizona. His interest had been tweaked by these new territories that settlers were starting to consider, and Samuel kept notes of everything he saw and did, eventually publishing a book about his travels. Samuel's prose gave his readers a peek into a landscape still relatively new in the American experience. One night, Samuel wandered away from camp. "I fancied myself shut out from the whole world, wrapped in an impenetrable veil of mystery. Scarcely a breath of air sighed. . . . Even the melancholy chirp of the cricket was hushed; the cuckoo and the plaintive whip-poor-will had forgotten their songs, not even the rustle of a leaf disturbed the quiet which reigned supreme."[77]

Novelist Zane Grey lived in Arizona for many years and lovingly incorporated the Arizona landscape into many of his books. In one novel, Grey spoke through Hettie Ide, a new settler from California. Grey positioned Hettie on a large rock on the edge of the Mogollon Plateau looking over the desert. Like Samuel, Hettie was seeing the Arizona landscape for the first time.

> How the summer winds roared above and back of her, now low, now high, deepening upward with the denser growth of forest!
>
> But it was the desert that enchanted Hettie. . . . Yet how soft, how marvelously purple and gray, how grandly the slope fell for league on league, widening, rolling, lengthening, descending, down to the blazing abyss of sage and rock and canyon.
>
> Sage and grass in the foreground gave that vast valley its softest beauty, its infinite charms, its mistiness and brilliance, as if drenched with dew. How like troops of great beasts appeared the isolated green cedars and the lonely jutting rocks, some gray, others red. This valley was a portal down to the dim unknown. On each side it swelled to ranges of foothills, themselves like trains of colossal camels trooping down to drink. They were rounded, soft as clouds, gray and pink and faintly green, without a tree, a rock to mar their exquisite curve.[78]

Zane Grey had Hettie and her mother, Ina, travel from California, by horse and wagon, seeking a healthier climate for Ina. Their trip across the Mogollon Plateau, was not the two-hour jaunt today's I-17 motorists enjoy.

> The travelers rode into rough forest land, where the main grade was uphill, but the apology for a road plunged down so often into dry hot ravines that the general ascent had to be taken for granted.

The forest consisted of cedars, oaks, piñons, and scattered pines. . . . Travel was exasperatingly slow. In some places the road was not safe, and the women had to get out and walk. . . . At length the cedars and piñons gave place to a heavier growth of pines. Here the real forest began, and except for the difficulty of travel, it was vastly satisfying to Hettie.[79]

On the desert floor, Samuel Cozzens found the landscape and the slumbering air oppressive. "Nature seemed not only to have lost her voice, but to have plunged into an eternal sleep, from which there was no awakening—a slumber at once so painful and mysterious, that I could have easily fancied the whole world dead, and I alone the only living, breathing thing left upon its pulseless surface . . . I felt as though a nightmare was oppressing me." Samuel sat there, fighting the impending sense of doom. Then suddenly, "the quick, snarling bark of a coyote, upon some far-off mesa, fell upon my ear." Samuel snapped out of his trance-like state and with "a thrilling sense of freedom and relief," sprang to his feet and made his way back to camp.[80]

Hettie Ide found the opposite while climbing the Mogollon Plateau. "The air grew clearer, less oppressive. . . . Massed foliage, like green lace, dark-brown seamed boles of pines, patches of sunlight on the white grass, the red of a tufted flower, like a stiff brush dipped in paint, and golden aisles of needles up and down the forest held . . . a never-failing delight."[81] As the sun set, she too experienced Samuel's veil of mystery. "A glory of gold and purple cloud . . . distant, broken, carved, where a lilac haze in transparent veils and rays spread from the sinking sun. She looked through that haze into an obscurity baffling and compelling, where shadows might be mountains and the purple depths beyond conception."[82]

Interstate 5: Celestials and Terrestrials

In the late 1850s, owners of the Central Pacific Railway were struggling to complete the railroad track eastward from Sacramento, California (Exits 513–531), across the Sierra Nevadas, in a corridor similar to that of today's I-80. It was a catch-22 situation of needing money to finance construction, but not being able to get the financing without a certain amount of track laid. Then, one of the principals of the company had

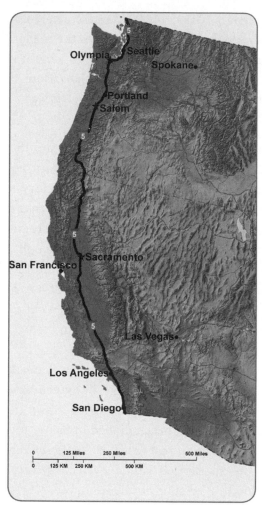

Interstate 5

a brain wave, albeit one that bought into the prejudicial, stereotypical ideas of the times. Why not hire Chinese immigrants? Yes, they were small in stature and did not weigh very much, but surely if the Chinese people could build the Great Wall of China, they could build a railroad. And yes, conditions for the construction crews bordered on slave labor camps, but thousands of Chinese immigrants had already arrived in Northern California where they worked as domestics and gardeners. Here was a ready labor pool ripe for exploitation.

It happened over and over all along the Pacific Coast. Throughout the area served by today's Interstate 5 from the Washington–British Columbia border to the California–Mexico border, immigrants filled many of the menial jobs Americans either did not want or for which there were

"Celestials" preparing to flee to safety in the wake of anti-Chinese demonstrations in Seattle in March 1886. (Courtesy of the University of Washington Libraries, Special Collections Division.)

not enough workers to fill the demand. In the case of the railroad company official, he insisted that fifty Chinese immigrants be given jobs. It cost about forty dollars per person for passage from Hong Kong on a freighter, which the hiring company willingly paid. The company then allowed the Chinese laborer to work off his passage for one hundred dollars. How could a business lose? Chinese crews quickly outperformed their white counterparts and by the time construction ended in 1869, over twelve thousand Chinese laborers worked for the railroad. Not only did they work harder than their American counterparts, but they were less prone to sanitation-related diseases, mainly because they insisted on being able to wash up after a day's hard work, and they drank tea, which meant boiled water. Their diet of vegetables, rice, and dried fruits was also healthier than the carbohydrate-rich but nutritionally poor American diet of beans and bread. Chinese laborers quickly gained a nickname: the celestials. Their American counterparts became the terrestrials. When the railroad to California was completed, many Chinese laborers moved north to railroad construction sites in such places as Spokane and Seattle.

The thousands of Chinese laborers pouring into California sent for their families, establishing vibrant communities in places like San Francisco (via Exit 522 to I-80). Here, many established some form of retail operation, whether it was a restaurant, a vending cart selling sweet-meats, or a store with trade goods from Asia. But while people enjoyed the cuisine and snapped up the likes of jade and rice paper paintings, they still did not recognize the Chinese people as equals. Chinese residents were not allowed to stake a goldfield claim or become American citizens. From the growing Chinese community in San Francisco, Chinese immigrants fanned out up and down the coast, taking whatever jobs would give them an economic toehold in their new country.

In 1899, Rudyard Kipling headed north from San Francisco to fish. He took a coastal steamer to Portland, Oregon (Exits 295–308), where he visited a fish-packing house on the coast. He found the plant completely staffed by Chinese immigrants who with an economy of motion, beheaded, gutted, and canned salmon. Rudyard "was impressed not so much with the speed of the manufacture as the character of the factory. Inside on a floor ninety by forty, the most civilized and murderous of machinery. Outside, three footsteps, the thick-growing pines and the immense solitude of the hills."[83]

Rudyard rented a carriage, and with two companions, headed out to a fishing hole. "Half a mile from this city of fifty thousand souls we struck (and this must be taken literally) a plank road that would have been a disgrace to an Irish village."[84] After the plank road came six miles of macadamized roads—the 1899 version of I-5 in Oregon, winding along the Willamette River (I-5 crosses the river at Mile Marker 282.5), with many farm wagons heading to town with "bunches of tow-haired, boggle-eyed urchins sitting in the hay behind," [85] But Rudyard decided to exit his "interstate" and take a side road to the fishing hole. Here, he found little evidence of road making. "There was a track—you couldn't well get off it, and it was all you could do to stay on it."[86] Today, Rudyard's "track" is probably a street in Portland.

In nearby Washington State, terrestrial anger against Native Americans and Chinese celestials working in the fishing, lumber, and service industries eventually boiled over in a 1919 general strike. The Chinese had come to work on the railroads and done the unthinkable—they had stayed! They had become good, hard-working members of communities up and down the I-5 trace, but they were perceived as taking jobs away from "real Americans." Sino-phobia forced many Chinese laborers out of their jobs. It had happened before—and would happen again. Generations earlier, Spanish priests had busily herded Native Americans into the missions along today's I-5 in Southern California to see to their well-being. The Native Americans found their day ordered by the mission bells: bells for meals, for work, for prayer. It was a regimented existence beyond their comprehension. Not only did they work to provide food for the mission, they often worked to produce the goods the mission sold to make money, whether it was soap, weaving, adobe bricks, or olive oil. Overseers were sometimes very cruel in enforcing the work schedule. By 1823, twenty-one missions stretched from San Diego (Exits 1–26) to Sonoma north of San Francisco; more than twenty-one thousand Native Americans lived and worked at the missions, producing the trade goods necessary to keep the California economy going. As elsewhere in the mission system, workers were not paid. But as settlers poured into California, the demand for land overwhelmed the mission system, which occupied the choicest real estate along the coast. The Mexican government ordered an end to the missions in 1833, virtually destroying the lives of the thousands of Native Americans who had lived and worked under the mission system. Wealthy settlers took over mission lands and Native Americans choosing to stay with the land became peons. Most migrated inland.

Then along came the waves of immigration in the latter half of the nineteenth century, and with it demand for more laborers to provide the comforts of life. From their base in San Francisco, Chinese immigrants made their way south along the I-5 trace into various aspects of the service industry as gardeners, domestic servants, hotel and restaurant staff, and launderers. They also provided much of the labor in the fledgling vegetable, fruit, and flower industries of Southern California. Gradually, Chinese immigrants and their families of the mid-1800s made their way up through the economic food chain, the jobs they had abandoned now taken over by new waves of immigrants from Asia, Mexico, and Europe. Between 1908 and 1913, about five thousand men, many of them immigrants, labored every day to build the aqueduct needed to supply the growing Los Angeles area (and ensure its continued growth) with water. Part of the job entailed tunneling through five miles of mountain north of the city. Food would not keep in the desert heat, so these men were frequently served spoiled food. Through a labor strike and fatalities, somehow, those in charge managed to keep the project going. The Big Ditch officially opened in November 1913.

With the onset of the Great Depression, thousands emigrated west from the dust bowl states in search of work. Suddenly, California officials had more than a million migrants on their hands. Then World War II broke out and there were more jobs than there were workers. Those of Japanese heritage living in I-5 states were moved inland to relocation camps for the duration of the war. Meanwhile, the migrant Americans working in the fields enlisted or took factory jobs for the defense industry. Mexicans took their place in the fields. A new era of migration along the I-5 trace had begun.

Interstate 93: Melvina and Laura, Sarah and Grace

Critics complained that she wrote like a man; fans put the book on the top of the bestseller list for two years. Few confessed to having read it, yet everyone was reading it! "It" was *Peyton Place* by Grace Metalious, a thirty-two-year-old mother of three and "housewife" from a small town in New Hampshire. The book's opening pages introduce its main characters and the setting in the fall of 1936, a time when young women from Peyton Place dreamed of a nice wedding, a husband who worked at the local mill, a handful of children, and life as a stay-at-home mom. Those who wanted to leave dreamed of the big city and a job as a clerk—where they would find a husband and settle down to become stay-at-home moms. Some left town to "visit" with family elsewhere while they delivered children out of wedlock. For Allison MacKenzie of Peyton Place, future dreams included life as a famous novelist in the big city of New York City. A husband would be nice, but was not essential.

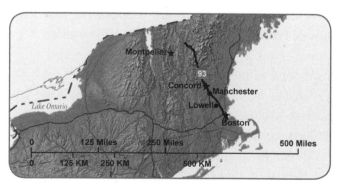

Interstate 93

Melvina and Laura, mill hands in the spinning room of the Amoskeag Manufacturing Company of Manchester, New Hampshire, photographed on May 21, 1909, by Lewis Wickes Hines. (Courtesy of the Library of Congress.)

A century earlier, young women all over New England had similar aspirations, but many of them flocked to mills in a handful of cities along what is today's Interstate 93—places like Manchester, New Hampshire (Exits 13–9) and Lowell, Massachusetts (Exit 44). It was hard, demanding work, but also a way to earn enough money to get a marriage off on the right foot financially, or support their siblings and parents still at home.

For the young women of Grace Metalious' *Peyton Place*, the way out of town was over a winding gravel road that led to other very similar small towns nestled in New England's mountains; the other alternative was to take a train. The story had been much the same a century earlier. Most young women walked or took a carriage ride to the nearest train station for the trip south to a job in a mill. In the earliest days, along what is today's I-93 corridor from Vermont to Massachusetts, mill jobs were not that far away. In 1830s Vermont, there were eighty textile mills plus knitting factories. Then the grasslands of the West opened up where larger flocks of sheep could roam freely with less supervision and care, and the wool could be sold more cheaply. Farmers from Vermont and nearby New Hampshire listened to Horace Greeley and headed west. Many smaller mills shut down and the young women moved to larger

Interstate 93, as it travels through Franconia Notch, is the only two-lane stretch of interstate in the nation. Engineers pressed for four lanes, but environmentalists recognized the need to protect the valley. Environmentalists won. The result: two lanes, no passing, no left turns.

mills in places like Manchester. Millwork was considered a better future than life on a struggling Vermont or New Hampshire farm. In a situation quite different from conditions immigrant laborers found on the Pacific Coast, paternalistic mill owners in New England often provided housing, recreation, and cultural events, and a job. They built boarding houses for the girls and strictly enforced regulations to ensure that only respectable young women were employed. Older women, usually widows, kept the boarding houses.

While mill hands Melvina and Laura had different last names, they lived near the Amoskeag mill at the same address in Manchester, possibly indicating that, in their case, an extended family all worked at the mill. Their last names indicate their families had been part of the large French-Canadian migration to mill jobs in Vermont and New Hampshire. In Melvina and Laura's time, the route south from Quebec to these mill towns was well served by rail. Places like Manchester where Melvina and Laura ended up could be reached in a couple of days from Montréal. If you were a lady of means, the rail company provided a ladies-only car, where you could relax in a parlor setting and enjoy a cup of tea. If you were a mill girl, you sat on a rough wooden bench in the coach clutching your belongings. Rail travel was a more practical alternative to the rugged conditions on the road traced by today's I-93.

Once in Manchester, Melvina and Laura became two of the more than seventeen thousand workers at the Amoskeag Manufacturing Company. Started in 1838, the company operated thirty mills in the area, producing cotton and woolen textiles. By the time Melvina and Laura went to work for the company, it was the largest textile producer in the world, turning out more than five million yards of cloth every week. To put the weekly tally in perspective, that is the equivalent of 2,841 miles of cloth or fifteen trips on I-93 from end to end.

Sarah Hale had another passion: poetry. She is the author of "Mary Had a Little Lamb."

A 1907 labor law restricted the hours women and children could be made to work to fifty-eight a week. Soon, lower wages in Southern mills, the invention of rayon, and the unwillingness of companies to modernize sounded the death knell for textile mills all over New England. In 1936, Amoskeag shut down, putting eleven thousand people out of work. A group of Manchester citizens subsequently acquired the old mill property and leased space to small companies wanting to set up shop in Manchester. They managed to attract more than one hundred businesses.

For another young woman of Manchester, mill work was not an option, the mills did not yet exist when her life went into crisis mode. In 1823, Sarah Josepha Hale found herself a widow and mother of five children. She was thirty-four years old and very good at keeping house and raising children. What was unusual in Sarah was her education. In an era when girls learned to read and write, if they were lucky, Sarah's brother had recognized the thirst for knowledge in his sister. He came home each evening from his classes at Dartmouth College and taught his sister

> Women in 1900 could not vote, enter a club, restaurant, saloon, tobacco shop, or hotel unless escorted by a male. Yet over five million women worked away from home in shops, factories, and offices—eighteen percent of the total U.S. workforce.

everything he had learned that day. Now Sarah needed to support her family. She tried a millinery shop. That did not work. Then along came the opportunity to edit a ladies' magazine in Boston. She placed four of her five children with relatives and headed to Boston to edit a magazine designed to further the education of women.

Today's I-93 continues south from Manchester past other former mill towns like Lowell and Lawrence (Exit 44) before going underground in the Big Dig across Boston. Melvina and Laura's families probably stopped at the first large mill town they encountered—Manchester—because mills were always hiring. Other mill girls came from further away; the Irish potato famine sent many young women and their families to New England mills. Posters in English and Scottish mills advertised jobs in the textile mills of New Hampshire, with good wages for spinners, weavers, and dyers.

Francis Cabot Lowell founded his textile mill in Massachusetts in 1814—the first to turn raw cotton into cloth all under one roof. It did not take long for the new town of Lowell to became a major textile and industrial center. By the time British author Anthony Trollope toured the mills in Lowell, they had been churning out textiles for fifty years. He was surprised by the appearance of the women and girls working in the mills. "They are not only better dressed, cleaner, and better mounted in every respect than the girls employed at manufactories in England, but they are so infinitely superior as to make a stranger immediately perceive that some very strong cause must have created the difference. . . . They are not sallow, nor dirty, nor ragged, nor rough."[87]

Just down the road in Boston, mill girls could earn considerably more money working on stage. In the 1880s, an entrepreneur by the name of B.F. Keith began producing wholesome family-oriented shows in Boston that became known as vaudeville. But if you happened to add pretty women in skimpy costumes that just happened to come off, you had burlesque. Boston would never be the same!

> The men and women of Boston could no more do without their lectures than those of Paris could without their theatres. It is the decorous diversion of the best ordered of her citizens. The fast young men go to clubs, and the fast young women to dances, as fast young men and women do in other places that are wicked; but lecturing is the favorite diversion of the steady-minded Bostonian.[88]

Today, several interstate exits serve Manchester, New Hampshire. The Amoskeag mill buildings where Melvina and Laura worked were partially demolished over the years, but the home where the girls lived behind the mill appears to still stand as a residence. While I-93 loops around Manchester, its offspring, I-293, cuts through downtown Manchester over some of the former mill property and within a couple of blocks of where Melvina and Laura once worked and lived. Sarah Hale continued to edit *Godey's Lady's Book* until 1877, two years before her death at the age of ninety-one. During that time, she worked tirelessly to improve the welfare of women. She also successfully campaigned to have Thanksgiving declared a national holiday and began the drive to preserve Mount Vernon.

By following the lives of two very different fourteen-year-old girls from New Hampshire, Grace Metalious exposed daily life and its undercurrents in a small town through the residents' strengths and weaknesses. Grace wrote a sequel, following those young girls from *Peyton Place* into adulthood. As for her own fate, Grace's journey along the I-93 corridor eventually took her to Boston where, unable to overcome personal demons, she died in 1964.

Interstate 57: Cairo Bound

In 1890, the U.S. Census calculated that just under sixty-three million people lived in the United States. Yet only three years later, the paid attendance at the Columbian Exposition in Chicago almost reached twenty-six million. People came to ride the world's first Ferris wheel, with its cars as big as a modern-day bus, sample some new foods, in-

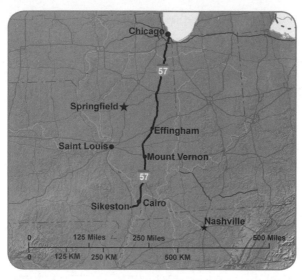

Interstate 57

cluding crackerjack and hamburgers, learn about the role of women in a modern society, and take in the wonders of the mechanical pavilions. Everywhere you turned, electricity and the idea of progress were intertwined. A seventy-foot tower of light bulbs drew millions as did the first phonographs and the telephone. In the Transportation Hall, the development of wheeled vehicles was there for all to see in a long line of handcarts, farm wagons, omnibuses, coaches, dogcarts, buggies, phaetons, hearses, sleighs, bicycles, wheelchairs, and baby carriages. If it rolled on a roadway, it was there—from all corners of the world. Russian carriages sat alongside sedan chairs from Colombia. But tucked in with centuries of wheeled history sat a new wonder: the electric carriage. The manufacturers of two electric carriages and an electric tricycle that had been included in the exhibit periodically took a display vehicle for a drive around the fairgrounds, especially if they sensed a sale. Horses stampeded to get out of the way, girls lined up to get a peek at the dashing driver and men rubbed their chins, contemplating how one of these new vehicles would look in the stable back home.

Visitors could also sample other cultures, through art, theatrical reviews, foods, and what would today be called a living-history display. Given the popularity of all things Egyptian at that time, one of these displays, in particular, became very popular: the "Street in Cairo" allowed visitors to wander through a Cairo marketplace, barter for goods, eat Egyptian fare, and see the North American debut of exotic dancing.

At 250 feet high, George Ferris' first wheel towered over the 1893 Columbia Exposition in Chicago. The Ferris wheel's thirty-six cars could each carry sixty persons and were about the size of a modern-day bus. (Courtesy of the Paul V. Galvin Library Digital History Collection, Illinois Institute of Technology.)

> Chicago is known as the "windy city" because of all the puffery and hot air expended by politicians and in the press to woo support for the Exposition. It has nothing to do with winds off Lake Michigan.

The World's Columbian Exposition in Chicago in 1893 shaped much of the century to come, and in many respects, set the stage for twentieth century interest in improved roadways which, in turn, spawned the interstate system. The Chicago of 1893 was an industrial hub for railroads, steel making, and grain, meat, and lumber trans-shipment. Its people reflected the decades of migration into the American West: By 1890, seventy percent of Chicago's population had either been born in another country or were the children of a foreign-born Chicagoan. It was a grimy, hard existence marred by slum conditions, and labor and civil unrest. Easterners routinely thumbed their noses at Chicago, so the city set out to improve its image with a world's fair.

While everything about the Exposition shouted technological progress, fair goers still got there the old-fashioned way—usually by steamship or rail, or a combination of the two. Special Exposition Flyers (trains) took fair goers from East-Coast cities to Chicago at the unheard of speed of eighty miles per hour. Westerners had a couple of railroads from which to choose. But for anyone coming up from the Southern states, the most viable option was the Central Illinois Railroad's steamship service from New Orleans with a switch to a railcar at Cairo, Illinois (Exit 1). The Central Illinois was a major north–south interstate of its time, connecting the Mississippi River system with a Great Lakes port.

Cairo (pronounced locally as Kay-ro) sits on a flat spit of land shaped like a slightly curved little finger where the Mississippi and Ohio Rivers meet. As such, Cairo flourished as a river town and major commercial hub for Southern Illinois and parts of Missouri and Kentucky. Its location also made the town an important military center during the Civil War.

From Cairo, the Central Illinois Railroad headed north to the Columbian Exposition along a trace similar to today's Interstate 57, depositing passengers at rail stations in Chicago, from which they could secure

> At the junction of the two rivers, on ground
> so flat and low and marshy, that at certain
> seasons of the year it is inundated to the housetops,
> lies a breeding-place of fever, ague, and death. . . . A
> dismal swamp, on which the half-built houses rot
> away: cleared here and there for the space of a few
> yards; and teeming, then, with rank, unwholesome
> vegetation, in whose baleful shade the wretched
> wanderers who are tempted here droop, and die, and
> lay their bones . . . a grave uncheered by any gleam of
> promise: a place without one single quality, in earth
> or air or water, to commend it: such is this dismal
> Cairo.
>
> —Charles Dickens, 1842 (1874: chapter 12)

> Cairo is a brisk town now; and is substantially built,
> and has a city look about it which is in noticeable
> contrast to its former estate, as per Mr. Dickens'
> portrait of it. . . . Her situation at the junction of the
> two great rivers is so advantageous that she cannot
> well help prospering.
>
> —Mark Twain, 1870 (1883: 117)

> The road in [to Cairo] was lined with battered houses
> and unpainted tenements. Aged black men sat on
> porches and stoops on old sofas and rocking chairs,
> waiting for death or dinner, whichever came first.
>
> —Bill Bryson, 1989 (1989: 52)

transit to a hotel or the fairgrounds. The Central Illinois still runs today, its tracks sitting to the west of I-57 until near Dongola (Exit 24) where I-57 takes a more easterly route toward Chicago. For much of their trace to Chicago, both roadways cut through what has been known since the first settlers arrived as Egypt or Little Egypt. A preacher visiting in 1799 seems to have made the first reference, calling the area the Land of Goshen, referred to in the Bible as the best land in Egypt, given to Joseph's family by the pharaoh. An incredibly bad winter in the northern part of Illinois in 1830–1831 led to wagon trains heading south into the Land of Goshen for much-needed food for both people and livestock, and seed for the coming spring. These settlers knew their Bible and referred to themselves as the sons of Jacob heading into Egypt to buy corn. Other Egyptian place names of that era soon appeared on the map: Dongola (Exit 24) and Karnak (Exit 18). The town of Thebes sits off to the west along the Mississippi River. And then there is Lake of Egypt Road (Exit 45) and the Lake of Egypt recreation area.

Interstate 57 continues northward across a narrow bay on Rend Lake (near Exit 77) through miles and miles of flat Illinois cornfields. Rend Lake did not exist in 1893 for Exposition travelers to admire; it was created by the U.S. Army Corps of Engineers, to ensure a dependable water supply in this area. Construction began in 1965 and the lake was filled in the early 1970s. Interstate 57 crosses through a state wildlife management area created as a result of the lake.

At Effingham (Exits 159–162), I-57 shares lanes with I-70 for a few miles before again turning northward to skirt around Champaign and Urbana (Exits 237–238). At this point, I-57 again parallels the tracks of the modern-day Illinois Central Railroad until the Chicago suburbs are reached near Exit 340. In Chicago, I-57 becomes part of the Dan Ryan Parkway, until it merges with I-94, not too far from the former Columbian Exposition grounds on Lake Michigan.

"Little Egypt, the Bewitching Bellyrina" was the name of the most famous "hootchie-kootchie" dancer at the Exposition. Some people disliked the idea of their part of Illinois being linked with a woman of "ill-repute" who wiggled the way Little Egypt did, but millions came to see her. Oscar Hammerstein hired her after the Exposition to play herself on Broadway; Hollywood made a film about her in the 1950s. Elvis Presley even sang about her in the 1964 movie, *Roustabout*. A generation later, Colonel Potter of "M*A*S*H" fame worried about the camp's water tower that had more shakes than Little Egypt.

A young woman, Johanna Wisthaler of New York, spent time at the Columbian Exposition, and recorded her impressions for a book. She loved the idea of being able to walk by castles and pagodas, learning about other manners of dress, foods, and customs. As for the "Street in Cairo," she found it imposing yet picturesque with upper stories over-

LITTLE EGYPT.

Newsboy

327

NEW YORK.

A photo of the legendary dancer, Little Egypt. (Courtesy of the New York Public Library.)

hanging shops selling goods from Egypt, Arabia, and Sudan. "Donkeys and camels were engaged in carrying visitors who chose to admire the busy thoroughfare seated on the backs of these animals. The native camel-drivers in their national costumes moved around and mingled with the strangers—which gave the populated street a peculiar charm to the eye."[89] While she saw replicas of the temple of Luxor, some fake mummies, and an Algerian and Tunisian village, propriety stopped her from commenting on any broadsheets advertising Little Egypt's show.

Like Johanna, people came to the Exposition to experience the world and all the new wonders of that world. Manufacturers took advantage of the crowds to introduce new products. Aunt Jemima syrup, cream of wheat, shredded wheat, Juicy Fruit gum, and Pabst beer all started appearing on American tables after the Exposition. The beautification of cities movement grew out of the fair, its grounds sculpted by Frederick Law Olmsted. The concept of an amusement park in beautifully landscaped grounds eventually led to the development of Disney World. Life changed in other ways. Columbus Day was first introduced as a holiday as a result of the Exposition. Scott Joplin played piano at the Exposition, working out a new form of music he called ragtime. The Pledge of Allegiance was introduced, and a young man by the name of L. Frank Baum stored up his impressions of the Exposition as inspiration for the Emerald City in *The Wizard of Oz*.

The Exposition represented a transitional phase for Americans. Its emphasis on the technology of the future wrapped up nicely in consumerism, helped craft the twentieth century as the United States slipped from an agrarian society to a technologically driven nation. It also marked a transition for America's roads. People went to the fair in the horse-and-buggy age and came away in the automobile age.

Coast to Coast
Automobile Traffic Begins

Get Out and Get Under

17458—"Why! Good Afternoon! Yes it is a shame,
He should have fixed that before we came."

"A dozen times they'd start to hug and kiss and then the darned old engine it would miss" (lyrics to a tune popular in 1913, Clarke and Leslie, no date). (Courtesy of the Library of Congress.)

IN 1900, there were forty-five states; the population was seventy-six million. The average hourly wage was twenty-two cents, and automobiles cost about fifteen hundred dollars. Some automobiles were even sold as kits for the new owner to assemble. Eight thousand cars shared the roads with fourteen million horses and hundreds of thousands of bicyclists. Trucks and buses had not been invented yet, and there were no gas stations. In many parts of the country, local residents viewed someone driving through town in an automobile with suspicion. The driver had to be a "shady" character or a millionaire with more money than sense. Vermont decreed that an adult waving a flag had to walk in front of every automobile. Tennessee required a week's notice if a motorist was going to take a trip. In Pennsylvania, the Farmers' Anti-Automobile Association advocated the use of Roman candles at night in rural areas. Motorists should send up a candle, wait ten minutes to make sure the road was clear and then proceed with caution, blowing the horn and sending up more Roman candles at appropriate intervals. Some cities banned them outright. San Diego set speed limits at eight miles per hour to try and control speed demons on bicycles. If found guilty, culprits could expect a fine of fifty dollars and up to thirty days in jail. Meanwhile in Chicago, six drivers took part in the first official automobile race on November 28, 1895 from Jackson Park (Chicago) to Evanston, Illinois, and back. J. Frank Duryea, developer of the first gasoline-powered vehicle won the fifty-four mile race (and $2,000). Today's I-94 traces the route that first automobile race followed. In California, the *Los Angeles Times* predicted that the "smart set of motoring"[1] would participate in the Los Angeles to Coronado endurance race. Thirty vehicles completed the 180 mile trip in two days. (Despite the fact that it was a race, participants respected the twenty miles per hour speed limit.) The third day, competitors raced on a one mile track in Coronado, much to the delight of spectators. Today, this route of a century ago has

The *Chicago Times-Herald* produced the first road map as we know it, in 1895, to identify the route for the Chicago to Evanston automobile race the newspaper sponsored.

been streamlined to 116 miles, easily completed in about 90 minutes, traffic permitting, on Interstate 5.

The next big automobiling challenge was an intercoastal drive. Alexander Winton, whose company was the leading manufacturer of automobiles in the United States, with production of 100 vehicles in 1899, attempted the first coast-to-coast road trip in 1901. Beginning in San Francisco, he made it into the Nevada desert—about five hundred miles—before getting hopelessly bogged down in sand and ending his quest after ten days.

A few years later, a young, recently married doctor from Vermont, Horatio Nelson Jackson, sat in a San Francisco gentleman's club sipping his drink and contemplating a challenge he had just accepted. He had put his money and his convictions on the line, having accepted a fifty dollar bet that he could drive an automobile across the United States from San Francisco to New York in three months. After explaining things to his wife, Horatio put her on a train for New York and started looking for an automobile to buy, but they were still so scarce that he had to settle for a used Winton with worn tires. Next, Horatio hunted up a bicycle mechanic who had some experience with gasoline engines and took a few quick driving lessons. Four days later, loaded down with all the equipment he thought they would need, Horatio and his mechanic left San Francisco.

In 1903, paved highways did not exist across the United States. There were two million miles of roads, but only about six percent, mostly in the East, were improved. The rest were little better than dirt paths. In the Connecticut Valley, now served by I-91, Boston and New York urbanites could ride in relative comfort on roads of gravel or macadam (a seven-to-ten-inch layer of tightly packed crushed rock covered with sand, clay, or finely crushed stone, which was then rolled into the crushed rock layer). This kind of roadbed was rare, so whether traveling in a comfortable carriage or new motorized vehicle, or on a bicycle, breakdowns were

J. Frank Duryea, winner of the first automobile race, sits holding the tiller of his vehicle. The gentleman in the bowler beside him is the race's umpire. It had taken nine hours in snow and a very cold wind to complete the fifty-mile course. (Courtesy of The Henry Ford.)

a fact of life: road surfaces and conditions simply could not handle a motor vehicle's speed. Getting out and under the automobile to see what was wrong became a regular occurrence.

Horatio and his mechanic/co-driver initially wandered around quite a bit, in part because road maps and directional road signs had not yet become commonplace. Their only navigational tool was a compass. The other part of the problem was the road network itself: it was not really a network. Roads had been built haphazardly, usually radiating out from population centers and frequently not connecting with anything in particular. After a rather lengthy jaunt north to find the easiest way across the mountains, and avoid the desert that had brought Alexander Winton's attempt to an end, Horatio and his mechanic eventually hooked up with what today is I-80 in Wyoming. It had taken them thirty-eight days to get this far. Here, they encountered some of the worst conditions: deeply rutted trails strewn with boulders and roads that were being used as irrigation ditches. At one point, Horatio tried driving cross country

The slough of despond. On a Michigan road in the early 1900s. (Courtesy of the Michigan Department of Transportation.)

using bundles of sagebrush under the wheels for traction. Every few days, they stopped to make repairs to the Winton or order new parts directly from the factory.

By Nebraska, mud posed the biggest obstacle. Nebraska had one of its wettest summers on record in 1903, and as Horatio wrote to his wife: "The mud was a cementlike mass that stuck to things like the best Portland. And it seemed to have no bottom. The car sank in it clear up to the battery boxes—that is, nearly to the tops of the wheels."[2] In a subsequent letter Horatio told his wife he was going to have "half a ton of Nebraska clay"[3] washed off the car. From Illinois eastward, Horatio called the roads child's play and the pair arrived in New York in the early morning of July 26, 1903. It had taken sixty-three days, twelve hours, and thirty minutes. Horatio won his bet (but never did collect his winnings). He reunited with his wife and became the darling of New York, enjoying his fifteen minutes of fame. His much-repaired Winton automobile eventually ended up in the Smithsonian. But Horatio obviously had the thrill of the open road in his blood. A few months later, he was arrested in Burlington, Vermont for breaking the speed limit of six miles per hour. He paid a five dollar fine plus court costs.

About the same time that Horatio Jackson was making history, a growing number of Florida car owners decided they had had enough. Florida's roadbeds frequently consisted of three to four inches of hard-packed sand, but rain turned these roads into quagmires, and in dry conditions it was not uncommon to have to pull off the road to let the dust from the sandy roadbed settle so the driver could see what was ahead. In 1909, eighteen car owners banded together to race from Tampa across Florida to Jacksonville. It was to be a round trip. The goal of the drivers—and of the newspapers sponsoring the race or vehicles in the race—was to raise public awareness about road conditions and lobby for better highways. Today, via I-95 and I-4 (or I-10 and I-75), the same journey takes about four and a half hours each way. In 1909, it took four days, and publicity from the race did prompt Florida to start building highways.

With people like Ransom Olds and Henry Ford turning manufacturing production lines on their ears with new techniques and lower costs, the automobile went from curiosity to commonplace. The rapidly growing number of automobile owners demanded road improvements, both to the road surface and in the creation of a network of roads that actually connected with each other, not ending in a farmer's barnyard as sometimes happened. The idea of a truly national, coast-to-coast highway did not occur to anyone until automotive accessories manufacturer Carl Fisher suggested one in 1912. His Indianapolis Motor Speedway was a success; why not build a highway spanning the nation to promote the automobile and a new age of travel in North America? Fisher and Henry Joy, president of the Packard Motor Car Company, wanted the most direct route possible. This was not to be a scenic tour; it was to be a direct, high-speed gravel roadway between New York and San Francisco. Communities along the selected route would receive free construction materials if they provided the equipment and manpower to build their portion of the highway. To assist in fund-raising and promote national awareness of the project, the decision was made to call the new road the Lincoln Highway. It would start in New York's Times Square, then head west in as direct a line as possible through Philadelphia, Pittsburgh, and Fort Wayne, around Chicago to Omaha, Cheyenne, Reno, and Sacramento to San Francisco.

On October 31, 1913, the *San Francisco Examiner* reported: "The Lincoln Highway, which promises to be a lasting monument to the automobile industry, and one of the greatest developments ever made in this country, will be officially dedicated tonight by every city, town and hamlet between New York and San Francisco. The widespread enthusiasm with which the highway project has been received throughout the country is the best indication of its ultimate success."[4]

By 1914, the word on the Lincoln Highway was concrete. A horse might not mind a dusty or muddy roadbed, but an automobile did. Henry Joy redirected his energies toward educating the country about the importance of concrete roadways and the need for federal involvement in road construction. To make his point, he had "seedling miles" of the new highway built with a concrete surface to show the nation the superiority of a paved road. The Lincoln Highway was completed in 1916, with some sections transgressing from the original routing as a result of political persuasion. For the first time, a truly national road existed. That year, an automobile drove the entire Lincoln Highway in five days; today, I-80 traces much of the same corridor.

In other places, terrain coupled with the automotive technology of the time proved the biggest obstacles. This was the case in San Diego.

> Pikes Peak, a mountain in Colorado accessible from I-25, is named after Zebulon Pike who explored the area in 1806. At fourteen thousand feet, Pike believed the mountain could not be scaled. With that kind of a challenge, early automobile enthusiasts set out to prove him wrong, holding races up its slopes. And, just to really prove him wrong, a Texan named Bill Williams pushed a peanut up Pikes Peak with his nose in 1929. It took twenty days and one hundred and seventy pairs of trousers before Bill and the peanut reached the summit.

The city sits on a strip of land bordering San Diego Bay hemmed in by a series of mountain ranges rising abruptly behind the Bay. In 1910, two young Texans, Harold and Bud, decided to drive to San Diego in a Model T Ford. But first, they had to get over the mountains. A Model T used gravity to feed gas into the carburetor. If the car had to go up too steep or too long an incline, the engine quit. Harold and Bud solved the problem by having Bud lie on a fender with a can of gas. As they made their way uphill, Bud poured gas into the carburetor as required to keep the engine running. It was a fairly risky solution; the road was rough and Bud could have been thrown off the fender. There was also the danger that with all the jostling he would accidentally pour gas on the hot engine, setting everything on fire, including himself. Harold and Bud, and the Model T made it, but they liked the view from the top of one mountain so well they pitched their tent and stayed a few days to admire the scenery and make repairs before continuing on to San Diego. Drivers on today's I-8 can admire the view Harold and Bud liked so well as they navigate across the mountains of Southern California toward San Diego.

The conditions Harold and Bud experienced in their motor trip to San Diego had long been a sore point with local residents, who began lobbying (and vying with Los Angeles) for a Southern transcontinental highway. The Dixie Overland Highway project began on the East Coast in Savannah in 1914 after the local automobile club went on a road trip across the state to Columbus on the Alabama border and discovered that roads only existed for about half of their journey. Club members decided to lobby for a road from Savannah to Columbus. But, if a road could be built across one state, why not across the country? Why not all the way to the Pacific? At that time, no road or railroad crossed the South from coast to coast. Other states along the proposed route were contacted and an association formed. Lobbying began in earnest. By February 1917, Georgia's portion of the Dixie Overland Highway was complete, including the road from Savannah to Macon, now I-16.

With the discovery of oil in Oklahoma and Texas, fuel for automobiles became very inexpensive. Trucks and buses began appearing on the nation's roadways, and automobiles became more reliable and comfortable. People could not wait to get their first automobile and enjoy the freedom of long distance travel, family road trips, and shopping ex-

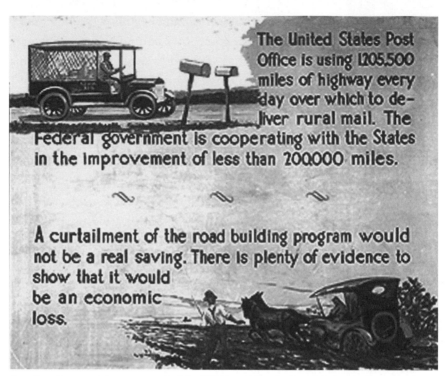

The United States Post Office is using 1,205,500 miles of highway every day over which to deliver rural mail. The Federal government is cooperating with the States in the improvement of less than 200,000 miles.

A curtailment of the road building program would not be a real saving. There is plenty of evidence to show that it would be an economic loss.

An advertisement that was part of the U.S. Postal Service's campaign to improve the nation's roads. (Used with the permission of the Online Image Gallery, American Association of State Highway and Transportation Officials, Washington, D.C.)

cursions downtown without having to hitch up the carriage. For women, it was not so much the ability to vote as it was their new runabout that gave them the freedom they so desired. Young people immediately recognized the advantages of the automobile in distancing themselves from parental control.

While the number of motor vehicles in operation continued to climb, roads still did not exist in parts of the country, particularly in desert locales or areas of sparse population like Arizona and Montana. In some places, plans to build highways did not materialize until the number of automobiles locally reached the point where roads became a necessity. Elsewhere, delivering mail became the impetus for road construction. The federal Rural Free Delivery Program stated that rural mail service would be offered along "good" roads. People living along roads that did not qualify started demanding repairs and upgrades to their roads. By 1903, eighty-six hundred mail carriers traveled two hundred thousand miles a day, serving five million people. The Federal Aid Law of 1916 provided states with funds to improve roads that were or could be used to deliver the mail between centers with a population of twenty-five hundred or more. This legislation set a spending cap of $10,000 per mile (except for bridges over twenty feet long). Since the roads were generally in rural areas, the Department of Agriculture provided road-building funds. The Post Office Appropriation Bill of 1919 upped the allowable cost per mile and extended the definition of eligible roads to include most roads used for postal delivery.

But despite these improvements, there was still no real network of roads. As did the mail, motorists traveled beyond county and state boundaries, but the roads they used did not always connect at a boundary between jurisdictions, and the quality varied considerably. Good roads associations popped up all over the country, generally promoted by rural residents wanting to end their isolation or businessmen wanting to entice rural dwellers into the urban areas to spend, spend, spend. Elections were won and lost based on road conditions in a particular jurisdiction. In 1916, Congress finally offered funding to build roads if the

Motorists crossing into Nevada in 1926. A journal kept by one of these unidentified motorists complained that "the road was found to be all up, no down . . . a stop [was necessary] every mile to let the clutch pedal cool off." (Courtesy of the Bancroft Library, University of California, Berkeley, Online Archive of California.)

Trucks also went into service doing road maintenance. This dump truck from 1921, one of the first models with hydraulic capabilities, belonged to the road department in Howell, Michigan (Exit 137 off I-96). The truck had thirteen forward gears and six reverse ones. (Courtesy of the Howell Carnegie Library, Howell, Michigan.)

states would match the federal contribution. To take advantage of the offer, some states had to create a department to look after roads. (If a state department of highways or transportation did not exist, the counties probably looked after roads, leaving an uneven patchwork of standards and, frequently, mismanagement.) In Nevada's case, legislators established a department of highways in 1917, but only gave it $20,000 and the use of convict labor for road repairs and construction. When the money ran out, so did any repairs. Six years passed before a pothole was again filled in Nevada. California, on the other hand, voted in an eighteen million dollar bond issue for a statewide road system declaring that "California should be in the vanguard of the march of twentieth century progress."[5]

America's entry into World War I slowed road development, draining resources and manpower from state budgets. In some ways, the delays caused by the war allowed the technology of road construction to catch up with the challenges posed by the landscape in various parts of the country. Not everyone had General Braddock's resources when he traveled through Pennsylvania in 1755 with a corps of seamen equipped with block and tackle to hoist his supply wagons up steep hills. Nor did motorists want to carry around sagebrush for traction as Horatio Jackson had done in 1903. Automobiles were more sophisticated and engineers had finally figured out how to span the deeper valleys and build longer tunnels in places like West Virginia. These technological advances opened up previously isolated areas to economic development and travel. West Virginia, for instance, designated 4,600 miles of roads as part of the state road system in 1917. By 1933, this number had grown to 35,766 miles. World War I also brought the potential of the truck to everyone's attention. Until the U.S. Army started shipping matériel to East Coast ports via truck, companies had not recognized the advantages the truck offered over rail transport. Suddenly, everyone from the milkman to the guy delivering wood or coal realized the advantages of a gas-powered truck. More speed and more cargo room meant more deliveries and, presumably, happier customers.

Road construction in some states continued to lag behind the desires of the nation's motorists. Still digging itself out from pre–Civil War borrowing and the hardships of Reconstruction, Virginia found itself with some of the worst roads in the nation. Only one road—the turnpike through the Shenandoah Valley, now I-81—had a hard surface. In 1921, one national automobile association advised its members to avoid Virginia. The state took the criticism to heart, creating the Virginia State Highway Commission and setting aside twelve million dollars for road construction. A fifty million dollar bond issue was suggested. State Senator Harry Byrd campaigned against borrowing the money and won the state governorship on the issue. Shortly after taking office in 1926, Governor Byrd was instrumental in getting a four-and-a-half cent gasoline tax passed. In the next two years, that tax generated twenty-five

Not everyone in Virginia in the 1920s wanted improved roads. Near Dumfries (Exit 152 off I-95), a group of tow truck owners blew up a section of new road to help preserve their customer base.

million dollars for road improvements. Virginia undertook an aggressive campaign of road repair and soon had one of the best road networks in the nation.

With the assignment of highway numbers by the federal government in 1926, existing roads acquiring a number received basic upgrading. A little more than half of the surface of U.S. Route 80 from Tybee Island, Georgia, to San Diego, California, for instance, was still a gravel, sand, or topsoil surface. Local authorities used lime to keep the dust down and the gravel in place. This was a major, 2,671-mile coast-to-coast road across a part of the country that enjoyed a relatively warm climate, which presumably meant an easier construction and maintenance environment. Fledgling highway departments borrowed the organizational structure for road maintenance from the railroads; work crews lived along the road assigned to them and maintained their section as required by traffic volume and Mother Nature. In Southern California, a road crew lived beside a section of plank road that crossed the desert from San Diego to Arizona. Crew members had one assignment: shovel drifting sand off the planks. Road crews along today's I-8 deal with similar problems in a more automated fashion.

In New York, development of the Bronx River Parkway pioneered two major safety innovations: lanes of traffic separated by a median and the concept of limited access. Overpasses eliminated dangerous intersections. When completed in 1925, it was the first roadway of its kind in North America. But the ever-growing number of automobiles and trucks pushed those same engineers into a whole new area—traffic. It continued to increase and speed up. In 1928, Woodbridge, New Jersey (Exit 11 from I-95/New Jersey Turnpike) became the site of the first cloverleaf to be used along an American highway. This major invention allowed traffic to merge smoothly onto and off busy thoroughfares. The growing use of automobiles meant people were no longer confined to streetcar routes or train schedules. More speed and better access meant those seeking a better way of life, away from the less-than-optimal conditions of housing surrounding a factory or an urban tenement, could live in the suburbs. In New Jersey, workers had been commuting into Manhattan on the Hoboken Ferry across the Hudson River as early as the 1830s. Stagecoach lines served the ferry, connecting many New Jersey towns with the ferry dock. With the advent of the automobile, grids of small uniform houses soon dotted the rural landscape. The suburbs were declared the way of the future. For those seeking work, the automobile also provided a freedom their ancestors had not enjoyed.

Franklin Delano Roosevelt took office at the age of fifty-one, at a time when the nation's two biggest crises of the twentieth century, the Great Depression and World War II, seemingly consumed his every waking moment. Yet, this middle-aged president was able to visualize a quite different American landscape. Roosevelt invoked the metaphor of the road ahead in his second inaugural address in 1937 when he asked the nation: "Shall we pause now and turn our back upon the road that lies ahead? Shall we call this the promised land? Or, shall we continue on our way? For 'each age is a dream that is dying, or one that is coming to birth.'"[6] Roosevelt's vision of the road ahead included four-lane, coast-to-coast highways. If the United States was to flourish as a world power, it needed a first-class road network that would make a whole day's journey seem "but a few strides." Good roads now had an economic reality attached to them. The nation would only be as strong as its economy, and its economy depended on being able to move raw materials and finished goods.

By the end of the Depression, the average price of an automobile had dropped to about six hundred and thirty dollars, thanks, in part, to cost-saving production changes by the automakers in Michigan and partly because people were buying the cheaper vehicles from product lines. But their vehicles were getting older. Americans were hanging on to their cars, trying to make them last until times got better. Even the Joads from John Steinbeck's *Grapes of Wrath* owned a vehicle. Today's I-20 traces part of the path many migrant workers took as they headed west in vehicles held together with wire and hope in search of the promised land—usually a vegetable field in California.

In the 1930s, as part of massive make-work programs, construction crews straightened highways, made them wider, and sometimes paved the surface for the first time. In signing the 1938 Federal Aid Highway Act, Roosevelt authorized a feasibility study of a network of six transcontinental superhighways: three running north–south and three running east–west. Roosevelt acted on the subsequent report "to meet

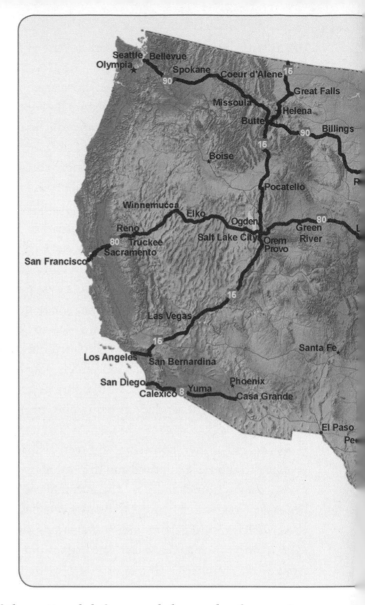

Interstates of
chapter 4

the requirements of the national defense and the needs of a growing peacetime traffic of longer range."[7] The report recommended building limited-access roads four lanes wide where traffic exceeded two thousand vehicles a day and beltways around major cities.

By 1939, the nation's thirty-one million vehicles zipped along at speeds unimagined even a decade earlier. The Pennsylvania Turnpike opened in 1941, with no posted speed limit. Granted, the turnpike was fairly straight, with gentler curves and easier grades than the norm, and limited access to boot, but it helped set a trend—even more speed.

The concept of the turnpike had been around almost as long as had roads; they had been introduced in the United States in the 1790s. Now, with the advent of motorized travel and the increase in traffic, particularly by commuters, state governments again turned to turnpikes to help pay for high-speed, multi-lane highways where demand warranted. Roads were wearing out faster than state governments could build them.

The onset of World War II created more jobs than there were people to fill them—and further emphasized the importance of moving people and goods quickly and efficiently. Modern mechanized warfare meant fast-moving convoys. It also meant, for the first time, the potential evacuation of large population centers in the United States. Suddenly, oceans were no guarantee of homeland safety. The Federal Aid Highway Act of 1944 authorized the development of a national system of interstate highways. The proposed interstates would connect the large urban areas and industrial centers. And unlike what was happening in many other industrialized countries, America's interstates would go through cities rather than bypass them. With surprising foresight, legislators also mandated that the system link with highways in Canada and Mexico. The interstates would improve national defense through the more efficient movement of troops and equipment, and provide a means for massive civilian evacuation, if required. Military vehicles and the movement of goods by truck to coastal ports were extremely hard on existing roads. To compound the problem, the wartime scarcity of steel led to the removal of reinforcing rod from pavement. But as Roosevelt planned for the end of the war, he knew his network of four-lane highways was one very good way to ensure a nation's continued safety and to provide soldiers with jobs when they returned to civilian life.

There were hints of what was to come. Toll roads sprang up in California, New Jersey, Ohio, West Virginia, and New York. Sometimes they worked; sometimes they did not. Six months after the Ohio Turnpike (now part of I-90) opened in 1955, bureaucrats realized truckers were avoiding it in favor of nearby roads. Fees where too high, they complained. And since automobiles had generally moved onto the turnpike, there was less traffic on the older roads the truckers were using. Authorities set out to woo truckers over to the turnpike with hot shower facilities and special parking lots. In West Virginia, tolls from the turnpike between Charleston and Princeton (now part of I-77) did not even cover operating costs in the early years. In Pennsylvania, the new turnpike across most of the state was a success. It was a similar story in New Jersey, because of the heavy traffic on other roads. Texas and California took a wait-and-see attitude.

Other hints of the future appeared. By the early 1950s, Americans collectively drove several hundred billion miles a year. Roads could not keep up with the massive growth in traffic. Highways started bypassing urban centers to reduce travel times, and time was money in the booming trucking industry. To compound the growing congestion on the nation's roads, auto sales increased dramatically. By 1955, Detroit was selling nearly eight million cars a year—up by two million over the previous year and a whopping four times the sales of 1946. There were now almost sixty-three million vehicles on a road system still flirting with the horse and buggy days of road design. It was time to catch up with Chuck Berry's Maybellene, who by 1956 was "motorvatin' over the hill . . . in a Coupe de Ville."[8] The sedate rhythm of earlier road travel had given way to a faster beat. So had travel on the roadways of the nation.

Interstate 80: Twenty-Seven Days and Counting

October 3, 1872, in a London gentlemen's club: Phileas Fogg, the hero of Jules Verne's *Around the World in Eighty Days*, finished his game of cards as he contemplated what he had just done. He had traded in his orderly existence for a mad dash around the world—in eighty days. Phileas ran home, packed a bag, grabbed his valet, Passepartout, and headed for Paris. Fifty-three days later, Phileas and Passepartout, now accompanied by a young woman named Aouda and shadowed by Detective Fix, arrived in San Francisco. In their subsequent dash across the

San Francisco Bay as Phileas Fogg, the protagonist of Jules Verne's *Around the World in Eighty Days*, would have seen it on arrival in the United States. (Courtesy of the Library of Congress.)

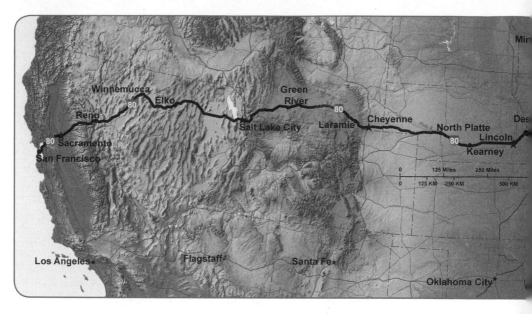

United States, Phileas Fogg and his companions followed a route very similar to today's Interstate 80 from San Francisco eastward. In writing a trans-American race into his book, Verne was well ahead of his time, but what makes the cross-country trek of Phileas and his companions all the more remarkable is that Jules Verne disliked travel. His one trip to the United States brought him to New York with a side trip to Niagara

The road beside the rail line Phileas Fogg used in California had been put there for a reason. The railway built it in the 1860s to bring supplies to advancing railroad crews blasting and leveling their way eastward toward Promontory, Utah. The railroad company needed the road, but was not averse to recouping some of the cost of actually building its own supply road. It decided to open the road to public traffic and charge tolls on freight traffic to Donner Lake. Given the exploding volume of goods starting to move along this new transcontinental corridor, the toll road soon generated one million dollars a year in revenue.

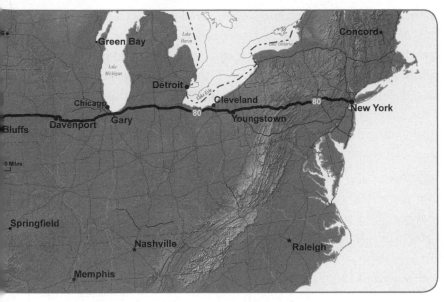

Interstate 80

Falls. Verne, however, liked to do research. He described Phileas' trip across the United States in meticulous detail, even down to the accurate train schedules, and sold millions of copies in dozens of languages.

Phileas and his travel companions left San Francisco on the train from Oakland Station. At that time, the train to New York was the only option for someone in a hurry. Roads were little better than trails and did not necessarily connect in a logical string from San Francisco to New York. As Phileas remarked, a journey that used to take six months, around the tip of Cape Horn, could now be accomplished in seven days by train. Phileas had twenty-seven days left in which to reach London. He and his companions passed through Sacramento at night, having taken six hours to get there from San Francisco. (Today, on I-80, it takes about eighty minutes, depending on traffic.) They "saw nothing of that important place, the seat of the State government, with its fine quays its broad streets, its noble hotels, squares, and churches,"[9] but did note that the countryside was not very hilly.

A few years later, one of the first successful female journalists, Elizabeth Cochrane, alias Nellie Bly, decided to see if she could beat the fictional Phileas Fogg's record. By day fifty-three she had retraced his steps to San Francisco. Despite her rush, as she passed through California by train, she had time to notice the rail bed as smooth as velvet, running down valleys as "straight as a sunbeam."[10] For Phileas, the route continued on toward the mountains and Nevada. "The railway track wound in and out among the passes, now approaching the mountain-sides, now suspended over precipices, avoiding abrupt angles by bold curves, plunging into narrow defiles, which seemed to have no outlet."[11] This was the same route many early pioneers took across the mountains. It was also the trail taken by adventurers heading to gold rushes in both Nevada and California and the silver rush in Nevada.

For the miners, there was another mode of transportation: donkeys or burros as they were also known. In 1861, someone decided that with all the sand lying around in Nevada, maybe camels would be an option. Thirteen camels imported from Mongolia soon resulted in city ordinances in places like Virginia City (Exit 13) banning the camels when streets were the busiest in an attempt to deal with spooked horses and donkeys.

Meanwhile, Nellie Bly and her travel companions sat back to "admire the beautiful country through which we were passing as swiftly as cloud along the sky, to read, or count telegraph poles."[12] Her well-orchestrated trip, designed to boost her newspaper's readership, had been planned down to the minute. Trains waited, and meals (and champagne) were delivered to her seat on the train. Adoring fans gathered at every stop to catch a glimpse of Nellie. "I only remember my trip across the continent as one maze of happy greetings, happy wishes, congratulating telegrams, fruit, flowers, loud cheers, wild hurrahs, rapid hand-shaking and a beautiful car filled with fragrant flowers attached to a swift engine that was tearing like mad through flower-dotted valleys and over snow-tipped mountains, on-on-on! It was glorious!"[13]

But, *Around the World in Eighty Days* would not have been a successful pot boiler if Jules Verne had done the same kind of precision planning for Phileas and his companions. They entered Nevada at about nine o'clock the next morning, fifteen hours out of San Francisco. (The timing today on I-80 is a little over three hours.) They reached Reno, Nevada (Exits 8–21), at midday where the train stopped to allow passengers to eat breakfast at what must have been the 1872 version of McDonald's—they were only given twenty minutes. Reno was a relatively new town when Jules Verne had Phileas and his companions stop there. Founded in 1868 as a railroad town, it was named after a Union officer from Virginia, General Jesse Lee Reno who was killed during the Civil War. In the early 1900s, Reno started gaining a reputation as a marriage and divorce center. Today, it serves as a vacation hub for the nearby Sierra Nevadas and Lake Tahoe.

Beyond Reno, Jules Verne described the railroad as "running along the Humboldt River, passed northward for several miles by its banks; then it turned eastward, and kept by the river until it reached the Humboldt Range, nearly at the extreme eastern limit of Nevada."[14] Today's I-80 traveler through this stretch can see the same views Phileas and his companions would have seen from their seats on the train. The next major stop was near the Great Salt Lake of Utah. At seventy miles long and thirty-five miles wide, the Great Salt Lake sits at thirty-eight hundred feet above sea level. Its water is about seven and a half times saltier than the oceans. Jules Verne had Phileas take the time to describe the Great Salt Lake for readers: "Thence the passengers could observe the vast extent of this interior sea. . . . It is a picturesque expanse, framed in lofty crags in large strata, encrusted with white salt—a superb sheet of water."[15]

Verne did not have Phileas mention the Bonneville Flats, possibly because they were not that well known when the research for the book was done. But once the gasoline engine was introduced, motorists looked at the smooth, flat surface of hard-packed salt and saw a perfect raceway. Barry Oldfield set the first land record at the Bonneville Flats in 1910 at 131.7 miles per hour. Interstate 80 motorists can best see the flats from a viewing area at Mile Marker 166.

At Ogden (Exit 120), Phileas' train rested for six hours. He was now nine hundred miles from San Francisco. It had taken him two days. Today's I-80 motorist takes about twelve hours. From Ogden, I-80 crosses the Wahsatch Mountains into Wyoming, across the same trace Jules Verne used in his book. Phileas and his companions kept on chugging past Green River (Exits 89–91), across the North Platte River (near Mile Marker 229), and through Cheyenne (Exit 358). Here Verne had Phileas remark that this was the "highest elevation of the journey, eight thousand and ninety-two feet above the level of the sea."[16] It had taken three days and nights for Phileas and his companions to get to this point, 1,382 miles from San Francisco; today's I-80 shaves a couple of hundred miles off Verne's calculations. Phileas estimated he was at least four days and nights from New York City.

In Nebraska, Jules Verne added Sioux Indians to the story having them threaten the train. In true pot-boiler fashion, Phileas and his companions survived. They continued on, generally following the future I-80 route. But before he could leave the Great Plains, Verne added a washed out bridge to Phileas' wows. He was now fifty-nine days into his journey; only twenty-one days remained in which to reach London, and they still had to sail across the Atlantic. But the prescient Verne came to their rescue in the form of a sled rigged as a sailboat. It was "a curious vehicle, a kind of frame on two long beams, a little raised in front like the runners of a sledge, and upon which there was room for five or six persons. A high mast was fixed on the frame, held firmly by metallic lashings, to which was attached a large brigantine sail. This mast held an iron stay upon which to hoist a jib-sail. Behind, a sort of rudder served to guide the vehicle. It was, in short, a sledge rigged like a sloop." Verne went on to explain that when the trains were blocked by snow, these sledges made for rapid transit of the frozen plains, slipping over the "prairies with a speed equal if not superior to that of the express trains."[17] Phileas and his companions caught the next train out of Omaha (Exits 442–454) and got back on track, so to speak, through Des Moines (Exits 121–142) and onward to Chicago (Exits 126–161).

Nellie Bly enjoyed a short respite on her train trip across country, giving a few interviews and waving at adoring fans who came out to catch a glimpse of her. In Chicago, she drank the last of her coffee, dressed leisurely, and on opening her stateroom door was quite surprised to "see the car quite filled with good-looking men."[18] For Phileas and his companions, Chicago was a quick change of trains. They chugged closer to their goal over the trace of today's I-80 crossing "Indiana, Ohio, Pennsylvania, and New Jersey like a flash, rushing through towns with antique names, some of which had streets and car-tracks, but as yet no houses."[19] At 11:15 on December 11, Phileas and his companions arrived at the docks in New York; their ship had left at 10:30. They were too late! Verne added a bit more suspense and a hair-raising trip across the

The reception for Nellie Bly on completing her trip around the world. (Courtesy of the Library of Congress.)

transatlantic, having Phileas and his companions burn their ship board by board to stoke the boilers and make it in time. After more plot twists, Phileas eventually won his bet and settled down to married life with Aouda. Nellie Bly, Phileas' real-life counterpart, enjoyed the limelight and attention, making it from coast to coast in one hundred hours and fifty-six minutes. "I took off my cap and wanted to yell with the crowd, not because I had gone around the world in seventy-two days, but because I was home again."[20] Mr. and Mrs. Jules Verne sent their congratulations.

Interstate 8: An Ocean Voyage to Arizona

It takes about five hours of driving on Interstate 8 through the freeways of San Diego, over mountain peaks and valleys, and across desert and more desert before reaching Casa Grande, Arizona. In the spring and summer of 1874, it took Martha Summerhayes a few months. The newly married Martha (or Mattie, as her husband called her) was heading off with her husband, Second Lieutenant Jack Summerhayes, to his posting

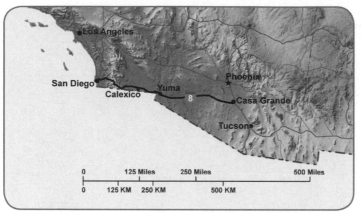

Interstate 8

at Fort Apache, near Phoenix, Arizona. The first part of the trip across country from New York to Cheyenne in the Wyoming Territory was by train. A wagon—the fort's ambulance—pulled by four mules brought them from the train station into Cheyenne. Logic dictates that you should be able to then go from Cheyenne to Fort Apache in a fairly direct north–south route. You could today: down I-25 to I-10 to Phoenix—about eighteen hours of hard driving. Not for Mattie.

In June 1874, she and her husband left Cheyenne by train for San Francisco. At that time, there were no railroads in Arizona. Troops sent there, either marched overland or took the train to San Francisco and then a steamer down the coast, and up into the Gulf of California to Fort Yuma. From there, soldiers either marched or boarded another steamer for the trip up the Colorado River before disembarking and marching to the post. The U.S. Army Corps of Engineers tried several times in the early 1850s to find a suitable route into Arizona from California, but nothing seemed feasible. It would be 1883 before rail service finally reached Arizona. After a layover in San Francisco, Mattie boarded the *Newbern* for the voyage to Arizona. It took a week to get to the tip of the Baja Peninsula. Mattie was confined to her stateroom the entire week with seasickness. San Diego was not mentioned and was apparently not even a port of call for the *Newbern*. At that time, San Diego was not that old, having been founded about the time California became an American possession in 1864. The military subsequently decided to make use of the deep, natural harbor and the city developed around the harbor facilities. For Mattie, it was now the middle of August and "insufferably hot." In the Gulf of California, sleep below decks became impossible. It was

Desert driving before the construction of I-8. (Courtesy of the Bancroft Library, University of California, Berkeley.)

not any easier on the deck. "[O]ur mattresses were brought up by the soldiers at night, and spread about. The situation, however, was so novel and altogether ludicrous, and our fear of rats which ran about on deck so great, that sleep was well-nigh out of the question."[21] By this time, the food supply had also deteriorated. "[W]hen the steward went down into the refrigerator, which was somewhere below the quarter-deck, to get provisions for the day, every woman held a bottle of salts to her nose, and the officers fled to the forward part of the ship."[22] Mattie lived on baked sweet potatoes for the remainder of the voyage.

On August 26, Mattie started her journey up the Colorado River on a riverboat bound for Yuma. Today, Yuma sits at about the halfway point on I-8. Founded in 1854, the city and fort had only recently been named Yuma when Mattie stayed there in 1874. "Yuma" is thought to come from the Spanish word *humo*, for smoke, from the Native American practice of using clouds of smoke to induce rain.

For Mattie, Yuma was a slice of heaven. Here was a hint of green grass, a clean bed, a proper bath and, best of all, fresh food. "I can never forget the taste of the oatmeal with fresh milk, the eggs and butter, and delicious tomatoes, which were served to us."[23] The town was apparently

With only three inches of rainfall a year, Yuma receives as much rain in a decade as many places see in only a year. It would take nineteen years, for instance, for Yuma to reach the annual rainfall total of Miami, Florida. As a result, the surrounding landscape is dry, sandy, and sparsely vegetated. The nearby mountainsides show the effects of wind rather than water erosion.

Mattie's slice of heaven: Fort Yuma photographed from Yuma City. (Courtesy of UCR/California Museum of Photography.)

the only place relatively fresh vegetables could be found in the Arizona Territory. The Yuma area of today has irrigated farmland with water diverted from the Colorado and Gila Rivers. Presumably, Mattie would be happy to find fresh veggies at restaurants along I-8. (Exits 14–1 serve Yuma.) Army officers on the ship had warned Mattie that Yuma was the hottest place on the planet. She described the roads in the morning as "white with heat," but here she could recline on a shaded piazza and rest during the day. Over and over Mattie heard the tale of a soldier stationed in Yuma who had died and gone to live with the devil. But, he had only been there a little while when he returned to Yuma to beg for his blankets, having found hell so much cooler than the place he had left. Yuma is officially the sunniest place in the United States with an average of 242 clear days a year. Another traveler named Hiram Hodge passed through Yuma in 1874, the same year as Mattie. He encouraged anyone with ailments to consider wintering in Yuma once it became more accessible.

Today's interstate motorist in Arizona would think nothing of continuing on eastward on I-8, across the Sonoran Desert to where it merges with I-10 near Casa Grande, and take a little jog up and over to Fort Apache. Mattie probably would have been delighted to load all her worldly possessions into an air-conditioned van or pickup and head off for what would probably be a four-hour trip. Instead, after a few days of rest in Yuma, she boarded a riverboat and continued up the Colorado River. Eighteen days later the boat pulled into Fort Mojave (near present-day Lake Havasu), and the long trek across the Mojave Desert to Fort Apache began. On October 4, she saw Fort Apache for the first time. It had been two months since she left San Francisco and four months since she had last seen Cheyenne. Mattie was tired, dirty, and sunbaked, the heat having "destroyed both our good looks and our tempers."[24]

By 1877, Mattie Summerhayes had a two-year-old son. After spending time with her family on Nantucket, Mattie and her son returned to Arizona. An overland stagecoach road had opened up east of San Diego, sparing Mattie and young Harry the rigors of a sea voyage. The stagecoach was very crowded. "I tried to stow myself and my little boy and my belongings away comfortably, but the road was rough and the coach swayed, and I gave it up. There were passengers on top of the coach, and passengers inside the coach. One woman who was totally deaf, and some miners and blacksmiths, and a few other men, the flotsam and jetsam of the Western countries."[25] The constant jolting and swaying made her son sick, and the other passengers helped her hold him. After being on the road for about eighteen hours, the stage stopped near dawn to change horses and driver and, despite the breakneck pace, was apparently late in reaching this way station.

The new driver sped up even more. And there were no runaway truck ramps, as there would be today, to save the coach. "The road was narrow and appeared to be cut out of solid rock, which seemed to be as smooth as soapstone; the four horses were put to their speed, and down and around and away we went. I drew in my breath as I looked out and over into the abyss on my left. Death and destruction seemed to be the end awaiting us all. Everybody was limp, when we reached the bottom." The stage stopped and the passengers were given an opportunity to catch their breath. As the driver explained, "we are an hour late this morning; we always make it a point to 'do it' before dawn, so the passengers can't see anything; they are almost sure to get stampeded if we come down by daylight."[26] Mattie later learned that the road, long desired in the area, had been cut out of solid rock. Only one man could drive the stagecoach over this stretch of road and always at night, so the passengers could not see outside. Martha wrote: "I did not inquire if there had ever been any accidents. I seemed to have learned all I wanted to know about it."[27]

Topography helps explain the lack of a good road east from San Diego for so many years. Mountains rise abruptly behind San Diego Bay followed by what in Mattie's time was known as the Imperial Desert, an area of constantly shifting sand dunes. A canal into the Imperial Desert opened in 1901 and helped turn this wasteland into an intensively farmed agricultural belt with truck crops, cotton, sugar beets, and animal feeds being the main crops. It is now known as the Imperial Valley. The completion of the Hoover Dam in 1935 brought more canals and more agriculture to the area.

Before the Imperial Desert became the Imperial Valley, drifting sand was the main problem for road travelers. Workmen laid down planking over the dunes in the first attempts to make a passable road. Initially, the planking was in two strips, each about twenty-five inches wide to accommodate two wheel paths, but if a wheel happened to slip off the planks, the automobile inevitably had to be dug or pulled out of the sand. Then work crews tried planking eight feet wide. A bit better. Crews laid even wider planking in some areas to allow a vehicle to pull off when meeting another automobile. California gave the six-mile stretch of plank road its own maintenance crew: their task was to keep shoveling the shifting sands off the planks.

In 1919, Joseph Chase recorded his journey on horseback along this plank road. He had trouble convincing his horse to step on the planks. "The planks had warped and loosened, and he was kept on a continual dance of nervousness: still they were a great boon for without them the five miles of shifting sand would have consumed as many hours."[28] Joseph took the time to observed the landscape. A "mist of sand was ever curling off [the dunes] and drifting in airy waves and feathers. . . . The whole mass of the sand was enveloped in this fairy-like veil creeping like smoke, weaving in dainty frills and spirals. . . . The color was wonderful in purity and sheer power of mass. The smooth, large outlines of pale yellow, the water-like transparency of cobalt shadow, and the soft brilliance of the early morning."[29]

During her time in Arizona, Mattie Summerhayes came to appreciate the desert landscape and the people of Arizona. Her husband subsequently served at posts in Nebraska, New York, and Florida. Mattie dutifully packed up household and children and moved with him. But in 1919, on writing her memoirs, a hint of melancholy crept into her words.

> Sometimes I hear the still voices of the Desert. . . . I hear, in fancy, the wheels of the ambulance crunching the small broken stones of the malapais, or grating swiftly over the gravel of the smooth white roads of the river-bottoms. I hear the rattle of the ivory rings on the harness of the six-mule team; I see the soldiers marching on ahead. . . . But how vain these fancies! Railroad and automobile have annihilated distance . . . the Arizona as we knew it, has vanished from the face of the earth.[30]

Interstate 90: And Ain't I a Woman?

Interstate 90 runs across the top of the United States, from coast to coast. In doing so it serves cities like Boston (Exits 22–15), Albany (Exit

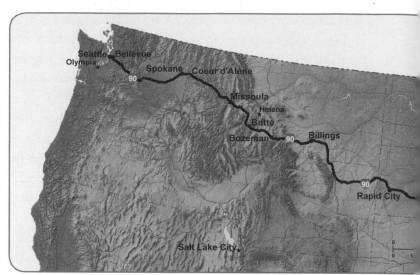

Interstate 90

A mother and child pose in a Wyoming wheat field in 1908; photographed by J. E. Stimson. (Courtesy of the Wyoming State Archives.)

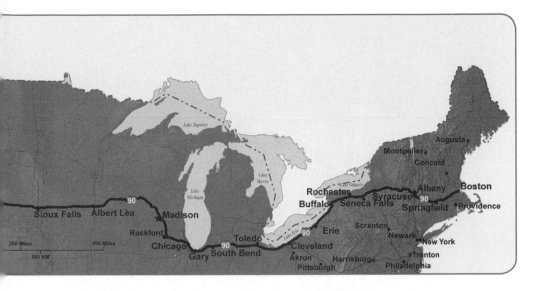

6), Buffalo (Exits 51–53), Chicago (Exits 1–19), Coeur d'Alene (Exits 15–13), Spokane (Exits 286–272), and Seattle (Exit 3). In June of 1851, women traveled along the future I-90 trace, and up many of the roads and rail lines that connect into today's I-90 at interchanges in Ohio and Pennsylvania to attend a gathering on women's rights in Akron, Ohio (Exit 172). The women's rights movement had grown out of the antislavery movement, and many Abolitionists were also there that day, including Sojourner Truth. Sojourner's strong Christian faith had helped her through her years of suffering and hardship as a slave in New York State. Now, at the age of fifty-four, she added her voice to the growing cry for women's suffrage.

According to one account of the day, ministers in attendance spoke of the superior intellect of men and the manhood of Christ. Sojourner rose from her seat in a back corner and pointed a finger. "That man over there says that women need to be helped into carriages, and lifted over ditches, and to have the best place everywhere. Nobody helps me any best place. And ain't I a woman?" She had her audience's attention. Sojourner continued. "Look at me! Look at my arm. . . . I have plowed, I have planted and I have gathered into barns. And no man could head me. And ain't I a woman?" Everyone listened intently so Sojourner continued. "I have borne children and seen most of them sold into slavery, and when I cried out with a mother's grief, none but Jesus heard me. And ain't I a woman?" The women in the church cheered wildly.

A photo of Sojourner Truth. NASA named the 1997 Pathfinder Mars rover *Sojourner* to honor this legendary woman, who traveled all over the United States to promote the rights of women and all African Americans to participate fully in society. Sojourner means "traveler."

Sojourner gestured toward a man in black. "He says women can't have as much rights as men. 'Cause Christ wasn't a woman. Where did your Christ come from?" When there was no response she raised her voice. "Where did your Christ come from? From God and a woman! Man had nothing to do with him!" By this time, the cheering in the church was deafening. Sojourner continued. "If the first woman God ever made was strong enough to turn the world upside down all alone, these women together ought to be able to turn it back and get it right-side up again. And now that they are asking to do it the men better let them."[31]

Interstate 90 connects the stories of an inordinate number of women in places like Boston and Chicago and every little town and cabin along the way who, like Sojourner, put their mark, however small or large, on the social landscape of their time. They and their daughters plowed, chopped wood, comforted, suffered, campaigned, and carved out business empires in a man's world alongside of, or in spite of, the husbands, brothers, and sons who traveled the same road. Ironically, at the time when women campaigned for full suffrage, the automobile probably gave them their greatest freedom.

Interstate 90 begins its three-thousand mile trek across the country in Boston, at Logan International Airport. Not far from I-90's departure point, Miss Farmer's School of Cookery once taught all branches of "cookery and household technique." Her sights set squarely on the almost invisible majority of American women—housewives—Miss Farmer's goal was to improve their lot and their diet. Anyone working for a living could look elsewhere for training. The first twelve editions of *The Fanny Farmer Cookbook* sold nearly four million copies and her lasting legacy became the standardized level measurements. Before Fanny's time, recipes frequently contained instructions for a lump of butter the size of a walnut or a teacup full of milk. Fanny insisted on consistent, exact measures in all of her recipes. A whole new industry sprang up as women clamored for accurate measuring utensils.

Interstate 90 continues westward through Massachusetts, crossing the Hudson River then skirting around Albany, New York, through lands that once belonged to tribes of the Iroquois Confederacy. Iroquois women tended the crops and distributed food. This included the game men provided by hunting. Because they essentially controlled the food supply, women had considerable say in political decisions. With the arrival of Europeans in North America, Albany became a way station for travelers on the Hudson River and those using the railways from Boston and New York. The town provided a place for women heading to the spas at Saratoga Springs to spend a comfortable night in a hotel bed before continuing their journey. It was also the starting point for those heading west on the Erie Canal, which runs along the Mohawk River as it crosses New York. Those bound for the Michigan Territory could ride a canal boat through to Buffalo and then board a lake boat bound for such ports as Detroit, a disembarkation point into the Michigan Territory. Early wagon trains heading west also got one last load of supplies in Albany—until the frontier edged westward and centers further west took over this role. With all this traffic, Albany flourished.

During her travels in 1828, Frances Trollope and her companions boarded a canal boat at Schenectady (Exits 25–26). It was an all-day and overnight trip via the canal to Utica (Exit 31). (Today's I-90 traveler makes the journey in about an hour.) Once aboard, Frances made a discovery.

> There is a great quietness about the women of America. . . . but somehow or other, I should never call it gentleness. In such trying moments as that of "fixing" themselves on board a packet-boat, the men are prompt, determined and will compromise any body's convenience, except their own. The women are doggedly steadfast in their will, and till matters are settled, look like hedgehogs, with every quill raised, and firmly set as if to forbid the approach of any one who might wish to rub them down.[32]

It was in Albany that Susan B. Anthony was denied permission to speak at a temperance meeting. Her treatment prompted Susan to add women's rights to her causes. A few years earlier, Elizabeth Cady, from Johnstown (Exit 27), had learned all about discriminatory laws while working in her father's law office. Elizabeth eventually married Henry Stanton (but had the word "obey" removed from the wedding vows) and moved to Seneca Falls (Exit 41) where she and Lucretia Mott, another advocate of equality for women, convened a women's rights convention in 1848. The first two days of discussions took place in Seneca Falls; subsequent meetings were held in Rochester (Exits 45–47). The Declaration of Sentiments detailing the inferior status of women and calling for extensive reforms emerged from these meetings, launching the women's rights movement in the United States. Women's Rights National Historical Park (NY Exit 41) commemorates those fateful days in July 1848.

From Seneca Falls, I-90 sets a flat, straight course to Rochester and then onward to Buffalo and along the south shore of Lake Erie through the flat lowlands and miles of vineyards. The interstate passes briefly into Pennsylvania, past Erie (Exit 22). During World War II, Erie became a hub of wartime production as women set aside their domestic aprons for heavy industrial aprons and a job in support of the war effort. Women also moved out of the kitchen in nearby Ohio. By the end of World War II one of every three defense workers in Ohio was female. Interstate 90 continues to hug the south shore of Lake Erie through Ohio and into the rolling hills of Indiana and Illinois.

In Chicago, I-90 passes the University of Illinois and its famous Hull House. While Susan B. Anthony, Elizabeth Cady Stanton, and Lucre-

Amelia Bloomer, of Seneca Falls, actively promoted the need for a change in women's dress in her various publications on women's rights and social reform. The split skirt covered by a long tunic gave way to a shorter skirt and knee-length undergarment that soon became known as bloomers. This gave women more freedom of movement and enabled them to participate in the latest craze sweeping the Western world—bicycling. (Courtesy of the Library of Congress.)

tia Mott campaigned for women's rights, two young women from Chicago quietly went about the task of improving the lives of thousands of working-class immigrants. In 1889, Jane Addams and Ellen Gates Starr opened a day nursery in Hull House (Exit 52), a vacant residence on Chicago's west side to help low-income workers and immigrants struggling to make ends meet. Eventually including thirteen buildings and a playground, the facility had a gymnasium, community kitchen, boarding facilities for working girls, crafts, music, arts, and college-level courses. Hull House even sponsored one of the first little-theater groups in Chicago and Benny Goodman took his first music lessons there. Young social workers flocked to Hull House for training. Ellen Gates Starr, the artistic side of the duo, firmly believed the bleak, monotonous existence of a factory job could be counterbalanced through artistic expression. Jane Addams, a passionate labor reformer, fought for the regulation of sweatshops, the opening of free employment offices, and factory inspec-

Jane Addams went international, serving as chairperson of the International Congress of Women in 1915 and participating in the founding of the American Civil Liberties Union in 1920. The world recognized Jane Addams' lifetime achievements in 1931 when she became a cowinner of the Nobel Peace Prize. (George Grantham Bain Collection, Library of Congress.)

tions. She also advocated for the eight-hour workday for women. Hull House continued its exceptional work until 1963 when the University of Illinois expanded into Chicago. Hull House and an adjacent dining hall became a museum complex; the organization relocated its headquarters and decentralized its operations throughout the city.

On leaving Chicago, I-90 steps northward through Wisconsin, where it crosses the Mississippi River into Minnesota. In the late 1800s, many women passed through Chicago on their way west, though usually not by their own choice; women rarely initiated a move to the frontier. While some did persuade their husbands to remain where they were, many others packed up home and family and headed into the unknown. Countless others stayed behind, becoming "gold rush widows," waiting to join their husband on a new farmstead in Kansas, in the California gold fields, or further north in the lumber towns of Oregon and Washington. Many were left destitute, never hearing from their husband again. For other women, heading west was the perfect way to escape a life of restriction in East Coast society. Others came for the money. A visit to the Wild West Show at the Columbian Exposition in Chicago in 1893 inspired some to make the journey west. A white woman arriving in a Western camp or town usually prompted all the men to spruce up their appearance. This could include washing and shaving for the first time in months or simply finding a clean shirt.

Wagon trains west frequently took on a holiday atmosphere, especially in the early weeks in the warmer months. Women whose normal day involved twelve to sixteen hours of farm labor, cooking, and cleaning, suddenly found themselves with long days of relative idleness, only interrupted by morning and evening meal preparation and caregiving duties for younger or sick family members. Some women read or wrote letters to family and friends back home. Many knitted or learned to knit. Others simply took the time to absorb the passing landscape. At a top speed of a couple of miles an hour, the scenery could be admired at leisure. Despite this short, possibly idyllic time in their life, the trip west for these women was by no means something to be romanticized; it was long, exhausting, and dangerous. The biggest fear for most women who headed west was the possible death of their husband. A contemporary account from the 1850s hinted at the naiveté of many of those making the trip.

> The amount of suffering that they must undergo is incredible; and it is painful to see the women and children who crowd the wagons, without the slightest idea of the difficulties that obstruct their path. There sits the mother patient and contented; the daughters blooming with health; the children petting a favorite dog, who springs into the wagon at their call: the grown son with his ox whip in hand, watching the resting team, and the father standing by the roadside, with his thick muddy boots and black beard of some day's growth, but with an air of indomitable resolution.[33]

Once at their destination, women usually concentrated on the chores associated with feeding and clothing their family. On top of this, they frequently helped clear the land, build the first shelter, whether of sod or lumber, and tend stock or work to establish the family business. An Englishwoman, Isabella Bird, spent time in the Rocky Mountains in the late 1870s. At one point she supported herself by acting as cook and

An illustration of Isabella Bird from her book recounting her adventures in the West. Isabella was a real rebel for her time. Not only was her costume considered scandalous, with the long bloomers under her skirt, but she rode a horse astride like a man, although she would sometimes switch to a side saddle posture when approaching civilization. (The word "astride" was considered socially unacceptable in Isabella's time. Polite society simply did not include that word in a conversation.) (Courtesy of the Denver Public Library, Western History Collection, Z-75.)

housekeeper for a group of snowbound ranchers/hunters. "My room is easily 'done' but the parlour is a never-ending business. I have swept shovelfuls of mud out of it three times today. There is nothing to dust it with but a buffalo's tail, and every now and then a gust descends the open chimney and drives the wood ashes all over the room."[34] Her room consisted of an unheated shed near the main cabin where it was normal to wake up with her face frozen to the blankets with several inches of snow on the floor and on her bed. One of Isabella's jobs as cook was to ration food, which in some instances meant serving one scant meal a day when supplies ran low, particularly the two staples of her kitchen: flour and coffee. The men provided game when they could find it. Isabella described the typical mountain woman as "lean, clean, toothless."[35]

In Wyoming, I-90 cuts a wedge out of the northeast corner of the state, a drive from border to border of about three hours through the rolling grasslands. Wyoming holds the distinction of being the first state to grant suffrage. Wyoming women were the first to vote, hold public office, and serve on juries, although the jury duty was short-lived— initially. It seems women imposed stiffer sentences or fines and men serving on the jury with them were not allowed to drink, smoke, or chew tobacco in court. After a few months of complaints from the men on juries, the right of women to serve on juries was taken away and not restored until 1950.

Wyoming became a territory in July 1868; very soon afterward a suffrage bill was introduced in the legislature. While some thought it was a publicity stunt to attract more settlers to Wyoming or a joke, the bill passed in December 1869. When Wyoming applied for statehood in 1888, it was feared that the application would not be approved if women continued to have the right to vote, but Wyoming was not budging without its women; Wyoming became a state in 1890, with full suffrage. Wyoming women continued to pile up firsts: first woman to hold a state elective office in 1894, first female state legislator in 1911, and first female state governor in 1925. Nellie Taylor Ross was elected to replace her late husband as state governor when he died in office. She served the final two years of his term. In 1933, she became the first female director of the U.S. Mint, a post she held for twenty years, overseeing the construction of Fort Knox in Kentucky to protect the nation's gold reserves. Wyoming celebrates November 29, Nellie Taylor Ross's birthday, as a state holiday.

From Wyoming, I-90 crosses into Montana, passing through Billings (Exits 452–446), Bozeman (Exits 309–305), and Missoula (Exits 109–104) before exiting into Idaho's northern neck and then into Washington State near Spokane. Towns along I-90 in this area were settled in the 1860s as supply depots or as access points to nearby resources. In Missoula's case, the resource was lumber. Between 1909 and 1918, seventy thousand to eighty thousand people homesteaded in Montana. By 1922, sixty thousand had left. As had happened in neighboring Wyoming, Montana women took the initiative in furthering women's rights. The first woman, elected to the U.S. House of Representatives, Jeannette Rankin grew up on a ranch near Missoula. In 1968, Jeannette, then eighty-seven, led a march on Washington to protest the Vietnam War. From Montana, I-90 crosses Washington State, past Spokane into Seattle where it meets up with I-5 and comes to an end. Seattle contributed the first woman elected mayor of a large U.S. city. Bertha Knight Landes served from 1926–1928.

As a young lady in the 1830s, Caroline Elizabeth Thomas Merrick saddled up her horse to go for a morning ride with a female cousin. Her father would not hear of it.

> "You will do nothing of the kind. You have no brother here to ride with you, and it is improper for two young ladies to be seen on the public road alone so early in the morning". . . . We were obliged to submit to his authority without protest, though I was ready to say, "There is a word sweeter than mother, home, or heaven, and the word is liberty." Contrast that with the freedom of the modern girl on her bicycle![36]

Caroline wrote her memoirs in 1901, at a time when the occasional automobile probably rolled by her parlor windows. Her granddaughters, however, certainly made use of their bicycles, giving them a freedom Caroline seems to have envied. If she had lived in a different era, Caroline probably would have been less malleable to her father's will as she

Interstate 20

drove her new horseless carriage out of the stable and headed off with her cousin to enjoy the freedom inherent in motorized vehicles. But, whether it was Fanny Farmer in Boston, or Susan B. Anthony and Amelia Bloomer in Seneca Falls, Sojourner Truth in Akron, Jane Addams in Chicago, Nellie Taylor Ross in Wyoming, or thousands of Marthas and Belles settling in the Dakotas and Great Plains, all along the trace I-90 now carves in the landscape the sentiment was the same: they were equal. They plowed, chopped wood, comforted, suffered, campaigned, and carved out lives in a man's world. Each worked in her own way to turn the world right side up again. They made a difference.

Interstate 20: Expectation and Hope

By the 1930s, hungry men and women carrying their belongings or pushing baby carriages piled with the remains of a household, the kids straggling along behind, walked the nation's highways. Others drove ramshackle vehicles, the household goods strapped to the top and sides. A million people took to the relatively new network of U.S. highways during the worst years of the Great Depression in search of food and shelter. As in the rest of the nation, families from the eastern end of what is now Interstate 20—the Carolinas, Georgia, and Alabama— made their way westward along roads that had already seen the migrations of the 1800s as disaffected African Americans, poor sharecroppers, and the drunkards, gamblers, profane swearers, and idlers Texas had wanted to

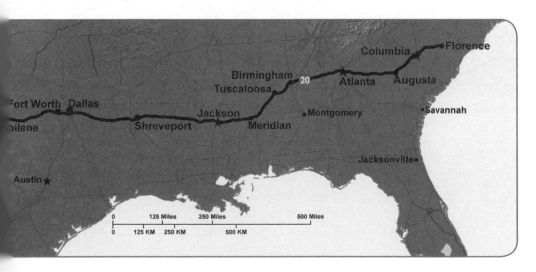

"Being unable to afford a car in America is the last step before living out of a plastic sack" (Bill Bryson, 1989: 139). This photograph taken in May 1937 by Dorothy Lange, Farm Security Administration, showed migrants bound for California. (Courtesy of the Library of Congress.)

> The cars of the migrant people crawled out of the side roads onto the great cross-country highway, and they took the migrant way to the West. In the daylight they scuttled like bugs to the westward; and as the dark caught them, they clustered like bugs near to shelter and to water.
>
> —John Steinbeck, *The Grapes of Wrath* (1971: 430)

keep out made their way west with expectations of a better life. Now, desperate families, looking for their next meal headed west as well. If they could not find work picking cotton or vegetables in Mississippi or Louisiana, they kept going. During the Great Depression, farm labor, when you could find it, in the dust bowls of Oklahoma and Northern Texas paid only $1.25 per day with no housing, but if one could somehow get all the way to California, a day's labor on a vegetable or fruit farm paid $2.95 and included rudimentary housing. To laborers and farmers who had had practically everything they owned repossessed, this was the promised land. Thousands migrated. Eventually, this trail of expectations became I-20 from Florence, South Carolina, to Pecos, Texas.

As today's I-20 does, the road west for these migrants crossed the Red River into Texas at Shreveport, Louisiana (Exits 26–11). Thousands had used this route as their portal into Texas in the last century seeking farmland and a new future. Now the Red River became just one more river to cross between desperation and a possible job at the end of the trail. Many found a few days work in the cotton fields and vegetable patches of Eastern Texas. Others kept on going. Crossing Texas from east to west was a particular challenge. The straightened and more streamlined Texas portion of I-20 today is 636 miles long. Think of the challenge in the 1930s, in an overloaded vehicle that had seen better days, its tires patched and repatched, the highway drifting in and out of every sorry little town along the way. Everyone is tired, coated with dust and hungry, and cramped into a tight little corner of the family car or truck. Kids who should be in school are not; grandparents who should be rocking on a porch back home in the Carolinas are not. The bread that should be rising in the oven and the soup that should be simmering on

You drive and you drive and you're still in Texas tomorrow night.

—Jack Kerouac (Charters, 1995: 213)

Children heading west with their impoverished family, 1936, as photographed by Dorothy Lange. (Courtesy of the Library of Congress.)

the cook stove for the evening meal are cherished memories. And Texas seems to go on and on and on. Many did not make it; the vehicle ran out of gas and the family ran out of money to pay for it. Good intentions and shattered dreams littered the roadsides along with worn out tires and busted axles. When this happened, all able-bodied family members fanned out looking for work, food, anything to improve their lot. They camped out at night in or around the stalled vehicle and prevailed on local soup kitchens and hospitality for a warm meal and whatever else they could get.

At the end of the I-20 corridor just west of Pecos, Texas (Exits 42–39), those who had made it this far crossed into Arizona and then California. A single mother with three children who drove west in search of work, along what is now the I-20 corridor, said it best: "Anybody as wants to work can get by. But if a person loses their faith in the soil like so many of them back there in Oklahoma, then there ain't no hope for them. We're making it all right here, all but for the schooling, 'cause that boy of mine, he wants to go to the University."[37] Expectation and hope; they had reached the promised land.

Interstate 55: Crossing Over

A bridge on Interstate 50—the Memphis-Arkansas Memorial Bridge—crosses the Mississippi River at Memphis, Tennessee. It is the only bridge on the interstate system to be on the National Register of Historic Places and is the longest Warren truss-style bridge in the United States. When it opened on December 17, 1949 it substantially reduced anxiety levels for the thousands of people crossing the river each day. The new bridge replaced one-lane wooden roadways suspended outside the steel framework of the nearby Harahan Railroad Bridge. The lanes were very narrow with only a low wooden railing to keep vehicles and their occupants from "crossing over" in more than one sense of the words. The wooden planking on these lanes did not fit together tightly, so anyone making the trip could see the muddy Mississippi one hundred feet below. The planks also rattled. But the worst was when a train crossed the bridge; automobiles on the bridge would start to vibrate. Many motorists and their passengers must have wondered if the last sound they heard would be the roar of a freight train. To add insult to

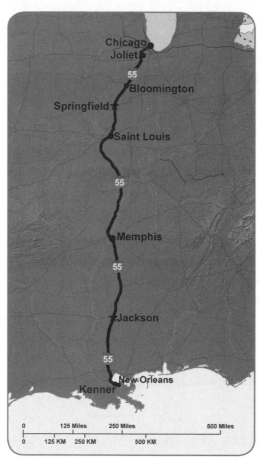

Interstate 55

terror, for the first six years of the bridge's existence, it cost twenty-five cents per automobile to use the roadway. A trip across the almost mile-long bridge in a vehicle must have invoked the names of quite a few saints for anyone afraid of heights, especially when sparks flew from the engines of the trains passing safely within the steel framework of the inner part of the bridge. In 1928, sparks from a train did set the roadway on fire, the creosote-soaked planking making the blaze hot enough to twist the steel. Repairs were made and the bridge reopened to vehicular traffic in a few months.

A rail bridge had existed across the Mississippi River at Memphis since 1892, but motorists had to wait until 1917 when the Harahan Bridge opened with its dual rail and vehicle lanes. The automobile lanes were an afterthought, at least for the railroad company forced to add them to the planned rail bridge. If the company wanted the bridge license, it had to include automobile lanes. But, the Harahan and the later Memphis-Arkansas Memorial Bridge connected more than Tennessee with Arkansas. As an essential element on the north–south rail and road grid from New Orleans to Chicago, the bridges provided a conduit for the flow of the musical stylings emanating out of the South when African American musicians headed north to work in the clubs of Chicago. Louis "Satchmo" Armstrong, Nat King Cole, Jelly Roll Morton, King Creole, Bessie Smith, Chuck Berry, and even Elvis probably crossed the river on these bridges.

The Memphis-Arkansas Memorial Bridge, on which I-55 crosses the Mississippi River, appears on the far left of this photograph from the Library of Congress's Historic American Engineering Record collection. The Frisco Bridge is pictured center and the Harahan Bridge is on the right. Because of heavy river traffic, bridge engineers had to line up the piers of the three bridges. (Courtesy of the Library of Congress.)

Today's I-55 begins near Baton Rouge, Louisiana (Exit 1), where it curves away from I-10. It then cuts almost due north past Jackson, Mississippi (Exit 104), into Tennessee. In the days of Louis Armstrong and Bessie Smith, the highway north from New Orleans (U.S. Route 61) traced the Mississippi River to the west of the current I-55 routing, but joined up with I-55's footprint in downtown Memphis (Exit 12) before heading across the Mississippi on the infamous Harahan Bridge. U.S. Route 61 and I-55 are one and the same northward from the Memphis-Arkansas Memorial Bridge through Arkansas until I-55 Exit 63. From there to St. Louis, the two highways intertwine along the west bank of the Mississippi before I-55 cuts across Illinois for Chicago. (U.S. Route 61 continues up the Mississippi.) It was always considered good luck for African American travelers to make a pit stop along this stretch of the road into Chicago to rub the nose of the Lincoln statue in Springfield, Illinois (Exits 100–92). Doing so was guaranteed to bring good fortune.

Slaves brought the musical stylings of Africa and the Caribbean to America, building on and adapting their cultural heritage with each passing generation. Especially in Louisiana, existing Spanish, French, and Cajun heritages added to the musical mix. Slave work songs and songs making fun of their masters blended with Underground Railroad songs. Spirituals evolved into gospel hymns adding in tambourines, drums, perhaps pianos to the cappella singing characteristic of spirituals. Many of the delegates heading to the 1930 National Baptist Convention in Chicago, including those crossing on the rail and road bridges at Memphis, heard a concert of gospel music for the first time. It was received so enthusiastically by the audience that any resistance to this new styling melted away. The heritage of lyrical songs of the slaves gradually evolved into jazz, blues, and rock and roll, their complex rhythms and intricate patterns beyond anything attempted by European musical styles of the times. The Louisiana zydeco heritage added to the blend rolling out of the South. Each genre built on the other, their interpreters paving the way for future generations of performers. Success in Chicago clubs became the ultimate goal for many of these Southern musicians toiling in Louisiana juke joints or the French Quarter of New Orleans. In Chicago, they could make a decent living and have their music accepted by everyone; the popular African American dance bands of the era and their accompanying soloists frequently had large fan bases among white audiences. Chicago also had a large and fairly stable African American population, thanks to the post Civil War migration northward. This made accommodation and acceptance within the city easier.

The riffs, the musical phrasings, the laments and hurt that crossed the Mississippi River in Memphis changed the face of music forever. Here on the old Harahan Bridge with its own shake, rattle and roll, and the roar of the freight engines, and the later Memphis-Arkansas Memorial Bridge, the rich Southern musical traditions crossed over to a white audience.

Interstate 77: High Gear

"It is remarkable that, although the Americans, as a people, travel more, perhaps, than any other nation, so little attention is paid by them to safety in transit. . . . As long as the rampant spirit of competition and desire to outvie their fellows, which prevails amongst a large class of Americans, is tacitly, if not openly, encouraged by the governing powers, such a state of things must exist, and will probably increase."[38] Tourist John Benwell was reacting to his experiences on American steamboats where he witnessed barrels of pine pitch being loaded on board. Once

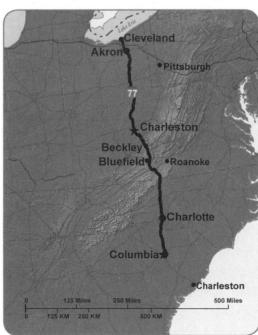

Interstate 77

Speed and alcohol don't mix. This 1922 automobile accident resulted in the discovery of several cases of moonshine. (Courtesy of the Library of Congress.)

the furnaces were started up, the pitch was poured into the fire to produce even more "caloric" and increase the speed of the boat, involved in an impromptu race with another boat that had pushed away from the dock at the same time. Even the passengers got into the act, urging their vessel onward in a race up the river.

The nation John set out to explore in the 1850s, also loved its liquor. Many people still declined to drink tea, and coffee, while widely consumed, was usually strong enough to rot even cast-iron palates. Drinking water was not always the safest, especially if traveling; liquor provided a viable option for young and old. All along the corridor served by today's Interstate 77, from the shores of Lake Erie in Ohio, through the Virginias and Carolinas, general stores and taverns readily sold liquor by the jug, and almost every farm along the way had a "facility" for turning grain and fruit into an alcoholic beverage, whether it was whiskey, brandy, or wine. In the liquid form, corn, grain, or fruit could easily and profitably be transported to market, whether it was out of the hills of West Virginia or along the piedmont in places like Charlotte, North Carolina. Whiskey made an appearance at every event from births to

> Hogs like the corn mash used to make alcohol so moonshiners frequently had to build a fence around the still. In one case, the moonshiner was too late; a hog had fallen into the mash and drowned. With a shrug of his shoulders, the moonshiner carried on, ignoring the dead hog. The results must have been pretty good, because from then on, strong liquor was frequently greeted with a satisfied swipe of the mouth and the exclamation: "It must'a had a dead hog in it!"

deaths; it was used to celebrate a marriage and served in church and at graveside at funerals. Young and old enjoyed their daily tipples.

The 1840 U.S. Census revealed that North Carolina produced more than one million gallons of distilled and fermented liquors annually. This compared to about one hundred thousand gallons in South Carolina and nearly one hundred and seventy thousand gallons in Virginia. Moonshine totals unknown. While restrained drinking had long been considered beneficial throughout the South as a preventive measure against "the bilious fevers" common in warmer climes, the population of North Carolina in 1840 was just over seven hundred and fifty thousand. That works out to one and a quarter gallons of legally distilled alcohol for every man, woman, and child in the state, never mind the huge illegal trade.

Not everyone approved. First Lady Lucy Hayes from the northern end of the I-77 corridor in Ohio acquired a nickname after she refused to

> What would Bart Simpson write on the blackboard if he had gone to school in 1860s North Carolina?
>
> "Touch not, taste not, handle not." —The golden rule for dealing with alcohol, assigned as a blackboard writing exercise to youngsters in Confederate schools in 1862.

serve liquor in the White House. The press heard her husband, President Rutherford B. Hayes, comment on the lemonade his wife kept serving at official functions. Lemonade Lucy made up for the lack of alcohol with elegant dinners that had Washington politicos and socialites fighting for invitations. She also set a new standard for White House entertaining.

Charles Dudley Warner, a sometime-collaborator with Mark Twain, traveled through the I-77 area in Virginia and North Carolina in the 1880s. He remarked on the woods being full of grog shanties selling "native brandy." In town, the local saloon was known as the "tippling house" or "doggery." The "Saturday night frolic" at the local doggery was common practice.

By 1900, Charlotte, North Carolina (Exits 1–12), had a population of eighteen thousand served by fifteen saloons. The prohibition vote in July 1904 in Charlotte gave voters two options: absolute prohibition or an outlet run by the city where residents could buy alcohol. It was a bitter election, pitting the wets against the drys. The wets were depicted as "morally stunted." Total prohibition won the day and Charlotte remained dry until September 1947 when voters approved the opening of seven Alcohol Beverage Control stores in Mecklenburg County.

In one of the more unusual pairings of interests working together for the same cause, North Carolina moonshiners collaborated with the Anti-Saloon League, ministers, and the Women's Christian Temperance Union during the 1933 state elections. Even the parties split on the issue. Dry Democrats worked with dry Republicans and the wets banded together on the other side of the issue: whether to repeal the statewide prohibition. With determination and a campaign budget of $8,000, the drys ultimately prevailed in most of the state. Not even a personal request by President Roosevelt, who tried to use his overwhelming popularity in North Carolina to persuade voters to repeal prohibition, could topple the grassroots, get-out-the-vote campaign waged from kitchens and meeting halls throughout the state. As for the moonshiners, they apparently became part of the dry campaign in an effort to protect their own business interests.

In Virginia, prohibition began in 1916, three years before the rest of the country. Revenuers traveled through the state collecting taxes and destroying stills. But instead of destroying the industry, moonshining became even bigger business. The Franklin County Conspiracy of 1935 sold a lot of newspapers with sensational headlines when charges were laid against dozens of revenue agents and other government officials who had been bribed by moonshiners. Franklin County, south of Roanoke (Exit 32, northbound; Exit 81, southbound) became known as the "wettest" place in the United States.

With so much pressure to deliver the goods—and avoid capture by the authorities—moonshiners turned to something that would give them more "caloric," turning in the farm wagon and the mule team for a racy little number from Detroit with a lot of horse power, designed to navigate the curvy hill country of the Virginias and the Carolinas through which I-77 rolls. But as prohibition came to an end, drivers who had gotten their adrenalin rush behind the wheel ferrying moonshine out of the back hills, found themselves without an outlet. In 1948, this need for more caloric led to the birth of NASCAR. Like many of the other early NASCAR stars, Robert Glen "Junior" Johnson learned to drive delivering his father's distilled efforts to customers. After serving time in prison for moonshining, Junior turned to NASCAR as an outlet for his need for caloric.

In Junior's day, new cars were in short supply. Since spectators probably would not take too kindly to seeing brand new cars smashed up on the track, speedway drivers turned to cars driven on public roads. Just about all of them were sedans that had seen better days. Often, the car was used during the week as the family vehicle and then driven to the track for the Saturday night race. All the windows still held their glass; the seat belt was frequently a piece of rope or an airplane pilot's harness. Roll bars, while mandated, were usually not installed. Sometimes, drivers rented vehicles for the Saturday night race. Fans piled into the local speedway in overflowing cars and trucks, and on hay wagons pulled behind tractors.

Today, the family sedan no longer takes to the track. Saturday night races have given way to race weekends that see fans pouring into nearby parking lots and temporarily converted farmer's fields to create massive tent cities and tailgate parties. Moonshine has given way to the ubiquitous can of beer. Speedways along the I-77 corridor include those at Charlotte, North Carolina, and Martinsville (Exit 14) and Bristol (Exit 40) in Virginia. Meanwhile, Mooresville, North Carolina (Exit 36), has developed into a NASCAR hotbed with many team garages located in and around this city just north of Charlotte. Pit crews learn their trade at Mooresville's NASCAR Technical Institute and fine-tune their cars and teams for the coming season.

Officials estimate the economic impact of NASCAR at five billion dollars in North Carolina alone, providing twenty-four thousand jobs in the state—not bad for a business that started out on winding back roads that today feed into the I-77 corridor. Tourist John Benwell of the 1850s predicted that the need for caloric would only increase. He was right; it did. A nation always enthralled with speed continues to indulge its passion.

Interstate 15: Happy Trails

Parts of Interstate 15, from San Diego, California (Exits 1–12), to Sweetgrass, Montana (Exit 397), might look vaguely familiar to passing motorists, even if they have never been this way before. Images along the interstate are embedded in our memories of time spent in front of the television, eyes glued to the screen at the movie theater or idly flipping through a magazine. This is where Butch Cassidy and the Sundance Kid roamed and the Rifleman made his small town safe. The boulder-strewn landscape and deserts along the way recall the likes of Hopalong

Visualize Wile E. Coyote, arms crossed, eyebrows arched, rubbing his chin as he peers over the ledge where this hiker from 1925 sits admiring the scenery in Zion National Park. (Courtesy of the California Museum of Photography, California Online Archive.)

Interstate 15

| 0 | 125 Miles | 250 Miles | 500 Miles |
| 0 | 125 KM | 250 KM | 500 KM |

Cassidy, the Lone Ranger, Roy Rogers, Thelma and Louise, and Wile E. Coyote. Those soaring cathedral rocks appear as a backdrop in commercials selling everything from next year's automobile model to the latest and greatest in high tech. Desert scenes crop up in beverage commercials, and the rolling grasslands of Big Sky Country in tobacco advertisements of another era.

Lured to the Los Angeles area, in the early 1900s, by sunshine and incentives from the Chamber of Commerce, the fledgling movie industry soon began to spread out from the studios and back lots springing up in the suburbs. Motion picture companies and some actors bought land nearby, particularly ranches with enough variation in the landscape suitable for anything the early plot lines demanded. But as plots and the technology of making a movie evolved, directors looked farther afield for their settings, particularly the Westerns riding across Saturday matinee screens. Zane Grey, father of both the Western romance novel

The hot, dry winds that sometimes blow through the Los Angeles area are named after the Santa Ana Mountains. Air rushing down off high plateaus compresses at lower altitudes and heats up, becoming a Santa Ana. Los Angeles writer Raymond Chandler's detective, Philip Marlowe, could always expect to get a case to solve when a Santa Ana turned people's thoughts to murder and mayhem.

and movie, insisted his stories be filmed at the location in the book. In doing so, he introduced Hollywood to his West. The Mojave Desert near the California–Nevada border, the Valley of Fire in Nevada, and the Zion Canyon area of Utah drew the celluloid buckaroos anxious to capitalize on dramatic settings along what is now I-15. In the early days, trains frequently took care of transporting film crews and actors out of Los Angeles to a nearby location. But as the comfort and technology of road travel evolved, and televisions started popping up in living rooms all over the world, film shoots wandered further afield from their Los Angeles studios. Today, John Wayne and John Ford could mosey up I-15 into *Stagecoach* country in an RV.

South of the Los Angeles area, I-15 skirts the eastern flank of the Santa Ana Mountains. Before the population of the area exploded, the Santa Anas frequently provided a backdrop for many of the early Westerns. Interstate 15 then passes along the Temescal Valley and the Rainbow Valley to Escondido (Exit 27) and on to San Diego, a distance of about one hundred miles. To the north of Los Angeles, I-15 swings up through Cajon Canyon and then in a northeasterly direction toward Las Vegas. Leonard Slye probably did not think too much about the landscape in this area when he headed to California in 1930 to visit his sister. His family stayed to pick fruit in the Great Depression and Leonard kept practicing on his mandolin and guitar. By 1937 he had signed with Republic Pictures as a singing cowboy. Together with Dale Evans, Trigger, Bullet, and sidekick Pat Brady and his trusty jeep Nellybelle, Leonard Slye became King of the Cowboys making over one hundred movies as Roy Rogers. Happy trails for Roy and Dale included family life near

Victorville (Exits 150–151). (Exit 151A takes motorists along Roy Rogers Drive while Exit 161 connects with the Dale Evans Parkway.) From here it was an easy commute along part of the famous U.S. Route 66 into Los Angeles and the various studios and sets circling the city. In later years, this stretch of U.S. Route 66 became I-15, for much of the way from San Bernardino (Exit 109) through the Cajon Canyon and up over Baldy Mesa and onward to Victorville. Built before Las Vegas was anything more than a small rail center in the desert, U.S. Route 66 then headed in a southeasterly direction for Arizona, avoiding Nevada altogether. But, by the time the interstates came along, Las Vegas was a major destination for Californians. Consequently, at Barstow (Exits 178–183), I-15 cut to the chase and headed straight across the Mojave Desert for Las Vegas.

Author Bill Bryson calls this stretch of California akin to "driving across the top of an oven."[39] Interstate 15 twists through a scruffy landscape scattered with huge rounded, gray boulders sleeping amid the brown tufts of grass. Occasionally, a waterfall glints in the sunshine. The interstate levels off into the high desert, with sagebrush and trailer parks scattered like so much stubble across the landscape. Long narrow ranges of mountains separated by deep valleys run parallel to each other. This ridge-and-valley topography has been described as, "an army of caterpillars crawling northward out of Mexico."[40] The interstate climbs over caterpillar backs all the way to Nevada. Motorists' ears pop. Long, gray and brown vistas stretch beyond the horizon, Las Vegas (Exits 36–58) glinting in the distance. The brighter than bright natural light of this area has served film crews well. Everything from *Viva Las Vegas* with Elvis Presley to *Diamonds are Forever*, *The Ballad of Cable Hogue*, *Cool World*, *Con Air*, *Rush Hour 2*, *Ocean's Eleven*, *The Mexican*, *America's Sweetheart*, and *Miss Congeniality 2* have made use of Las Vegas loca-

Nearby Hinkley (Exit 179) played a pivotal role in the film *Erin Brockovich*. It was here that the power company and the real-life Brockovich butted heads, resulting in a lawsuit and handsome settlement for the town and a feature role in the movie starring Julia Roberts.

tions. And of course, there is the current crop of television shows set in Las Vegas that periodically venture out of closed studios in California to take advantage of Las Vegas settings.

Las Vegas means "the meadows" in Spanish. The location was well known by travelers, because the meadows were a good spot to camp, and had nearby artesian springs. From a camping ground, it became a Mormon fort to protect the mail run from Los Angeles to Salt Lake City before turning itself into a rail town in 1905 and then the Las Vegas of today, thanks to Benjamin (Bugsy) Siegel building one of the first luxury hotels on what would become the Strip in 1946. Until that time the fortunes of the quiet town near the Boulder Dam (now Hoover Dam) construction site had alternately flourished and waned. But with a luxury gambling facility, better transportation including the new I-15, and more and more people escaping to the desert to live in air-conditioned comfort, Las Vegas never looked back.

Heading out of Las Vegas to the northeast, I-15 passes the entrance to Valley of Fire State Park (Exit 75). Named for the red, orange, and white sandstone formations, the park's eerie shapes of brilliant red sandstone have been used in Western and sci-fi movies, including a *Lost in Space* movie and *Star Trek Generations*. Film and television crews used Kanab, Utah (Exit 16), as their headquarters while shooting such famous flicks as *Butch Cassidy and the Sundance Kid* and some Clint Eastwood films. The *Rifleman* TV series was shot here as well. Butch Cassidy crews used a ghost town south of Zion National Park (Exit 40). Created in 1909, Zion was one of the first national parks. The Virgin River carved the canyon in the park with subsequent fine-tuning by the elements over the millennia. The canyon is up to twenty-four hundred feet deep and half a mile wide. Native American cliff drawings and ancient fossils have been found along the canyon walls. Stone columns, hoodoos, and arches stand sentinel over nearby Cedar Breaks (Exits 57, 75), a natural amphitheater about two thousand feet deep and three miles in diameter. Native Americans called it the Circle of Painted Cliffs; on a hot day, the rock strata glow in shades of golds, orange, red, pink, and a brilliant white, but as the day wanes, they turn to blues and violet.

Film credits for this area range from Tom Mix movies to *Thelma and Louise*, with John Wayne, Matt Dillon, Grizzly Adams, the Outlaw Josie Wales, God (in *The Greatest Story Ever Told*), and a few inter-planetary

> "Say, did God make this country?"
>
> "Of course He did," said her companion, rather startled by this unexpected question.
>
> "He made the country down in Illinois, and He made the Missouri," the little girl continued. "I guess somebody else made the country in these parts. It's not so well done. They forgot the water and the trees."
>
> —John and Lucy Ferrier discussing Utah's landscape in "A Study in Scarlet"

apes from *Planet of the Apes* thrown in for good measure. Up the road a few miles, the real Butch Cassidy, alias George Leroy Parker, called Beaver (Exits 109–112) home. His Hole-in-the-Wall Gang held up banks and trains, sometimes sharing their loot with the less fortunate.

Salt Lake City, Utah (Exits 297–318) sits between Great Salt Lake and the peaks of the Wasatch and Oquirrh Mountains to the east and southwest. Both ranges can be seen from the interstate. Sherlock Holmes made his first appearance in 1887 in "A Study in Scarlet," but the case did not occur in the British Isles. Utah, specifically the area around Salt Lake City, captured the honor of introducing the genius of the world's first consulting detective. The inevitable film in 1933 generally ignored most of the plot and came up with its own storyline.

Interstate 15 continues up the eastern side of Great Salt Lake, curving gently in to touch it near Exit 354. The lake covers more than seventeen hundred square miles, its size varying according to fluctuations in the rate of evaporation and the flow of the three rivers that feed it. Great Salt Lake is like a bathtub sitting in the sun with no drain; rivers flow into the depression but then the water evaporates leaving a salty brine. Around Salt Lake City, construction of I-15 dramatically shortened travel times into the city, reviving smaller communities like Kaysville (Exit 331) and Farmington (Exits 325–327). Between Bountiful (Exits 320–321) and Layton (Exits 332–334), engineers upgraded an existing four-lane stretch of road to interstate standards. Anyone who watched the 2002 Winter Olympics on TV will remember the incredible vistas in this area; Salt Lake City and nearby Park City (Exit 307) hosted many of the events. Since 1981, Park City has also hosted one of the most re-spected festivals for innovative films: The Sundance Film Festival.

In Idaho, the browns and grays of Utah gradually turn to hues of green as I-15 passes through Caribou National Forest, from the Utah border to Pocatello, Idaho (Exits 69–71). Adjectives like vast, huge, and endless start entering the vocabulary to describe the horizon. Towns become farther apart; so do service centers. Contrary to its name, Cari-bou National Forest does not have any caribou. It never did. A miner, by the name of Caribou Jack, liked to tell tall tales about the caribou in Northern Canada. Caribou Jack struck it rich in 1870 with a major gold find. In the next twenty years, fifty million dollars in placer gold made its way out of these slopes and prompted the development of roads into the area as yet another gold rush brought miners, companies, and aux-iliary services to this part of Idaho. Caribou Jack's name lives on in the Caribou Mountains and in Caribou National Forest. The forest of timber and sagebrush covers one million acres in Idaho, Utah, and Wyoming.

Just past Humphrey (Exit 190), I-15 starts line dancing with the Con-tinental Divide. Up to this point, the watersheds along I-15 flow into the Pacific, but at the border with Montana at Monida Pass (elevation: 8,870 feet), I-15 crosses over to the Atlantic side of the Divide. Then, just south of Butte at Deer Lodge Pass (elevation: 5,879 feet), I-15 steps back over the Divide again only to dance back to the Atlantic side almost imme-diately at Homestake Pass (elevation: 6,368 feet) and Elk Park Pass (el-evation: 6,364 feet) just to the north of Butte. From this point onward, I-15 remains on the Atlantic side of the Continental Divide, through the Deer Lodge National Forest and onward to Helena (Exits 192–193). *Run-away Train*, a film from 1985 was nominated for three Academy Awards. Starring Jon Voight, Eric Roberts, and Rebecca de Mornay, the film used the prison museum in Deer Lodge and the rail yards in Anaconda. *Diggstown* with James Woods and Lou Gossett Jr. used the same prison a few years later. Other movies shot in the Deer Lodge area include *Fast-Walking* with James Woods and *The Last Ride* with Mickey Rourke.

In the 1890s, Helena boasted that it had more millionaires per cap-ita than any other place in the United States, thanks to the huge gold, copper, and coal deposits nearby. (At that time, coal was still used to heat homes and people were starting to wire their homes for electricity and the telephone with copper.) Helena's original name could serve as

> Montana shares a distinction with Nevada, its neighboring I-15 state: they were the last two states to implement a maximum daytime speed limit. The 1980s oil crisis forced their hand: if they did not enforce a fifty-five mile per hour speed limit, federal highway funding would dry up. After the federal government removed this cap on speed limits in 1995, Nevada established seventy-five miles per hour as the upper limit for rural interstates. A court challenge to Montana's vague upper limit of a speed that was "reasonable and prudent" also forced Montana to set the upper speed limit at seventy-five miles per hour.

a movie town name in a Western: Last Chance Gulch. A group of gold miners founded the town in 1864. Appropriately, one of the great movie cowboys, Gary Cooper of *High Noon* fame, was born on a ranch near Helena.

In *The Big Sky*, Pulitzer Prize–winning novelist A.B. Guthrie Jr. called Montana, "a raw, vast, lonesome land, too big, too empty."[41] Guthrie's bestselling novel about trappers in the American West eventually reached the silver screen in 1952 starring Kirk Douglas. This was the golden age of Hollywood Westerns. The fast waters of the Missouri River used in the filming of *The Big Sky* and the open spaces of Montana epitomized the West and Westerns in moviegoers' eyes. In 1961, Guthrie granted permission to use Big Sky as part of what became a very successful promotional campaign: Montana became Big Sky Country.

Snowcapped mountains, their craggy ridges looming over boulder-strewn foothills, deep jagged canyons, soaring cathedrals carved out of rock, gently rolling hills spotted with sagebrush and grasses, oceans of desert, Big Sky Country. From start to finish, I-15 offers a palette to delight and stimulate with shades of cobalt blue, magenta, gentian violet, burnt sienna, and raw umber. But it is also a palette of movie heroes and screen legends of another era, who, with their faithful companions, cantered across black and white television sets every Saturday morning for millions of youngsters who watched their heroes round up the bad guys and set the world aright for yet another day. Everyone breathed a sigh of relief as the hero rode off into the sunset, sometimes serenading his lady, enjoying the moment and the anticipation of happy trails.

Interstate 68: In a Cat's Eye

Cumberland, Maryland, started life in the 1750s as Fort Cumberland. (George Washington commanded the fort at one time.) As an early transportation hub, Cumberland prospered. The National Road, which passed through the Appalachians at Cumberland into the Ohio Valley and beyond, was a main gateway for settlers heading west. It was also the western terminus of the C & O Canal, built as a transportation link between Washington, D.C., and the interior. Today, Cumberland sits at about the halfway point along Interstate 68 in the Maryland Panhandle. Interstate 68 starts in Hancock (Exit 82) at an I-70 exit ramp. It then heads west through Cumberland (Exits 46–43) and Frostburg (Exits 34–33), crossing into West Virginia and ending in Morgantown (Exit 1) where it meets up with I-79. In doing so, I-68 provides an alternate, slightly more southerly routing to the heavy traffic on I-70.

Besides being a centuries-old transportation hub and gateway for travel across the continent, Cumberland has another serious claim to fame. It seems that the area has a tendency to produce world marbles-playing champions. For the uninitiated, marbles are shot within a spe-

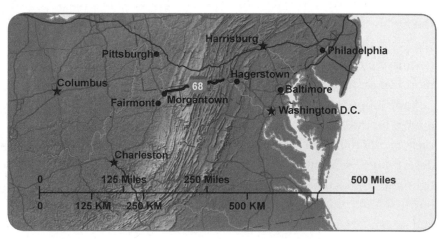

Interstate 68

cific area or along a course with the back of the hand resting on the ground. Sometimes, the goal is to shoot the marbles into a hole. If this sounds vaguely familiar, it might be because marbles has been credited with spawning present-day games, including golf, bowling, and billiards. Marbles playing makes Cumberland's connection with the adjacent corner of West Virginia all the more important, because West Virginia has huge reserves of silica sand and natural gas. Industrious West Virginians looked at these reserves and set out to become the leading producers of marbles—enough alleys, aggies, and cat's eyes to keep those marbles-playing Marylanders happy, as well as most of the world. Before losing much of their market to cheaper marbles from China, West Virginia plants (and plants in central Illinois) turned out about three hundred and fifty million marbles a year. That is about two hundred a minute for the statistically inclined. But when was the last time you watched or played a game of marbles? Why the huge production?

The National Marbles Championship in Cumberland sometime in the 1930s. Photograph from the Herman and Stacia Miller Collection. (Courtesy of the Mayor and City Council of Cumberland, Maryland.)

Marbles players and games of Chinese checkers account for a few million marbles each year but not three hundred and fifty million. Most marbles end up in other products, including one that routinely appeared along roadsides for almost one hundred years before being supplanted by twenty-first century technologies. Did you ever wonder how those reflective road signs worked—not the reflective aluminum signs or the computerized message boards of today—the older-style signs where the letters seem to be made of rows of little reflective circles? Marbles.

The use of marbles in a reflective capacity on the road goes back to about 1900. One way to make the rear end of your vehicle visible in the dark was to take a bunch of glass marbles, paint one side with that new-fangled aluminum paint, and then glue the marbles to the back of your carriage or wagon. The lanterns or headlamps of approaching vehicles reflected in the marbles and the driver knew a slower-moving vehicle was ahead. The technology was adopted for automobiles and trains, and road signs. The rows of backlit circles on the taillights of many vehicles today and in the electronic message boards along the interstates reflect this marble-using heritage. But how does the world use up so many marbles every year? What about that rattling noise when you shake an aerosol can? Glass marble. It does not corrode or rust. Glass marbles are sometimes used as ball bearings, because they do not require lubrication, and they have been known to help a sluggish oil well produce. Even funeral homes routinely use a few marbles to help slide heavy caskets into place.

At one time, of the world's twenty-one marble factories, fifteen were in West Virginia. Most of these factories extended along a line from the Maryland border across the state to the Ohio border, with many of them just south of I-68. Now, only a couple of marble factories survive, concentrating on collector marbles, having conceded defeat in the industrial marbles market to cheaper Asian imports.

Collectors prize a good cat's eye. A cat's eye is a special kind of marble. It has a green or blue swirl in the center shaped a bit like a cat's eye. But a different kind of cat's eye also saves lives. That row of reflectors set into the pavement or along the side of the road are also known as cat's eyes. They reflect light helping vehicles stay the course. Their name is associated with a twist of fate that led to their invention. An Englishman in the 1930s was saved from driving off the road by a cat's eyes, which he spied through the heavy fog.

Thomas Jefferson was apparently very proud of his collection of cat's eyes, and George Washington, John Adams, and Abraham Lincoln played marbles whenever they could. Their passion for the game easily translates into today's golf enthusiasts, but could any of these presidential mibsters have predicted the evolution of marbles from a popular game of skill to the red trace of taillights? Perhaps as they admired a prized alley before a flickering candle or lamp, relaxing in an easy chair, and sipping a favorite drink, a glimpse of the future glimmered between their fingers.

Interstate 78: Stop, Go, and Run Like Crazy

Garrett Morgan never met George Carlin, which could be a good thing, although being able to eavesdrop on a conversation between the pair would probably have been enlightening, no pun intended. Garrett Morgan, considered by many to be the father of transportation safety technology, invented the modern-day stoplight; George Carlin, the acerbic, frequently profane, wordsmith comedian, hated stoplights. "When did this . . . [expletive] start? I only noticed them about a month ago myself and I'll be honest with you, I don't stop for them any more. I did for about a week; didn't like it."[42] George also hated tollbooths. Given that Interstate 78 from the Holland Tunnel in New York, through New Jersey and into Pennsylvania has tollbooths and one of the only stoplights on the interstate system, George was at his caustic best when describing a road trip through the Garden State. "You can't make any gas mileage in New Jersey; you're in a constant state of slowing down! By the time I get to Pennsylvania, I need a[n expletive] . . . brake job!"[43]

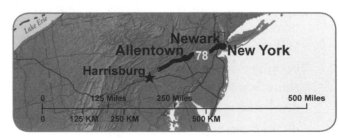

Interstate 78

A traffic-control system similar to that designed by Garrett Morgan at work in a Denver, Colorado, intersection. (Courtesy of the Denver Public Library, Western History Collection, X-23634.)

Garrett Morgan would probably see a trip along I-78 differently. In the early 1900s, as horse-drawn buggies tangled on the nation's roadways with automobiles, vehicle safety became an issue. Until that time most people were more concerned with the safety of the road itself. Were bridges safe? Was the roadbed smooth enough that the horse would not fall into a huge hole or the buggy lose a wheel? Could a horse-drawn cart make its way up a hill? Would the roadway wash away after a rain? Traffic at intersections was not that big a deal and who knew it would be an issue if you did not stay in your own lane of traffic.

Garrett Morgan, an African American sewing-machine repairman and garment company owner, living in Cleveland, Ohio, produced clothing on equipment he had designed himself. With success came profitability, and Garrett purchased an automobile around 1920. Suddenly, Garrett became more aware of the hazards of the roadway, including intersections. It was every motorist, buggy driver, pedestrian, and bicyclist for him or herself when it came to traffic. After witnessing a horrific accident between a horse and buggy and an automobile, Garrett put more thought into the problem. He received a patent for his electric traffic signal in November of 1923, a t-shaped pole with three positions: stop, go, and run like crazy if you were a pedestrian. His signal consisted of a tall pole with wooden flags with "stop" printed on them. The flags were raised and lowered via a crank. When a flag was at the bottom, it was the equivalent to today's green; at the very top it matched today's red. Half mast was the equivalent of a yellow signal today. This third position halted traffic in all directions to give pedestrians a few moments to get out of the way. A policeman from Utah had patented a red–green electric traffic light as early as 1912 and it had been installed in Cleveland in 1914. In Detroit, a four-way, three-color light had gone into service in 1920, so when Garrett came along with a more efficient electric signal mechanism in 1923, it didn't take long for his initial stop, go, and run-like-crazy settings to evolve into the red, green, and yellow of today, with red on top, then yellow and green.

So how did a traffic light end up on an interstate highway? According to the guidelines, there are not supposed to be any. But, sometimes, when interstate traffic mixes with urban traffic even a roadway designated an interstate needs a traffic signal; that is what happened at the eastern end of I-78 where the Newark Bay Extension of the New Jersey Turnpike bumps up against the Holland Tunnel into New York. Westbound traffic crossing into Hoboken, New Jersey, has a couple of lights to contend with on entering I-78. From the Tunnel, I-78 passes by Newark, New Jersey (Exits 58–57), and crosses over into Allentown, Pennsylvania (Exits 58–54), before merging with traffic on I-81 outside of Harrisburg, Pennsylvania.

Garrett Morgan lived until 1963, which was long enough to know the interstates were coming, but not long enough to see the full system in

> In a predominately Irish neighborhood in Syracuse, New York, traffic lights appeared at intersections in the 1920s, but were always vandalized. Irish residents objected to the red light's position atop the green, which they viewed as representative of Britain's oppression of Ireland. City officials finally gave up and installed special traffic signals with the green light on top.

operation. If he were alive today, Garrett would probably approve of the advances in traffic management the interstates have wrought. Garrett benefited financially from his invention, eventually selling it to General Electric for $40,000; the U.S. government even recognized his contribution to traffic safety with a special citation. As for George Carlin, he commented that after he stopped paying attention to red lights in New Jersey, he started "getting a whole lot better mileage."[44] Garrett Morgan would not approve.

Interstate 76 East: Glory Road

Devout Pennsylvanians called it the Glory Road. After putting up with steep hills, sharp turns, and dangerous intersections, the four lanes cutting through the Alleghenies must have seemed heaven sent. And then there was the increased truck traffic. Industry throughout the country had ramped up to support a possible war effort, and trucks had taken over the highways. Anyone trapped behind a convoy of trucks grinding up a mountainside knew the frustrations and dangers of the existing two-lane roads, especially when patience ran out and motorists pulled out to pass right into a head on collision. The Lord's name certainly must have been invoked at least once on every trip over the mountains of Southern Pennsylvania in the 1930s. But all that changed in October 1940 when the Glory Road opened for business. The ten-to-fourteen hour trip between Pittsburgh and the East Coast could now be accomplished in a fraction of that time. There was no fanfare on that day in October. President Roosevelt had been invited to speak, but officials delayed the actual ceremonies until after the election that year.

The forerunner of what is now Interstate 76 East, from Philadelphia,

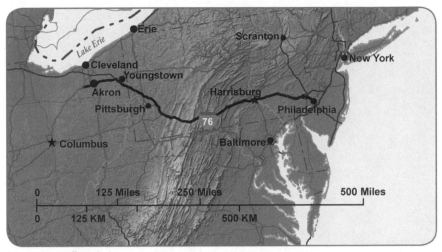

Interstate 76 East

Pennsylvania, to Akron, Ohio, the Glory Road was desperately needed. Roads had not kept pace with either the volume or the technology of vehicles of the 1930s, and despite the Great Depression, automobile ownership continued to increase. In Southern Pennsylvania, one of Roosevelt's make-work programs tackled the road over the Alleghenies to Pittsburgh, a crucial steelmaking hub for the nation and the military. In Pennsylvania, almost nine hundred thousand people were unemployed or in part-time jobs; highway construction would put many of these workers back on a payroll. And then there was the shot in the arm the local economy would receive with all those workers pouring into the area. Pennsylvania had a lot of Electoral College votes, and federal funding for a superhighway across the state made Democratic sense, especially if Roosevelt ran for a third term. But there was a catch to any funding: the highway had to be completed before the next gubernatorial election to help the Democratic candidate. With seventy million dollars in funding and a no-nonsense commissioner overseeing construction, laborers, supplies, and equipment flooded into the state.

It was an almost impossible feat, yet it took only twenty-one months to complete 160 miles of four-lane, limited-access highway from Middlesex (fifteen miles west of Harrisburg) to Irwin (20 miles east of Pittsburgh), through a mountainous terrain and the freeze–thaw cycles of two winters and springs. The commissioner in charge of construction "sent 'cats' and bulldozers racing over the Appalachian slopes like Nazi

Waiting for the Glory Road to open; motorists lined up waiting for midnight at the Pittsburgh interchange on October 1, 1940. (Courtesy of the Pennsylvania Turnpike Commission.)

tanks in the Ardennes, ordered concrete flushed over roadbeds that had been given scarcely the winter to settle."[45] One of the first tasks had been to acquire the thirty-four miles of a partially completed railroad from the 1880s; this included seven tunnels through the mountains that had to be drained and cleaned out after sitting dormant for so many years. Property was acquired, overpass contracts let, and the right-of-way cleared, drained, and graded. Work went on around the clock with portable lighting plants powered by generators hauled to areas not yet served by electricity. Contractors kept mechanics and spare parts on site to make sure all equipment ran as it should. Engineers, geologists, and inspectors also stayed on site around the clock in case they were needed. Everything about the highway broke new ground. For the first time, a highway was designed based on vehicle operation, rather than on the terrain. Long, sweeping curves promoted safety at high-speeds and allowed for safe stopping distances. The right-of-way was to be two hundred feet with ten-foot shoulders and a ten-foot median. Motorists had to have a sight line ahead of them of at least six hundred feet. Exit and entrance ramps twelve hundred feet long provided room for chang-

In the days when villages were protected by walls, moats, bridges, and, sometimes, a gate, one type of early traffic-control device was a spiked barrier or pike across the road. It helped guard against sudden attacks. Sometimes, these spiked barriers were manned to oversee those travelers passing along the road. It wasn't long before someone caught on to the idea of charging a fee for travel through the barrier or pike. When the fee was paid, the pike would be turned open to allow the traveler to pass.

ing speeds. There would be no intersections, which meant that for the first time, engineers had to design a variety of overpasses. They created 307 bridges and culverts, and diverted a channel of the Juniata River.

At Everett (Exit 149), engineers decided to cut their way through Clear Ridge rather than build another tunnel. The decision to excavate resulted in the removal of over one million cubic yards of debris. To give that figure perspective, the average dump truck holds twenty-five cubic yards. It took the equivalent of forty-four thousand dump trucks to remove all the rock and dirt from Clear Ridge and turn it into Clear Ridge Cut.

Time called the Pennsylvania Turnpike, "America's greatest highway."[46] Except in the tunnels, you could drive the turnpike's entire length if you wanted to at ninety miles per hour without shifting gears once. There were no intersections, traffic lights, pedestrians, or steep hills to worry about. For truckers who had once ground the gears on the old highway, the steepest grade was three percent. You went through the Alleghenies, rather than over them! The debris cleared out of dynamited slopes now filled in nearby valleys to provide a more level roadbed, and the curves were so gentle, motorists and truckers did not have to reduce speed. Some stretches were as straight as an arrow. Test drives over the roadway reached speeds of one hundred miles per hour. The military even tried it out. A training exercise in 1940 had a National Guard convoy drive to Bedford (Exit 146) to prevent its capture by hostile forces.

Despite the postponement of opening ceremonies, the commissioner in charge decided to open the Pennsylvania Turnpike anyway. With only six hours of advance notice, motorists lined up at each end to be among the first to drive Glory Road. At the eastern end, a reporter for the *Harrisburg Telegraph* recorded the big event. "At midnight, two black cats ambled across the gleaming cement. A minute later, a ticket-seller dropped his arm in the gesture of an automobile race-starter, and traffic was under way."[47] From start to finish, it was a marvel of modern ingenuity and engineering—the longest uniformly planned road in the nation. On its opening, *Time* was almost effusive.

> A 10-ft. centre strip, soon to be hedged with small fir trees, divides the four lanes into two. No signboards mar the way or confuse the eye—its only borders are the misty, pine-edged hillsides of the Alleghenies. Ten smart Esso stations, finished Pennsylvania-Dutch fashion in native wood and stone, specialize in restroom toilet seats sterilized by ultraviolet ray after every use.[48]

The first Sunday after its opening, churchgoers from all along the route left their place of worship that morning and headed for the turnpike in such numbers that tollbooths ran out of tickets and operators started giving motorists hand-written notes. And then there was the problem of getting off the turnpike. After zipping along to the next exit, motorists discovered long lines waiting to pay the toll and get back home for Sunday dinner. In the end, some twenty-seven thousand Sunday drivers checked the road out that day, about twenty-four thousand more than traffic planners had estimated for average daily traffic counts. The Glory Road was a hit!

For the first time, an American road was more advanced in engineering than the capabilities of trucks and cars of that time. Although not enforced at first, speed limits were soon mandated. It did not take planners long to start talking about extending the road all the way to Philadelphia and Pittsburgh, and shortly after the end of World War II, construction began. After being folded into the interstate system, further upgrades were done to the tunnels, eliminating some with rock cuts and bypasses, and twinning others. Elsewhere, engineers added truck lanes. The war had brought gas and tire rationing, and a booming economy. Truck traffic had overtaken automobile traffic on many highways. Now, it threatened to overwhelm the road infrastructure of America.

The Interstate Highway Era

Motorvatin' Over the Hill

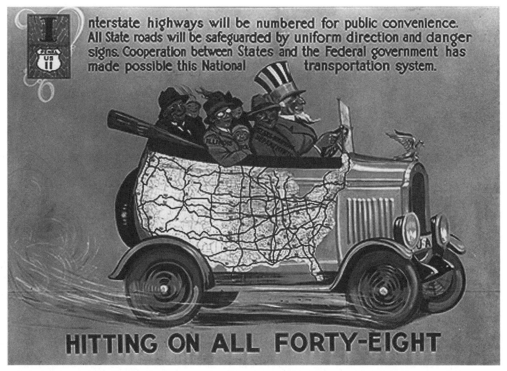

A U.S. Department of Agriculture promotional poster reassuring motorists that they would be able to find their way around on the new interstate system. (Courtesy of the Online Image Gallery, American Association of Highway and Transportation Officials, Washington, D.C.)

A T A TIME when Chuck Berry's Maybellene was "motorvatin' over
the hill . . . in a Coupe de Ville," President Eisenhower was worried
about the nation's roads. In the chill of the postwar era, the very real
potential existed for the government to order the evacuation of a large
city. Except for Los Angeles, New York, and Chicago, no expressways
existed to carry people out of the large urban areas to safety. High-speed
roads were also needed for military traffic. Eisenhower firmly believed
that an efficient transportation system was essential for the well-being
of the United States.

Congress, meanwhile, continued to dither about how best to upgrade the nation's roads mainly as a result of ongoing political disputes
with the various states about who should pay. Those lobbying for better roads—the trucking industry, automobile associations, and other
special interest groups—had so many specific agendas that they rarely
acted together. But Eisenhower persisted. Expressways were quickly
becoming a necessity, and only the federal government could accomplish a unified coast-to-coast system. In July 1954, Eisenhower sent Vice
President Richard Nixon to speak in his stead to the annual gathering of
governors. Nixon read a text prepared by President Eisenhower, which
described the nation's highways as "inadequate locally, and obsolete as
a national system."[1] Congress had allocated increased funding for highway construction during the last decade, but progress was slow. To re-
solve the problem, Eisenhower proposed an interstate system to meet
the growing demands on the country's road network. His plan called for
fifty billion dollars to be spent over ten years, in addition to the seven
hundred million dollars the federal government already spent annually
on the nation's roads.

Eisenhower's suggestion to the governors to think outside the box
and consider a transcontinental road system of the magnitude he envisioned sent everyone scurrying off to study the whole issue. How would
the funds be raised and allocated? Some governors had already consid-

ered asking the federal government to get out of the highway business or stop collecting gas taxes so states could have the revenues. Lobbyists for the gas and tire industries, and transportation companies joined the debate. To compound the problem, auto sales increased dramatically. In 1953, consumers drove 3.3 million new Ford, Chevrolet, and Plymouth cars off sales lots and onto the nation's roads. Collectively, Americans drove five hundred and fifty billion miles that year on a road system still flirting with the horse and buggy days of road design. The American Road and Transportation Builders Association concurred with Eisenhower's assessment of the situation, estimating that thirty-two billion dollars needed to be spent to repair the federal-aid highway system. Just to keep up with repairs, some forty thousand miles of roadway needed total rehabilitation every year. If that was not bad enough, two thirds of the twelve thousand bridges on the national system had been deemed unsafe for transport trucks. A new, improved interstate highway system was needed.

Eisenhower later wrote: "Its impact on the American economy—the jobs it would produce in manufacturing and construction, the rural areas it would open up—was beyond calculation."[2] The proposed interstate highway system would facilitate the efficient transportation of goods and people, reduce economic losses from detours and traffic jams, save lives through fewer accidents and "meet the demands of catastrophe or defense, should an atomic war come."[3] But a Republican administration and Democratic Congress meant very little headway on Eisenhower's commitment to an interstate system. In early 1956, everyone finally agreed to work together to get things started. It was none too soon. As President Eisenhower wrote in his State of the Union address that year, there were now sixty-one million motor vehicles on a road network that could no longer keep up. Highway construction was essential to maintain the "personal safety, the general prosperity, the national security of the American people."[4] The interstates would change the face of America.

As conceived, the interstate highway system had three goals: promote national defense, link all state capitals and cities with a population of more than fifty thousand with Washington (in 1956, 224 cities met this criteria), and, wherever possible, connect with the major thoroughfares and cities of Mexico and Canada. About forty-one thousand miles of interstate highways were to be developed, divided among forty interstates varying in length from over three thousand miles to just a handful of miles. The planned interstates represented a fraction of the nation's 3.6 million miles of roads, but were expected to carry twenty percent of all traffic. Those involved in planning the new system were well aware of the tremendous costs involved, particularly in urban areas and over difficult terrain. Bridges and tunnels, and sheared-off mountains did not come cheaply. The federal government agreed to pick up ninety percent of the overall cost, which amounted to twenty-eight billion dollars. The gas tax increased by one cent per gallon, and highway user tax revenues would help pay for the system.

The 1956 Federal-Aid Highway Act eventually made its way to Eisenhower's bedside in Walter Reed Army Medical Center on June 29, 1956, where he was recovering from intestinal surgery. No observers witnessed the signing; no cameras even recorded the event, yet Eisenhower's signature put the money in place to begin a project eventually described as one of the wonders of the modern world, eclipsing even man's first step on the moon in its impact on the twentieth century and on the daily lives of every American. President Eisenhower had succeeded in creating the National System of Interstate and Defense Highways.

Although there would be exceptions, standards for the new interstates were to be strictly followed. This included controlled access with no traffic signals, intersections, or rail crossings. There had to be at least two lanes of traffic in each direction, with a median and wide shoulders. Rest areas had to be spaced out along the highways, and grades and curves were to be safe at high speeds with no blind hills. (The federal government added a codicil of sorts in 1965 with the passage of the Highway Beautification Act. States wanting to continue to receive federal aid for interstates had to improve the view from the road: no junkyards or landfills left unscreened, or garish outdoor advertising. Extra funds were provided for landscaping with trees and shrubs.)

While the engineering aspects of road construction had moved forward since the days of the Pennsylvania Turnpike construction in the 1930s, the massive equipment needed to carve this much roadway out of the landscape and the science of pavement and interstate maintenance were very much in their infancy. The amount of heavy equipment needed to do the job was unprecedented and almost overwhelming. In

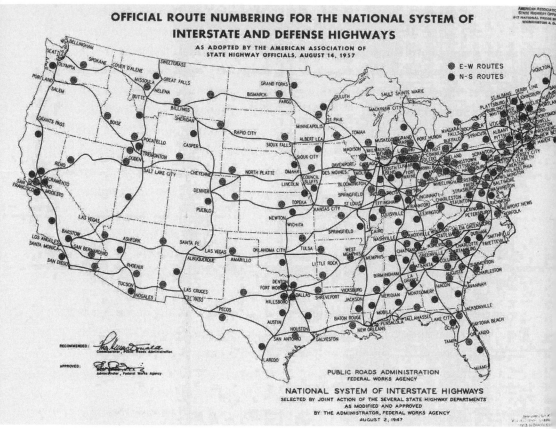

The Dwight D. Eisenhower System of Interstate and Defense Highways, as initially designed in 1957.

other places, where an existing roadway only needed upgrading, small, easily maneuvered, more articulated equipment was required. Engineers developed machines to do more than one aspect of road construction and maintenance. Caterpillar Co. established full production of its heavy earth-moving equipment in Decatur, Illinois, in 1956, transforming the city (now on I-72) from the soybean capital of the world into a highway equipment hotbed of innovation and production. The ripple effect carried down through the parts manufacturers, tire companies, and engine manufacturers; they all benefited. The economy soared. Concrete and asphalt companies experimented to find the right mix for each particular environment. A seven-mile test roadbed near Ottawa, Illinois (on I-80), proved invaluable in providing many of the answers. Army-supplied heavy vehicles circled endlessly on the test track to simulate real-time conditions.

By August 1958, construction crews had completed 1,952 miles of the interstate highway system; another 3,159 miles were under construction, but costs were rising. The interstate construction bill for 1959 was expected to top $7.1 billion—a little more than half what Americans were probably going to spend on new cars that year. The American Road and Transportation Builders Association estimated that by 1960, nine hundred thousand Americans would be employed building the interstates: about half of those working on the actual roads, with the remainder producing the goods and services needed to keep road crews working. During the 1960s, the system grew by forty miles a week. By 1965, twenty thousand miles of interstates had opened to traffic. Number crunchers determined that each mile had cost an average of $1,141,000. Some urban sections had cost as much as $50 million a mile. The entire system was expected to cost $46.8 billion. By 1980, road builders were almost done; forty thousand miles were completed. But not everything went smoothly. The creation of I-90 across Boston, with its various tunnels and bridges, resulted in what is known as the Big Dig. This fifteen-mile stretch of interstate, with its various permutations, technical problems, extensive cost overruns, and community protests, took forty-one years from the groundbreaking in 1962 to the opening of the tunnels to Logan Airport in 2003. It still leaks and has had serious problems with its concrete ceiling.

In carving I-15 out of the landscape from San Diego, California, to Sweetgrass, Montana, planners managed to accomplish all three of Eisenhower's interstate goals. While parts of the route already existed as other highways and, in some instances as old rail beds, much of I-15's trace cut through virgin territory, adding a new footprint to the landscape. The highway jigged in Utah to connect military job centers near Ogden with the interstate system. In Arizona, it jogged by Grand Canyon National Park, but did travel through the Virgin River Gorge. Here, the Virgin River had to be rechanneled twelve times to accommodate a roadway that included some of the longest bridges in the system and canyon walls so close that they almost touch the pavement. These construction challenges added up to the most expensive strip of the interstate highway system when originally built in the 1970s. Despite the changes to the river, this portion of I-15 also reflected a growing environmental consciousness. *Arizona Highways* later commented that, in diverting the river, engineers had managed to enhance, "rather than distract from nature's handiwork."[5] Interstate 15 construction ended south of San Diego at the Mexican border; its northern terminus already connected with highways leading into the developing energy fields in the Canadian province of Alberta and the booming cities of Calgary and Edmonton. Within the United States, commuters around Los Angeles, and between Los Angeles and San Diego, now had another limited-access thruway to crawl along and a speedy exit to that gigantic, neon pleasure palace in the desert: Las Vegas.

In a pattern that repeated throughout the nation, small towns on I-15 that had once been too far from Salt Lake City or Provo, Utah, for an easy daily commute suddenly saw their populations double. In Idaho and Montana, the night sky began glowing with more than starlight or the northern lights as small oases of fuel, home-cooked meals, strong coffee, and well-lit parking lots big enough to wrangle a herd of transports sprang up at interchanges amid the rolling grasslands. Bypasses meant many downtown cores withered; some died as the commercial center crawled toward the nearest interstate exit. Small local restaurants and gas stations were supplanted by national chains sporting an architecture designed to attract motorists: fast-in, fast-out, takeout meals, big washrooms, vending machines, hot showers, well-lit parking lots, chains identically configured, easily identified at a distance in time to make the decision to exit. The golden arches era had arrived, the similarity of the commercial enterprises at each interchange beginning to blur with a sameness of architecture and menus coast to coast.

In a 1968 article updating readers on the progress of the interstate system, *National Geographic* likened the magnitude and scope of the program as akin to trying to explain New York City to an ant: incomprehensible. *Time* called it the "biggest public works program since the Pharaohs piled up the pyramids."[6] It turned out to be the largest earthmoving project in history—forty-two billion cubic yards of material were excavated to build an eventual 46,000 miles of highway with 54,663 bridges and 104 tunnels. The original forty interstates consumed enough concrete to build a fifty-foot wall around the equator nine feet thick.

Interstates had to be built to consistent standards: limited access, four lanes each twelve feet wide, paved shoulders, and capable of handling speeds up to seventy miles per hour. Overpasses had to be at least sixteen feet high to accommodate military vehicles and grades were to be such that a military vehicle would not lose speed going up hill. Sometimes, this proved difficult to accomplish, especially when existing freeways suddenly found themselves designated as interstates. In Pennsylvania, the Harrisburg-York-Baltimore Expressway became I-83. Built before interstate standards were established, there have been problems with the Expressway's conversion. The Pennsylvania Department of Transportation worked hard to widen the roadway, introduce modern road-building technologies, and eliminate the likes of Dead Man's Curve in York (formerly near Exit 15) to bring the highway up to current standards, which now includes the ability to cope with the one hundred thousand or more vehicles using I-83 every day.

In Denver, Colorado, an older interchange onto one of Denver's major east–west streets found itself becoming the link between I-25 and I-70—without upgrading. Its ramps were short and its curves tight. It soon became a chronic accident site, dubbed locally as the Mousetrap. Things became so bad that in the days before interstate video monitoring, Denver police built an observation tower in the middle of the Mousetrap to keep an eye on the three hundred thousand vehicles using the interchange daily. Then, in the early hours of an August morning in 1984, a truck carrying armed torpedoes overturned on a Mousetrap ramp. Both interstates were closed for several hours, and the Mousetrap made national headlines. Something had to be done. By 1998 (and millions of dollars later), the approaches of both interstates into the Mousetrap had been realigned, high-occupancy vehicle lanes added, and traffic was up to three hundred and forty thousand vehicles a day, already surpassing the long-range estimates of planners.

Many existing roads that morphed into interstates reflected the technology and mindset of a bygone era, when the landscape dominated the road rather than the road dominating the landscape. Pre-1956 roads typically took the path of least resistance, curving around hills and lakes, finding soils and rock formations that could most easily form a solid roadbed. Grades were gentle, roads rarely straight. By the time states began folding these existing roadways into the interstate system and planning for new sections of highway, the mentality had become damn the torpedoes, full steam ahead—quite literally. Motorists traveling through Arizona on Interstate 40 can still admire the Bristol Mountains, because of something Nikita Khrushchev did in 1963; he signed the Limited Test Ban Treaty. Interstate 40 in Arizona follows the trace of U.S. Route 66 through the Bristol Mountains. In the early 1960s, when atmospheric testing of nuclear weapons was still allowed, scientists and road engineers had what they thought was a eureka moment. Why not vaporize anything that got in the way of a good, flat, straight highway along this stretch of U.S. Route 66? Arizona was not far away from Nevada's testing grounds, population density in the area was relatively low, there was nothing but sand all over the place, and there sat the Bristol Mountains right in the path of a potentially flat stretch of interstate highway. Plans to vaporize some of these mountains proceeded to the point that invitations were sent out to dignitaries and bunting ordered for the reviewing stand. The twenty-two nuclear warheads planted along a two-mile stretch of roadway had one hundred and thirty-three times more power than the two bombs dropped on Hiroshima and Nagasaki. The mushroom cloud created by their detonation would have had a diameter of over seven miles, but the interstate highway would be fifteen miles shorter! And then Krushchev picked up a pen and signed the treaty. All of a sudden, vaporizing the Bristol Mountains could become a huge provocation in the Cold War era. Engineers went back to the drawing board and the scientists went back to Nevada and underground testing.

By 1996, the interstates were estimated to have cost $329 billion—$58.5 billion in 1957 dollars—a sum relatively close to original estimates. Once built, local taxes were expected to pay for annual maintenance of the highways, though this plan eventually caused problems in some states that could not generate the revenue necessary to keep their roads in good condition. "It's like giving a Cadillac to a guy making $1,000 a year and saying, 'O.K., you take care of it,' declared one road expert."[7] Many more interstate highways than originally proposed would be built. Some of the original forty interstates wound up being longer than intended, some shorter, balancing out to a current total of 46,717 total miles of interstate highways.

"Look at an interstate map."

"Why interstate?"

"Why do you think the interstates were built? Not so the Harper family could drive from Aspen to Yellowstone Park on vacation. So the Army could move troops and weapons around, fast and easy."

"They were?"

Reacher nodded. "Sure they were. Eisenhower built them in the fifties. Height of the Cold War thing, and Eisenhower was a West Pointer, first and last."

"So?"

"So you look where the interstates all meet. That's where they put the storage, so the stuff can go any which way, moment's notice. Mostly just behind the coasts, because old Ike wasn't too worried about parachutists dropping into Kansas."

—Jack Reacher discussing the interstate highway system with his traveling partner in Lee Child's *Running Blind* (2000: 347–348)

Roads once designed to evacuate cities in the event of a nuclear attack, now evacuate millions in the path of an oncoming hurricane. They also speed up the physical and economic recovery in the storm's aftermath. A 1996 report estimated that every dollar spent on interstate highway construction had been, at that point, returned sixfold to the American economy. Today, nearly every good or service uses an interstate at some point in reaching the American consumer. The interstates have created a truly national marketplace and made shipping and warehousing more economical. In doing so, retail competition has increased and consumers have more options. Every dollar invested in interstate highways yields an average annual reduction of 23.4 cents in product costs. And, because many interstate highways cut right through cities, they are widely used by commuters.

Interstates of
chapter 5

In 1900, there were eight thousand motor vehicles in the United States. By 1945, there were forty million. By 1965, just as the first stretches of interstates were opening to the public, the number had risen to ninety million, an increase of 5.7 percent a year during a period when yearly population growth averaged 1.7 percent. Today, ninety-one percent of

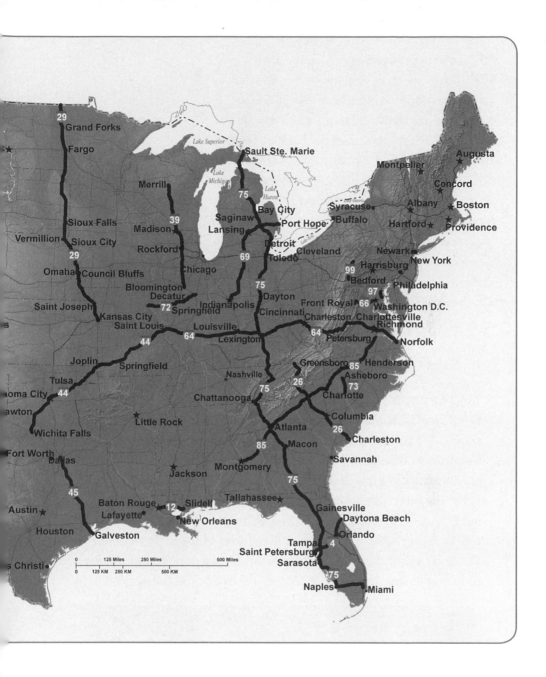

all person miles of travel are in a private passenger vehicle. Motorists clock an annual seven hundred and three billion vehicle miles on Eisenhower's interstate system. While Maybellene was motorvatin' over the hill in her Coupe de Ville, an agriculturally oriented society changed into an industrialized, high-speed nation in perpetual motion.

In 1957, the average rush hour speed on all Los Angeles freeways and streets was twenty-four miles per hour. By 1964, road conditions had improved to the point that this increased to thirty-one miles per hour, but Detroit automakers came up with a couple of schemes to bring it still higher. One plan called for computer punch cards controlling passenger capsules in a tube that would glide along at forty-five miles per hour. Another plan used the same punch cards to steer cars along a computerized superhighway. No word on how many punch cards it would take, or what would happen if they got out of order.

Interstate 99: If Blue Is North, Which Way Is Yellow?

Imagine trying to make your way from Boston to Phoenix to visit Aunt Edna and Uncle Stanley. Sounds easy. Leave Boston Saturday morning, following a road map and directional signs on the interstates to travel in a southwest direction. After some hard driving, you pull into their driveway in Phoenix a few days later. But there is a catch to this road trip; it's 1920. The interstates do not exist and there are very few directional road signs—just colored bands on a few utility poles along the road, but you do not know what they mean. Where does blue go? Is red the road to Phoenix? What about yellow? Occasionally, a signpost does appear with names of towns and arrows pointing off in all directions.

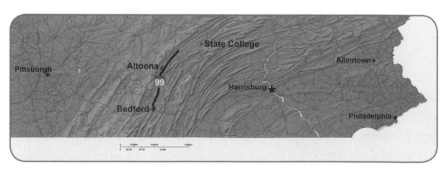

Interstate 99

An example of highway signage from the early 1900s. (Courtesy of the Michigan Department of Transportation.)

Such was the situation for millions of Americans buying into the new American dream of an automobile in every garage. They burst onto the roads with little idea of how to reach their destination. Main highways usually had names, such as the Lincoln Highway, the National Road, and the Valley Turnpike. By the mid-1920s, over two-hundred and fifty named trails, including the Robert E. Lee Highway, Atlantic Highway, Dixie Highway, Pacific Highway, and Yellowstone Trail, had been sponsored by organizations and now appeared on the national road maps. The problem was that written signage was largely non-existent; each group painted a colored band on utility poles to mark a given route. But gaily striped utility poles did not help motorists who did not know which color matched which highway. In New England, state highway departments marked north–south routes with a blue band, east–west ones with red, and what they called "intermediate" routes with yellow. That did not necessarily mean a blue band on a utility pole meant the same thing in Nebraska or Georgia. Finally, in 1925, the American Association of State Highway Officials decided to end this haphazard system of road identification. The time had come for road numbering, which went hand in hand with the need for consistency in another relatively new addition to the road landscape: directional signage. The Joint Board on Interstate Highways recommended a numbered system in October 1925: even numbers would appear on east–west highways and odd numbers on north–south highways. The smallest numbers would be in the east and north. This plan was adopted, and uniform numbered signage replaced the colored stripes on utility poles. The smallest odd number was given to U.S. Route 1, which hugs the Atlantic Coast. The smallest even number, U.S. Route 2, follows the U.S.–Canada border.

When the interstates came along, they needed distinct identifiers. Those busy road-numbering bureaucrats decided to keep the same north–south, east–west, odd and even numbering conventions but to work in the opposite direction with the lowest odd number on the West Coast and the lowest even number in Southern Florida. The goal was to avoid confusion with the older highway network. Interstates would be given one- or two-digit numbers, with the longer ones ending in zero or five. A bypass around a built-up area on an existing two-digit interstate would have an additional digit appended on the front of the interstate number. In the case of Syracuse, New York, for instance, I-81 cuts through downtown, while I-481 circumvents most of the heavy congestion as it loops around the southeast edge of the city.

So, with a numbering plan in place, how did Interstate 99 end up in the middle of Pennsylvania? The odd number identifies it as a north–south route, but it sits between I-79 and I-81. Could it not have become a three-digit interstate highway to keep to the numbering convention? Not according to Pennsylvania Congressman Bud Shuster, chair of the U.S. House Committee on Transportation and Infrastructure in 1995, who made an end run around the American Association of State and Highway Officials (the organization which normally assigns interstate highway numbers), and included plans for I-99 and its number in the National Highway Designation Act of 1995. Shuster wanted an interstate in his district and since no suitable two-digit number was available, he chose ninety-nine.

Still a work in progress, I-99 originally connected Bedford, Pennsylvania, with Bald Eagle, Pennsylvania, along the U.S. Route 220 corridor, a winding, hilly road that had been designated for priority upgrading as early as 1991. Ongoing construction is extending I-99 further north and improving its connection to I-80 and State College, Pennsylvania, home of the main Penn State campus and the Nittany Lions, a football team that garners massive fan support and some massive traffic jams on game days. As for Bud Shuster, he decided his work was done and retired after fourteen terms of office; his son succeeded him in Congress. Interstate 99 has been officially designated as the Bud Shuster Highway.

Interstate 85: Richmond Is a Hard Road to Travel

The June 18, 1956, edition of *Time* featured the recent medical travails of President Eisenhower, even putting a smiling Ike on its cover, amid assurances the president was recovering nicely from his recent health scare and surgery. Mention was made of his approval of the legislation

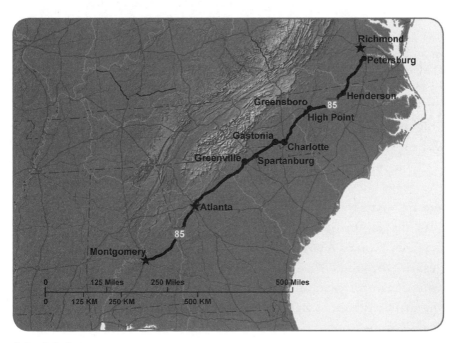

Interstate 85

The state capitol in Montgomery, Alabama, where Jefferson Davis became president of the Confederacy and civil rights advocates gathered a century later. (Courtesy of the Library of Congress.)

authorizing creation of the interstate highway system, but it was not "big" news. In another small article at the end of the national section, *Time* updated its readers on the bus boycott in Montgomery, Alabama.

Six months earlier, Rosa Parks had refused to give up her seat on a municipal bus to a white passenger. She had been on her feet all day and did not want to stand up for the trip home. She was also tired of the way African Americans were being treated. Rosa Parks was arrested and fined ten dollars. A boycott of Montgomery buses by African American residents resulted. Their demands were simple: first come, first served when it came to seats and African American drivers for the routes serving mainly African American neighborhoods. White passengers could still sit in the front of the bus, but African American passengers wanted to be treated courteously and with dignity. The economic effects on a transportation system where African Americans made up seventy-five percent of the ridership were staggering. The boycott ultimately lasted over a year resulting in a Supreme Court ruling that it was illegal to segregate any form of public transit.

The bus boycott organized by parishioners of a downtown Baptist church and their pastor, Dr. Martin Luther King Jr., proved a major boost for the fledgling civil rights movement, ironically in a city also known as the cradle of the Confederacy. A few blocks away from Montgomery's Civil Rights Memorial, a brass star marks the spot where Jefferson Davis stood as he was sworn in as president of the Confederacy in May 1861. Davis had arrived in Montgomery a few days earlier on a train from Atlanta, following a route similar to that taken by present-day Interstate 85. A few months later, Davis again took the train, this time to Richmond, Virginia, which was the new capital of the Confederacy. His routing took a few jogs as no direct rail line existed between Atlanta and Richmond in 1861. Despite this lack of a direct route, rail travel was still the best option for the notoriously frail Davis.

Present-day travelers can find the Civil Rights Memorial and the Alabama State Capitol Building off of Exit 1 on I-85. From there, I-85 continues to Atlanta, Georgia (Exits 68–104), Spartanburg, South Carolina (Exits 70–77), and Charlotte (Exits 34–40), Greensboro (Exits 121–128), and Durham (Exits 173–179), North Carolina, before slipping into Virginia and coming to an end in Petersburg, where it merges with I-95 just south of Richmond. This trace generally takes I-85 along the fall line between the rolling piedmont and coastal plain. Because its route carries it through only Southern states, I-85 is sometimes called the official interstate of the South, since it connects the Southern center of the universe (Atlanta) with three Southern capitals: Montgomery, Alabama, Raleigh, North Carolina, and Richmond, Virginia. If he had traveled by stagecoach in 1861, Jefferson Davis would have perhaps gone through Augusta, Georgia, and Columbia, South Carolina, then headed back up to Charlotte and perhaps Greensboro, North Carolina, and on to Petersburg and Richmond, Virginia. What today would be about a ten-hour trip took days in 1861. The road to Richmond did not get any easier for the hundreds of thousands of Union troops, for whom the city was the ultimate goal. One of the most popular Union marching songs became "Richmond Is a Hard Road to Travel."

Then pull off your overcoat and roll up your sleeve,
For Richmond is a hard road to travel.

Union forces finally reached Richmond in April 1865, but not before turning Southern roadways into a wasteland of burned bridges and muddied thoroughfares. During Reconstruction, Southern states made concerted efforts to drain, grade, and macadamize their roads, beginning with the major highways. In Mecklenburg County, North Carolina, through which I-85 passes, it cost about two thousand dollars per mile to upgrade the roads. Convict labor was used by the county at a cost of about twenty-one cents per convict per day, which included food, clothing, guards, a road supervisor, and medical care as required. By the time the interstates came along, the I-85 corridor was essentially in place thanks to a series of highways built in the first wave of highway construction before World War II.

Symbolically, Richmond also proved to be a hard road to travel for Rosa Parks and the thousands of people who came together in Montgomery in 1956. It took 381 days, but they walked and car pooled and boycotted to end segregation on buses in Alabama and kick start the civil rights movement throughout the nation, including the cities all along the I-85 corridor. In the former Confederate capital of Richmond, it took court orders to segregate schools. In Greensboro, students took up the civil rights cause at chain-store lunch counters in early 1960. Lunch counter sit-ins soon spread to nearby Raleigh-Durham and Charlotte. The tactic eventually worked. On July 25, 1960, the first African American ate a meal while sitting at a Woolworth's lunch counter. Over the next seven days, three hundred more received service at the same counter. The Montgomery bus boycott had taken patience and organization. A few weeks into the boycott, one elderly African American woman was asked whether she was tired of walking everywhere. She responded: "My soul has been tired for a long time. Now my feet are tired, and my soul is resting."[8]

Interstate 75: Color-Coated Road Trip

Marcia remembers summers spent in Southern Florida with her grandmother in the 1950s. She also remembers the drive north every August. Of Italian descent, Marcia tanned to a rich brown after several weeks

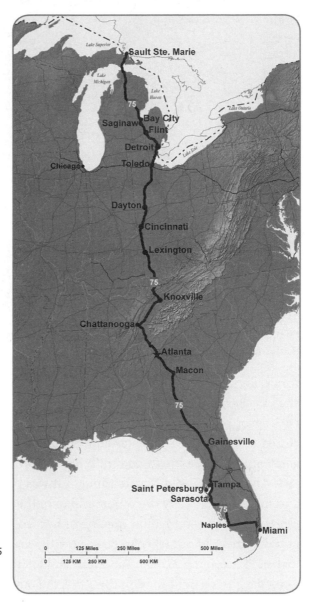

Interstate 75

of running around in a bathing suit on a Florida beach. Marcia's grandmother, on the other hand, covered up to keep her skin as fair as possible,
to accompany her slim good looks and bleached blonde hair. Marcia was
more interested in sandcastles and playing in the surf than the fact that
she was getting browner and browner as each day passed. But Marcia's
grandmother noticed, especially as the time drew near to head north. To
further complicate the situation, Marcia's mother, a hairdresser, spent
long days on her feet at work. She came home tired with little energy

Stopped alongside the road on the trip north in August 1957. Marcia sips from a plastic cup while a stuffed elephant peers over her shoulder. Her constant companion, Mr. Rabbit, pokes an ear above the passenger seat.

for dealing with her daughter's straight, dark hair on a regular basis, so she gave her a really curly perm a couple of times a year that left Marcia with a mop of dark, frizzy hair in the Miami humidity. Short trips to the corner store found Marcia standing by the curb while her grandmother went in to get the bread and milk, or whatever supplies they needed that day. Five-year-old Marcia thought it was because she was so small and might accidentally break something in the crowded store. But, the storeowner refused to allow anyone of her "color" in the store and her grandmother did not want to be seen with what to the casual observer looked like a young African American child. Rather than defending her granddaughter's right to be in the store, or going elsewhere for the daily groceries, the older woman left Marcia outside on the sidewalk.

In late August, Marcia and her grandmother piled into what was always the current year's model of the Oldsmobile convertible and started the trip north to Marcia's family and the beginning of the school year. Not only was it a long drive for an older woman to make, but the era in which the drives were made added an element of danger; in parts of the South, it was not safe for a white women to be seen traveling with what appeared to be an African American child.

Interstate 75, from Miami heads north up Florida's west coast, through Georgia, Tennessee, Kentucky, and Ohio and on to the northern tip of Michigan. It traces routes that have long been used by vacationers either heading to Southern sun or the shores of the Great Lakes. In the 1800s, railroad companies aggressively promoted the areas their lines served along this corridor as the ultimate tourist destination. With the advent of the family car and clever marketing by automobile manufacturers, railroads, and fledgling state tourism boards, people started to think about family vacations. Governments set lands aside for national and state parks and forests; and politicians discovered the publicity they could garner with a photo opportunity of them fishing in Michigan or enjoying a beach in Tampa. Tourism mushroomed. This was the great twentieth-century addition to travel: the annual family road trip. In the post-war era, rising standards of living meant more disposable income. Many households used these extra dollars for leisure-time automobile travel. Better roads and cars spawned tourist destinations specifically designed for motorists. States started promoting their natural attractions in a bid to woo these extra dollars into their local economies. Many states adopted slogans: the Sunshine State (Florida), the Golden State (California), the Land of Zane Grey (Utah). State bureaucrats and tourism officials agitated for better roads to speed tourists—and their dollars—toward their waiting retail and service sectors. In Florida, luxury resorts along the coast gave tourists the chance to live like the rich and famous for a few days. Suddenly, people were motoring down the precursors of I-75 to reach the beach. Along the highways, the multi-story hotel on Main Street gave way to the drive-up-to-your-door motor inn. A new word entered the vocabulary: motel. Roadside businesses sprang up to serve this new motoring public: McDonald's, Howard Johnson's, Holiday Inn, Burger King, and national chains of gas stations instead of small, family-owned and operated garages.

African Americans also discovered the lure of the family vacation. Enterprising publishers released two series of travel guides: one for white travelers and another identifying African American-owned businesses, and those that accepted African Americans with the same courtesy afforded whites. This included the location of African American-only beaches, resorts, and lodging. One such facility, the Ben T. Davis Beach, sat between Clearwater and Tampa at the eastern end of the causeway across Old Tampa Bay (accessible off Exit 274). Here, with Tampa as a backdrop and not far from the port, African Americans were allowed the use of this narrow but beautiful beach.

For Marcia and her grandmother, the trip north had the appearance of a white woman traveling with an African American child, something that was simply not done in that era. The Southern interstates had been approved, but were still under construction, so the two of them took what would today be considered the back roads, but were the main thoroughfares of the 1950s. Particularly in the South, whenever they approached a built-up area, Marcia hid. If they were just slowing to drive through a town, her grandmother barked out the command: "Get down!" and Marcia would scrunch up in the space under the dash on the passenger side. If they had to stop for gas or food, Marcia's instructions were to "get in the back!" Here, she curled up in a little ball on the floor behind the driver's seat and stayed as quiet as a mouse. In an era before drive-through windows or take-out counters, the pair never ate in restaurants, probably because of her grandmother's own prejudices, but also not wanting to risk the embarrassment of being thrown out if the diner did not serve "coloreds." Instead, Marcia's grandmother went in alone and bought sandwiches, fruit, and candy to keep her granddaughter fed. When they stopped for the day, the grandmother found a motel and hustled Marcia into the room.

Marcia remembers her fascination with the motels of that era. She particularly loved the look of the motor courts with the individual cabins, their shutters and trim painted different colors. She so desperately wanted to stay in one of these "dollhouses" that she begged her grandmother to let them stay in one for a night. Grandmother relented. Marcia remembers the brightly painted trim, the little peaked roof, and her devastation when the door swung open. There was no pink dollhouse furniture, no tea set, no toys to play with, and no lacy ruffles on the window! The room was unpainted and plain, with a bed, a toilet, and a sink. She burst into tears.

These trips continued for a handful of summers, until Marcia and her family moved. By that time, her grandmother had a new man in her life and was uninterested in spending the summer with her granddaughter. Marcia still makes periodic trips to Florida to walk along the beaches of her childhood, with her own adult daughter. She remembers her grandmother, not too fondly, as a strict disciplinarian, hung up on appearance and image, with a rather odd sense of how to spend quality time with her granddaughter. Despite Marcia's age and innocence, her grandmother did not attempt to hide the reality of their road trips. "It wasn't a game," Marcia commented years later, "she was legitimately concerned for our safety, but I don't think it ever occurred to her to color-coat the reality of our summer road trips for a little girl."

Interstate 4: Mouse Congestion

About the same time Washington bureaucrats were planning the interstate highway system, another visionary, Walt Disney, was mulling over the possibility of carving a kingdom out of undeveloped land in the middle of Florida. The official interstate highway map of 1956 indicated Florida would be well served by two north–south interstate highways and two east–west interstates, one of them—Interstate 4—stretching from Daytona Beach on Florida's Atlantic coast, through what was then a small city called Orlando, to Tampa on the Gulf coast. In doing so, it

Interstate 4

Roy Disney (*center*, pointing) inspects the property that would become Disney World. (Courtesy of the State Archives of Florida.)

would connect the two north–south interstates 75 and 95. Interstate 4 replaced U.S. Route 92, a highway commissioned in 1924 that had gradually evolved out of the original trails crossing the middle of the state.

Begun in late 1958, I-4 was completed in February 1965. Part of the trail that eventually evolved into I-4 had been cleared in the 1830s, with regular military patrols to protect both the road and travelers from Seminole Indians, who were active against encroachment into their traditional territories. This older roadbed ran from Palatka (south of Jacksonville), an important trading post and transportation hub on the St. Johns River, to Tampa, where a fort had been built in 1824 to oversee the removal of Seminole Indians from the area. This was the fringe of America's Southern frontier. But these soldiers carving the cross-Florida trail out of the wilderness in the 1800s could not have imagined more than one hundred and eighty thousand vehicles a day on their trail, never mind that they were motorized and going to see a mouse in suspenders! Even those planning the interstate system in the 1950s in Washington could not have envisioned this happening.

In 1963, Walt Disney, then sixty-one, told an interviewer that the "fun is in always building something . . . We're always opening up new doors."[9] At that time, Disney employees were looking at a tract of land near Orlando, Florida, an area blessed with plenty of lakes and sun, and surrounded by orange groves. In 1964, Disney Productions began building something new for Walt on the twenty-eight thousand acres he had purchased the year before. In its first full year of operation, Disney World attracted twelve million visitors—more people than lived in Florida at that time. Orlando residents were suddenly dealing with bumper-to-bumper traffic in a state where all roads now seemed to lead to their front door. Other theme parks soon added to the congestion and strain on facilities. In 1971, when Disney World opened, Orlando had 5,854 hotel rooms. In less than a year, that number more than doubled. Today, Disney World alone has thirty-five thousand hotel rooms.

At its eastern end, I-4 begins a couple of miles from the Intracoastal Waterway in Daytona, then crosses over I-95 and heads in a southwesterly direction. In its march toward Orlando, I-4 crosses Tiger Bay State Forest, a swamp with embedded pine islands and ridges. The ridges, which run across I-4, date from the changes in sea level during the Pleistocene period. It is also an important wildlife protection corridor for threatened and endangered species including the black bear and bald eagle. Wildfires in 1998 severely damaged the forest and restoration work is ongoing. Interstate 4 then skirts the cities of De Land (Exit 118) and Deltona (Exits 111–108), before crossing Lake Monroe and plunging through Orlando on its final mad dash for the theme parks. The trip from Daytona to Orlando usually takes about fifty minutes. Orlando's name honors a sentry killed during the Seminole wars. First settlement in the area began about 1844.

From the Gulf Coast, I-4 begins in downtown Tampa, in a corner of the city once known as the cigar capital of the United States. After passing through Tampa's suburbs and a few citrus groves, I-4 skirts Plant City (Exit 22) and Lakeland (Exits 38–27). Once a major cotton-producing center, Plant City became famous for its strawberries; even today, three quarters of the strawberries sold in the United States during the winter months come from Plant City. Strawberries also helped Lakeland's economy expand in the late 1880s, as did the introduction of seedless grapefruit. The area continues to be one of the most important citrus growth and production centers in North America. From Lakeland, I-4 continues in a northeasterly direction, through citrus groves toward the Magic Kingdom. Along this stretch, I-4 crosses Green Swamp, one of the most important wetlands in Florida. Because of its higher elevation, the swamp acts like a water tower, providing the underground pressure necessary to supply freshwater to most of Florida's population. This pressure also prevents saltwater from intruding into this all-important aquifer. Travel time from Tampa to Orlando averages about seventy-five minutes.

Motorists used to race through Florida's interior to reach Daytona Beach or Tampa. Now, these two ends of the interstate have been overshadowed by the theme parks built on what was once bucolic farm country and miles of orange groves. By October 1995, Disney World welcomed its five hundred millionth visitor. To keep up with the growing demands, parts of I-4 have been widened, lanes have been added, and entrance and exit ramps reconfigured to cope with higher speeds and increased traffic. The environment is also a concern in any future road construction: I-4 crosses environmentally sensitive wetlands on both approaches to Orlando. Neighborhoods have also banded together to protect their communities and lobby for responsible road development. Meanwhile, video surveillance and service patrols help authorities keep traffic moving as smoothly as possible for the millions of motorists on their way to see the famous mouse in suspenders.

Interstate 12: Saint Peter Does Not Serve Gumbo

A Louisianan was standing at the Pearly Gates talking to Saint Peter. Just as the Louisianan was about to walk through the Gates, he turned

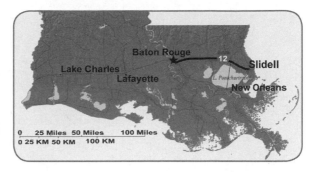

Interstate 12

0   25 Miles 50 Miles   100 Miles
0 25 KM 50 KM   100 KM

and asked Saint Peter: "Do you serve gumbo in heaven?" Saint Peter heaved a great sigh and replied that gumbo was not yet available in heaven. The Louisianan did an about face and headed straight back to his home state.

Slaves taken from the Congo called okra *quingombo*. The okra pod, when cut into thick slices and cooked, becomes a natural thickening agent. Because okra's flavor complements tomatoes, seafood, ham, chicken, rice, peppers, and onions, the *quingombo* used by Louisiana slaves to thicken their soups and stews evolved into gumbo to describe the dish itself. Gumbo soon migrated to the tables of white planters and became synonymous with the bayou country. It made an appearance at the fanciest dress balls, where it was served at sunrise along with strong coffee to revelers facing a long drive home after a night of dancing and socializing. From plantations on the Mississippi River, those making their way home could head east along a trace served by today's Interstate 12. That road of the 1800s went as far east as Ponchatoula. In writing about her childhood in 1840s New Orleans, Eliza Ripley recalled heading home at dawn from a dance at a plantation. "Laughing wide-awake girls and tired fathers and mothers started homeward at the first blush of dawn, when they could plainly see their way over the roads. I started too early from a party the year before, and the buggy I was in ran over a dust-colored cow lying asleep in the road."[10]

Interstate 12 begins just outside Baton Rouge at Exit 159 from I-10. From there, it loops around the north side of Lake Pontchartrain to connect to both I-59 and I-10 at Slidell, Louisiana. Total distance: 85.5 miles. Driving time: a little more than an hour. For long-distance travelers, it provides a fast, easy alternative to driving through New Orleans. Because I-12 does little more than loop around New Orleans and Lake Pontchartrain, passing through flat, pine-forested countryside, many

The road around Lake Pontchartrain, near Mandeville (Exits 63–65), as it appeared in 1937. (Courtesy of the State Library of Louisiana.)

question why, given the interstate guidelines, it is not a three-digit extension of I-10.

Interstate 12 is also known as the West Florida Republic Parkway. In the late 1700s, this area was part of the Spanish colony of West Florida. While Spain encouraged immigration by offering land grants that were quickly snapped up by English-speaking Americans, the government of Thomas Jefferson bided its time until so many Anglophones poured into the area that Spanish speakers would be in the minority. In 1810, Anglo-Americans in Baton Rouge declared the Republic of West Florida. President James Madison quickly acted to annex the lands for the United States. The settlers who followed all contributed to the multiethnic "gumbo" that became Louisiana society: French, German, Spanish, and Italian settlers, as well as what became the largest Hungarian community in the United States ended up along the I-12 corridor. Some owned plantations; others eked out a subsistence existence with small farm plots supplemented by fishing and hunting at nearby Lake Pontchartrain.

At 625 square miles, Lake Pontchartrain is about half the size of Rhode Island, hence the length of the loop created by I-12. Because Lake Pontchartrain is connected to the sea, its water is mildly salty, and the lake provides much of the seafood that ends up on New Orleans tables—and in Louisiana gumbo. The Lake Pontchartrain Basin Maritime Museum at Madisonville (Exit 57) exhibits frontier life in this area, and towns like Slidell, Ponchatoula, and Denham Springs (Exits 83, 40, and 10, respectively) offer antique hunters a chance to stroll historic main streets, some established in the eighteenth century.

Anyone driving on I-12 may have to hunt for gumbo. The usual array of fast-food outlets crowds the exits. But chances are the nearest mom-and-pop restaurant will have it on the menu. As for the gentleman who did an about face at the Pearly Gates: "If you don't have no more gumbo and no more jambalaya, what hell Cajun gon' eat that's any good, hein. Oh M'sieu, ça c'est awful!"[11]

Interstate 72: Ribbons of Concrete

President Thomas Jefferson started the ball rolling when he sent planners off to study the first proposed highway in the United States, a road running west from Baltimore into Ohio and points westward. Jefferson wanted this new national road to be as smooth as possible. At a time when road builders routinely left stumps and boulders in the paths carved out of the wilderness and local residents maintained the roads with whatever implements and knowledge they might have about roads, this was a tall order. When construction finally began in 1816, stumps

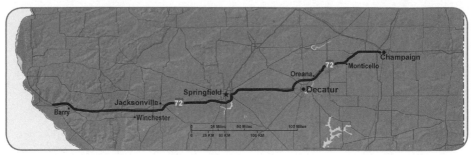

Interstate 72

were duly hauled out and rocks and boulders rolled to the sides of the right-of-way. Aided by teams of oxen, hundreds of laborers cleared the route of other debris and dug a foundation one foot deep and twenty feet wide. This cleared area was then filled with two layers: the first of rounded rocks no more than seven inches in diameter, all fitted tightly together, the second a dense layer of three-inch stones. And to make sure no one cheated and tried to wedge in a larger rock, inspectors measured every rounded rock. These rock layers were then covered with very fine rock dust or sand, which, once wetted down, made everything stick together and provided a relatively smooth surface after being compressed with a heavy roller. This technique created what was called a macadam road. Laborers working on what became known as the National Road kept this process up for 131 miles, and although it was time-consuming and laborious, it provided a stable road surface that was passable in any weather.

In the 1890s, an Ohio gentleman experimenting on his own came up with a powdery blend he called "artificial stone." When you added water and mixed well, the powder hardened into a stone-like surface. A local road builder blocked off a street in their hometown into a five foot square grid and filled in the grid with this new product. Storeowners were so impressed, they asked for more. Word spread and the concrete paving industry was born. By this time, horses had replaced the oxen used to build Jefferson's National Road. Trucks came next along with more automated construction methods. The make-work programs of the 1930s reverted to manual labor as much as possible to provide the maximum number of jobs. For example, rather than use a truck to deliver concrete, a contractor might hire convoys of wheelbarrow-toting laborers to carry the concrete from the mix site to the pour site. On other road construction sites, the contractor might opt for brick paving, again to maximize the need for manual labor. But, developments in concrete technology and the arrival of petroleum-based products, such as asphalt, would soon relegate brick paving to the realm of landscape architecture.

Then along came the proposed interstate highway system, with its massive proportions and tight deadlines. The labor-intensive techniques of the past would not suffice. The project called for big thinking. A company already producing track-type tractors for farmers and tanks for armies expanded into making road graders. Earth-moving equipment soon followed—big earth-moving equipment. To capitalize on the obvious market presented by the proposed interstate system, Caterpillar

Construction of the first macadamized road in America, in Maryland, in 1823. The gentleman on the left measures a rounded rock by slipping it through a ring he holds to make sure it meets the specified diameter. The painting is by Carl Rakeman. (Courtesy of the U.S. Department of Transportation.)

Co. set up full production of such equipment in a fairly central location—Decatur, Illinois. Ironically, it would be another thirty-five years before an interstate highway served Decatur—in this case Interstate 72 approved in 1991. With an additional extension a decade later, I-72 now serves a corridor from Hannibal, Missouri, to Champaign-Urbana, Illinois.

Although first built primarily of concrete, like all the other interstates, I-72 now reflects a blend of concrete and asphalt surfaces. (Missouri and Illinois both used concrete on more than ninety percent of their highway surfaces during the initial construction phase of the interstates.) But, in the rush of the early years to get the interstate system built, the emphasis was rarely on quality, especially of the sort that would allow the highway to outlast its projected twenty or twenty-five year lifespan. By the 1980s, the nation's first interstates started falling apart, and the vehicles on them were increasingly sophisticated and capable of higher speeds. This combination made many of the roadbeds, especially the interchanges, obsolete and dangerous. Technological advances and petroleum shortages led to innovations in the equipment used to build and repair roads and in the ability to recycle asphalt. Advances had also been made in concretes with more resistance to salt damage and longer durability. Today, over seventy million tons of asphalt paving material are recycled every year; the machines to do this did not exist until push came to shove and it became expedient to recycle and conserve. While asphalt goes down faster, especially with the new techniques in widespread use, the continued importance of asphalt to the nation's roadways became readily apparent in 2006 when many road-building and reconstruction efforts across the nation ground to a halt due to a shortage of concrete; rebuilding efforts in the wake of Hurricane Katrina had consumed available supplies.

Strict standards now exist for road surfaces, in an attempt to provide more safety to the traveling public and reduce the strain on future state coffers. But quality control comes with a price. In the case of I-72, states, businesses, motorists, and the federal government all want to see it expanded in both directions deeper into Missouri and into Indiana. While considered a relatively small expansion, especially when compared to the magnitude of the original interstate system, the reality of the cost and the potential strain on state and federal budgets could see the expansion of this particular ribbon of concrete extend well into the 2030s.

Interstate 29: Rocky Road and Mocha Almond Fudge

An ice cream factory in a small town off Interstate 29's Exit 144 in Le Mars, Iowa (population about 9,300),produces more ice cream in one facility than anywhere else in the world: about one hundred million gallons every year. That's several thousand truckloads of ice cream moving along I-29 every year on its way to American waistlines. Then consider the fact that all the other plants in the United States produce an additional 1.5 billion gallons of ice cream annually. No matter how much you smother it in chocolate sauce, that's a lot of ice cream trucking along U.S. interstates. It also reflects a mantra of the modern era of transportation: if you got it, a truck brought it.

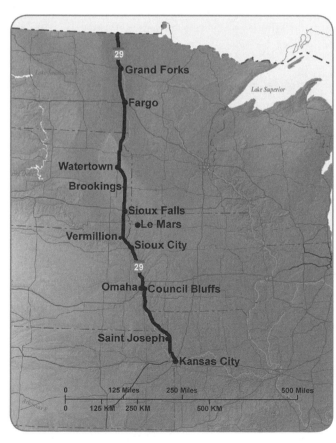

Interstate 29

The original delivery wagon for Wells' Dairy Inc. in 1913; the company now produces one hundred million gallons of ice cream a year. (Courtesy of Wells' Dairy, Inc.)

As a major corridor for trucking agricultural produce from Missouri, Iowa, and the Dakotas to markets, and as a NAFTA link with Canada, through the equally agriculturally inclined Manitoba, Interstate 29 from Kansas City, Missouri, to the North Dakota–Manitoba border tracks through and by places like St. Joseph, Missouri (Exits 56–43), Council Bluffs, Iowa (Exits 56–53), Sioux Falls, South Dakota (Exits 81–77), and Fargo, North Dakota (Exits 67–60). With such a route, I-29 truckers carry more than their share of soybeans, corn, and ice cream. But you are not going to see huge ice cream storage facilities along I-29; trucks have become rolling warehouses with just-in-time production geared to keep up with demand.

Interstate 29 provides easy continental access to this part of Iowa opening the state up to further industrial development. The arrival of the interstate also resulted in the construction of service stations and restaurants at interchanges, and huge truck transportation facilities sprang up along I-29. Shipment of agricultural goods out of the I-29 corridor also increased. Many small towns not connected to an interstate lost the economic battle for survival. In the Dakotas, for instance, all large communities (by Dakota standards) are on interstate highways.

> The town of De Smet (Exit 132 off I-29) became the town in *Little Town on the Prairies* by South Dakota native Laura Ingalls Wilder. "'And now let's make some ice cream,' Manley said. 'You stir it up, Laura, and I'll gather up hailstones to freeze it'" (from Wilder, *The First Four Years* 1971: 55).

While having an interstate highway in the area has generally not increased tourism along the I-29 corridor, branding itself as the ice cream capital of the world certainly helped Le Mars, Iowa. About twenty-five thousand pilgrims belly up to the ice cream bar at the end of the factory tour in Le Mars, trying to decide which flavor they want. (Despite a huge selection, vanilla is still the most popular, followed by chocolate.) To put the annual production at Le Mars into perspective, if each of those twenty-five thousand visitors stayed at the bar until they consumed their share of the annual production, they would each have had about one hundred and twenty-eight thousand servings of ice cream. In a nation where ten percent of all citizens have confessed to eating ice cream for breakfast, over a lifetime, consuming that many servings of ice cream is probably not so far fetched. But, if driving a vehicle burns off about 144 calories an hour, that's a lot of interstate driving to burn off just one scoop of ice cream, especially for a nation that also enjoys its gooey toppings and crunchy cones.

Interstate 39: Connecting the Dots

While touring Wisconsin in the early 1840s, a gentleman who wrote under the pseudonym of Morleigh found his sleep frequently disturbed by groups of Northern European immigrants who gathered in a local tavern to sing songs from the homeland. After hours, they would take to the streets and serenade anyone within listening distance until the wee small hours.

> One night I was roused from my slumber by a band of those sons of harmony; they marched past, singing the national hymn of Nor-

way, a wild and melancholy air, and as the singers retreated ... the music had a peculiar plaintive and solemn effect. I afterwards heard it was a band of Norwegians, who were thus chanting their favourite airs as they marched away into the woods in search of their new homes.[12]

Several generations later, the descendants of this band of Norwegians, and of the immigrants from Switzerland, Germany, other Scandinavian countries, and the Cornish of Southwest England who settled this part of the Midwest had succeeded in turning states like Wisconsin and Illinois into agricultural powerhouses of corn and milk production. Eventually, interstates crisscrossed the woods where Morleigh's sons of harmony once searched for their new homes. But there was one catch: the new interstates seemed to cluster serving the middle part of Illinois (I-55, I-57, I-64, I-70, and I-74) but not necessarily connecting very efficiently to another cluster of interstates in Northern Illinois and Wisconsin (I-43, I-80, I-88, I-90, and I-94). No one had "connected the dots." By 1984, it had become clear that something had to be done. Funding was found to begin construction to upgrade U.S. Route 51, a north–south highway in central Illinois and Wisconsin, to interstate standards. By 2000, Interstate 39 had been extended to connect places like Bloomington (Exit 2) and La Salle (Exits 52–57) in Illinois with Stevens Point

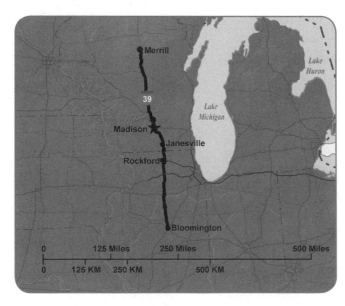

Interstate 39

Connecting the dots, 1964; these children sit on their school's lawn drawing Highway 51 with the Wisconsin River and Rib Mountain in the background. Upgraded sections of Highway 51 later became I-39. (The interstate highway would appear in the background if this photo was retaken today.) Rib Mountain sits near I-39's Exit 190. (Courtesy of the Wisconsin Historical Society, Image 23514.)

(Exits 158–161) and Wausau (Exit 192) in Wisconsin, and to join the surrounding interstate highway clusters. The agricultural heartland of both states could now ship produce to markets more efficiently. As for Morleigh, it seems he misjudged the sons of harmony. Morleigh noted meeting groups of Norwegians on the roads, "who have emigrated from their own forests to locate themselves in the only difficult and impracticable belt of woods in Wisconsin; they have already made some little clearing, but I think their labour and time quite thrown away."[13]

Interstate 45: Two Sights and a Look

The only interstate trips you remember are the ones in which something goes wrong. Isaac Cline, chief meteorologist of Galveston, Texas (Exit 1), felt much the same way one summer evening in late August 1900 as he scanned the skies from the rooftop of his office in downtown Galveston. "No one ever remembered a nice day. But no one ever forgot . . . the thud of walnut-sized hail against a horse's flank, or the way a superheated wind could turn your eyes to burlap."[14] Although a tropical storm had been reported over Central Florida, it was a beautiful evening on Isaac's rooftop: temperature at 90.5°F, wind at 13 to 15 miles per hour from the north, barometric pressure of 29.818 mm/hg, and light scattered cloud cover. The storm would probably move to the Atlantic. To use a Texas expression popular in Isaac's time, it was two sights and a look away— far away and nothing to worry about.

A few days later, children played in the strengthening surf and adults walked down to the beach to look at the high tides. The air was muggy, with temperatures still hovering around 90°F. Soon, someone reported waves splashing over the beach into the roadway. The public beach house

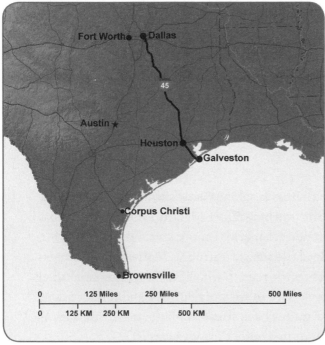

Interstate 45

Traffic clogging I-45 northbound, ahead of Hurricane Rita in September 2005. (Courtesy of FEMA/Ed Edahl.)

and pier broke apart. Still, there was no need for concern. Life went on as usual. But that night, the wind and rain arrived, bringing the Gulf waters. By morning thousands were dead.

It was not so much a case of not evacuating in the path of an oncoming hurricane, but in not believing that such a violent storm could actually occur. There had been stories, but everyone knew stories frequently exaggerated the truth. Even Christopher Columbus had been accused of embellishing his encounter with a Caribbean hurricane. Evacuation would have been possible. This city in the sand that had created a life for itself on a small island in the Gulf of Mexico was well served by rail and roadway over a two-mile bridge to the mainland. From there, a well-maintained road continued on to Houston (Exits 26–57) and points further north, as did the rail line, following a route similar to that of today's Interstate 45. It was also possible to travel along the coastline by rail or road, and coastal steamers connected Galveston with Houston. As the furthest point inland that was accessible to a loaded steamer, Houston thrived as a transshipment hub. In 1857, Frederick Law Olmsted had reported that the road from the steamboat landing was the busiest in Texas. He found stuffed cotton sheds and huge piles of baled cotton all along the waterfront. Even in Olmsted's time, Houston already exhibited signs of wealth with its fine residences and stores. Its roads, however, were a different story. As one 1874 account put it, Houston's roads had an "unusual capacity for muddiness,"[15] and given the rivalry between the two cities, Galvestonians called Houstonians "mud turtles." The railroad hastened Houston's transformation into a prosperous city. It opened up Texas and the rest of the continent to a city that had long existed because of its links to the Gulf of Mexico.

The Galveston of Chief Meteorologist Isaac Cline's day was a trim and elegant seaside city, with many long piers jutting out into the Gulf. Carts pulled by mules brought unloaded goods from schooners anchored in through the shallow waters to docks and warehouses. The weather was "never disagreeably intense," and city hotels and beaches offered "seductive bait for travelers."[16] Despite its tourism potential, Galveston's livelihood in 1900 rested squarely on its port facilities. Even pirate Jean Lafitte had recognized Galveston's strategic importance. Once known as the Galveston Buccaneer, Lafitte stationed about one thousand men on Galveston Island. The Mexicans even appointed him governor of the island. During his tenure, the smuggling trade thrived, as did the slave trade.

Texas communities had long been held back by a lack of transportation facilities. Then, what started as a pirate hangout became an international port served by ships sailing throughout the Gulf, and to Atlantic cities and Europe. Cotton, cottonseed oil cake, tallow, cattle, wool, and hides left the port while lumber, salt, coffee, iron, tin, and crockery flowed into Galveston. This trade required land-based transportation facilities to and from the port, hence, the network of road and rail facilities crossing Galveston Bay in 1900.

In the aftermath of the 1900 hurricane, Galveston's long-time rival, Houston, took advantage of the situation to trumpet itself as a much safer port, further inland. It also had the advantage of being closer to the newly discovered Texas oilfields in nearby Beaumont (Exit 48). In a 1900s version of rock, paper, scissors, oil trumped cotton and Galveston would never be the same. Meanwhile Galveston got to work, building a seawall seventeen feet high, protected by a boulder field twenty-seven feet wide. City engineers also decided to raise the entire city. Workmen manually lifted over two thousand buildings, including a large church, setting them down on newly built foundations of trucked-in fill. Both projects taxed the engineering skills of the day.

A few years later, the road between Galveston and Houston became U.S. Route 75, the Gulf Freeway. There was still not much thought to evacuations, but by the time U.S. Route 75 evolved into Interstate 45, the need to plan for evacuations had come to the fore as one of the goals of the interstate highway system. Granted, in the Cold War era in which much of the planning for the interstates took place, bureaucrats and politicians placed more emphasis on evacuating cities in case of a missile attack or nuclear incident. The need to out run a massive weather event was not a priority. However, in September 2005 and again in 2008, that is exactly where millions of Gulf Coast residents found themselves— stuck in traffic on I-45 with lots of time to contemplate the taillights ahead of them as they headed north through the rolling landscape of Central Texas toward Dallas where I-45 links up with I-30.

Given the lack of zoning in Houston's past, the city sprawled out to mammoth proportions, necessitating a vehicle to get around town, which in turn led to a network of freeways, highways, access roads, and interstates. On a normal day, this network of roads sort of works, but in September 2005, and to a lesser extent in 2008, as the exodus ahead of a hurricane got underway, gridlock ruled. If the only memorable interstate highway trips are the ones in which something goes wrong, Houstonians were about to store up some major memories. In 2005, Houston residents found themselves moving northbound at an average speed of less than two miles an hour. It became one of the slowest evacuations in U.S. history, despite all lanes being opened to northbound traffic. Hurricane Rita approached at a faster pace than people could flee her path. Vehicles that had run out of gas sat abandoned by the road. An interstate that barely accommodates the daily rush hour traffic simply could not cope. The 2005 gridlock prompted emergency preparedness organizations all over the United States to re-evaluate their own plans or lack thereof. This necessarily includes the role of the nation's interstates. In Houston's case, Rita moved inland to the east and spared the I-45 corridor from the worst destruction. Three years later, Hurricane Ike struck near Galveston, breaching some of the defenses put in place after the deadly 1900 hurricane, but again Houston and much of the I-45 corridor escaped the worst of the storm. Two sights and a look worked.

Interstate 44: Pause and Exhale

Think of it as a multi-layered interchange, roads heading off in all directions. Dry air traveling east on one level of a four-lane highway comes to an interchange where warm moist air just happens to be traveling north from the Gulf of Mexico on a lower four-lane deck of its own. At the point where the two "interstates" merge, they can kick up quite a storm as the moist air on the lower deck swirls upward into the drier air on the upper deck. There are now eight lanes of traffic heading into a spiraling ramp up ahead. As with traffic on two interstate highways that merges at high speeds, the combined mass of wind becomes bigger, stronger, and in this case, faster. Sometimes, it pauses as if in rush hour traffic, before exhaling and moving forward or dying out altogether.

On May 3, 1999, strong winds carrying a great deal of moisture flowing northward at about five thousand to ten thousand feet got sucked upward by stronger, drier winds traveling east at twenty thousand feet. The merging of winds happened over the Interstate 44 corridor, southwest of Oklahoma City. When the two winds merged into each other at right angles, they started a spiral effect that got bigger, stronger, and

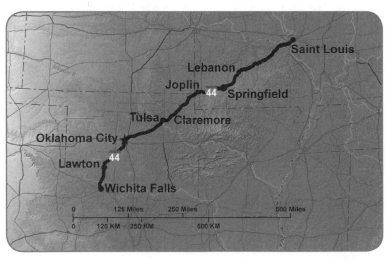

Interstate 44

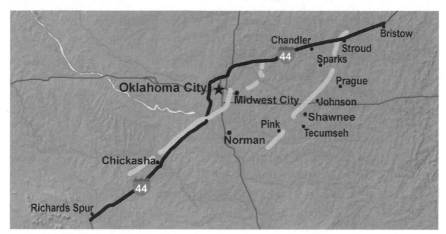

Tornado locations in Oklahoma, May 3, 1999. Interstate 44 appears in the lower left, then tracks to the northeast along the same line as the tornadoes.

nastier. Together, the air masses created one of the biggest tornado episodes in history, now known as the Oklahoma Tornado Outbreak of 1999.

The biggest of the seventy tornadoes spawned that day first paused over Chickasha (Exit 83). It exhaled with what one reporter called "demonic persistence. . . . The Chickasha twister settled in like a plow, ripping an 80-mile gash northeast through a corner of Oklahoma City and several suburbs over an endless four hours."[17] Interstate 44 travels north from Wichita Falls, Texas, to Oklahoma City, and then turns northeast through Tulsa and on to Joplin, Missouri, and St. Louis; this path puts it in what is known as Tornado Alley. That May afternoon, the tornado followed the interstate corridor from Chickasha northward to about Exit 110, before cutting through Oklahoma City and finally exhaling its last breath as it wiped out whole subdivisions. This particular tornado's winds at one point reached 301 miles per hour, putting it in the strongest category, F5, on the Fujita tornado scale. That same afternoon another tornado, this time an F3, crossed I-44 south of Oklahoma City. As it cut a swath across farmland, the tornado literally did a quickstep to the right to blast the bridge at Exit 107 and destroy a nearby outlet mall. It then just as adroitly quickstepped back to the left and continued on its way, before exhaling its last gusts in fields near Moore (Exit 110).

For motorists on I-44 that day, sheltering in the crotch of an overpass seemed the obvious place. Big mistake. Winds actually pick up speed as they funnel under an overpass, the structure creating a wind-tunnel effect similar to that experienced on an urban street with high-rise buildings. Considerable debris is sucked beneath overpasses during tornadoes. Deaths occurred at three interstate highway overpasses that day, including Exit 107, where the tornado had quickstepped right then left. Others were killed along the highways because they didn't see it coming. One woman on I-44 was sucked out of her sports car and tossed into a nearby field. (Experts advise getting off the highway and seeking shelter in as solid a structure as possible.)

The survivors along the F5's path that day, who had ridden out the tornado huddled in hallways, bathrooms, and basements, subsequently described a surreal, frozen in time moment that left them with a sense of disbelief that they had actually survived. *Time* picked up the story of one surviving family. "'It felt like the tornado was hovering over our house,' which it was. Then the pause ended, there was a roar 'like it exhaled,' and . . . [the] house imploded."[18] Pause and exhale. Whole communities had simply disappeared.

Interstate 64: Disturb Not Their Dreams

One of Virginia author Rita Mae Brown's characters in *Whisker of Evil*, the Reverend Herbert C. Jones, voices a strong local sentiment: "I hated it when they built I-64. Sliced in half some of the most beautiful farms in Albemarle County, and in all the counties from Tidewater to St. Louis, Missouri. More traffic. More pollution. More accidents, especially up on Afton Mountain. They can build the road straight as an arrow but they can't do squat about the fog."[19]

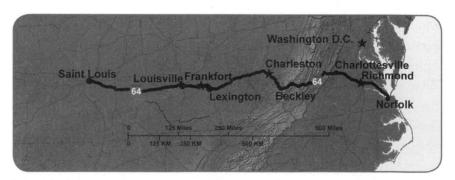

Interstate 64

The Virginia Department of Transportation memorial to its fallen workers. Photographed by Tom Saunders in 2005. (Courtesy of the Virginia Department of Transportation.)

But they try—to do something about the fog, that is. Signs all along Interstate 64 as it crosses Virginia's Afton Mountain advise motorists to be alert, turn on their headlights, and reduce speed when fog is present. The Virginia Department of Transportation is even trying an in-pavement lighting system in which roadside sensors detect low light conditions, as in one of the famous Afton Mountain fogs. In-pavement lighting turns on to define the edges of I-64.

Afton Mountain takes its name from the river in Scotland of the same name, immortalized by Robert Burns.

> Flow gently, sweet Afton! amang thy green braes,
> Flow gently, I'll sing thee a song in thy praise.[20]

Given its scenic beauty, it seems appropriate that the Virginia Department of Transportation chose a lookout on Afton Mountain to place a memorial to its fallen workers.

About forty-three thousand people die each year on the nation's roads. Driver inattentiveness is usually the cause. This includes talking on a cell phone, being distracted by something happening within the vehicle, and driver fatigue. Such inattentiveness also puts road crews at risk. Interstate 64, from Norfolk, Virginia, through West Virginia, Kentucky, Indiana, and Illinois, to St. Louis, Missouri, sees its share of roadside tragedy. In Illinois, for instance, almost seven thousand car accidents occur yearly in road construction zones. In 2005, twenty-six people died within these Illinois construction zones, most of them motorists who failed to slow down as required. Fines are hefty and can include license suspension. Some states are now also installing cameras to catch work-zone speeders. Still, despite public service campaigns such as Missouri's "Give Them a Brake," signage, the presence of state troopers, flashing lights, luminescent whirligigs on roadside posts, barriers, and enough orange fluorescence to light up all of Afton Mountain, road crews take their lives in their hands every time they step on an interstate, the speed and volume of nearby traffic creating wind suction that even grabs at the workers' clothing. In Virginia's case, 131 road workers died between 1928 and 2005. State troopers also complain of the danger they face in standing just inches from the traffic whizzing by when they pull someone over. In fact, troopers stand a greater chance of being hit by a vehicle than a bullet while on the job.

For many of the forty-three thousand traffic-related deaths, a roadside memorial frequently becomes a hastily built cross, a few plastic or silk flowers, some ribbon, a teddy bear. These roadside markers act as beacons, drawing the eye of passing motorists, perhaps warning of dangers lurking at that spot, and providing the grieving family and friends with a symbol at the place of death, made more significant by the sudden, unexpected nature of that death. In Virginia, legislation restricts the use of these markers, but has not been strictly enforced. Roadside markers are only removed if, in law enforcements' eyes they put motorists at risk, perhaps by being too big or flamboyant.

Virginia's memorial to its road workers sits amid native perennial wildflowers at a scenic overlook on Afton Mountain between Mile Markers 103 and 104, not far from where Rita Mae Brown situates the fictional Reverend Herbert C. Jones in Crozet (Exit 107). The memorial portrays three workers in hard hats, with an open profile at one end, emblematic of the "missing" worker. From the walkway around the memorial, visitors can look down into the bucolic valley, interlaced with creeks and overshot with every shade of green in the color palette during the warmer months.

> My Mary's asleep by the murmuring stream,
> Flow gently, sweet Afton, disturb not her dream.

Interstate 26: The Circle of Life

With an average width of two hundred and fifty feet, it takes a little over twenty-one miles of interstate right-of-way to gobble up one square mile of countryside. (Interchanges take even more land.) That might not sound like much in a country of 3.5 million square miles, but to put it in perspective, 484 regulation-size football fields fit in a square mile. Interstate 26, from Charleston, South Carolina, to Johnson City, Tennessee, is 349 miles long. This means that, interchanges aside, at a minimum, the I-26 right-of-way gobbled up 16.6 square miles along its total length. If this right-of-way had all been turned into football fields instead of an interstate highway, the University of South Carolina Gamecocks, at Columbia (Exits 111–101), could theoretically play every regular-season game on a different field for the next 618 years.

Football turf aside, in the right-of-way along I-26, a distinctive ecosystem flourishes, nourished by runoff from the pavement and providing vegetative cover in the median, along the shoulders, and in the circles created by on and off ramps. Plants that might not otherwise thrive do

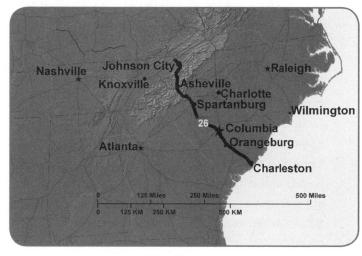

Interstate 26

Wildflowers, marsh grasses, and trees provide a habitat for hosts of insects, amphibians, birds, and small animals within yards of passing traffic. This photograph shows the view from an I-26 interchange near Charleston, South Carolina.

well when they receive the extra water running off the pavement. Others take over the cleared shoulders of the roadway. The vine that ate the South, otherwise known as kudzu, smothers other foliage and covers anything that gets in its way with a green blanket of large leaves and vines. Imported from Asia by a well-intentioned Department of Agriculture in the late 1920s, kudzu was supposed to be a nourishing feed crop for livestock that would revitalize the soil and help impoverished farmers recover from the boll weevil infestation that had wiped out cotton crops. The government even paid farmers eight dollars an acre to plant the stuff. The kudzu took off—quite literally. Capable of growing a foot a day in summer and thriving in drought conditions, the vines soon enveloped anything that stood still, smothering other vegetation, utility poles, and abandoned buildings. Today, it is considered a noxious weed.

Small animals and distinctive vegetation find sheltering homes in the circles created by on- and off-ramps. Like much of the shoulder and the median, these circles provide an area where humans rarely tread. Many small creatures spend their entire lives in these protected spaces. If the space happens to be marshy, colonies of frogs and other amphibians settle in, and plants that enjoy such conditions, like the Venus flytrap, which is indigenous to coastal Carolina, take hold.

All the states along I-26 have wildflower beautification programs. The Tennessee Department of Transportation has a permanent roadside landscaping program to improve aesthetics along interstates and reduce landscaping maintenance. Its emphasis is on wildflower preservation and propagation. Poppies, daisies, cosmos, lilies, and other native species wave in summer breezes along the medians. Sometimes, vegetation specifically planted to reduce the need to mow, such as crown vetch, blankets and nourishes the shoulders and median, its mauve-pink blossoms brightening the summer landscape. Other native wildflowers blend in with the roadside grasses: goldenrod, phlox, violets, and Queen Anne's lace.

Taller foliage in the median screens oncoming traffic and helps prevent crossover accidents. Shrubs and trees include rhododendron, azaleas, and various conifers, depending on where you are along I-26. Cypresses, oaks, magnolias, and tulip trees thrive in the lowlands along the coast, while further inland pines, maples, hemlocks, and beeches take over. In the Great Smoky Mountains and across the Blue Ridge, patches of conifers dominate the right of way. To hide the clear-cutting on pine plantations, loggers plant a few dense rows of pines at the edge of their lots to protect the sensibilities of passing motorists. Elsewhere, a high berm of earth or sand runs parallel to the road to hide unsightly clear-

 Queen Anne, Queen Anne, has washed her lace
(She chose a summer day)
And hung it in a grassy place
To whiten, if it may.

—from "Queen Anne's Lace," a poem by Tennessee poet Mary Leslie Newton (1874–1944) (in Ferris, 1957)

cutting. South Carolina also likes to plant palmettos along its medians. The palmetto became the state tree after Fort Moultrie, built of palmetto logs, helped save Charleston from the British in 1776. The British underestimated the fort due to its appearance, and their cannonballs sank into the soft palmetto logs, which absorbed most of the impact.

Reptiles find warmth (and death) on the pavement when temperatures are lower. For larger animals, such as raccoons and deer, the dash across the pavement is a race with death. Meanwhile, buzzards and crows watch for those that did not make it, and hawks circle looking for prey in the shortened grasses of the road shoulders. Despite the barrier created by the highway, the circle of life continues.

Interstate 97: How Many Petals on a Black-Eyed Susan?

He loves me, he loves me not. Will the answer be "yes" or "no"? In Maryland, girls doing petal-pulling prognostications with the state flower—the black-eyed Susan—will discover that it is indeed true love, because the black-eyed Susan has an odd number of petals—thirteen to be exact. That is one of the things that caught the attention of Maryland legislators in 1918 when it came time to choose a state flower. After some debate, they picked the black-eyed Susan (*Rudbeckia hirta*), not because it happens to brighten the summer landscape all over Maryland, but because those sharp-eyed legislators noticed that the flower's colors (black and gold) match those of Maryland's flag and the family crest of Lord Baltimore, the state's founder. And a careful count revealed thirteen petals on a black-eyed Susan—exactly the same number as original colonies. The choice was made.

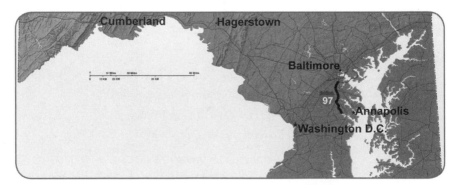

Interstate 97

Sometimes called a coneflower, black-eyed Susans brighten Maryland rights-of-way through-out the warmer months. (Courtesy of the National Park Service, Shenandoah National Park.)

In 1986, when the Maryland State Highway Administration introduced its Wildflower Program, the black-eyed Susan was naturally included as the dominant species in the mix broadcast along roadsides and in the medians of the state's highways. This included along Interstate 97, a heavily trafficked commuter route between Baltimore and Annapolis. At just under eighteen miles long, it is the shortest interstate highway and the only interstate entirely within one county (Anne Arundel County). Meanwhile, over three hundred acres of medians and roadsides in the state have been seeded with a mix of annuals, biennials, and perennials including cosmos, poppies, primrose, larkspur, yarrow, cornflower, and daisies. This reduces the amount of mowing (and the related pollution from mowers), promotes wildlife habitats along highways, and presumably gives rush-hour commuters on I-97 something a little more aesthetically pleasing to look at than the taillight neon up ahead.

Interstate 66: Stonewalling

It was a beautiful Saturday evening. Near what is now Exit 53 on Interstate 66, a Union soldier lying on the ground enjoying the July night sky called it "one of the most beautiful nights that the imagination can conceive." The soldier lay amid thousands of others, all waiting for morning. "The sky is perfectly clear, the moon is full and bright, and the air is still as if it were not within a few hours to be disturbed by the roar of can-

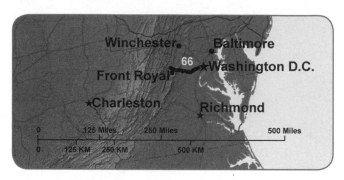

Interstate 66

non and the shouts of contending men."[21] By nightfall of the next day, 460 Union soldiers lay dead, 1,124 were wounded, and 1,312 were listed as missing. On the Confederate side, 387 would never see the bright full moon again. Another 1,582 lay wounded, and 13 were listed as missing. Unreported casualties probably added another two thousand names to these totals. The First Battle of Bull Run had ended—and not as expected in Washington. Union forces had been stopped from capturing the small town of Manassas, Virginia, with its vital rail and road links into the Shenandoah Valley and to Richmond. Walt Whitman watched the Union retreat into Washington, in the drizzly rain of Monday July 22, 1861, "their clothes all saturated with the clay-powder filling the air—stirr'd up everywhere on the dry roads and trodden fields by the regiments, swarming wagons, artillery, etc. all the men with this coating of murk and sweat and rain, now recoiling back . . . a horrible march of 20 miles, returning to Washington baffled, humiliated, panic-struck. . . . The sun rises, but shines not."[22]

The day before, the momentum of the battle had shifted, one side breaking into disarray and reforming its lines, then the other. While Confederate Brigadier General Barnard Bee rallied the troops, General Thomas Jackson halted his Virginia brigade behind the crest of a hill and remained there for most of the day. Why he did so remains a mystery. Jackson, being a stickler for procedure is one possible answer: no one had yet ordered him forward. He continued to wait. At one point, Bee gestured toward Jackson's brigade exclaiming that there stands Jackson like a stone wall. Just exactly what Brigadier General Bee meant is also unclear. Some say he was praising Jackson and his troops for not budging; others claim he was being sarcastic, furious that Jackson's force had not moved forward to aid the crumbling Confederate lines. In any event, the name stuck.

"The sun rises, but shines not." An image of the Union retreat down Warrenton Turnpike from Bull Run in July 1861. This illustration appeared in the August 10, 1861, issue of *Harper's Weekly*.

By the end of the day, the Union forces blinked first and retreated along the Warrenton Turnpike, now replaced by Interstate 66. As one of the best hard-surfaced roads of its time, the Warrenton Turnpike connected Washington with Front Royal (Exit 13), passing through a string of small Virginia towns including Manassas (Exit 47) and Warrenton (Exit 43). It was along this thoroughfare that Walt Whitman witnessed the disarray of the retreat the next day.

After the First Battle of Bull Run, Stonewall Jackson entered the history books and the verb "stonewall" crept into dictionaries, to indicate the action of preventing the progress of something, hindering or blocking. The two forces met again a year later for the Second Battle of Bull Run, this time with a decisive Confederate victory. The battlefield became a national park accessed from Exit 47 of I-66, which skirts the park's southern flank. The Warrenton Turnpike gradually evolved into a numbered state road and then into U.S. Route 29. Then, along came the interstates and the path of Union retreat became a commuter corridor as I-66, extending for seventy-six miles from Front Royal, Virginia, to downtown Washington.

By the time engineers planned I-66 in the 1960s, "stonewalling" was very much a part of the modern vernacular. It applied to everything from football plays to filibustering politicians. It also applied to irate environmentalists and landowners with a bad case of NIMBY—not in my back yard. There were no problems with the I-66 construction until it neared Washington. To plan for future development, engineers wanted eight lanes on a new bridge across the Potomac to connect the ever-spreading suburbs with the proposed inner beltway and I-95. A four-lane section of interstate cuts a swath about two hundred and fifty feet wide across the landscape. Eight lanes meant a pretty big footprint—one large enough to draw the opposition of environmentalists and suburban residents in the area of the proposed highway. The stonewalling began. As opposition to the project gained strength, engineers went back to the drawing board. Eventually, a compromise was reached in which the interstate would be built, but with only four lanes, extensive landscaping, and noise barriers. Near Washington, engineers put the roadway below grade to further minimize its impact. Hiking and biking trails were to be built near the right-of-way, and the median was wide enough that it could accommodate a branch of the Washington light-rail commuter service. High vehicle occupancy was also to be encouraged. However, I-66 would not connect with other freeways as originally planned. Opposition had already scuttled the inner beltway; I-66 as it now exists dumps motorists into an urban street not far from the Watergate complex in downtown Washington.

Almost two hundred thousand vehicles use I-66 daily within suburban Washington, and expansion plans are once again afoot. While some sections expanded to eight lanes over the years, bottlenecks still routinely bring motorists to a standstill. In a post-9/11 world, elected officials and Washington residents have also been reminded of one of the original objectives of the interstate system: the evacuation of large populations in case of enemy attack. The older stretches of I-66 are not up to the challenge of such an evacuation, especially the Roosevelt Bridge section in Washington. Now, as neighborhoods rally to stonewall expansion into their back yard, all options are on the table, including tolls, further emphasis on high occupancy vehicle lanes, and improved mass transit. On one hand, expanding I-66 could relieve congestion in the suburbs along its path; on the other, any move to accommodate increased traffic would certainly increase noise and air pollution, not to mention the expanded footprint of a bigger I-66. But this time community activists have another weapon in their arsenal: limited tax dollars. In the case of I-66, in 2004, after years of planning and promises, Virginia's Department of Transportation agreed to spend what it could: the $43.9 million in available funds went toward improving 3.8 miles on the worst stretch of interstate near Manassas. Closer to Washington, the debate continues as politicians, engineers, and neighborhoods try to find a viable solution to an inevitably vicious circle: improved roads mean more suburban expansion, which means more commuters, and definitely leads to more concrete and asphalt covering the landscape.

In July 1861, on the day Thomas Jackson acquired his nickname, his men eventually left their cover behind the hill and entered the battle. One of Jackson's last instructions to his brigade that day was to "yell like furies" when they charged. Jackson had an innate sense of the landscape in which he maneuvered his troops. Time and again he outwitted opposing forces with his deft feints around, and use of, topographical features. However, Jackson also appreciated the value of a good road, especially in an era when troops marched to war on foot. He also appreciated the value of a good roadway in retreat, or in today's case, in case of evacuation. Will neighborhood activists and environmentalists along I-66 be able to make their case against the thrum of traffic? Or, will those in favor of an expanded I-66 get the green light? Who will yell the loudest: environmentalists and communities practicing good environmental stewardship, or commuters stuck in traffic, engines idling with a different view of environmental stewardship? The distinctive yell that Jackson's men came up with that day became the infamous rebel yell. The tone-deaf Jackson called it one of the best sounds he ever heard. The stonewalling continues.

Interstate 69: Shake, Rattle, but Don't Roll

Drifting off the road is the single largest contributor to interstate accidents. Once vehicles do start to drift, most end up rolling over. Of the drivers involved, over half either fall asleep at the wheel due to boredom or fatigue, or they become distracted. The remainder are either speeding or something else happens as in hydroplaning, tire blowout, or they

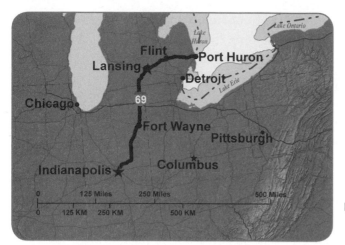

Interstate 69

Getting out of the ditch before the invention of the cell phone and tow truck. (Courtesy of the Library of Congress.)

> Suddenly I realize I'm goin' sixty miles an hour
> and I don't remember the last five minutes.
> I'm—I can't seem to—keep my mind on it.

—Willy Loman in *Death of a Salesman* (Miller, 1949: 13)

> I drove along in that state of semimindlessness that
> settles over you on interstate highways.

—Bill Bryson, *The Lost Continent* (1987, 173)

> I was driving along, you understand? And I was
> fine. I was even observing the scenery.... And then
> all of a sudden I'm goin' off the road! I'm tellin' ya, I
> absolutely forgot I was driving. If I'd gone the other
> way over the white line I might've killed somebody.
> So I went on again—and five minutes later I'm
> dreamin' again.

—Willy Loman in *Death of a Salesman* (Miller, 1949: 13)

swerve to miss something ahead and lose control. Common distractions include fumbling with a cell phone, reaching for something, looking at a map, children, eating, and cigarettes. The majority of these drivers are male, and most of the accidents occur on weekends.

In test after test since the 1980s, indentations along the shoulder of the highway, about half an inch deep, have proven effective in reducing the number of accidents where a vehicle drifts off the road, whether because of fatigue, inattentiveness, or bad weather.

Any major roadwork involving federal funds must include noise abatement measures if the sound is deemed excessive for nearby residents or buildings with special functions, such as hospitals. Noise abatement measures include berms, vegetation, and concrete or wooden walls, usually as high as the exhaust stack on a transport truck. Sixty-seven decibels is the ceiling beyond which a substantial reduction in noise is required. To put this into perspective, sixty-seven decibels is just about where an alarm clock or lawn mower weighs in on the sound-volume scale. Yet in somewhat of an anomaly in the federal noise abatement legislation for roads, the corrugation along the shoulder is designed to make a noise of seventy-five to eighty decibels inside the average passenger vehicle—quite a bit louder than the alarm clock from hell or the annoying neighbor with a lawn mower. The tests have been so conclusive, with an estimated fifty-five to seventy-five percent reduction in accidents, that rumble strips are now mandatory for any construction, reconstruction, rehabilitation, or resurfacing of rural highways in about half of the United States. They also are fairly inexpensive to install, costing only about fifty cents to a dollar apiece, which has helped increase their use.

So, with federal and state governments haggling over the funding and timing of the proposed expansion of Interstate 69 from its present 356-mile trace through Port Huron (Exit 199), Lansing (Exits 87, 91, and 95) and Coldwater (Exit 13), Michigan, and Fort Wayne (Exits 109–102) and Muncie (Exit 41), Indiana to connect with the Mexican border, probably in Laredo, Texas, it is a given that those corrugated rumble strips will be included as the interstate makes its way through Kentucky, Tennessee, Arkansas, Mississippi, Louisiana, and Texas. This alignment will turn I-69 into a major NAFTA corridor, giving an economic boost all along its path and relieving NAFTA traffic on neighboring interstates that are becoming crowded. It will also help cement the primacy of Texas as the state with the most interstate highways (seventeen overall) and interstate highway miles (3,233.45).

Rumble strips go by several official names depending on the configuration, including sonic nap alert pattern or SNAP, and continuous shoulder rumble strip or CSRS. Sometimes, the pattern of indentations is continuous; in other instances they are spaced out in groups. When they are continuous, there are about 5,260 indentations per mile. Tests by the Michigan Department of Transportation showed that continuous indentations, if milled into the concrete or asphalt, are the most effective, because the tire has a chance to sink into the groove and transmit vibrations to the steering wheel. They also emit more noise, even in snow and ice conditions, where the strips are useful edge-of-the-road guides for drivers and snowplow operators in bad weather.

Placement close to the edge of the lane has proven most effective, as opposed to a foot or more from the lane's edge. Drift-off crashes happen almost equally to the left and right, so rumble strips are important on both shoulders. Some states have also experimented with rumble strips between lanes. And then there are the experiments with fuzzy-logic based virtual rumble strips where the vehicle is programmed to re-act if the driver "drifts." Michigan has also tested painted rumble strips and discovered that in poor weather, the painted strips "pop up" at you like an airport runway making an excellent edge-of-road guide. In the words of one Michigan Department of Transportation employee, when it comes to rumble strips, you need to "mill it, move it, paint it, and measure it."[23]

Interstate 73: Getting It Right

An October 1961 review of progress on the nation's interstate highway system referred to it as an autocrat and a sacred cow, saying that no one dared stand in its way. While acknowledging that many of the na-tion's roads, and certainly the compulsion to be on the move constantly were a legacy from the first pioneers, nothing was allowed to impede a nation in a hurry. "Family homesteads, a town's ancient elms, historic monuments were sacrificed to spare the passing motorist a few minutes' delay. Bypasses and underpasses and overpasses snaked through and around the cities."[24] The review further noted that in the rush to secure

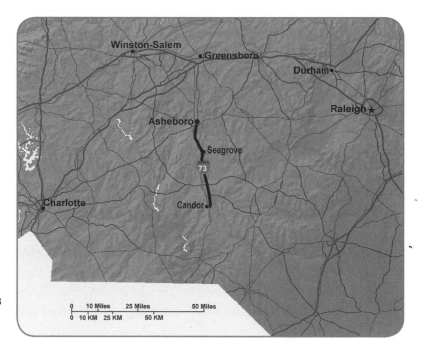

Interstate 73

The importance of getting it right. Speeders on an 1870 version of an interstate. (Courtesy of the Library of Congress.)

federal funding, some states had gone a little overboard, citing Nevada in particular, where three overpasses were in question: one led to a railroad shanty, another to a ranch, and a third to an abandoned bordello.

In the 1950s and '60s, safe, efficient, utilitarian interstates were the ultimate goal so a nation constantly on the move could indulge its passion. The landscape was of secondary importance. Function trumped aesthetic qualities, and the high speeds on the growing interstate system made it more and more difficult for motorists to appreciate, even connect with the passing landscape. This important relationship was in danger of being lost. But gradually, with a growing push from environmentalists and taxpayers, people began to realize that maybe this approach needed to be changed. In building an interstate across an existing landscape, the interstate created a new landscape, but maybe a better job needed to be done in integrating the old with the new. Maybe the existing local natural and social ecology needed to have priority. Suddenly, the proposed elimination of a park or possible degradation of an endangered species' habitat, the destruction of a neighborhood were no longer acceptable. In the 1960s, highway expansion through run-down neighborhoods was usually deemed "urban renewal," and it was definitely less expensive to expropriate slums than to push through a part of town with more expensive real estate. Now, it's a struggle to balance quality of life and the environment with economic progress.

When the new Interstate 73 was planned in the early 1990s, its route led from Cincinnati, Ohio, to Myrtle Beach, South Carolina. A few adjustments and political compromises later, government agencies have now identified a preferred route in some states, but other states still have not made the new interstate a priority. While twenty-six miles near Asheboro, North Carolina, have been signed as I-73, not all of this stretch of highway meets interstate standards and is therefore not all recognized by federal officials as truly an interstate. As far as the rest of the trace I-73 will leave on the landscape, a lot has changed since the days when a buffalo trail or wagon road through a farmer's field could automatically morph into a highway and then an interstate.

In the Carolinas, the proposed I-73 will track south from near Roanoke, Virginia, through Greensboro to the stretch already signed as I-73 around Asheboro, then on to Rockingham, North Carolina, before cutting across I-95 toward Myrtle Beach, South Carolina. To get to this point in the planning, officials from the Federal Highway Authority held several public meetings and then met with what officials called "a significant number of church congregations, service organizations, and social fraternities and sororities."[25] Considerable research also went into the impact the proposed route would have on the natural and human environments, particularly since the Great and Little Pee Dee River basins are involved. Of all the possible alternatives, the preferred trace affects the smallest area of wetlands (384 acres), farmland (1,708 acres), and historically significant land. It also has the lowest cost of all the alternatives. Construction of the South Carolina portion alone will still cost an estimated $2.4 billion, but is now expected to bring seventy-seven hundred jobs to a high unemployment region and $4.1 billion in economic impact, an almost two-fold return on investment.

Novelist and North Carolinian Thomas Wolfe hated the impact of highways on the rural landscape, the "great glittering beetles of machinery drilling past forever in projectile flight." Wolfe also recognized the lost connection between the motorist and the passing landscape, with "unknown nameless lives hurtling on forever, lost forever, going God knows where!"[26] Additional tweaking will almost certainly take place along the proposed I-73 corridor before bulldozers move in for the kill. In the meantime, environmentalists, taxpayers, and politicians continue to express their opinions to the Federal Highway Authority as it struggles to maintain an equitable balance between economic growth and the social and ecological landscape so many of us take for granted.

"Every little vista, every little glimpse that we have of what lies before us, gives the impatient imagination rein, so that it can outstrip the body and already plunge into the shadow of the woods and overlook from the hill-top the plain beyond it" (Robert Louis Stevenson, "Roads"). The road leading westward from Kansas City in 1909, now served by I-70. (Courtesy of the Library of Congress.)

The Red Trace of Taillights

O N TODAY'S interstate highways, would a middle-aged Robert Louis Stevenson lean forward to catch a first glimpse of the view around the next bend on Interstate 77 in West Virginia, or would he be concentrating on getting to his destination on time? Would he take the time to appreciate the silver mist rising up from the valleys as the warming sun slides between the green hilltops? What about his contemporary Mark Twain? Would he notice the dead air of the Nevada deserts from the air-conditioned comfort of a pickup truck on Interstate 80? He would probably have a window open a crack to accommodate his smoking habit and he'd pull into a truck stop for his ham and eggs—boots, jeans, and shirt safely in place. In 1861, it took Twain three weeks to reach Nevada, traveling a distance of about two thousand miles from his Missouri hometown. Today, he could comfortably drive the same distance in about three days.

In all fairness, neither Stevenson nor Twain had yet reached that exalted status of maximum appreciation that comes with middle age when they first wrote of their travels in the United States, yet the roads they did travel appealed to their sense of anticipation. Stevenson called it *Sehnsucht*—the anticipation of what lies ahead—the prospect or desire

to see what is beyond the next bend in the road, the distant horizon. While the ability to perceive the passing landscape and its many elements changes from generation to generation, that sense of anticipation, of constantly seeking what is ahead, remains. It is what sends millions of Americans off on holiday road trips to visit family, attractions, or a place they simply have never been. Anticipation sent early European colonists across the Atlantic and over the Piedmont onto the Great Plains. *Sehnsucht* sent Frances and Anthony Trollope off to explore North America. It sent Horace Greeley west to see what conditions were really like, and it put John Boyle O'Reilly into a canoe drifting down the Connecticut River. It propelled Gary and Ezra along what is now Interstate 40 and it prompted the first cross-country road adventures in a motor vehicle.

Charles Kuralt and Bill Bryson understood *Sehnsucht*. Kuralt likened interstate travel to being able to drive from coast to coast, "without seeing anybody or meeting anybody."[1] For him, life began at the exit ramps, but, from 1967 to 1980, Americans waited from week to week to see what Kuralt would discover next on his rambles along America's back roads. Bill Bryson is well-known for his perceptive yet humorously irreverent take on the American landscape. In his world, an interstate trip becomes an epic journey of "unrelenting tedium, in a baking steel capsule on a ribbon of highway."[2] Yet this is the same guy who sees "gumdrop hills"[3] in Virginia, and finds "thick and stifling" heat in Washington, which he likens to "being inside a vacuum cleaner bag."[4] All of Bill's senses enrich his writing and his readers' vicarious discovery of what is around the next bend.

They knew what *Sehnsucht* was all about in 1939. The New York World's Fair was "Building the World of Tomorrow"—tomorrow being 1960. One of the biggest attractions was Futurama, with its glimpse into life as it would be in that far away place called the 1960s. Millions came to see for themselves what the future held. Here was the first commercial television broadcast. Homes actually had attached garages and were built of the latest in wood products—plywood. They were set in tidy new suburbs and equipped with wondrous new forms of automation. Ford and General Motors displayed richly upholstered, flashy automobiles to take workers from that new home in the suburbs to a job in the city. Walking to a destination would be a thing of the past, and if you did have to walk, it would probably be on an elevated sidewalk.

Futurama presented a glimpse of what was to come: the red trace of taillights disappearing off into the sunset over a gray ribbon of concrete. Automobiles of the 1960s would use a network of magic motorways—divided highways with vehicles moving at speeds of one hundred miles per hour. Highway intersections were obsolete with grade crossings separated from the lanes of traffic. Headlights would not be necessary, because magic motorways had their own lighting. One vision of the 1960s had layers of elevated roadways with the top tier for high-speed, long-distance travel and the bottom layer for local, slower traffic. Futurama fired up the public's imagination. These magic motorways were the future.

Fast forward. It is 2050. Vehicles on the interstates glide by about two feet apart, all programmed to the speed limit. Everything flows as a unit at a constant speed. No taillight boogie here. Sensors maintain the distance on all sides from the other vehicles. In a special truck lane convoys of driverless, computer-operated transports flash by. Sensors in the roadway and in the vehicles monitor everything. The electronic message boards that were so popular in the early years of the twenty-first century have been replaced by onboard display panels that relay messages on traffic and road conditions directly to the vehicle's dashboard.

Now, planners struggle to figure out how to accommodate projected traffic loads safely, in a way that will help promote state economies yet stay within state and federal budgets. There are well over two hundred million vehicles in the United States on an interstate highway system originally designed with less than half that number in mind. Billions of dollars will be spent in the coming decades to make interstates safe at higher speeds with higher traffic volumes. This means additional lanes, rebuilt overpasses, exit ramps that can be negotiated at higher speeds, road sensors to monitor traffic and weather conditions, wider medians, wider shoulders, better guardrails, computerized message boards, and camera surveillance. It also means driver education. While this perpetual motion along our highways will have a monetary price tag, it should not have a human one.

In the early years of the twentieth century, the future of road travel was often depicted visually as a ribbon of concrete to nowhere, disappearing off into the sunset, the surrounding landscape, stark and futuristic. Today, for many motorists staring out their windshield, the

> Forty years ago, that interstate down there didn't exist. . . . [T]he road didn't cut through the land like that interstate. It moved with the land, you know. It rose, it fell, it curved. Cars didn't drive on it to make great time. They drove on it to have a great time.
>
> —Sally the Porsche in the film *Cars*

vehicles ahead blur, their taillights melding into one continuous stream as they chase the sunset.

For Teddy Roosevelt, *Sehnsucht* meant adventure. But if you no longer had youth and vigor, or Stevenson's middle-aged sensibilities, not to despair. Roosevelt firmly believed that much remained for the individual who had "warmed both hands before the fire of life."[5] From a comfortable vehicle or a smoother pathway, an older traveler could still appreciate the passing landscape—perhaps the red sunset over a desert landscape, its afterglow shining on the same canyoned battlements the Native Americans had first admired, and used to their advantage. Teddy Roosevelt's distant cousin, Franklin Delano Roosevelt, also understood the pleasure and freedom of the open road, of discovering what was around the next bend or over the next hill. Though separated slightly in age, both men witnessed the excitement of the first automobiles. For FDR, the automobile represented a freedom taken from him by his disability. He had always been interested in cars, and although not very good at it, FDR loved to drive and frequently campaigned in his car. In his later years, he had a blacksmith install hand levers so he could continue driving despite his paralyzed legs. This gave him back the independence he had lost; the open road was his once again. Acquaintances were always impressed by FDR's detailed knowledge of the American landscape, much of it acquired firsthand. For Teddy Roosevelt, who would die prematurely of heart disease, the road ahead represented the joy of living. As he proclaimed a couple of years before his death, the open road was "his who has the heart to demand it."[6] Here was his sense of prospect, his anticipation of the woods that overlook the hill beyond, of the red trace of taillights.

Acknowledgments

In 1841, Charles Cist, Clerk for the District Court of Ohio, was preparing a Cincinnati business directory for publication. In the course of researching the city's businesses, Mr. Cist visited a vendor who made "bratwurst, knackwurst, leber wurst and sour-krout" and promised to include him in the directory. Unfortunately, due to a compilation error, this did not happen. A few months after the release of the directory, Mr. Cist encountered the now-disgruntled businessman, who told him: "Your correctory not wort one cent. How do people know where he kits his sour krout?"

Every interstate highway has myriad stories to tell and every one of the millions of interstate travelers could contribute an anecdote or two of their own. This book's content represents only a small cross-section of those tales, selected to tweak the interest of readers desirous of learning about the traces of the interstate highways that carve through the American landscape. Any errors or omissions in the telling of those tales, as in the anecdote above, are the author's responsibility.

Mr. Cist acknowledged his error in the preface to a revised directory in which he commented: "I must expect every man who has his sour-krout left out, will also be apt to pronounce this volume 'not wort one cent.' It behooves me, however, to refer to what is in it, rather than what has been left out." As Mr. Cist did, I would also like to acknowledge what this book contains, or rather, what it reflects: the patience and skill of my sounding board, my mapmaker and technical wizard husband Don, the love and encouragement of good friends, the talent of my agent Sorche Fairbank, the support of John Byram and the staff at the University Press of Florida, and the advice of the reviewers. Finally, here's to Amelia, the start of it all.

Notes

To the Reader

1. Conroy, *The Water Is Wide*, 221.
2. Stevenson, "Roads."

Chapter 1. Early Road Travel: Pluck, Patience, and Profanity

1. As quoted in *Barracuda Magazine*.
2. Lawson, *A New Voyage to Carolina*, 19 of 180.
3. Bartram, *Observations on the Inhabitants*, 12.
4. As quoted in Clark, *Benjamin Franklin: A Biography*, 120.
5. Trollope, *Domestic Manners of the Americans*, 164 of 186.
6. Ibid., 144 of 186.
7. Ibid., 12 of 186.
8. Johnson, *Ante-Bellum North Carolina*, 131.
9. As quoted in Etten, "Grand Rapids in 1844–1845."
10. As quoted in Mencken, "Geographical Names," para. 1.
11. Ibid., para. 9.
12. Ibid., para. 1.
13. Cozzens, *The Marvellous Country*, 165.
14. Hodge, *Arizona as It Is*, 155.
15. From "The Ballad of Davy Crockett," by Bill Hayes.
16. As quoted in *Columbia Encyclopedia*, 2001.
17. As quoted in Abbott, *David Crockett*, chapter 11.
18. As quoted in Reader's Digest, *American Folklore and Legend*, 159.
19. As quoted in Abbott, *David Crockett*, chapter 11.
20. As quoted in Abbott, *David Crockett*, chapter 11.
21. Johnson, *Ante-Bellum North Carolina*, 96.
22. Bartram, *Observations on the Inhabitants*.
23. Trollope, *Domestic Manners of the Americans*, 127–128 of 186.
24. Trollope, *North America*, 30 of 196.
25. Debar, *The West Virginia Hand-Book*, 22 of 78.
26. Olmsted, *A Journey through Texas*, 15–16.

27. Warner, *On Horseback*, chapter 1.

28. Dickens, *American Notes*, chapter 9, 163.

29. Ibid., chapter 9, 164.

30. Ibid., chapter 9, 164.

31. Trollope, "The Courtship of Susan Bell."

32. Irving, "Rip Van Winkle."

33. Gilman, *The Poetry of Travelling*, 81.

34. Ibid., 84.

35. Ibid., 85.

36. Ibid., 85.

37. Colt, *The Tourist's Guide*, 137.

38. Ibid., 146.

39. *Time*, "Saratoga Spa."

40. *Visitors' and Automobilists' Guide Book* as quoted in Lewis, *Divided Highways*, 281.

41. Colt, *The Tourist's Guide*, 153.

42. Ibid., 149.

43. Ibid., 151.

44. Ibid., 158.

45. Ibid., 213.

46. Gilman, *The Poetry of Travelling*, 87.

47. Olmsted, *A Journey through Texas*, 32.

48. Ibid., 28.

49. Ibid., 36.

50. Ibid., 30.

51. Ibid., 30.

52. Ibid., 30.

53. Morleigh, *A Merry Briton in Pioneer Wisconsin*, 28.

54. Ibid., 29.

55. Ibid., 35.

56. Ibid., 56.

57. Ibid., 57.

58. Ibid., 60.

59. Ibid., 61.

60. Mevis, *Pioneer Recollections*, 9.

61. Ibid., 9.

62. Ibid., 49.

63. Ibid., 12.

64. Ibid., 12.

65. Ibid., 32.

66. Ibid., 83.

67. Ibid., 107.

Chapter 2. Interstate Commerce Develops: This Little Piggy Went to Market

1. As quoted in Hulbert, *The Paths of Inland Commerce*, chapter 1.
2. Johnson, *Ante-Bellum North Carolina*, 73.
3. As described in Inman, *The Santa Fe Trail*, 76.
4. King, "Glimpses of Texas, I," 304.
5. Twain, *Roughing It*, 376.
6. Twain, "Snodgrass' Ride on the Railroad."
7. Muir, "Crossing the Cumberland."
8. Debar, *The West Virginia Hand-Book*, 64 of 78.
9. Trollope, *North America*, 28 of 196.
10. Pollard, *The Virginia Tourist*, 89 of 98.
11. Ibid., 74 of 98.
12. Ingersoll, "Rocky Mountain Mules," 932.
13. Ibid., 935.
14. Cozzens, *The Marvellous Country*, 101.
15. Ibid., 101.
16. As quoted in Sharp, "Desert Trails," 3 of 10.
17. As described in Inman, *The Santa Fe Trail*, 58.
18. Bird, *A Lady's Life in the Rocky Mountains*, 34.
19. Ibid., 123.
20. Ibid., 161.
21. Ibid., 195.
22. Ibid., 28.
23. Ingersoll, "Rocky Mountain Mules," 936.
24. Bird, *A Lady's Life in the Rocky Mountains*, 29.
25. Ibid., 30.
26. Ibid., 32–33.
27. Ingersoll, "Rocky Mountain Mules," 935.
28. Text of Pease's letter is available from the Texas State Library and Archives Commission. <www.tsl.state.tx.us>. Accessed May 8, 2006.
29. As quoted in Santella, *The Chisholm Trail*, 17.
30. Howard, "The Rush to Oklahoma," 391.
31. King, "The Great South," (July): 261.
32. Ibid., (July): 281.
33. Grey, *The Man of the Forest*, 356.
34. Clark, *Cowboy Poetry, Classic Poems & Prose*.
35. Grey, *The Man of the Forest*, 356.
36. Dickens, *American Notes*, chapter 12, 196.
37. Olmsted, *A Journey Through Texas*, 12.
38. Trollope, *Domestic Manners of the Americans*, 15 of 186.
39. Ibid.
40. Ibid., 18 of 186.
41. Ibid.

42. Ibid., 16 of 186.

43. Dickens, *American Notes*, chapter 11, 189.

44. Trollope, *Domestic Manners of the Americans*, 35 of 186.

45. Ibid., 17 of 186.

46. McMurtry, *Roads*, 70.

47. King, "The Great South," (December): 152.

48. Rebecca Latimer became the first woman to serve in the U.S. Senate when she served briefly in 1922 until a permanent replacement could be found for a vacant seat.

49. Felton, *Country Life in Georgia*, 75.

50. King, "The Great South," (August): 406.

51. Ibid., (August): 406.

52. Ibid., (August): 399.

53. Goldfield et al., *The American Journey*, 343.

54. Metalious, *Peyton Place*, 1.

55. As quoted in McNair, *New Hampshire*, 54.

56. Burt, *Burt's Illustrated Guide of the Connecticut Valley*, 137.

57. As quoted in the U.S. Forest Service's, "History of the Green Mountain National Forest."

58. Clemens, *A Connecticut Yankee*, 657.

59. Trollope, *Domestic Manners of the Americans*, 161 of 186.

60. Clemens, *A Connecticut Yankee*, 657.

61. Trollope, *Domestic Manners of the Americans*, 161 of 186.

62. Macleod, *Harper's New York and Erie Rail-Road Guide Book*, 1 of 52.

63. Ibid., 2 of 52.

64. Ibid., 2 of 52.

65. Ibid., 2 of 52.

66. Ibid., 4 of 52.

67. Ibid., 4 of 52.

68. Ibid., 24 of 52.

69. Ibid., 31 of 52.

70. Ibid., 5 of 52.

71. Ibid., 38 of 52.

72. Ibid., 39 of 52.

73. Ibid., 36 of 52.

74. Ibid., 51 of 52.

75. Stevenson, *Across the Plains*, chapter 1.

76. O'Reilly, "Canoeing Sketches."

77. Ibid.

78. Burt, *Burt's Illustrated Guide of the Connecticut Valley*, 20.

79. O'Reilly, "Canoeing Sketches."

80. Ibid.

81. Burt, *Burt's Illustrated Guide of the Connecticut Valley*, 120.

82. O'Reilly, "Canoeing Sketches."

83. Ibid., 243–259.
84. The North Carolina Board of Agriculture, *North Carolina and Its Resources*, 122 of 186.
85. Trollope, *Domestic Manners of the Americans*, 118 of 186.
86. Lanman, *Adventures in the Wilds*, 97.
87. Ibid., 100.
88. Clinton, *A Winter from Home*, 20.
89. The North Carolina Board of Agriculture, *North Carolina and Its Resources*, 183 of 186.
90. The North Carolina Land Company, *A Statistical and Descriptive Account*, 4.
91. Ibid., 120.
92. Ibid., 70.
93. Lanier, *Florida: Its Scenery, Climate, and History*, 238.
94. Whittier, "On Receiving an Eagle's Quill from Lake Superior."
95. Wisthaler, *By Water to the Columbia Exposition*, 25 of 69.
96. Trollope, *North America*, 78 of 196.
97. Ibid., 78 of 196.
98. Ibid., 104 of 196.
99. Dedmon, *Fabulous Chicago*, 32.
100. As quoted in Stein, *Chicago*, 25.
101. John Stephen Wright, a Chicago businessman, as quoted in Chicago Historical Society's, "Queen of the West Once More."
102. Twain, Twainquotes.com.
103. Stevenson, *Across the Plains*, 10 of 40.
104. Kipling, *American Notes*, 91.
105. Ibid., 93.
106. Quote 37505, Bartleby.com, from *The Columbia World of Quotations*, accessed July 2006.
107. Stegner, *The Big Rock Candy Mountain*, 29.
108. Sandburg, *Complete Poems*, 3.
109. Trollope, *North America*, 80 of 196.
110. Ibid., 85 of 196.
111. Ibid., 95 of 196.
112. Ibid., 93 of 196.
113. Whittier, "On Receiving an Eagle's Quill from Lake Superior."

Chapter 3. Roads Cross the Continent: Root Hog, or Die

1. Greeley, *An Overland Journey*, 64–65.
2. Hulbert, *The Paths of Inland Commerce*, chapter 8.
3. Johnson, *Ante-Bellum North Carolina*, 39.
4. Ibid., 39.
5. Stephen Austin paraphrased from Ward, *The West*, 64.
6. Stevenson, "New York."
7. Greeley, *An Overland Journey*, 168.

8. Ibid., 88.

9. Ibid., 23.

10. Territorial Kansas Online 1854–1861.

11. Greeley, *An Overland Journey*, 35.

12. Territorial Kansas Online 1854–1861.

13. Greeley, *An Overland Journey*, 55.

14. As quoted in Carpenter, *Utah*, 58.

15. Stevenson, *Across the Plains*, 38 of 40.

16. Ibid., 39 of 40.

17. Greeley, *An Overland Journey*, 158.

18. Clinton, *A Winter from Home*, 55.

19. Lanman, *Adventures in the Wilds*, 125.

20. Ibid., 128.

21. The North Carolina Land Company, *A Statistical and Descriptive Account*, 134.

22. Clinton, *A Winter from Home*, 55.

23. Greeley, *An Overland Journey*, 168.

24. DeBar, *The West Virginia Hand-Book*, 12 of 78.

25. Ibid., 3 of 78.

26. Ibid., 3 of 78.

27. Quote 8311, Bartleby.com, from Bartlett, *Familiar Quotations*.

28. DeBar, *The West Virginia Hand-Book*, 17 of 78.

29. Ibid., 18 of 78.

30. Thompson, "Glimpses of Western Farm Life," 686.

31. Ibid., 685.

32. Ibid., 685.

33. Stevenson, *Across the Plains*, chapter 1.

34. Clinton, *A Winter from Home*, 58.

35. Thompson, "Glimpses of Western Farm Life," 679.

36. Ibid., 681.

37. Meeker, *Ox-Team Days on the Oregon Trail*, 165.

38. Ibid., 32.

39. Ibid., 39.

40. Ibid., 39.

41. Ibid., 63.

42. Ibid., 63.

43. Ibid., 195.

44. Crumpton and Crumpton, *The Adventures of Two Alabama Boys*, 30.

45. Ibid., 31.

46. Ibid., 38.

47. Trollope, *Domestic Manners of the Americans*, 85 of 186.

48. Ibid., 81 of 186.

49. Ibid., 83 of 186.

50. Ibid., 81 of 186.

51. Ibid., 173 of 186.

52. Ibid., 80 of 186.

53. Boynton, *Journey through Kansas*, 86.

54. Greeley, *An Overland Journey*, 78.

55. Ibid., 78.

56. Ibid., 98.

57. Ibid., 111.

58. Ibid., 114.

59. Ibid., 165.

60. Ibid., 116.

61. Ibid., 117.

62. As quoted in Brown, *Wondrous Times on the Frontier*, 32.

63. Greeley, *An Overland Journey*, 170.

64. Ibid., 78.

65. Atwater, *Incidents of a Southern Tour*, 33.

66. As quoted in Somerville, *Illinois*, 34.

67. Pollard, *The Virginia Tourist*, chapter 1.

68. Warner, *On Horseback*.

69. Pollard, *The Virginia Tourist*, 25 of 98.

70. Ripley, *Social Life in Old New Orleans*, 110.

71. Ibid., 108.

72. The North Carolina Board of Agriculture, *North Carolina and Its Resources*, 286.

73. King, *The Great South*, 183.

74. Ibid., 183.

75. Ibid., 183.

76. Ibid., 183.

77. Cozzens, *The Marvellous Country*, 291–292.

78. Grey, *Nevada*, 134–135.

79. Ibid., 132.

80. Cozzens, *The Marvellous Country*, 291–292.

81. Grey, *Nevada*, 132–133.

82. Ibid., 119.

83. Kipling, *American Notes*, 59–60.

84. Ibid., 61.

85. Ibid., 61.

86. Ibid., 61.

87. Trollope, *North America*, 161 of 196.

88. Ibid., 146 of 196.

89. Wisthaler, *By Water to the Columbia Exposition*, 41 of 69.

Chapter 4. Coast to Coast Automobile Traffic Begins: Get Out and Get Under

1. As quoted in the San Diego Historical Society's Web site. Accessed July, 2006.

2. Duncan and Burns, *Horatio's Drive*, 95.

3. Ibid., 101.

4. Gayness, "Celebration To-Night."

5. The California Highway Commission as quoted in Davies, *American Road*, 200.

6. From a report to Congress in 1939 titled *Toll Roads and Free Roads*, as quoted in Weingroff, "Essential to the National Interest," 2 of 15.

7. Roosevelt, "Second Inaugural Address."

8. Lyrics from the Lyrics Depot Web site. <www.lyricsdepot.com>. Accessed July 18, 2007.

9. Verne, *Around the World in Eighty Days*, 217.

10. Bly, *Around the World in Seventy-Two Days*, chapter 17.

11. Verne, *Around the World in Eighty Days*, 217.

12. Bly, *Around the World in Seventy-Two Days*, 84 of 89.

13. Ibid., chapter 17, opening para.

14. Verne, *Around the World in Eighty Days*, 218.

15. Ibid., 226.

16. Ibid., 242.

17. Ibid., 264.

18. Bly, *Around the World in Seventy-Two Days*, 85 of 89.

19. Verne, *Around the World in Eighty Days*, 271.

20. Bly, *Around the World in Seventy-Two Days*, last para.

21. Summerhayes, *Vanished Arizona*, chapter 3.

22. Ibid., chapter 3.

23. Ibid., chapter 3.

24. Ibid., chapter 6.

25. Ibid., chapter 23.

26. Ibid., chapter 23.

27. Ibid., chapter 23.

28. Chase, *California Desert Trail*, 299.

29. Ibid., 299.

30. Summerhayes, *Vanished Arizona*, chapter 33.

31. All of Sojourner Truth's quotes in this section are taken from her speech, "Ain't I a Woman?" <http://afgen.com/sojourner1.html>. Accessed September, 2005.

32. Trollope, *Domestic Manners of the Americans*, 160 of 186.

33. Clinton, *A Winter from Home*, 55.

34. Bird, *A Lady's Life in the Rocky Mountains*, 237.

35. Ibid., 53.

36. Merrick, *Old Times in Dixie Land*, 11.

37. Caption on photograph LC-USF34-009871-E, Library of Congress.

38. Benwell, *An Englishman's Travels in America*, 14 of 86.

39. Bryson, *The Lost Continent*, 249.

40. As quoted in Charlet, "Great Basin-Mojave Desert."

41. As quoted in Edwards, "Should They Build a Fence Around Montana?"

42. Carlin, "What Am I Doing in New Jersey?"

43. Ibid.

44. Ibid.

45. *Time*, "Glory Road."

46. *Time*, "The Call of the Road."

47. As quoted in Kitsko, "The Pennsylvania Turnpike."

48. *Time*, "Glory Road."

Chapter 5. The Interstate Highway Era: Motorvatin' Over the Hill

1. As quoted in Weingroff, "The Man Who Changed America, Part I."

2. As quoted in Weingroff, "The Man Who Changed America, Part II."

3. As quoted in Weingroff, "The Man Who Changed America, Part I."

4. As quoted in Weingroff, "The Man Who Changed America, Part II."

5. As quoted in Weingroff, "Dwight D. Eisenhower System of Interstate and Defense Highways Engineering Marvels."

6. *Time*, "The Great Road."

7. *Time*, "Ode to the Road."

8. *Time*, "Double-Edged Blade."

9. De Roos, "The Magic Worlds of Walt Disney," 207.

10. Ripley, *Social Life in Old New Orleans*, 262.

11. Saxon et al., *Gumbo Ya-Ya*.

12. Morleigh, *A Merry Briton in Pioneer Wisconsin*, 33.

13. Ibid., 29.

14. Larson, *Isaac's Storm*, 123.

15. King, "Glimpses of Texas I," 408.

16. Ibid., 403.

17. *Time*, "Funnel of Death."

18. Ibid.

19. Brown, *Whisker of Evil*, 17.

20. The poem "Sweet Afton" was taken from Bartleby.com. <www.bartleby.com>. Accessed June 19, 2006.

21. As quoted in Davis, *First Blood: Fort Sumter to Bull Run*, 126–127.

22. Ibid., 150.

23. As quoted in Morena, "Rumbling Toward Safety."

24. As quoted in *Time*, "One for the Roads."

25. Text from an FHWA press release, issued on May 30, 2006.

26. As quoted in *Time*, "One for the Roads."

Chapter 6. The Red Trace of Taillights

1. Quote 3332, Bartleby.com, from Simpson, *Simpson's Contemporary Quotations*. Accessed July 2006.

2. Bryson, *The Lost Continent*, 9.

3. Ibid., 105.

4. Ibid., 114.

5. Roosevelt, *Foreword*.

6. Ibid.

Bibliography

Abbott, John. 1874. *David Crockett: His Life and Adventures*. New York: Dodd, Mead & Co. Project Gutenberg text. <www.gutenberg.org>, accessed July 18, 2006.

Adams, Andy. 1903. *The Log of a Cowboy: A Narrative of the Old Trail Days*. Boston and New York: Houghton, Mifflin and Co. Project Gutenberg text. <www.gutenberg. org>, accessed January 2006.

Andrews, Robert, Mary Biggs, and Michael Seidel, eds. 2001. *The Columbia World of Quotations*. New York: Bartleby.com.

Atwater, Horace Cowles. 1857. *Incidents of a Southern Tour*. Boston: J.P. Magee. Making of America, University of Michigan Library, Ann Arbor, Michigan. 1996. <www.hti.umich.edu>, accessed May 2005.

Ayer, Eleanor H. 1997. *Celebrate the States: Colorado*. New York: Benchmark Books–Marshall Cavendish.

Bales, Richard F. 2002. *The Great Chicago Fire and the Myth of Mrs. O'Leary's Cow*. Jefferson, NC: McFarland & Co.

Barracuda Magazine. No date. "The Lincoln Highway." <*www.barracudamagazine. com/lincoln-highway.htm*>, accessed May 16, 2005.

Barry, Dave. 1999. "The Walt 'You Will Have Fun' Disney World." In Fred Setterberg, ed., *America True Stories of Life on the Road*. Redwood City, CA: Travelers' Tales Inc.

Bartlett, John, comp. 2000. *Familiar Quotations*. New York: Bartleby.com.

Bartram, John. 1751. *Observations on the Inhabitants, Climate, Soil, Rivers, Productions, Animals, and Other Matters Worthy of Notice Made by Mr. John Bartram, in His Travels from Pensilvania [sic] to Onondago, Oswego and the Lake Ontario in Canada*. London: J. Whiston & B. White. Early Canadiana Online. <www.canadiana. org>, accessed July 18, 2006.

Bennet, James. 1909. Speech to the Minisink Valley Historical Society, February 21. <www.portjervisny.org>, accessed August 23, 2005.

Benwell, John. 1857. *An Englishman's Travels in America: His Observations of Life and Manners in the Free and Slave States*. Project Gutenberg text. <www.gutenberg. org>, accessed July 26, 2004.

Bird, Isabella. 1881. *A Lady's Life in the Rocky Mountains*. New York: G.P. Putnam's Sons. Project Gutenberg text. <www.gutenberg.org>, accessed October 2005.

Bly, Nellie. 1890. *Around the World in Seventy-Two Days*. New York: The Pictorial Weeklies Company. Electronic edition, University of Pennsylvania Library, A Celebration of Women Writers. <http://digital.library.upenn.edu/women/bly/world/world.html>, accessed October 2005.

Boynton, Charles. 1855. *Journey through Kansas with Sketches of Nebraska*. Cincinnati: Moore, Wilstach, Keys & Co. Making of America, University of Michigan Library, Ann Arbor, Michigan. 1996. <www.hti.umich.edu>, accessed July 2005.

Brown, Dee. 1991. *Wondrous Times on the Frontier*. Little Rock, AR: August House Publishers Inc.

Brown, Rita Mae. 2004. *Whisker of Evil*. New York: Bantam Books.

Browne, John Ross. 1864. *Adventures in the Apache Country: A Tour through Arizona*. New York: Promontory Press.

Bryson, Bill. 1989. *The Lost Continent*. New York: Harper & Row, Publishers.

Burt, Henry. 1867. *Burt's Illustrated Guide of the Connecticut Valley*. Northampton, MA: New England Publishing Company. Making of America, University of Michigan Library, Ann Arbor, Michigan. 1996. <www.hti.umich.edu>, accessed August 2005.

Carlin, George. 1988. "What Am I Doing in New Jersey?" HBO special.

Carpenter, Allan. 1978. *Louisiana*. The New Enchantment of America series. Chicago: Children's Press.

———. 1979. *Utah*. The New Enchantment of America series. Chicago: Children's Press.

Channing, Steven, and the editors of Time-Life Books. 1984. *Confederate Ordeal: The Southern Home Front*. Alexandria, Virginia: Time-Life Books.

Charlet, D.A. No date. "Great Basin-Mojave Desert." <http://biology.usgs.gov/s+t/SNT/noframe/gb150.htm>, accessed November 15, 2005.

Charters, Ann, ed. 1995. *The Portable Jack Kerouac*. New York: Viking Books.

Chase, Joseph S. 1919. *California Desert Trails*. Boston: Houghton Mifflin Company. Online edition, Göttinger Digitalisierungs-Zentrum, <www.gdz.sub.uni-goettingen.de>, accessed November 2005.

Chicago Historical Society. No date. "Queen of the West Once More." <www.chicagohs.org>, accessed January 20, 2006.

Child, Lee. 2000. *Running Blind*. New York: The Berkeley Publishing Group.

Clark, Badger. 2005. *Cowboy Poetry, Classic Poems & Prose*. Greg Scott, ed. Cowboy Miner Productions.

Clark, R.W. 1983. *Benjamin Franklin: A Biography*. New York: Random House.

Clarke, Grant, and Edgar Leslie. No date. "He'd Have to Get Under—Get Out and Get Under." <http://americanhistory.si.edu/onthemove/collection/object_916.html>, accessed August 2005.

Clemens, Samuel. 1891. *Roughing It*. Hartford, CT: Americana Publishing Co. American Memory, Library of Congress. <http://memory.loc.gov>, accessed November 2005.

———. 1889. *A Connecticut Yankee in King Arthur's Court*, as reprinted in *The Family Mark Twain*. New York: Harper & Row Publishers Inc., 1972.

————. 1883. *Life on the Mississippi*, as reprinted in *The Family Mark Twain*. New York: Harper & Row Publishers Inc., 1972.

Clinton, Charles. 1852. *A Winter from Home*. New York: John F. Trow, Printer. Making of America, University of Michigan Library, Ann Arbor, Michigan. 1996. <www.hti.umich.edu>, accessed May 2005.

Coastal Carolina University, BB&T Center for Economic and Community Development. 2009. "CCU Estimates Economic Impact of I-73 Construction." Press release. January 29.

Colt, Mrs. S.S. 1871. *The Tourist's Guide through the Empire State*. Albany, N.Y.: Mrs. S.S. Colt. Making of America, University of Michigan Library, Ann Arbor, Michigan. 1996. <www.hti.umich.edu>, accessed March 2004.

Cozzens, Samuel Woodworth. 1876. *The Marvellous Country; or, Three Years in Arizona and New Mexico*. Boston: Lee and Shepard. Making of America, University of Michigan Library, Ann Arbor, Michigan. 1996. <www.hti.umich.edu>, accessed July 18, 2006.

Crumpton, H.J., and W.B. Crumpton. 1912. *The Adventures of Two Alabama Boys*. Montgomery, Ala.: The Paragon Press. Documenting the American South, University of North Carolina at Chapel Hill. 2004. <www.docsouth.unc.edu>, accessed November 2005.

Davies, Pete. 2002. *American Road*. New York: Henry Holt and Company.

Davis, William C. 1983. *First Blood: Fort Sumter to Bull Run*. Alexandria, Virginia: Time-Life Books.

Dean, Leon W., ed. 1956. *Vermont History*, XXIV(4) (October). <www.vtonly.com>, accessed August 16, 2005.

Debar, Joseph Hubert Diss. 1870. *The West Virginia Hand-Book and Immigrant's Guide*. Parkersburg, W.V.: Gibbens Bros. Making of America, University of Michigan Library, Ann Arbor, Michigan. 1996. <www.hti.umich.edu>, accessed June 15, 2001.

Dedmon, Emmett. 1953. *Fabulous Chicago*. New York: Random House.

De Roos, Robert. August 1963. "The Magic Worlds of Walt Disney." *National Geographic*.

Dickens, Charles. 1874. *American Notes*. New York: Peter Fenelon Collier, Publisher.

Disney/Pixar Films. 2006. *Cars*.

Doyle, Arthur Conan. 1887. "A Study in Scarlet," as reprinted in *The Complete Sherlock Holmes*, Vol. I. New York: Doubleday & Co., 1960.

Duncan, Dayton, and Ken Burns. 2003. *Horatio's Drive: America's First Road Trip*. New York: Alfred A. Knopf.

Edwards, Mike W. May 1976. "Should They Build a Fence Around Montana?" *National Geographic*.

Eggleston, Edward. 1871. *The Hoosier Schoolmaster*. Project Gutenberg text. <www.gutenberg.org>, accessed June 2006.

Etten, William J. 1926. "Grand Rapids in 1844–1845." In *A Citizens' History of Grand Rapids, Michigan*. A. P. Johnson Co.

Federal Highway Administration. Press release from May 30, 2006. <*www.i73insc.com*>, accessed July 1, 2006.

Felton, Rebecca Latimer. 1919. *Country Life in Georgia in the Days of My Youth*. Atlanta, Georgia: Index Printing Co. Documenting the American South, University of North Carolina at Chapel Hill. 2004. <www.docsouth.unc.edu>, accessed July 18, 2006.

Ferris, Helen, ed. 1957. *Favorite Poems Old and New*. New York: Doubleday & Co. Inc.

Fowler, William. 1877. *Women on the American Frontier*. Hartford, Conn.: S. S. Scranton & Co. Making of America, University of Michigan Library, Ann Arbor, Michigan. 1996. <www.hti.umich.edu>, accessed May 2006.

Gayness, Stuart. 1913. "Celebration To-Night Will Inaugurate Campaign for Great Undertaking." *San Francisco Examiner*. Published October 31, 1913. <www.ugcs. caltech.edu>, accessed May 16, 2005.

Gilman, Caroline Howard. 1838. *The Poetry of Travelling in the United States*. New York: S. Colman. Making of America, University of Michigan Library, Ann Arbor, Michigan. 1996. <www.hti.umich.edu>, accessed March 2004.

Goldfield, David, Carl Abbott, Virginia DeJohn Anderson, Jo Ann E. Argersinger, Peter H. Argersinger, William Barney, and Robert M. Weir. 1998. *The American Journey: A History of the United States*. New Jersey: Prentice-Hall Inc.

Greeley, Horace. 1860. *An Overland Journey, from New York to San Francisco in the Summer of 1859*. New York: C.M. Saxon, Barker & Co. Making of America, University of Michigan Library, Ann Arbor, Michigan. 1996. <www.hti.umich.edu>, accessed December 2005.

Gregg, Josiah A. 1844–1845. *Commerce of the Prairies*. Kansas Collection Books. <www.kancoll.org>, accessed December 2005.

Grey, Zane. 1909. *The Last Trail*. New York: A.L. Burt Company.

———. 1920. *The Man of the Forest*. New York: Grosset & Dunlap.

———. 1928. *Nevada*. Toronto: The Best Printing Co.

Hamilton, Virginia. 1985. *The People Could Fly American Black Folktales*. New York: Alfred A. Knopf.

Hodge, Hiram. 1877. *Arizona as It Is; or, The Coming Country*. Making of America, University of Michigan Library, Ann Arbor, Michigan. 1996. <www.hti.umich.edu>, accessed August 18, 2005.

Howard, William Willard. May 18, 1889. "The Rush to Oklahoma." *Harper's Weekly*.

Howarth, William. July 1982. "The Country of Willa Cather." *National Geographic*.

Hulbert, A. B. 1919. *The Paths of Inland Commerce, a Chronicle of Trail, Road, and Waterway*. Project Gutenberg text. <www.gutenberg.org>, accessed May 2003.

Ingersoll, Ernest. April 1880. "Rocky Mountain Mules." *Scribner's Monthly*: 932.

Inman, Colonel Henry. 1897. *The Santa Fe Trail*. Project Gutenberg text. <www. gutenberg.org>, accessed February 2006.

Irving, Washington. 1907. "Rip Van Winkle." <www.bartleby.com>, accessed November 2000.

Johnson, Guion Griffis. 1937. *Ante-Bellum North Carolina: A Social History*. University of North Carolina Press. Documenting the South, University of North Carolina at Chapel Hill. 2004. <www.docsouth.unc.edu>, accessed July 18, 2006.

Jordan, Robert Paul. August 1971. "Oklahoma, the Adventurous One." *National Geographic*.

Kent, D. 1994. *Connecticut*. America the Beautiful series. Chicago: Children's Press.

King, Edward. December 1873. "The Great South." *Scribner's Monthly*, 7(2).

———. January 1874. "Glimpses of Texas, I." *Scribner's Monthly*, 7(3).

———. February 1874. "Glimpses of Texas II." *Scribner's Monthly*, 7(4).

———. July 1874. "The Great South." *Scribner's Monthly*, 8(3).

———. August 1874. "The Great South." *Scribner's Monthly*, 8(4).

———. 1875. *The Great South*. Hartford, Conn.: American Publishing Co. Documenting the American South, University of North Carolina at Chapel Hill. 2002. <www.docsouth.unc.edu>, accessed January 2006.

Kipling, Rudyard. 1899. *American Notes*. Boston: Brown and Company. <http://etext.lib.virginia.edu>, accessed April 20, 2005.

Kitsko, J.J. No date. "Pennsylvania Turnpike." <www.pahighways.com>, accessed April 23, 2006.

L'Amour, Louis. 1988. *Lonigan*. New York: Bantam Books.

———. 1992. *The Trail to Seven Pines*. New York: Bantam Books.

Lanier, Sidney. 1876. *Florida: Its Scenery, Climate, and History. With an Account of Charleston, Savannah, Augusta, and Aiken; a Chapter for Consumptives; Various Papers on Fruit-Culture; and a Complete Hand-Book and Guide*. Philadelphia, Penn.: J.B. Lippincott & Co. Making of America, University of Michigan Library, Ann Arbor, Michigan. 1996. <www.hti.umich.edu>, accessed May 2005.

———. 1885. *The Poems of Sidney Lanier*. Mary Day Lanier, ed. New York: Charles Scribner's Sons. Making of America, University of Michigan Library, Ann Arbor, Michigan. 2005. <www.hti.umich.edu>, accessed May 2005.

Lanman, Charles. 1856. *Adventures in the Wilds of the United States and British American Provinces*. Philadelphia, Penn.: J.W. Moore. Making of America, University of Michigan Library, Ann Arbor, Michigan. 1996. <www.hti.umich.edu>, accessed May 2005.

Larson, Erik. 1999. *Isaac's Storm*. New York: Crown Publishers.

Lawson, John. 1711. *A New Voyage to Carolina*. Project Gutenberg text. <www.gutenberg.org>, accessed February 2, 2003.

Legends of America. No date. "Tales of the Santa Fe Trail." <www.legendsofamerica.com>, accessed December 2, 2005.

Lewis, Tom. 1997. *Divided Highways*. New York: Penguin Books.

Macleod, William. 1855–1856. *Harper's New York and Erie Rail-Road Guide Book*, 8th edition. New York: Harper & Brothers. Making of America, University of Michigan Library, Ann Arbor, Michigan. 2005. <www.hti.umich.edu>, accessed July 20, 2006.

McFeely, W. 1990. *Ulysses S. Grant: Memoirs and Selected Letters*. Library of Congress.

McMurtry, Larry. 2000. *Roads: Driving America's Great Highways*. New York: Touchstone.

McNair, Sylvia. 1992. *New Hampshire*. America the Beautiful series. Chicago: Children's Press.

McNichol, Dan. 2006. *The Roads that Built America*. New York: Sterling Publishing Co., Inc.

Meeker, Ezra, and Howard R. Driggs. 1922. *Ox-Team Days on the Oregon Trail*. Yonkers, N.Y.: World Book Company. Washington Secretary of State. <www.secstate. wa.gov>, accessed July 2006.

Mencken, H.L. 1921. "Geographical Names." *The American Language*. New York: Alfred A. Knopf. <www.bartleby.com>, accessed November 2000.

Merrick, Caroline Elizabeth Thomas. 1901. *Old Times in Dixie Land: A Southern Matron's Memories*. New York: Grafton Press. Documenting the American South, University of North Carolina at Chapel Hill. 2004. <www.docsouth.unc.edu>, accessed January 2006.

Metalious, G. 1954. *Peyton Place*. New York: Gramercy Books.

Mevis, Daniel. 1911. *Pioneer Recollections*. Lansing, Mich.: Robert Smith Printing Company. American Memory, Library of Congress. <http://memory.loc.gov>, accessed March 2006.

Miller, Arthur. 1949. *Death of a Salesman*. New York: The Viking Press.

Mitchell, Margaret. 1938. *Gone with the Wind*. Toronto: The MacMillan Company of Canada Ltd.

Morena, David. September-October 2003. "Rumbling Toward Safety." *Public Roads*, 67(2). <www.tfhrc.gov/pubrds/03sep/06.htm>, accessed July 10, 2006.

Morleigh (pseudonym). 1842. *A Merry Briton in Pioneer Wisconsin*. London. American Memory, Library of Congress. <http://memory.loc.gov>, accessed July 18, 2006.

Muir, John. 1916. "Crossing the Cumberland." From *A Thousand Mile Walk to the Gulf*. New York: Houghton Mifflin Co. <www.sierraclub.org>, accessed July 2005.

North Carolina Board of Agriculture. 1896. *North Carolina and Its Resources*. Winston-Salem, N.C.: State Board of Agriculture. Documenting the American South, University of North Carolina at Chapel Hill. 2004. <www.docsouth.unc.edu>, accessed June 9, 2004.

North Carolina Land Company. 1869. *A Statistical and Descriptive Account of the Several Counties of the State of North Carolina, United States of America*. Raleigh, N.C.: North Carolina Land Company. Making of America, University of Michigan Library, Ann Arbor, Michigan. 1996. <www.hti.umich.edu>, accessed June 2003.

Olmsted, Frederick Law. 1857. *A Journey through Texas; or, A Saddle-Trip on the Southwestern Frontier*. New York: Dix, Edwards & Co. Making of America, University of Michigan Library, Ann Arbor, Michigan. 1996. <www.hti.umich.edu>, accessed July 18, 2006.

O'Reilly, John Boyle. 1890. "Canoeing Sketches." *Athletics and Manly Sport*. Boston: Pilot Publishing Company.

Parkman, Francis Jr. 1847. *The Oregon Trail*. Project Gutenberg text. <www. gutenberg.org>, accessed December 13, 2005.

Pollard, Edward Alfred. 1870. *The Virginia Tourist*. Philadelphia, Penn.: J.B. Lippincott & Co. Making of America, University of Michigan Library, Ann Arbor, Michigan. 2005. <www.hti.umich.edu>, accessed July 18, 2006.

Reader's Digest Association. 1978. *American Folklore and Legend*. Reader's Digest Association.

Ripley, Eliza. 1912. *Social Life in Old New Orleans*. New York and London: D. Appelton and Company. Documenting the American South, University of North Carolina at Chapel Hill. 2004. <www.docsouth.unc.edu>, accessed November 2005.

Roosevelt, Franklin Delano. 1937. "Second Inaugural Address." <www.yale.edu/lawweb/avalon/presiden/inaug/froos2.htm>, accessed July 18, 2006.

Roosevelt, T. 1916. "Foreword." *A Book-Lover's Holidays in the Open*. New York: Charles Scribner's Sons. <www.bartleby.com>, accessed December 1999.

Sandburg, Carl. 1970. *Complete Poems of Carl Sandburg*. Revised edition. New York: Harcourt Brace Jovanovich.

San Diego Historical Society. No Date. Home page. <www.sandiegohistory.org>, accessed July 2006.

Santella, A. 1997. *The Chisholm Trail*. Chicago: Children's Press.

Saxon, Lyle, Edward Dreyer, and Robert Tallant, comps. 1987. *Gumbo Ya-Ya*. Pelican.

Sharp, Jay. No date entry a. "Desert Trails. The Juan Bautista de Ana Trail." <www.desertusa.com>, accessed November 25, 2005.

———. No date entry b. "Desert Trails. A Wild and Diverse Landscape." <www.desertusa.com>, accessed November 25, 2005.

Simpson, James B., comp. 2000. *Simpson's Contemporary Quotations*. New York: Bartleby.com.

Slater, Rodney E. 1996. "Happy 40th Anniversary National System of Interstate and Defense Highways." <www.fhwa.dot.gov/infrastructure/40thannv.cfm>, accessed July 18, 2006.

Somerville, Barbara A. 2001. *Illinois*. From Sea to Shining Sea series. Chicago: Children's Press.

Stegner, Wallace. 1973. *The Big Rock Candy Mountain*. New York: Doubleday & Co. Inc.

Stein, R. Conrad. 1997. *Chicago*. Chicago: Children's Press.

Steinbeck, John. 1971. *Travels with Charley*. Pascal Covici Jr., ed., *The Portable Steinbeck*. New York: Viking Penguin Inc.

———. 1971. *The Grapes of Wrath*. Pascal Covici Jr., ed., *The Portable Steinbeck*. New York: Viking Penguin Inc.

Stevenson, Robert Louis. 1892. *Across the Plains*. London: Chatto & Windus. Project Gutenberg text. <www.gutenberg.org>, accessed July 18, 2006.

———. 1905. "Roads, 1873." From *Essays of Travel*. London: Chatto & Windus. <www.gutenberg.org>, accessed July 18, 2006.

———. 1905. "New York." From *Essays of Travel*. London: Chatto & Windus. <www.gutenberg.org>, accessed July 18, 2006.

———. 1907. *Travels with a Donkey. In the Cevenne*. London: Chatto & Windus. Project Gutenberg text. <www.gutenberg.org>, accessed July 18, 2006.

Summerhayes, Martha. 1911. *Vanished Arizona Recollections of the Army Life by a New England Woman*. Project Gutenberg text. <www.gutenberg.org>, accessed October 2005.

Swan, L.B. 1904. *Journal of a Trip to Michigan in 1841*. Rochester, N.Y. American Memory, Library of Congress. <http://memory.loc.gov>, accessed July 18, 2006.

Territorial Kansas Online 1854–1861. Home page. <www.territorialkansasonline.org>, accessed September 23, 2005.

Thompson, Maurice. 1878. "Glimpses of Western Farm Life." *Scribner's Monthly*, 16(5).

Time. August 5, 1935. "Saratoga Spa."

———. October 7, 1940. "Glory Road."

———. August 23, 1948. "The Call of the Road."

———. January 16, 1956. "Double-Edged Blade."

———. July 9, 1956. "The Great Road."

———. August 25, 1958. "The Quiet Highwayman."

———. October 6, 1961. "One for the Roads."

———. August 9, 1963. "The 100-Year Binge."

———. September 10, 1965. "Ode to the Road."

———. May 17, 1999. "Funnel of Death."

Time-Life Books Editors. 1995. *Tribes of the Southern Plains*. Alexandria, Virginia: Time-Life Books.

Trestrail, J. 1999. *Art of the State: Illinois*. New York: Harry N. Abrams, Inc. Publishers.

Trollope, Anthony. 1863. *North America, Volume I*. Philadelphia, Penn.: J.B. Lippincott & Co. Project Gutenberg text. <www.gutenberg.org>, accessed July 18, 2006.

———. 1864. "The Courtship of Susan Bell." *Tales of All Countries*. Chapman and Hall. Project Gutenberg text. <www.gutenberg.org>, accessed July 20, 2006.

Trollope, F. 1832. *Domestic Manners of the Americans*. Project Gutenberg text. <www.gutenberg.org>, accessed July 18, 2006.

Truth, Sojourner. 1851. "Ain't I a Woman?" African American History Web site. <http://afroamhistory.about.com>, accessed August 2006.

Twainquotes.com. No date. <www.twainquotes.com>, accessed April 2006.

United States, Department of Agriculture, Forest Service. No date. "History of the Green Mountain National Forest." <www.fs.fed.us>, accessed August 16, 2005.

Verne, Jules. 1873. *Around the World in Eighty Days*. Electronic edition, University of Virginia Library. <http://etext.lib.virginia.edu>, accessed May 2005.

Walker, Paul Robert. 2001. *The Southwest Gold, God, and Grandeur*. Washington, D.C.: National Geographic Books.

Ward, G.C., D. Duncan, and K. Burns. 2001. *Mark Twain*. New York: Alfred A. Knopf.

Ward, Geoffrey. 1996. *The West*. Boston and New York: Little Brown and Company.

Warner, Charles Dudley. July-October 1885. "On Horseback." *The Atlantic Monthly*, 56(333–336). Project Gutenberg text. <www.gutenberg.org>, accessed July 18, 2006.

Weingroff, Richard F. Summer 1996. "Creating the Interstate System." *Public Roads*, 60(1). <www.tfhrc.gov/pubrds/summer96/p96su10.htm>, accessed December 14, 2004.

———. March-April 2003. "The Man Who Changed America, Part I." *Public Roads*, 66(5). <http://222.tfhrc.gov/pubrds/03.htm>, accessed November 2006.

———. May 2003. "The Man Who Changed America, Part II." *Public Roads*, 66(6). <http://222.tfhrc.gov/pubrds/03/05.htm>, accessed November 2006.

———. January-February 2006. "The Year of the Interstate." *Public Roads*, 69(4). <www.tfhrc.gov/pubrds/06jan/01.htm>, accessed July 18, 2006.

———. March-April 2006. "Essential to the National Interest." *Public Roads*, 69(5). <www.tfhrc.gov/pubrds/06mar/07.htm>, accessed July 18, 2006.

———. No date. "Dwight D. Eisenhower System of Interstate and Defense Highways Engineering Marvels." <http://www.fhwa.dot.gov>, accessed November 16, 2004.

Whittier, John Greenleaf. 1894. "On Receiving an Eagle's Quill from Lake Superior." *The Frost Spirit and Others from Poems of Nature, Poems Subjective and Reminiscent and Religious Poems*. Vol. II of *The Works of Whittier*. Project Gutenberg text. <www.gutenberg.org>, accessed July 20, 2006.

Wilder, Laura Ingalls. 1971. *The First Four Years*. Copyright: Roger Lea MacBride. New York: HarperCollins Publishers.

Wisthaler, Johanna S. 1894. *By Water to the Columbia Exposition*. Project Gutenberg text. <www.gutenberg.org>, accessed January 2006.

Index

Dianne Perrier is a freelance writer and editor who splits her time between Ontario, Canada, and Fernandina Beach, Florida.